"*Beyond Therapy, Beyond Science* is a courageous and innovative work by a provocative and important thinker, challenging ideas fundamental to psychology as it has been traditionally practiced. Anne Wilson Schaef shares her own personal journey as well as her ideas and practice as a professional."
  —Carol S. Pearson, author of *Awakening the Heroes Within*

"*Beyond Therapy, Beyond Science* is yet another example of Anne Wilson Schaef's courage and intuition, as she once again moves into uncharted waters and deepens the process of healing in which our culture is engaged. I agree with all of it. I celebrate its insights. It deserves the widest readership."
  —Brian Swimme, author of *The Universe Is a Green Dragon* and
    coauthor of *The Universe Story*

"*Beyond Therapy, Beyond Science* is a courageous book. Schaef's work, like all good observation based on experience, rings true. For all who love science, curiosity, and the natural world, and are concerned about our planet, this is must reading."
  —Christian Northrup, M.D., Fellow of the American College of
    Obstetricians and Gynecologists

"Anne Wilson Schaef's name is synonymous with healing. This compassionate and courageous book sets a course beyond contemporary psychotherapy. Just the process of reading it offers a revelatory glimpse of what being alive really means."
  —Roy Scheider, actor

"I heartily recommend this book to all who know intuitively there is another way, but can't figure out how to get there. Schaef is there. She understands reductionist science and therapy and why they simply can't help us anymore. More importantly, Schaef writes from within a new paradigm. The way she writes and her content are beautifully congruent. She is emotionally brilliant. When we finish *Beyond Therapy, Beyond Science,* we not only have been inspired and excited by a new idea, we have participated in the writer's life. I closed this book in awe and with the unshakeable confidence that it is possible to live in process."
    —Diane Fassel, author of *Working Ourselves to Death*

"A fascinating and courageous account of the author's exodus from conventional psychotherapeutic practice to the liberation of Process Therapy. This transformation involves the repudiation of the paradigm of objective, deterministic, mechanistic science, in which the therapist becomes a codependent of his client in the maintenance of the addiction from which the client seeks release, to the paradigm of the therapist as participant with the client in the process of releasing the resources for healing within the person. Theoretic science has already moved from the first to the second paradigm, in consequence of the quantum theory of Relativity. This book confronts Psychology and Psychotherapy with the necessity of the same radical revision of its assumptions and practices. This is a harbinger of the revolution to come."
    —John L. Casteel, retired professor of practical theology,
        Union Theological Seminary

"*Beyond Therapy, Beyond Science* penetrates to the core of the healing process with wisdom, eloquence, insight, and heartfelt experience."
    —Phil Lane, Jr., associate professor/coordinator, The Four
        Worlds Development Project

Beyond Therapy, Beyond Science

Beyond Therapy, Beyond Science

A NEW MODEL FOR HEALING

THE WHOLE PERSON

Anne Wilson Schaef

HarperSanFrancisco
A Division of HarperCollinsPublishers

FIRST EDITION

Library of Congress Cataloging-in-Publication Data

Schaef, Anne Wilson.
    Beyond therapy, beyond science : a new model for healing the
whole person / Anne Wilson Schaef. —1st ed.
        p.   cm.
    Includes bibliographical references and index.
    ISBN 0-06-250782-6 (acid-free paper)
    ISBN 0-06-250833-4 (pbk.)
    1. Psychotherapy—Philosophy.   2. Compulsive behavior—
Alternative treatment.   I. Title.
    RC437.5.S3   1992
    616.89'14'01—dc20   90-56473
                                                                CIP

92 93 94 95 96 RRD(H) 10 9 8 7 6 5 4 3 2 1

Contents

v

I dedicate this book to my former clients (some of whom I even called patients)—all of them. I did the best I knew how to at the time, and I wish I had known more. Unfortunately, I was a "good" psychotherapist.

I dedicate it to the client who was using cocaine "socially" and "occasionally"; we agreed to work on her long-term family and psychological problems and ignore her cocaine use.

I dedicate it to the man who came to me when he felt crazy and who was on large doses of lithium. I worked with him to get him off the lithium, which helped him function better. Unfortunately, it wasn't until he came back to see me later because of another crisis in his life, after I had really become knowledgeable about addictions and started my own recovery program, that I recognized that his "psychological" problems stemmed from addictions and the addictive process. We confronted drug addiction, alcohol addiction, nicotine addiction, caffeine addiction, sugar addiction, relationship addiction, and money addiction, in that order, and he is now doing well. How many others like him slipped through, I don't know.

I dedicate this book to those clients and workshop participants on whom I used techniques, interpretations, control, and manipulation. These "tools" were what I was taught, and a part of me believed they would help. Until recently, I never recognized how "heady" they were for me, the "therapist."

I dedicate this book to all of my clients for whom I had goals and knew what was right for them and what would heal them. I was arrogant and out of line.

I dedicate this book to all those patients in back wards of mental hospitals where "they" said nothing could be done and I accepted what "they" said. I want especially to mention Albertina (long since dead, I'm sure), because thinking of her helped me know the structure of this book.

I was operating out of a series of assumptions that I was taught in my training that I now know frequently exacerbated the problem and facilitated my clients' adjustment into an addictive, sexist, racist, self-destructing society, and I am sorry for that.

To you, my former clients, and to myself, I make amends. This book is my amends and, therefore, an important part of my recovery as a psychotherapist.

Preface

This book is my attempt to describe a way of understanding ourselves that goes beyond psychology as we know it. It is my attempt to articulate a theory and practice of healing that is integrated with a holographic scientific paradigm.

We hear a lot these days about a "new scientific paradigm," a "new world order," and a "New Age." By trying to use old and new wisdom, we have sought to give voice to what is wrong with this human experiment and to heal ourselves and our planet.

Although physics and many of the higher sciences have progressively evolved beyond a postmodernist scientific paradigm, psychology, the social sciences, and the helping professions have remained stuck in a mechanistic, dualistic, reductionistic, cause-and-effect scientific model.

Both the New Age and recovery fields have had the potential to lead us into a psychology that goes beyond psychology as we know it and into an approach to understanding the human being as an integral part of a holographic universe. Both have failed to take this leap. Both have tried to change the *content* of what we think, while continuing to use processes and techniques that are firmly entrenched in a science whose limited understanding of the universe renders it incapable of resonating with fully functional and integrated human beings. New spiritualities and new psychologies have proliferated as rapidly as the problems they have tried to solve, yet they often have subtly supported and, in fact, exacerbated those problems.

The fields of psychotherapy, medicine, counseling psychology, psychiatry, social work, ministry, and even education have all attempted to improve the human condition and truly help people. Unfortunately, their helpfulness is limited by the very concept of science on which they are built. As many scientists are warning, this mechanistic, reductionistic scientific model is reaching a state of entropy. It is beginning to turn on and devour itself. The time has come for psychology and psychotherapy as we know them to change dramatically.

Helping professionals have not been unaware of the limits of clinical psychology and psychotherapy, but those were the best we had and the best we could come up with, given the paradigm we were working with. Most of us have sought to make basic changes in our professions and in the ways we work. And we have always attempted to make changes while clinging to models that simply could not support real change. We have not been courageous. We have been willing to change our interpretations, as in Jungian work, and we have not been willing to *stop interpreting*. We have been willing to change our techniques, and we have not been willing to *stop using techniques*. We have been willing to accept spirituality and yet we feel more comfortable with a spirituality that is manipulated and controlled, as is "New Age" spirituality.

If we truly want to be helped and be helpful, nothing short of a radical paradigm shift in the way we think and work will suffice. For over twenty years, I have been working with individuals, couples, groups, organizations, and total societal systems. Slowly, over that time, I have evolved a philosophy and way of working with people that is unique to and compatible with a holographic (holomovement) paradigm and that offers, I believe, a greater possibility for healing than anything that currently exists. This book is my first attempt to communicate *how* I work, why I work the way I do, and the surprising effectiveness of this Living Process approach.

I do not fool myself into believing that my way of working is any kind of end point in what we need to learn and for how we need to function as human beings. It surely is not. However, I do believe this work is an essential and necessary step in a movement to bring a paradigm that is addictive, consuming, sick, and entropic into one that is holographic, healing, and necessary for the healthy survival of individuals and the planet.

In order to develop it, I have had to face my own demons and the demons of my training as a clinical psychologist. I have had to stand up to my own fears; to my own complacency, my satisfaction with what "sold" or seemed to work; to my own profession, which I loved, and the beliefs and rules of that profession; to a welcome into the "New Age" world even while I sensed that much New Age work was just the same old wolf in sheep's clothing, worn by people who were really sincere and meant well; to the recovery field, where I thought I had found a home only to find a change in content and not in the *way* things are done; to endless numbers of people who told me that we were doing the same work, only to find that while we used the same words, what we actually *do* is radically different. Probably most significant, I have had to stand up to my own loneliness, my fear of not being enough and not trusting that the work I do actually resonates with a paradigm shift and needs to be presented to the professional world—most of all, to the people who continue to seek help from those who cannot help because they operate out of a paradigm that cannot possibly work.

My hope is that this work will allow us to begin to leave behind psychologies and even psychotherapies themselves that have, indeed, done some good but have kept us locked into a worldview that is destructive to all life and that ultimately cannot be healing.

Beyond Therapy,
Beyond Science

Although the events, locales, and personalities described in this book are accurate, some of the names and identifying details of individuals have been changed in order to protect their privacy.

Introduction

Writing this book has been a struggle and has taken longer than any of my other books. Yet I knew that the struggle was part of the "ripening" and needed its own time. Also, I have felt intuitively that this was a very important book for me, and I have had some fear in the writing.

I have always known that writing any book—at least the way I write books—is self-revealing, and I knew that this book would be even more so. Public self-revelation in an addictive society can be dangerous, especially if one is challenging the most sacred cows of the illusion.

On another level, I realized that this book will be the first written documentation of *what I do.* Up until now, the only way to know how I work with people has been to come to one of the Intensive workshops that I schedule or to train with me and learn experientially about my work. Because the work I do is participatory and the theory has evolved and is evolving out of what I do, it does not easily lend itself to writing and language—or, at least, I feared it would not.

Also, most of the writing that I have done has been descriptive. It has described my observations about what I see happening in individuals, groups, families, organizations, the society, and, more and more, the planet. I have hinted at the work I do, and I have never really attempted to communicate it on any large scale.

There is now an international network of almost five hundred people who have trained with me for a year or more. Many of these people are professionals from all disciplines who are now doing Living

3

Process work. In addition, there are several thousand who have attended Intensives and have been influenced by this evolving work. Yet most people who have any concern or interest in what I actually do with people have either had to surmise, project, imagine, judge, or wonder. So I might say that this book is my "coming out of the closet" about my work, and needless to say, there is no small amount of fear attached to doing so.

It was very important to me that I be able to write this book in such a way that the form would be congruent with the ideas I am attempting to communicate. I did not want to put new wine in old wineskins. Writing *about* a new paradigm truly requires writing *in* a new paradigm. That meant that I had to wait for "pieces of understanding" to fall into place so that the book would reflect where I am at this stage in my process as a person, as a recovering person, and as a recovering professional. (I question the term *professional* as I write it, *and* I am a recovering professional.)

The work that I do has not been theory-informed. My training in psychology encouraged "professionals" to accept or develop theory and to operate out of it. That approach results in a tendency to make theory static and holy. It offers security and breeds rigidity. Professionals who operate in this way become "theory-bound."

My work informs my theory. By doing what works, by being led by the people with whom I work and not trying to fit them into my "theory" or preconceived notions, I have been able to hear and see them and myself and have had constantly to reassess what I do and to be willing to change and modify endlessly. I assume this process will continue throughout my life.[1]

This process of constant modification has often been a struggle. It would have been easier to justify what I do by invoking some theory rather than by sharing what I have intuitively had to do by trusting my own process and then later (sometimes years later) discovering an evolving theory. Yet what I want to share with you is what I do, and I want to do it in a way that makes sense to me. In order to do that, I need to share my process of coming to write this book.

I was initially going to write a book on treating the addictive process. I believe that any change or growth process *has* to deal with the addictive process. As I travel around the world seeing what is being done (and not being done) with addictions, I realize that the work we are doing in the Living Process Network is not only unique, it may well be revolutionary. Hence, it seemed that it was time to communicate what we know about it.

Then I changed the title to *Confronting and Healing the Addictive Process.* I realized that we were talking more about "healing" than "treating" and that there was much that needed to be said about the underlying addictive process and how it functions. My rationale was (1) we need a unified theory about the process of healing from addictions, (2) my colleagues and I know a great deal about working with this constellation of diseases, and (3) no one, as yet, has done any major writing about healing the overall addictive process and where it fits into what we know about the helping professions. I still believe that this kind of book is needed, and I have expanded what I want to do with these ideas.

As I began to look more closely at what is actually being done with people in treatment centers, mental hospitals, private psychotherapy, and clinics from a perspective that had changed immeasurably because of my own active recovery process from relationship addiction, my attempts to Live in Process—doing my own deep process work and sitting with the deep process of others—I knew that I had to write this book from a larger perspective.

I also saw that it was not possible for me to write about what I was doing without trying to say something about the theoretical framework that has emerged from the work as I am now doing it.

My evolution as a feminist has helped me understand how dangerous it is for a theoretical framework to be mistaken for reality. First, I am leery and fearful of work that cannot state its assumptions clearly. Women, blacks, Native Americans, and other minorities have suffered greatly because unstated assumptions of the dominant culture have long passed for "reality," thereby negating theirs.[2] Next, there are theoretical frameworks that can't be put into practice. They are fascinating in the abstract, but their proponents really have no idea how to *live* the theory. Third, I find more and more people who are changing their theory or their words to be more congruent with recovery and the "new science" while continuing to use old techniques, approaches, and behaviors. They have modified their content and not their process.

Hence, I felt that it was important to try to articulate what is true for me at this point, what I am doing and why I am doing it (as far as I know). I then decided upon *Beyond Therapy, Beyond Science,* because by this stage in my thinking about these issues, I knew that the work

I was doing extended far beyond most psychotherapy as it is being practiced (and as I had been taught to practice it) and far beyond the scientific worldview on which I had been raised. I found what I had been taught to be hopelessly embedded in a worldview that produces procedures and techniques that are not only not helpful, they are actually harmful—much more harmful than we have previously imagined.

I began to see psychotherapy as the practice of the addictive process and was eager to "name" psychotherapy as the systematized practice of codependence (which I still see as valid) and to focus the book on what is wrong, at a very deep level, with psychotherapy and its philosophical and theoretical assumptions. I was going to write about what is *wrong* with psychotherapy, what therapists are doing *wrong* and why at some important metalevel it really is not working. I was in a right/wrong dualism, and I know that when I am in any dualism, I am in my addictive disease process. So I stopped and waited with *my* process.

During this waiting time, I began to collect the many letters I was receiving from people who were reading and responding to my books, people who had tried every form of psychotherapeutic, medical, or psychiatric cure and had not really begun to improve and feel right with their lives until they faced their addictive process. They often felt great relief when they named their addiction (Step One of the Twelve-Step program of Alcoholics Anonymous) and started recovery. I kept these letters and read and reread them because they so paralleled the lives and healing of the people with whom I shared Living in Process.

Finally, I realized that the piece I had to face was that I was (or at least had been) one of those therapists who had operated out of a reductionistic-mechanistic, postmodernist[3] scientific worldview. I was a "scientist," well-trained in the scientific method, and although I had evolved and changed in many ways, I realized that the very method I now saw as destructive is still deeply embedded in the marrow of my bones. Even though I have progressively moved away from ideologies and practices that I have come to believe are not only unethical but harmful, I continue to uncover hidden assumptions and resultant practices in myself that I, personally, can no longer tolerate in anyone.

I began to realize that I had participated in most or many of the assumptions, techniques, and beliefs that I would now attack and about which I feel so intensely. I am not without responsibility for what psychotherapy was or has become. This was especially difficult for me to admit to, because I have always been somewhat of a rebel and a seeker and have never felt completely accepted by the traditional power structure of psychology and psychiatry (nor have I wanted to be). I was *of* it but not *in* it. Why did I have to admit the wrongness of being *of* it when I was not getting the perks for being *in* it? Because, for my own sobriety, I need to be as honest as I can be and confront the addictive process in myself wherever I find it, and I was clearly seeing this addictive process in the way I had learned to practice psychotherapy.

I began to see how the work that I had been trained to do was not only compatible with but helped perpetuate and exacerbate an addictive society and that psychotherapy as we have known it has always been enmeshed in the problem. I could see that the helping professions are in the same relationship to an addictive society that the enabler is to the addict. We take the pressure off and keep things going just enough to prevent the society from "hitting bottom"; we continue to "prop it up" and allow it to stay in its addiction. Because the work of the therapist is so integrated into the addictive model, the way we do what we do is no threat to the addictive society. In fact, we enable that addictive, dysfunctional system.

Out of this awareness came my conviction that this book first and foremost must be written and dedicated to my former clients as part of my amends process in my recovery work about having been a psychotherapist. I need to make an amend for trying to operate out of a belief system that I was taught and that even then did not feel right to me, and also for what I did *not* know. Solid recovery requires that we take responsibility for everything we did while practicing our disease, even if we were unaware, ignorant, or in denial. I am clear that I will need to continue this amends process as I develop more awareness about the ways I continue to perpetuate the addictive process in the work I do, and yet the writing of this book is an important part of the healing process.

Let me say a little about the amends process as I have learned about it from the Twelve-Step program based on Alcoholics Anonymous.[4] Forgiveness, righting of wrongs, and owning our own behaviors are not new concepts. Those of us in recovery from any of a variety of addictions have learned that in order to achieve and maintain some sort of serenity in our lives, we must own what we wittingly or unwittingly have done to others when we were operating out of our "disease" and make amends when it would not harm anyone to do so. Prior to making amends, it is necessary to do the footwork of the previous seven steps of the Twelve-Step program. Then, we need to make a list of those we have harmed or wronged, including ourselves, and make amends.

The amends process, I believe, is a process of claiming our own lives, relinquishing our defensiveness, and doing what we need to do to become *right within ourselves*. Making amends is a personal act. We make amends for ourselves. Amends are not made to make others feel better, to change others' attitude toward us, or to elicit forgiveness. We make amends because *we* need to. We make amends because we know that our recovery, our growth, our development, cannot proceed unless we claim those things we have done of which we are not proud that have harmed others. We need to own that we have behaved in ways that have been alien to our beliefs, morality, and spirituality.

So this book itself is an offering of amends for my blind spots and my following of a system that was not good for me or others. I was not conscious, then, of the system out of which I was operating. Even though, to the best of my knowledge, I did everything I did out of the best of motives, I still have to own and claim that I now know that the psychotherapy model I was taught was not helpful and was often destructive.

I want to make it clear that I have not done anything horrendous as a therapist. In fact, I was considered to be a "good" therapist. I was dedicated, caring, concerned, energetic, curious, and involved in my work, and I had integrity. I just did not know that the assumptions out of which I was trained and operating were ultimately destructive to me and my clients and subtly supported a worldview that was destructive to the planet. When we treat people as things or "its," we are destructive to them.[5] So, because making amends is where I am in my recovery process about my work, I begin this book with an amend to myself and my clients. The book itself is my amends.

In addition, as I look at my own development, I can see some of the pitfalls I missed and others that I fell into without even realizing that I was falling. As Michael Lerner says, "What therapists often do is simply help people accommodate better to the social roles that therapists accept as fixed and inevitable."[6] Because of my active role in the civil rights movement and my firm commitment to feminism, I believed that I had enough awareness not to help people *adjust* to a sick society. I now believe that my arrogance in this awareness clouded my ability to see the subtle ways I was still buying into the system.

Because I have been and continue to be part of the problem, I began to see clearly that this book cannot be a book about what *they* are doing wrong. It must be a book about what *I* can no longer do, what I now do, and the theoretical understanding I have developed. I do not want to exacerbate the problems that exist in the field of psychotherapy —within ourselves, with each other as psychotherapists, or with those with whom we work.[7]

These behaviors are common among psychotherapists of whatever discipline, and I have been a part of these behaviors at times. I know behaving like this is a part of my disease. Whenever I think dualistically, am judgmental, and set up and take sides, I am operating out of the addictive process.

The option for my health and sobriety is to speak out of my experiences, what I know, and what is true for me, which is what I will attempt to do in this book.

Out of these struggles the structure of this book emerged for me. It is clear to me that its structure needs to reflect my theory and belief system, and my theory and belief system need to inform the structure of this book.

In Part I, I share my personal and professional journey as a therapist and that of moving beyond being a "therapist" to becoming a "recovering psychotherapist" (as in recovering from being a psychotherapist and ultimately leaving the field completely). This journey is not only personal; it has been reflected in and parallel to the development of the field of psychotherapy. I was trained in classical Freudian psychodynamic psychotherapy, moved into the cognitive behavioral therapies, then to humanistic and systems psychology, and then to transpersonal psychology, picking and choosing all the way. Civil rights and feminism helped me add new and important dimensions that resulted in my development of a new approach to working with people. Working with addictions, including my own, added a major piece that culminated in a major shift in perceptions and theory.

As I share my own professional journey, I will flag significant struggles, experiences, confrontations, fears, awarenesses, joys, insights, and turning points that I will later pick up, showing how they have contributed to the work in which I now participate.

Part II will explore of the work I now do, the Living Process work. I will describe deep process work and show how the approach that I have learned is effective with addictions and, beyond addiction, to living fully. The interdependence and interrelationship of the Living Process work and the work with addictions will be discussed in detail. I will relate this work to significant points in my professional development and show how the *process* of my joys, fears, confusion, trust, and pain have emerged and continue to emerge into the work I am doing.

Part III will explore the theoretical and philosophical issues and lessons that have emerged out of my own personal and professional journey and the work that I do.

In order to do my work I have had to recognize and explore the assumptions inherent in my training and the worldview out of which my education came. I have not *tried* to develop the "mind of the beginner" in the Zen Buddhist sense, yet I often found myself there. I believe that if I had known about this "empty cup" (emptying myself consciously so more can enter) and tried to develop it, I quite possibly would not have achieved this openness. I tried to reconcile the worldview out of which I had come with what I knew and what I was learning and experiencing. I saw how important it is to "name" our experience and our reality. As I did this I began to question what I see as violence done in the name of science and healing in the helping professions. I began to ask if psychologists and people in the helping professions are open to asking themselves the question, Is the unspoken worldview that underlies the assumptions from which I practice my profession perhaps, unwittingly, contributing to the very problems that I am committed to solve? If we are not open to struggling with this question and articulating our assumptions, we are, indeed, part of the problem.

I went through a period of being aware that there are some things (like "techniques" and interpretation) that I can no longer do and still be "in integrity with myself."[8] I struggled with how to be myself and be congruent with what I believe and what I know while naming what I am learning.

I began to uncover philosophical and theoretical positions[9] that supported what I had already "organically" discovered by doing what my life and work demanded, the theories that I discovered out of some of the painful and exhilarating shifts that had occurred in me in order to be in integrity with myself. I saw how we truly must move beyond psychotherapy and beyond science as we know it.

In this part, I will bring forward the previously stated threads of my own development, tie these threads into the work that I now do, and weave these together with some theoretical and philosophical explorations.

This part will include the following:

1. An exploration of the philosophy of science and the movement beyond a reductionistic, mechanistic, empirical, "modern" worldview. I will look at what David Griffin calls a "constructive, revisionary, postmodern"[10] scientific exploration, what is being explored as the "new paradigm," and at David Bohm's idea of the universe as a hologram or a holomovement.[11]

2. An exploration of the practice of psychotherapy as we have known it—its assumptions, contributions, and limitations.

3. The importance of social movements and changes in working with people.

4. The importance of understanding addiction and recovery from addiction and the interrelationship between addiction and the prevalent scientific worldview. I will also look at the relationship of recovery to emerging scientific models and the relationships of these models or philosophies to recovery as an interactive process.

5. The role of the spiritual in all of the above issues. A distinction between religion and how it supports the current limited scientific worldview will be explored, as will other implications for spirituality.

6. What all these philosophical and theoretical issues can mean when looked at as a whole process and part of the process of the whole.

I then want to voice some of my concerns and visions and my sense of the future implications of the ideas explored here.

The work I am doing has been a process. I have been through many levels of truth with it and am sure I will go through many more. My quest has not been to figure out some disembodied theory and then force myself, my work, and others into it. My work involves following the process wherever it leads and *then* discovering that there are ideas, theories, constructs, and philosophies that are congruent with my experience. I have come to these theories "embodied," in touch with my feelings and intuition and trusting both. I have been fully participatory in my work and the evaluation of it. I have done my deep process work; I have confronted my addictions and am actively in recovery. I have attempted to Live in Process, often "flying by the seat of my pants" and "living a life of faith."

Lest I misrepresent myself, I want to stress that I recognize the importance of logical, rational, left-brain functioning. The problem with these thinking functions, I believe, is where they come in the process. When we lead with our logical, rational minds and try to get our feelings, thoughts, awarenesses, behavior, and even spirituality to follow, we almost always get in trouble. When we do this, we almost always find ourselves firmly entrenched in the current mechanistic empirical paradigm. I have found that this kind of thinking is best done *following* the experience or the process of the knowing, as it is integrated into a life process.

When we decide first where we should go, we never get there.

Part I

The Rise and Demise
of a Psychotherapist

As I begin this part, I find myself a bit nervous and uneasy. I clean up my desk and look for distractions. Staying with those feelings, I am aware of uncertainty and fear. I am also aware that these feelings emerge when I referent myself externally. Will I be too vulnerable if I expose myself this way? Will my attackers and detractors find fuel for their fires (which they will do anyway, regardless of what I say or do)? I cannot control this, and yet it does engender fear and caution in me. I realize that the attacks that have been made against me, fortunately or unfortunately, had little or nothing to do with me or what I am saying. Will it seem arrogant to share my development and the emergent threads in that process? Perhaps, and I know of no other way to communicate the *process* of what I am now doing and how I have come to it. When we see only an end point or an advanced point of what someone is doing, we tend to ignore that getting there was a process and that the path is the way. The process *is* the participating fully in our part of the universe and *is* the information.

So I hope that this section will be read in the spirit of the Zen saying "When a wise man [*sic*] points to the moon, the fool ends up looking at his finger." What I am pointing to in this part is not my particular personality but to a process that has included many people, many ideas, and many paths. Please do not become overinvolved with the finger.

13

The Foundations for New Ideas

Sometime around the age of ten I had a very clear awareness of the work that I would be doing. I remember "knowing," and I also remember that I had no way to articulate what it was that I had discovered. As clearly as I can recall I had no anxiety about not being able to put words to my knowing. As I look back from my current understanding, I would say that this was an example of "trusting the process." I had no need of words for my knowing in fifth grade, so I tucked away the knowing and stayed busy with the full-time focus of being a ten-year-old.

I was always an eager and curious learner, as were my mother and father, and even though I went to very small schools (two- and three-room country schools), I believe that I had a good and broad education. Neither of my parents had a college degree. We came from a simple Arkansas "hillbilly" background, and our milieu was not one that had language for what my work would be. (Perhaps it does not exist even now.) Externally, I was not preparing myself for anything, and internally I felt very clearly in my process, whatever that was. My father was a "natural" electronics genius who found a way to get an on-the-job education by working for the U.S. government and doing research in electronics. My father taught me the basics of mechanistic science—a *way* of thinking. He taught me to state the problem clearly, reduce it to component parts, and to work on the problem until we could fix it. I grew up believing he could fix anything (which he could, mechanically). My mother was a poet, mystic, painter, and horse-woman. She taught me to trust my intuition, to respect animals and the earth, and to live with myself and the earth.

My father's wisdom was good for living with mechanics and technology and seeing their place in our lives. My mother's wisdom was good for living and giving me the foundations necessary for recognizing a Living Process System. I feel grateful to know both of these systems and their methods so intimately.

Early in my life, neither my mother nor my father really had any clear connection to the work that I knew I would be doing, and their approach was always to support my interests and curiosity and not to interfere with my path. My mother, in some ways, was a natural "psychologist." Whenever people did something that impinged upon our family, she would always say, "Try to see what is behind their behavior. See if you can understand why they are doing what they do." This, I believe, was an early contribution to my curiosity about what "made people tick." I now see that this was early training into interpreting others, the efficacy of which I now question.

Somewhere between fifth grade and high school, I latched onto the word *psychiatrist*. I was going to become a psychiatrist. My high school years were spent taking the necessary classes for entrance into and scholarships for a good pre-med program, knowing I would have to work and get scholarships to go to college. I also took on various "causes," whether personal or group, excelled in sports, and participated in every activity that was available to me. I learned as much or more in my "activities" as I did in classes, and this interaction of formal and informal learning has been a thread throughout my life.

I entered Washington University, St. Louis, as a premedical student in the fall of 1952. I was on my way to becoming a psychiatrist. Because I was going to medical school, I worked at the local hospital in the summers. This hospital was a small, Catholic community hospital and was very supportive of me. My first year I worked as a "special treatment nurse" and was assigned my "own" patients. I had complete care of them, did all their nursing procedures, and in my spare time was able to read medical books about their particular illnesses and discuss my learning with the nurses and physicians. I spent time in surgery, staff meetings, and, in general, was included into the operation of the hospital.

In my second year I worked in polio isolation. This was before the Salk vaccine was common, and we had an "epidemic" with three people in iron lungs and several other less severe cases. With my youthful, arrogant nonvulnerability, I considered myself safe and volunteered to work in isolation. Again, I learned a great deal.

My last summer at the hospital I was asked to work in the medical laboratory as a medical technologist. Within a few weeks, I was on call every other night and every other weekend. I was twenty years old, and I was making decisions about life and death. The first such decision was in relation to a blood transfusion for the wife of one of my favorite high school teachers. In a small town, there is no such thing as professional distance; we all just pitched in on everything that needed to be done. I learned about canceling dates to go to the hospital. I learned about being ready to leave work after a long day of running blood samples, setting up cultures, and gazing through the microscope at someone's urine and being called back on emergencies that kept me involved until the wee hours of the morning. I learned the exhilaration of working intensely with the medical team and the terror of a 2:00 A.M. drive to the hospital when I was drowsy from sleep. I learned what it meant to work in the medical world, and I also saw the seductiveness of medicine, the egocentrism of medicine, and how demanding a lover it could be. I also began to be uncomfortable with physicians and questioned whether I wanted to be one.

Throughout my college education, I associated mostly with pre-medical students, music students, and students who were active in the campus YWCA-YMCA. I worked hard in my classes, with major work in chemistry and zoology *and* a declared major in psychology, dated steadily, and was busy in extracurricular activities. I had opportunities to be on many national and international student committees, which broadened my parochial perspective and supported my deep family beliefs that we are all citizens of the world. I traveled, sang, explored my relationship with my spirituality, played, and studied hard. I moved into civil rights work in the mid-1950s and fought hard for causes in which I believed. I loved the university and what I was doing. College was a good time.

My favorite course as an undergraduate was comparative anatomy and embryology, taught by a marvelous German professor of the "old school," Dr. Vicktor Hamberger. Many years later, I realized why this was my favorite course: it was the *only* science course I had that was a *process* course. Every other science course studied dead or static phenomena or laws. The embryology course, while studying static serial cross sections, really studied the *process* of the development of the chick embryo and in doing so studied the *process* of evolution and development. I loved it.

When it came time to apply to medical schools, I found that I could not fill out the applications. Like accusatory reminders of a task undone, they sat on my desk for many months. I still was in touch with this inner knowing about my work, and I was progressively less clear that medical school was the vehicle for me. Just as the deadlines were pressing in upon me, I was called into the office of the dean of women. I had never been called into the dean's office, and I was terrified. What had I done? What had I done that she *knew* about? Was it the Vaseline on the toilet seats in the dorm? Was it sneaking through her dining room at night to get midnight snacks from the kitchen (totally forbidden, of course)? I decided to play it cool and let her show her hand first.

Happily, she had called me in to tell me that she was recommending me for a Danforth Fellowship, nicknamed the "Danny Grad Program."

After our meeting, I was so sure that this fellowship (which was for a year of self-development) was right for me, that I threw away all my medical school applications. Later I learned that there had been over six hundred sixty applications; sixty-some had been interviewed, and they had accepted eighteen. I was one of those chosen. Even though I did not have the language, trusting that this was right for me was a clear example of trusting the process.

I was sent to Maryland (I welcomed the chance to get to know another geographic area; my school was in St. Louis, and my home in Oregon) and the fellowship offered me the time and space to have a year for myself, explore another part of the country, work with the dean and counsel with students, be a troubleshooter for the dean on campus, test out love relationships, and try to get clear on what I should do next. I was learning to trust my process as a young adult.

Of the many important things I learned that year, what I learned about prayer seems particularly significant to me now. Because the Danforth Fellowship was somewhat identified with spirituality and I had been on the national executive committee of the United Student Christian Fellowship and the National Student YMCA-YWCA, local churches in Baltimore saw me as a potential new resource. For some reason, I was invited to lead retreats on prayer. Actually, while I had a lot of intellectual knowledge, I had done most of my praying by closing my eyes and just getting through it in church. I decided that if I was going to speak about prayer, I'd better find out what it was like. I committed myself to "try prayer" and set aside an hour each morning to see what it meant to me. Learning about important issues and concepts by participating has been an important facet of the way I learn. I believe this "exercise" in prayer was the first time that I consciously understood the differences among participatory (or open) learning systems, experiential learning systems (having someone else set up the situation in order to learn what you should by experience), and scientific learning systems (or abstract learning).

That "Danforth year" was just what I needed. I had time for myself, time to explore new areas geographically, interpersonally, and within myself. Relieved from the pressure of academia, I audited courses such as poetry and art that I had not taken time for in my heavily scientific pre-med curriculum. I pursued my music and acting by singing as a soloist in a church choir and acting in several local and campus musicals. Also, the interpersonal psychotherapy of Harry Stack Sullivan had its center right down the road, so I was exposed to lectures and seminars that were pushing beyond the individual focus in psychotherapy. This, coupled with the fact that one of the men I dated was undergoing Reichian therapy in the nude (orgone therapy) three times a week, gave me food for thought.

Two other aspects of this year were important to me: the money we were given to spend on others and the trust that was bestowed on us. We were given twenty-five dollars a month to spend on other people in any way we saw fit (in 1956–57 this seemed like a lot; even in 1989, I wonder how many foundations do this). The school where I was sent had many first-generation college students from rural communities. I bought myself a season ticket to the symphony with my own money and used my "gift money" to purchase a second season ticket; each time I went I took a new person with me. I did the same for the theater and the arts that year. This, again, was a participatory approach to sharing that I still practice.

The Danforth Foundation gave each of us a mandate to serve the campus and to grow as a person, and it trusted us to do that. Just how we did so was completely up to us. Our growing, learning, and seeing was in a *context*, it was *self-determined*, it was a *process* that could not be predetermined or determined by someone not in the situation, and it was *respectful*. These are key elements in the work I now do.

During this year, I *discovered* my decision about medical school. By not trying to *make* a decision, I let myself *discover* one. For years, I have said, "Our most important decisions are discovered, not made. We can make the unimportant ones, and we have to wait to discover the big ones." During this year I discovered that I simply could not go to medical school. I did not know why; I only knew that I could not do it, and I trusted that. I believe now that had I gone to medical school, it would have taken me even longer to unlearn what I have had to unlearn to do the work that I now do, and I question if it would have been possible at all.

After the Danforth year, I considered social work and psychology and finally chose graduate school in psychology. I was accepted into the program in clinical psychology approved by the APA (American Psychological Association) at Washington University in St. Louis and plunged into graduate work. My graduate and undergraduate education was paid for by scholarship, or I would not have been able to attend. I say this because I am so aware of how important it was for me to follow my path and pursue my education when, culturally, there was such great pressure on women to give up the pursuit of their own work. I recognized the pressures and responded to them, and always tried to follow my path.

I loved graduate school, and I loved psychology. My adviser in graduate school was the professor of experimental psychology, and he was concerned that because I was such a good "scientist" I would be wasted in clinical psychology (the experimental psychologists were seen as the "real," "true" psychologists, while the clinical psychologists were seen as "fringe" or "play" psychologists, although they far outnumbered the experimentalists). Because I loved and respected my adviser so much, it was difficult not to follow his "advice."

He and my former embryology professor, Dr. Hamberger, even set up a joint research project between the psychology and zoology departments (my two favorites), and I had a lab in each building. I was operating on the brains of chicken embryos, making various kinds of lesions in different locations, then hatching the eggs, and studying various conditioning patterns in a Skinner box that we had built and programmed. Probably the most exciting part of this study was when the chickens got loose in the basement of the psychology building and the secretaries tried to catch them.

As the first year of graduate school was the basic "science" aspect of psychology, I buzzed along quite smoothly and easily. I breezed through the comprehensives examination with top honors and was advised to skip a master's degree and move into completing the doctorate as soon as possible. That summer I was given a job at Arkansas State Mental Hospital in Little Rock and found myself plunged into a snake pit of racism, superstition, "lockup," and intrigue that I found to be unnervingly similar to conditions at Delaware State Mental Hospital outside Wilmington, where I had worked the previous summer.

Because I was listed as a "recreational therapist" in Delaware, I attended my first Alcoholics Anonymous meeting with "patients" there in 1957. The "patients" also taught me to play pool (although I was *death* on the table) and several card games. My favorite times that summer in Delaware were taking the old women from the "back wards" out for walks and sitting under the trees. They didn't seem "crazy" to me. Many of them were immigrants who could speak little or no English and who had become well adjusted to the hospital. Albertina, to whom this book is dedicated, was one of those old women.

In Little Rock, I was expected to help build up the almost nonexistent (before that summer) psychology department and *test* patients. One of my most enlightening experiences that summer learning about the cultural bias of intelligence and psychological tests. I found that what we called "testing the limits" was the only possible way to approximate getting valid results on poor Southern whites and blacks. I also learned some terribly "valuable" diagnostic information as I sat in on the psychiatric staff meetings: I learned that long fingernails are an important diagnostic "criterion" for schizophrenia (if people have long fingernails they are probably schizophrenic) and that oral sex of any kind is abnormal and people who indulge in it at all should be hospitalized. Also, there was a currently held psychiatric belief among the physicians that divorcing and later remarrying the same person was a diagnostic indicator of schizophrenia. I think it is easy to see how this early training stood me in good stead in my later work.

I went to several civil rights meetings while I was there and battled with many of my colleagues over civil rights. I remember once being invited to the home of a colleague, whose husband was a resident at the medical school hospital across the street from where I worked. He was working in Ob/Gyn in the clinic at the med school and mostly was delivering black babies. During dinner, he was complaining about "wasting" his time waiting for those women to deliver those babies and how he just used forceps in every delivery to "get it over with quicker." I was horrified and said so. A heated Southern discussion ensued. Needless to say, I was never invited back to dinner. I did discuss my concern with one of the faculty from the medical school. I wondered how many of those children have birth defects, learning disabilities, and impulse disorders because that particular doctor did not want to "waste" his time. It was clear to me that I could not separate my politics, personal ethics, and belief system from the work I was doing. Neither was it for that resident, and, somehow, his was just more integrated into the dominant belief system and seen as "normal" for that time and worldview. In many instances, I saw that the "scientific" worldview as it was then practiced was a lot more "political" than I had been taught.

Following that summer, I decided to take a year out from my doctoral work to attend Union Theological Seminary in New York City. My stated reason was that "an educated person should know what she thinks theologically." Down deep, I believe that going to seminary was just something I needed to do. I had no money, so I applied for a scholarship. I couldn't get any scholarship money unless I was in a specific program, so I was put in the M.R.E. program (Master of Religious Education—at that time, usually for women) and then was allowed to take the courses I wanted. I was given an assistantship in the Department of Psychiatry and Religion helping doctoral students design and analyze their final research projects as well as work on some of the director's pet projects. In addition, I did field work with a campus student organization in New Jersey and part-time work in the library.

The library job scared me to death; libraries just overwhelmed me. At that time, I was in the process of learning that I had had a reading disability as a child and that I was basically an auditory learner. I had almost total auditory recall, and reading was a struggle for me. My eyes worked against me in dealing with the printed word. However, having almost total auditory recall was a wonderful skill for a therapist and/or facilitator, and I have been grateful for it. Working in the library helped me become more comfortable with books. I had long since outgrown my perceptual learning problem, and my self-identity as not being a visual learner changed that year.

I took advantage of the opportunity to learn from the "greats" in theology: Tillich, Buber, the Niebuhrs, Bob Brown, Siever, Milenberg. I harvested from the theological minds that surrounded me and loved it. Because this work would not contribute to my doctoral degree, I did not feel any pressure to perform and worked for the sheer joy of learning.

Many doors were open to me that year. I discovered that because I was a full-time student at Union, I could take courses at Columbia and Teacher's College, which I never could have afforded otherwise, under an exchange agreement with Union. I then learned that the upper level courses were reserved for "their" doctoral students, unless I could get special permission from the faculty teaching the courses I wanted to take. Everyone I asked said yes, and I was able to study with some of the greats of the day.

In addition to going to school and work, I explored New York. The Cloisters, the Museum of Modern Art, and the Frick Museum kept me sane. I came to realize how much I loved nature and how my time in nature had always been a kind of gyroscope for maintaining my sanity. That year helped me know that I must have nature in my life and spend periods of time in nature to keep in touch with my roots and, as Paul Tillich would say, "the ground of my being."

Yet, I loved New York, too. Whenever I could, I went to the theater and museums, to concerts and films. I don't believe I learned much about *my* spirituality at Union Seminary; I learned theology (and there's a great difference). I learned much more about my spirituality by "doing New York."

Another "sanity check" that year was a colleague from the Little Rock experience who was getting her doctorate in counseling at Teachers College. We religiously scheduled a weekly lunch where we could look at the various insanities of our respective institutions. We are friends to this day. I found out how important it is to have persons outside the institutional systems in which I am enmeshed with whom to do "reality checks."

After that year at seminary, I decided I needed to go back to graduate school and finish up my course work in my area of focus, clinical psychology. I had one unit on alcoholism that was part of one class session, and, like many other professionals, I got from that unit the mistaken impression that I knew something about alcoholism and addiction. I returned to graduate school with a new husband, a baby growing in my belly, and a determination to get my requirements done for my doctorate. I received an NIMH (National Institute of Mental Health) fellowship in gerontology contingent upon my doing some research in gerontology, and that seemed all right. Mostly, I was knocking off the clinical requirements and loving every minute of it.

The birthing process may well have been my most important learning that year. I *hated* my doctor. It never occurred to me that I could change doctors. I thought when I was pregnant and consulted an Obstetrician that we were "married" for nine months. I don't think he liked me much either. Luckily, I had a Filipino resident who was related to one of my graduate student colleagues, and he attended me during most of the labor. The physician only arrived to catch my baby (of course, he was paid his full fee).

I learned a lot about process *and* powerlessness during that birthing. I also learned a lot about myth, heresy, and folklore. I started my "labor" early in the morning and felt no pain. I just felt regular "waves" going through my body. When they were about two and a half minutes apart, I called the doctor and reported in; I still felt no pain so believed that I was not having labor "pains." The hospital confirmed that I was dilating and in labor. I still didn't hurt, but there was a level of focus and intensity that was all-consuming and transcended time and space. Then the pains hit. I have a high threshold for pain—I have had many injuries and accidents—and I had never felt anything like this. If this was what people called labor pain, I couldn't imagine thirty or so hours of it. No one bothered to tell me that I had moved from labor to delivery and after ten or eleven of these contractions I would have a baby; they were hoping that the doctor would make it before I delivered. This was the point where I suddenly remembered that my grandmother had died in childbirth and my mother had almost died in childbirth (at the time it seemed irrelevant that there had been extenuating circumstances in both instances).

Between contractions, I quietly crossed my legs and with great calm announced that I had decided not to have this baby. No one seemed to pay much attention, but I was dead serious. I lay there with this huge belly heaving around and began—logically and rationally— to figure out how, over a period of nine months, I could reabsorb this fetus. I was willing to carry it around and take whatever time was necessary. A certain calm spread over me as I believed that I had "figured out" a solution to my present dilemma. Suddenly, I had another contraction, and that contraction challenged my whole education and worldview. Figured-out solutions were grand and could be very logical and rational; they just didn't always make sense. Also, I did not *control* this process. It was not just *my* process. I had a daughter who was living her process; we could participate in each other's process, and if either of us tried to control the process of the other, it would be destructive—even fatal. Both of my children have continued to help me learn this lesson again and again.

I have since discussed this with my daughter and told her that it was not that I didn't want *her*; I just was afraid of delivering a baby. How often I have relearned that when we do not deal with our feelings, we often project them in a destructive way.

When my first child was one week old, I had a call from the professor of the one course for which I had missed the final because I was giving birth. He said something like, "Are you going to laze around all your life? When are you going to get in here and take this final?" Immediately, I rose to the challenge and told him that I would be in the next morning. I greatly admired this professor. He was a real scholar, and I absolutely loved his course on Freud. He later told me that he and my adviser had been discussing me, and they were afraid that having this baby might mean that I would drop out of psychology. They hoped I wouldn't. I was grateful that he threw me just the right hook, and I jumped for it.

That summer I was scheduled for twelve hours of a practicum in a child guidance clinic with an excellent staff. That meant leaving my daughter with a woman from our church and her family. That was the hardest thing I ever did. I cried for days, and yet realized that she had the full attention of a mother, grandmother, and two sons every day. When I picked her up, she was always bathed, fed, and being walked in her carriage or played with in the house. She was probably getting more than I could have given her. Still, in my self-centeredness, I feared that everything should come from me. I realized that because I had my work, I was probably able to be more with her when I was with her, but in the 1960s there was little or no support for being a working mother. I was the only one from my Danforth group who was really following my own work *and* trying to be a wife and mother. Those were difficult, painful, and joyful times for me.

My agreement with my husband was that if we went back to St. Louis so I could finish my second year of clinical work, I would return to New York City so he could finish his education for the ministry. I was ready for my internship in clinical psychology and applied to four institutions in New York. I was accepted at three, and the other one wanted me as an intern *but* suggested that I stay home with my daughter and *then* come. (I still hate that kind of sexism. No one told my husband to wait a year.) I decided to accept the internship with David Wechsler at Bellevue Hospital because my husband was in school and with this internship I could get some income and fulfill a requirement for my doctorate at the same time.

Entering the World of the Professional

I will never forget how terrified I was when I first walked into Bellevue Hospital, especially before I was assigned my key. On my first morning there, I gathered with the other interns in the psychology office. They were all from "big" schools in New York City. I was twenty-six years old and felt about three. Suddenly, Wechsler's big voice boomed out: "Where's that little girl from the Midwest? I've never accepted anyone without an interview before. She looked good on paper, and she'd better *be* good." That set the tone for my time at Bellevue. My strong pre-med background had included physics and a good science and math emphasis, and that was what Dr. Wechsler needed for the research he wanted to do that year. I can't remember anything significant coming out of the work we did except that I got to know Wechsler quite well.

I was assigned to the adolescent ward. A young woman from Hunter and I were the only two female interns. At that time, women clinical psychologists were expected to work with adolescents or children, so we always were assigned to those wards. Working on these wards did allow me to work with two outstanding psychiatrists.

People who work with children and adolescents, I noticed, behave differently from people who work exclusively with adults, and it is usually those who work with adults who make up the rules and ethics. There is much less "objectivity" and more relating in settings where work is done with children and adolescents. This observation solidified my realization that there are some covert models of working with people that are not exactly consistent with the dominant models in psychology.

People on the staff at Bellevue often took kids home with them, shared their families with them, took them on excursions, held them, walked with their arms around them, and developed what would now be considered a "nonobjective, nonethical" dual relationship with them. Often, the staff became "friends" with the kids, and this friendship spanned years as they became a surrogate family. This training was my initiation into beginning to ask what a "therapeutic" relationship really means.

Again, I loved my work at Bellevue, and I was lucky to have many opportunities to feed my hungry curiosity. Somehow, in applying there, I had missed the fact that Bellevue was a *diagnostic* center. Long-term treatment was not done there. Individuals were diagnosed at Bellevue and sent to the outlying state hospitals for long-term treatment, but I wanted to be a therapist (or so I thought). How could I do that when no one stayed around long enough for me to therapize?

I talked with my supervisor and Dr. Wechsler, and they said if some patients were willing and if I could do the other work expected of me, we could arrange for a few patients to stay and have "treatment" with me. Frankly, looking back, I don't know how great this was for the patients. It did, however, offer them an opportunity to stay near their families, so they agreed. I had my "clients." I had a therapy supervisor from the psychology department who had a psychodynamic Freudian perspective. I decided I would like different perspectives on the same cases, so I was given permission to do whatever I could work out. So, in addition, I arranged to have a psychiatrist with an Adlerian orientation and one with a Jungian orientation give me additional supervision on my cases.

25

Other than fighting off the sexual advances of my psychology supervisor, this proved to be a good experience for me. Having three different perspectives relieved any one person of being the only and final word on how to conceptualize and what to do. Having them on the same cases left me lots of options to see what made the most sense to me. This setup, I believe, saved me from psychological and systemic dogmatism and focused the decision making on me and my client, a process that has, I believe, been of utmost importance in my development.

Because Bellevue was a diagnostic center, we did lots of testing. The usual battery was an Intelligence Scale (almost always a Wechsler, of course, sometimes a Stanford-Binet with children, and we were working on the WPPSI at that point), a Rorschach, a Figure-Drawing, and a Bender-Gestalt; others were sometimes used so we would be familiar with a range of tests to be used when indicated. We had one man on the staff who was a genius with the Draw-a-Person test. He could take one figure drawing and in a few minutes give us all the information we had required a whole battery to get. His information was valid and reliable. I learned that in spite of standardization and standardized procedures, the test was only as good as the person giving it. Because all the Wechsler tests were developed there, there was a certain "looseness" about their administration. Later, I discovered that other mental health clinics and hospitals were much more rigid than Wechsler ever was with those tests.

One of my most important lessons at Bellevue was that I didn't have the luxury of lounging around with a battery of tests. There was a lot of testing done, and we were expected to *produce;* because the new psychiatric residents were in need of so much support, I learned to do up to six full batteries a day and have them scored and written up by the time I finished the testing. At the time, it was a killer *and* it kept psychological testing in perspective for me. I never saw it as being akin to the coronation of the queen or some other splendiferous process. Up until I quit doing it entirely, it was just one tool among many to get information. I am very grateful for this perspective; psychological testing and even interpretations from it are, after all, a very small sampling of behavior.

As I was ready to leave Bellevue, I was recommended for a "plum job" that paid well at a children's residential treatment center. I was to go to the center two nights a week for a few hours until I completed my internship and would then work full-time. Early in my career there I began to uncover some suspicious information in the charts and after talking with some of the boys discovered that they were being sexually molested by the assistant director. When I met with the director about my findings, I was told that it was "my word against his" and that "my services would no longer be needed." I sent letters to all the board members and left, feeling I was abandoning the kids and not knowing what else to do. This was my first introduction to working in the field as a "real" professional.

My short stint as a psychologist in a residential treatment center was followed by three years as a school psychologist in Westchester County, New York. As a licensed school psychologist, I worked in Westchester during the day, took classes two nights a week at Teacher's College, Columbia, and tried to have some time with my daughter. In his last year of seminary, my husband was working weekends. His schedule was more flexible than mine, so he did more child care during the week and took our daughter to and from day care. I missed being with her and treasured our time together.

Initially, being a school psychologist did not seem to give me much opportunity to do what I really wanted to do. I was the sole psychologist for a high school of twenty-three hundred students three days a week and for a grade school of several hundred students one day a week; I was in the central office to do reports and meet with parents one day a week. I had the responsibility of doing the testing for all the special classes in the high school. Regular retesting was periodically required by law. Thanks to my training in efficient testing and report writing at Bellevue, this took little time. I then began to snoop around for other things to do.

When I first took the job, 10 percent of my work came from self-referrals through the structure of the school. When I left, three years later, 90 percent of my load was self-referral. I was able to get the required work done in 10 percent of my time and spent the rest of my time really working with kids and faculty. I worked with some of the kids off and on for two or three years. They taught me a lot.

One of my most important "teachers" was a very bright, sensitive young man who was an artist and a writer. When I discovered him, he was repeating *all* of the courses for the sophomore year. I called him in and discovered in him a beautiful and intuitive young man who was wonderful the way he was; he just didn't fit into the system the way *it* was. When I spoke with his parents, I discovered that they were both artists and realized that he was very much like them. He reminded me of a person who had no skin or flesh over his nerves. He poured out his creativity in beautiful art and poetry, which he shared with me.

He, his parents, and I agreed that if I could find a school that would accept and support him the way he was he could go there. I looked all over the United States and could not find a place for him. My pain in this awareness was second only to his and his parents'. In the middle of his second time through the same sophomore courses, he decided to quit school and join the army. I couldn't imagine what he would do in the army, but I could not think of anything else. Because this was his decision, his parents and I painfully agreed and supported him. Periodically, I would hear from him.

One night I dreamed about him. The next day his parents called and asked me if I had heard from him. I hadn't. They had just received his footlocker and some other things of his. A few days after that I walked out of my office, and there in the midst of the students who were hanging around waiting to be seen (much to the consternation of the administration, who sometimes saw this gaggle of kids as "untidy") was this young man. I burst into tears and rushed over to embrace him. He had been kicked out of the army. He had been reading Nietzsche and had written a paper about his response. His sergeant had found it and passed it on, all the way up to the commanding officer. Within two days he had been interviewed by the psychiatrist, the chaplain, and I don't know who else, and he was out of the army. They were afraid he was a subversive. He was still a little dazed. So was I. If there was ever a harmless person in the world, it was he. Was there no place in this society for this kid? And what did it say about this society if there was no place for him? Working with individuals had to be broader than *just* working with individuals. For healing to happen, we must have a society that has space for persons like this kid.

Another of my great teachers during these three years was a kid whom I had known by reputation my first year there and had never met. He was supposed to be the most intelligent student the school had ever had. His records showed that he had gone off the scale on every intelligence test he had ever taken. He came from a wealthy, intelligent dysfunctional family. His parents, though well educated, never left the house. In the fall of my second year as a school psychologist, he made an appointment to see me. I was flattered and excited to see what he would be like.

His first words upon entering the room were, "Where's the psychologist?" I told him that he was "looking at her," and he said "You can't be. You're too young. I expected someone with gray hair in a gray suit." As he sat in front of me, I saw a young man in pain, cautious, scared, suspicious, and careful. I looked him straight in the eye and said, "Andrew, I'm not as intelligent as you are. I know few people who are, and I won't compete with you on an intellectual level. But I may *know* more than you do, and I can listen. Shall we give it a try?" His whole body shook and shuddered (which I would now recognize as a deep process coming up), his eyes filled with tears, and a deep sigh went through him. I saw him two to three times a week for two years, and he was a great teacher for me. He graduated with honors and went off to an Ivy League school—to be a psychologist. He was a wonderful gift for me. I don't think I ever really knew what I was doing. At that time in my development I really had only had training in psychodynamically oriented psychotherapies and behaviorism. I am sure that I tried both on him at various times (little, if any, behavioral work, I'm relieved to say). I'm sure that I made stabs at analyzing, and—I hate to admit it—I am sure I tried my hand at "wise" interpretations. Mostly, to my credit, because I really didn't know *what* to do, I just listened and *cared*, a lot. I knew that the contact and the relationship were good for both of us, and we both learned something (I more than he, probably).

There was a lot that I didn't know. As I look back, it is clear that he came from a dysfunctional family, and I suspect one in which there was chemical abuse. I have a vague recollection of the use of prescription drugs on the part of his parents, probably alcohol too. In fact, I would now guess that he had a high probability of becoming an alcoholic. I didn't know about addictions then, and neither did my profession except in a very cursory way.

As I look back on my time at Bellevue, I can see so many cases that were presented at grand rounds there were cases of addiction: sex addiction, alcohol, food—all the addictions. Addiction was never mentioned, except occasionally with respect to alcohol, and then we looked at the organicity involved. As far as I can tell from some conferences I have attended recently, this is *still* the situation at many hospitals and medical centers. There is still no understanding of addiction.

And, we had no idea of what it really meant to come from an addicted family. Oh, we took family histories, of course, or the social workers did—division of labor, you know—but we only used them for diagnosis (as I say that, I wonder if even that is true); we really didn't *do* anything with the information. Much of the information we gathered was mainly used for mental masturbation. I don't believe we knew what to do with it, because we were working out of a model (still prevalent) that basically said if we *understood* a problem (and *sometimes* could make the client understand it), the problem was *solved*.

Also, here I was working with a kid who had a brain that wouldn't quit and who, naturally, stayed in that excellent head of his; never once did we really deal with his *feelings*. We talked, and talked, and talked. He had never had an opportunity to get beyond his logical, rational brain into his process and deep processes, which were rumbling around inside him. I didn't know about dealing with his and his family's addictions and his processes. I did the best I could, and I now wish I had known more.

My one day a week as a psychologist in the grade school was quite different than my three days at the high school. I dealt with some discipline and behavior problems, and most of my work was focused upon learning disabilities. I had had some training in these disorders in my graduate work and at Bellevue in the outpatient clinic, and, again, I felt more curious than competent. I was expected to test these kids, analyze the tests, and come up with a prescription for a cure—the old medical model. I will say, however, that when it came down to education, the teachers and the principal were more interested in working with the child's *process* than a "fix" or a "cure." One child I evaluated had a fascinating constellation of history, test scores, and scatter on the tests. He clearly was "something" (diagnostically), but I had no idea what. I suggested to the parents that we get a consultation from the Columbia Presbyterian Neuropsychiatric Institute in New York City (one of my professors from Columbia did research there) and see what they had to say. I was still operating out of the medical model that assumed if we could just get an accurate *diagnosis* we would know what to do; we would have the "fix."

I carefully wrote up my report and sent it off to the new Department of Pediatric Neurology. Within a few days I had a call from the *director* of the department. (I can tell you that I was scared to death.) "Who are you? What's your background? Where were you trained?" He threw these questions at me as though he was lobbing mortars over a wall. Shaking in my boots, I answered each question as calmly as I could. "Do you know what you have here?" he asked. "No, I don't. That's why I sent him to you," I replied. "This kid has a Straussian

Syndrome," he said, "You have described it so accurately I don't even have to see him." Silence. "What's a Straussian Syndrome?" I squeaked.

This interaction was followed by an invitation to come and meet with him personally. I was so *flattered*. Here I was, a little girl from Watts, Oklahoma (pop. 100), going down to meet with the head of pediatric neurology at Columbia Presbyterian Medical Center in New York City. Wow! The school district even gave me time off to do it (a clear indication of prestige). Dr. Gold invited me to sit in on the training program he ran for neurologists and pediatricians and asked if I would do some private work for him. Boy, was I important! I was completely seduced by the power of diagnosis and the medical model. I *loved* the figuring out, the assumptions, the cleverness, the trying this and that (medications, etc.), the power of knowing, the power that we *might* have a solution. I was hooked—Delacatto techniques, Straussian Syndromes, Ritalin, early infantile autism—I plunged into all of it.

For some time, I did a lot of work in the field of learning disabilities, and as I became more community based in my work, my focus became more one of working with the process of the child and helping other professionals work with the process of the child. Diagnosing can still be fun when I remember that it's really just like one of the science "games" I used to play around the dinner table when I was a child.

One of the important things I did learn during those years was to work interdisciplinarily. Because of my premedical background and having worked in hospitals all those years, I was and still am alert to physical components that need to be taken care of before anything else can be done. It's difficult to do emotional and spiritual healing with a dead body.

I have found that many adults carry their learning disabilities—or certainly their *reactions* to their learning disabilities—into their adult lives, and it is helpful to be able to spot the residuals. Even though many learning disabilities are outgrown, sometimes an adult can be referred to a visual perceptual specialist and get help.

Also, I have been grateful for my training in theology. I know of very few people who do not have some issues about religion to work through, even if religion is not thought to be "scientific" and, therefore, not appropriate for the "science" of psychology.

All in all, my three years as a school psychologist were good years. I liked the work, I believe I did a good job (as well as I could at the time), and they were pleased with me—until right at the end of my time there.

I had already decided to terminate at the end of the year and go back and finish up my doctoral work and had given my notice when one of the teacher counselors asked me if I would see one of the students who was a senior and a daughter of one of the faculty members. Of course, I said yes. The problem was, she was dating a "black" boy (this was the early sixties). He was one of the star athletes, well liked, easygoing. He lived in the projects and had no father, his mother worked hard, and he would probably get to go to college if he got an athletic scholarship. The kids were "cute" together and seemed to be genuinely good for each other. The young man's mother liked the young woman but was afraid of anything that might jeopardize her son's welfare and chances for college. The young woman's parents were initially very upset. They liked the kid; they just did not like that he was black. As they met with me they realized that the worst thing they could do was to become rigid and controlling.

The parents decided to back off and see what happened when the kids went their separate directions to college, but this wasn't good enough for the principal. He called the young man in and told him that he would personally see to it that if the boy had any contact with his girlfriend whatsoever, he would see to it that *no* college would even consider him for admission or for a scholarship. Both kids wound up in my office in tears. The young man was shaken to the core and terrified. I was outraged.

I marched right down to the principal and read him the riot act. (I don't remember what I said as I write this; I remember the feeling.) In the last months of my work there, this incident opened up a can of worms the likes of which one can only imagine. Up until this point, all my evaluations had been outstanding, but suddenly my supervisors were ordered to give me unsatisfactory ratings. The issue was that after three years, dependent upon these ratings, I would be eligible for tenure. Even though I had given notice to leave, they wanted to take no chances. The principal in the grade school refused to rate me down and took the matter to the school board. The supervisor of pupil personnel services in the high school was "relieved" of doing my final evaluation (he refused to cooperate), and it was given to a vice-principal who, credential-wise, was very shaky in his job. He came to me with tears in his eyes and begged me to give him permission to rate me down; he had to stay, and I would be leaving anyway. I told him to do what he had to do; he had to live with himself. I went to the school board; my secretaries were outraged and threatened to quit; the other psychologists became scarce; my social worker "friends" took a philosophical position; kids, parents, and teachers I had worked with were outraged. I left to go back to complete my doctoral work.

I bring up this incident because it obviously is a pattern in my life. I have never been willing to go along with things that I think are *wrong*. That, I feel okay about. I have always taken stands when I believed stands needed to be taken, even when they were unpopular and frightening to take. In a way, this book is one of those stands. And, I now question whether the *way* I do it brings on more garbage than needs to be generated. Is my *righteousness* part of my addictive pattern? Is it setting up a dualism or agreeing to participate in a dualism that is the addictive disease process? I don't know. I am continuing to look at this. I *do* know that Martin Luther, who said, "Here I stand, I can do no other," is one of my heroes, and I *do* know that one of my favorite posters in the 1960s and 1970s (actually still is) reads something like, "All that is necessary for the forces of evil to prosper is for enough good people to do nothing." I have always felt that I had an inner morality, an inner ethic, inner "light" that I could not deny or compromise that was core to my being. I still cannot blindly follow the "rules" when I believe they are wrong, and neither can my children. I believe the pain this causes from outside is second only to the pain that would be inflicted upon my very being from inside if I were not to function in this way.

I share this issue because I still struggle with it, and I also know that it is not possible to heal in isolation. If a work does not recognize that healing must exist in families, groups, organizations, communities, societies, the globe, and the universe, I believe it cannot be adequate. The scientific worldview in which all of us have been raised takes the organism out of context, tries to make it static (often kills it), and then studies it. This reductionism is not the way the process of the world operates—but I'm getting ahead of myself.

I left the East and school psychology behind me and went back to St. Louis to finish up the last of my course work for my doctorate in clinical psychology. My daughter was four years old, and my husband was an ordained minister. I signed up for the courses I needed and took a half-time job as supervising psychologist for the Youth Center at St. Louis State Hospital, where, again, it was my work that was the major source of learning. At St. Louis State Hospital I was privileged to work under the best administrator I have ever had. He basically gave me a free reign and behaved in a manner that said to me, "You are a competent professional. Go for it." He was later to become my second husband.

These were significant years for me. Testing the kids and working with them, attending staff meetings, and so on were not nearly enough to keep me busy in my half-time schedule. (Dr. Schaef later showed me a chart on the production of the staff, and even though I was working half-time, I was doing twice as much as any of his full-time staff. He kept charts on everything—later, he even had one on our sex life.) I began to branch out into staff development and community work for these kids.

I discovered that the staff who came on from 11:00 P.M. to 7:00 A.M. had never had any in-service training, and in an adolescent treatment center those were often difficult hours. Most of the attendants at that point in history were black, uneducated, and low income. I asked the hospital to pay them to come in an extra hour for in-service. The hospital refused. I asked the staff if they were willing to come in one hour early twice a week on their own time without pay to get some extra training; all accepted. We didn't do much, and it was great. We started with nuts and bolts like reading charts, understanding terms, and so forth. Then we went on to understanding psychological and psychiatric reports, following treatment plans, giving feedback from their shifts, and unofficial staffing of specific kids with whom they were having trouble, either difficult cases or especially interesting cases. This group contained some of the most eager learners I have ever had, and the center seemed to click along better.

Then I began to be aware of something in the staff meetings to which I'd always had an uneasy reaction and all at once could not bear to hear. (Isn't it strange how we might have been listening to something for years and it didn't bother us, and all of a sudden we *hear* it and we can't stand it?) What I suddenly could not stand was the phrase, "This kid is untreatable." Arghhh—suddenly I hated it. It was clear to me that *we didn't know what to do or our techniques didn't work.* What was said, though, was, "This kid is untreatable." I asked the staff to look at our dishonesty with ourselves, each other, *and* the kids and just simply to say, "We don't know what to do with this kid." As part of my popularity campaign and consciousness raising, whenever anyone said, "This kid is untreatable," I would say, "We don't know what to do with this kid." It was so clear to me that much of our psychiatric and psychological treatment was by-guess-and-by-gosh and we really didn't know what to do. How much easier it would have been on all of us if we only could have admitted it.

I also saw something that has become clearer and clearer to me. I saw that under the guise of scientific objectivity, psychology and psychiatry essentially functioned out of an emotional, judgmental base that often blamed and disrespected the client.

Again, I learned so much from the kids and the attendants. They almost always seem to have more information than the "professionals." Maybe this is related to that old Zen story about the professor who went to the Zen master to get Wisdom. The old master asked a student to bring two cups and some tea. He placed one cup in front of the professor and began to pour the tea. The cup filled, and he continued to pour. When the tea was running all over the table, the professor could no longer stand it, and he said, "Stop pouring? Can't you see the cup is full?" The old Zen master smiled and said, "And so it is with you. Only by emptying ourselves is there room for more to come in." I am so grateful for the freedom I had to explore in that job.

Another significant area of exploration for me during that time was the new realm of the human potential movement and humanistic psychology. Dr. Schaef himself was a seeker. He was always open to new ideas and new approaches and encouraged his staff to be also. We had a large psychodrama section of our department and excellent psychodrama facilities due to his support. He encouraged me to go to conferences, workshops, and training seminars and to explore. During those years, I had the opportunity to learn from Maslow, Satir, Rogers, Perls, Moreno, Haley, and many of the "greats." He supported my going "right to the horse's mouth," and I found myself plunged into a new world. I also participated in encounter groups, growth groups, human potential groups, sensitivity groups, and body work. At the American Psychological Association conventions and Humanistic Psychology Association conventions, I heard people on the cutting edge describe their work in great detail. I heard about nude marathon groups that specialized in "asshole gazing" (to help people get over their inhibitions), I heard about implosive and explosive therapy, I heard about aversive conditioning, and, I have to admit, much of it sounded crazy to me. During some of those years, Dr. Schaef was program chairperson for Division 29 of the American Psychological Association, and as his assistant, I was in charge of the "conversations in psychotherapy." Through this work, I not only got to know many of the "greats" of that time, I was able to present some of my ideas at the American Psychological Association's convention.

One of the things I discovered was that my adviser in graduate school had been right. It did seem as though many of the "big boys" in APA were there to screw the starry-eyed graduate students while their wives discreetly went shopping or lazed around the pool but always showed up on their arm at banquets. My last APA convention was in 1970, and I have not missed them.

Those years at St. Louis State Hospital were years of mind stretching and new discovery. I explored the work of the National Training Laboratories, group process (relating back to my work with the Campus YMCA-YWCA, where I was the group process and leadership trainer and was trained by the Y secretary, who was NTL-trained), sensitivity training, conflict management, and organizational consulting. This was like a homecoming for me, and soon I was accepted as a senior trainer in the NTL Network.

One of my great experiences in NTL was working with a trainer named Saul Siegel. He was not a person who was full of gimmicks, tricks, and techniques. He had the courage and security to let the group process take its course. Up until that point, my experience with group dynamics was a series of "experiential exercises" that were ways of getting us to learn what we were supposed to learn "experientially," that is, through experience and not just intellectually. I was thrilled with this new way of learning when I first encountered it and moved right into the techniques and gimmicks of NTL and the human potential movement as an old hand, because I had basically picked up these skills in the 1950s in college, but Saul had something new to teach me. He taught me to wait, and to watch and to listen and, most of all, to trust—to trust the group process and see where it goes. This learning has proved essential to my work.

I have since learned that the dynamics I learned to watch for, to name, and to pull out (such as power struggles, coalitions, and previously defined group roles) are processes that we find in an addictive system. These are group processes we find in groups operating addictively and are not usually found in process groups as I now participate in them. There is a great difference between group process and process groups.

NTL played an important role in my life for some years to come. As a senior trainer, I was invited to staff workshops and seminars for them in various parts of the country. These were always stimulating, and I always learned something. Saul had wanted me to be on the staff of NTL's major management workshops. I was very interested in organizational development and management, and although he pushed very hard for this, the administration of NTL decided that corporate managers would never accept a woman as a trainer. Women were not asked to staff major management workshops until much later.

Civil Rights, Feminism, Community, and Indian Medicine Women

About this time, I had again become active in the civil rights movement, and it, too, was a very important force in my life. My work in civil rights was a long, painful process, the most difficult part of which was facing myself. I was a White Liberal. I had always been on the side of the underdog and stood for what was "right." That was why I was always getting in trouble. But my black friends brought me up short. I realize now that much of my "rights" activity was wanting them to tell me that I was different. I wanted to hear that I was "not like the others." Well, two of my friends and colleagues wouldn't tell me that. They just kept saying, "You ain't got it yet." I raged, I cried, I pleaded, I tried to do the right thing, I complied, I threatened, I walked away, and still they said, "You ain't got it yet." I didn't even know what the "it" was I didn't get. I kept looking outside myself for the answer, and it wasn't there. Finally, I looked inside, and what I saw inside was pure *white*. I was pure white. I was racist. I think white; I perceive white; I have white privilege. I may fight for the underdog, I may take stands for blacks, I may even put my life on the line for civil rights, but unless I am willing to look inside and face the depth of my own racism, nothing is really going to change. I may not have *caused* racism, but I am racist by the very fact of being born white.

Even as I write these words I see how important this is to me and how grateful I am to those two who didn't let me off the hook. I see it as similar to some of the flack that I am getting now about "blaming the victim" when I say that the women involved in battering relationships have a disease and can't just look outside and blame the society. Of course the society is unfair and contributes to, even demands, this problem, but the strength and healing comes from looking inside first and owning our own reality and the ways we act out this system in ourselves. Women are victimized, and only *we* can integrate those experiences and transcend them.

I don't know whether my civil rights work did any good for any blacks (I hope it did), but it sure was good for me. Understanding that we *are* the system even when we do not like the system still informs who I am and the way I work. This work in civil rights is one of the threads that helped me to evolve a participatory way of doing my work and, even more important, a participatory scientific worldview.[1] It helped me to see that unless I am willing to ferret out the unconscious way I act out of the system, I will continue to inflict it upon myself and others.

During these years, NTL was doing workshops and consultations on racism. I was involved in several, and I realized that there were few black trainees in the NTL network, which I thought was a crime. If NTL or any other organization wanted to do work on racism, they should be using an equal number of black trainers. With the support of the midwestern and national organizations of NTL, three of us in St. Louis (Bob Schaef, Nick Calorelli, and myself), organized a program to train black trainers. We volunteered to train a group of black professionals to be part of the NTL network. I don't remember how long this program lasted or how often we met; I do know I liked doing it.

Two very important awarenesses came out of this work for me. This was the first time I had been called a "witch" in the positive sense of the word, and I liked it. The training group was amazed at how much I picked up on and was impressed and nervous about it. I have gotten that feedback all my life, and I now realize that what *I* see is available for anybody to see and I just have been given the gift to be present. When we don't have a lot of other stuff rumbling around in us and our minds are not too busy screening what we see through our theories and formulating theories and interpretations, we can just be present. Then, we see a lot.

Second, I discovered a pattern and a process in myself that was not new to me but I gave words to it during one of the training sessions. At one point, it appeared to me that one of the other senior trainers was taking over and controlling the group. I saw this as a call to arms and rose to the occasion. The trainees watched as a battle ensued. I didn't fight much, but when I did I expected to win. When we had settled the fracas, I turned to the group and said, "Take over, stand up for yourselves." I realized that I did not want the control, I just was not willing for anyone *else* to control anyone. I can see this theme emerging periodically throughout my life and can see how it has evolved into the work I do. I have come to believe any system that operates out of the illusion of control is an addictive system, and addictive systems are destructive to life. I strongly believe that oppression and control and manipulation of others is wrong, and much of my life has been devoted to the right of each of us to find our own destiny.

During the time I was involved in the human potential movement and NTL, I left my job at St. Louis State Hospital and took a job as director of the Adolescent Treatment Center at Alton, Illinois, working for the Illinois Department of Mental Health. One of my former professors of clinical psychology was assistant director of the Illinois Department of Mental Health and wanted me to help set up an adolescent treatment program in that region. I wasn't too eager to leave where I was, so I made a list of conditions (being hired at a Ph.D. level although I did not have my Ph.D., setting my own hours, a secretary so I could dictate reports, expenses paid for conferences and training, etc.). Much to my surprise, he accepted them. I learned how dangerous it is to ask for what I want. At the state level everything was fine, but at the local level everyone, even the superintendent of the hospital, resented my having asked for and received what I wanted. (Some of these trouble spots in my life make a lot more sense to me now that I understand addictions and adult children of alcoholics. I seem to be a trigger for active addicts and adult children.)

Somewhere during this time, I decided not to finish my Ph.D. in clinical psychology. Several factors were involved. Culturally there was Vietnam, civil rights, and the women's movement. Personally, I had a six-year-old and was pregnant with my son; I was working full-time, having an affair with my former boss, and running and attending workshops on the side. Writing a dissertation about some meaningless research did not seem worth it, and everyone advised against trying to do something "significant" for a doctoral project. "Just get it over with," they advised. Life was too important and too valid to waste it on "just getting it over with."

As I look back, I realize that I gave myself three externally referenced, meaningless excuses for not completing my Ph.D. at that time: (1) I had more clinical experience than any of the faculty, (2) I was as well or better known than any of them, and (3) I made as much money or more than any of them. I don't even know whether any of these "excuses" was true; they gave me the excuse I needed to stop. The real issue for me was that I felt that I would lose my soul if I did one thing more in that system. I didn't know why; I just knew that it was true. I said that I wanted to "make it" on a competence model not a credential model, and I already knew that there was something deeply wrong with psychology, a field I had loved and in which I had excelled.

Also, at that time in history there were many psychologists who were ABDs (all but dissertations) and had good jobs and good private practices. We had met all the educational requirements; we just had not written our final papers. And what did that really have to do with doing psychotherapy? I was doing work that I loved and exploring new ideas every day. The sun was in the heavens, and my feet were on the ground. What more could I ask? The late sixties and early seventies were times for me to find my own self and my own way. There was a lot going on in the world, and there was a lot going on in me. Writing a dissertation seemed like a meaningless exercise in futility and form.

Of course, in the work I was doing at that time, as I had been trained, I was enmeshed in techniques and exercises. Just tell me what you want to accomplish, and I will quickly design a technique or exercise to get at it. My mind thrived on figuring out and then "designing" an experiential learning. I "knew" how to get people to become more intimate (Just walk around and look one another in the eye. Touch someone's face where you see something going on or not going on). I could help people get to suppressed or repressed feelings (Just talk to a chair—Just try to break out of a circle). I could manipulate feelings (I see anger. Here's a bataka [a padded bat used by some therapists], beat the pillows). I analyzed, I interpreted, I manipulated, I put people through their paces, and—they loved me for it. *I* knew what was going on with them, *I* knew what they needed, *I* knew how to set up situations that would *make* them get what I knew they needed. I was caring, loving, and important. I was skilled, well-trained, and *essential*. What heady times these were! I had rejected the godlike setup of analysis and the medical model, and I had opted for the godlike model of the human potential movement and experiential learning. People *needed* me. I was so perceptive and so much sharper about picking up subtle awarenesses (much sharper than the clients themselves, I might add) that wherever I went, I was successful and people wanted to work with me. I had learned well, and I was good at what I had learned. People got better because *I* was so good, so loving, and so skilled. What a trip. I now see that these are all characteristics of a relationship addict.

I was plunged into one of the most important personal and professional phases of my life about this time. I became active in the women's movement. I became a feminist. The struggle for civil rights had prepared me well for a budding consciousness of women's rights.

An early awareness of women's issues came through my experiences with NTL. I was asked to be a senior trainer for a workshop with a community focus that was to be the most integrated staff NTL had offered up to that point, male and female, black and white. The other woman on the staff, Coleen (Cokey) Keibert, was wonderful and the kind of woman I always get pitted against. She was very competent, and she was also extremely *beautiful*. Because I was senior staff, I had a private room. Junior staff were supposed to share rooms, but because she was the only female junior staff, she had a single room and had to pay the difference. After the first day of staff planning, we both had noticed that many of the sentences of the male staff that day had begun, "I know Cokey and Anne will disagree on this but—" It sure seemed to us that we were being set up to battle with each other, so I invited her to move in with me, and we have been friends ever since. Two major events happened for me at that workshop. First, the blacks threw out the design and had a caucus. We whites didn't know what to do with ourselves, but the black caucus seemed busy. Not a thing was said when the black male staff members went with the black caucus. Two days later, the black women called a women's caucus, and we got a lot of static from the rest of the staff for going with the other women. I was sure glad I had a support person there and have insisted on one since that time, especially when I am going into the lion's mouth to clean his teeth.

The women's caucus was wonderful. The black women were *furious* with some of the white women for being seductive with some of the black men, and starting with that issue we slugged it out all day long, then went on to genuinely meet each other and deal with other significant issues. The sexism among the staff was rampant, and Cokey and I both needed the support of other women to deal with it. The black caucus was seen as legitimate. The women's caucus was not.

After that experience, Cokey and I decided to do some women's workshops together, and I was plunged up to my ears in women's issues. Almost everything I did for the next fifteen to twenty years revolved around women's issues. "Workshops" then (I'm now embarrassed to say) involved a series of exercises and techniques designed to elicit something (whatever we *thought* it was we wanted to elicit). We did collages, action sociograms, body exercises—all the "tricks and techniques" we had been learning along the way. These were not therapy. They were workshops and involved sharing and telling our stories.

The first workshop that we gave together was sponsored by NTL. We were asked to do a weekend workshop for interns' wives (their husbands were doing a year of training with NTL, and they wanted something for the wives). We were told that we were to increase their self-esteem and give them more confidence (which ironically, of course, we then felt competent to do). We must have succeeded, because unbeknownst to us, many of them called NTL after the workshop and demanded more workshops for women. We were accused of having put them up to it. (Neither of us was ever asked to do a women's workshop or any workshop again for NTL. It hurt us both very deeply because we had started the whole focus for women in NTL, and NTL was very important to us.) As I write this, I am aware of how much pain I have experienced in my profession when what I felt was right and moral for me did not coincide with the party line.

As for putting the women up to asking for more workshops, nothing could have been further from the truth. Our energy at that workshop was going into *survival*. There was so much pain and anger in that group that we were completely overwhelmed. I don't remember eating one meal that weekend. After each session, we would stagger back to our cabin supporting each other, flop on the beds, and collapse until the next session. Nothing in my training had prepared me to deal with the pain and rage that came out of these women. In *Women's Reality*, I say that the theories I learned in graduate school were "at best useless and at worst, harmful" in working with these women, and I still believe that to be true.[2] These women were hurt and angry all the way to their souls—*so was I*. Objectivity went out the window. I knew what they were talking about. I had lived it too. I was furious with the things that happened to me simply because I was a woman. Memories flooded in upon me as if a dam had burst. I realized that in order to do the work I was facing into, I would have to do my own work and that I had started on something from which there was no turning back. My work and my being were ultimately interrelated. I was launched full tilt into my rage phase. It was at this point that I made one of the most important decisions in my life. I felt that if I did not go into my rage and deal with it, I would lose my soul. It's akin to making the decision to put my sobriety first. I stopped and acknowledged that I had reached a point where I had to deal with my rage, and if it meant that I lost everything in my life—my kids, my husband, my house, all my professional contacts—whatever—I had to do it.

This was a terrifying period for me. My only *real* support was Cokey, with whom I did workshops, and she lived a thousand miles away. We spent a lot of time on the telephone. I realized that my terror came from several sources. I was overwhelmed with what was inside me. In my grandiosity, I believed that my rage was akin to an atomic bomb, and if I let it out there would be nothing but a wasteland with nothing living and no one with whom to relate. In the process of working with my own rage, I discovered that this fantasy was very common among women.

Also, I had to deal with others' reactions to my rage. They seemed more terrified of it than I was, and often there was a backlash of punishment that accompanied their reaction.

I tried therapy, but most therapists wanted me to talk *about* it, not experience it and go through it. I went to human potential workshops where we were "supposed" to deal with feelings and found that we were supposed to deal with feelings that had been elicited by the techniques the leaders knew and that there was a very narrow range of acceptable intensity and content to "feelings," especially when those feelings related to sexism.

Although my family was supportive, I did not want to drop my rage there. The only place it felt acceptable was in the workshops that I was co-leading with my friend. She was having the same difficulty, so we began to develop what I now see is a participatory model for working with groups.

At the beginning of the group we would announce that the group could not expect the usual kind of "leadership" from us. We did not have it "together" and were not rational, logical, and objective as the current prevailing model of "therapist" dictated. We shared that we ourselves were working on many of the same issues that members of the groups were working on and that if issues came up for us, we would work on them there. Out of necessity, we were unwittingly creating an egalitarian, participatory model. We did not sit down and say, "We are going to create an egalitarian, participatory model." We did it because we simply had no other choice.

Because we had been at this longer than some of the participants, we shared what information and knowledge we had gleaned about women's issues, and we shared our own experiences and outrages. We still used "exercises" and "techniques" similar to those we had learned in NTL and encounter groups, but much of our time was spent just "sharing." When strong pain or rage came up (what I now recognize as deep processes), we didn't know what else to do, so we just sat with the person, tried to contain and protect her, and rode it out. As I look back, I am sure that few, if any, persons really completed a deep process during that time, and we did the best we knew at the time; many felt it was the best option available. Also, I am embarrassed to say, we did holding down, pushing back (to provide resistance—we thought), and breaking-out exercises and a complement of other "techniques" that were in vogue at the time that I would now never do. Mostly we shared and found our commonality.

During this period, I made a commitment to myself to find out what was going on with women (myself included, of course). I decided to dedicate as many years as necessary to finding out what women were thinking and, most important, feeling. I was invited to do a lot of speaking engagements and consulting, and I had many opportunities to be in situations where only women were present. Very early on, I discovered that if even one man was present, women would not be honest. They would protect themselves.

At some point during this time, I made two important decisions that on the surface seem conflictual but paradoxically supported each other. I had reached my limit as clinical director of the Youth Center at Alton State Mental Hospital and was transferred to the regional office in East St. Louis to do community psychology in Region VII (which was very large). This meant that most of my time was spent out knocking around the boondocks trying to develop "community mental health resources." This could mean anything from sitting with some old men on the whittler's bench in a small town, to working with local ministers, to speaking about mental health to the women's clubs, to working with local teachers to try to be more effective with children with learning disabilities in the classroom, because most districts did not have any special resources. We were talking about preventive mental health and follow-up support systems for people who had been hospitalized. We were talking about the communities dealing with their own mental health problems because there were no "experts" around. We were talking about communities functioning as communities.

Early on, I realized that there was much more wisdom in those little farm communities than met the eye. When we had a kid who had been hospitalized ready to come back out into the community, I would wander out to his area. We knew that he would land right back in our laps if he didn't have support. It was my job to see what we could "mobilize" in the community. Often, I started with the old men in front of the store "sitting a spell." In the towns where people had come to know me, I was always warmly greeted. In the ones where I was a stranger, it took some time. I always was very honest about who I was and what I did. Then I would say something like, "You know that Thompson kid that started acting kinda strange and was hospitalized?" "Yep." "He's about ready to come out of the hospital." (I had worked hard on a philosophy in the hospital not to keep kids so long that they adjusted to the hospital system. I saw the hospital for adolescents as a short-term emergency measure whenever possible.) "We'd like for him to make it in the community. What do you think?" (It was impossible to break confidentiality, because everyone knew what was going on anyway.) There would be a pause, and then someone would say something like, "Well, you know that Thompson kid is sorta like the Harrison kid. That Harrison kid is thirty years old now, but he was kinda strange from the time he was born, and he's never been hospitalized. We all just keep an eye on him and make sure he never gets into trouble. Everybody in town knows his whereabouts and are always giving him treats. Maybe that would work with the Thompson kid." "Maybe."

About this time, I realized how many of the theoretical frameworks I had studied had nothing to do with life in the heartland. There were no high-falutin' therapists out here, and if there had been, they would have had to be unethical, by definition, as the ethics have been set up. The ethical model of the psychotherapist as needing to be isolated and having no social or other kind of contact may have been possible for an analyst operating in New York City, but it was not possible out here in the boonies. People used whatever resources they had, and those sources were more trusted and more effective if they were totally integrated into the community. This was "community." There were no secrets or masks. Everybody knew everyone else's business. I realized that the ethical model of working with people that is now in vogue simply did not apply. Objectivity was a fraud, and those of us working with people in those communities could not be protected by the "rules" of ethics. We had to deal with our feelings; we had to deal with our attractions; we had to deal with our dishonesties—everybody knew about them anyway.

I realized that in my women's workshops and in my community psychology work I was dealing with a very different model for working with people. I did not have the language at that time, and I now realize that it was what I would now call a "participatory" model. Those who were most trusted were not the authorities who supposedly "had it all together" (the people out there with their roots in the earth knew that was a hoax). They were willing to listen to information from someone they trusted, but they were not willing to be controlled or manipulated by some "authority." Neither were the women in my workshops. They'd had their fill of that.

My old down-to-earth hillbilly background stood me in good stead. I felt right at home with this way of functioning. This model of working with people was not new to me. I had seen it often in professionals who worked with adolescents and children. I knew it from my religious upbringing. Jesus always worked among those he knew the best and who came to him. He did not refuse to heal someone because they were a friend or a member of a close family. He worked with his "community," and people who were strangers became part of his community as he worked with them.

Then there was the Indian medicine woman who was an important part of my background on many levels. Indian medicine women always ministered to, worked with, and healed their village and their tribe. Their healing worked because they were *known* and trusted, or perhaps I should say their healing worked *and* they were known and trusted. This paradigm is not governed by cause and effect and control, manipulation, objectivity, and nonparticipation. These healers worked out of a different worldview from the modernist, mechanical, "objective" science I had been taught, and it felt better and more integrated to me.

Finally, there were the feminists. I was learning so much and healing so much within my feminist community, and because I was the only feminist therapist in town during those early years, many of my friends, social acquaintances, and professional colleagues asked to work with me. My husband and I were, in fact, for a short time clients of a psychiatrist who was in our social group and a casual friend. Dual, triple, or quadruple relationships were the norm, and they worked. Isolating and controlling a scientific patient-therapist relationship made no sense. These existing relationships were not an ethical or professional problem.

Working for the state of Illinois proved to be quite stressful. When I made an internal switch from a medical model to a growth model because of my work in humanistic psychology, I found it increasingly difficult to work in the hospital, so I switched to community psychology. A small shift in me had turned out to be a big shift for the hospital, and working there was stressful for both of us.

The model for the hospital was a modified psychodynamic medical model à la empiricism and reductionistic science. There were two major beliefs that ruled the way we operated. One was that people chose to be sick and were resistant to getting well because of their defense mechanisms, which were usually ego-syntonic (comfortable to them). So we had to fight their resistance to being healthy (stated quite simplistically, of course, but I believe quite accurately). With some, it just wasn't worth it to "fight" with them, so we just medicated, placed them on back wards, or "maintained" them. The other belief was that the medical model, when practiced from a rather simple cause-and-effect mentality, would work. If we could just find out *exactly* what was wrong, diagnose it accurately, then we could prescribe the proper "cure," and the patient would heal. Therefore, much emphasis was put on accurate diagnosis (still true today in many circles, I believe), followed by major confusion about what to do. Following the beautiful diagnosis, we slipped into a massive denial system because no one really knew what worked with these folks, but none of us admitted it, and the problem was always blamed on the patient, his or her resistance, and defense mechanisms or the part of the personality that really "wanted to be sick." I also believe that down deep most "professionals" believed that people who had been "damaged" in childhood never really healed and the best that could be hoped for was some kind of minimal adjustment.

Shifting Paradigms

As I worked in and learned from humanistic psychology, I found myself shifting to a "growth model." That model was very simple. That model said that the normal state for the human organism was to grow and change. Whenever that growth and change was inhibited, interfered with, or stopped, the organism showed symptoms. So our role as psychotherapists was not to fight and struggle against an organism who doesn't *really* want to get well or to "control" or "trick" that organism into growth and healing. Our role as therapists was to cooperate with what the organism wanted—its normal state—help it deal with whatever was blocking its growth and development and support its process. Instead of being adversaries, we were partners, and what the organism did in trying to get back on this track for itself was its business, not ours. Some organisms did some very strange things trying to get back on track, but it was only when *we* tried to "make sense" of what they did, intellectually and from our perspective, that it seemed strange. We really did not need to understand it at all. That was our problem and directly related to our control issues.

As I remember, that shift in my thinking and being occurred very suddenly over one weekend, and when I went to work on Monday, the patients looked different to me. I started to operate out of this new awareness—not really visibly that different—and my patients started improving more rapidly. A simple change of attitude and awareness within *me* seemed like magic. I was so excited and enthusiastic that I switched into my evangelistic mode. "The answer is in us. We have to look at *ourselves* and our *assumptions* and *attitudes*. Let's make these changes in ourselves and start a research program on one of the back wards. I'll participate! I'll head it up!" (I had no idea how to *do* these changes. I had *done* it [my process had done it], but I had no idea how to *do* it). I think it is easy to see how my working at the hospital became stressful for me and the hospital. I was no longer an easy cog in a system that was accustomed to grinding on in its usual way of grinding on. We both became eager to "try Anne in the community."

I have since learned that when I try to stagnate, block, or ignore my own process, I usually either get sick or get a good hard whack alongside the head, or both. This time I got a whack, which was getting sick. I was sitting in a staff meeting contemplating my hot pink, chartreuse, and black girdle (we wore them then, and one of the ways I got through those interminable meetings was to sit there and say to myself, "I have a hot pink, chartreuse, and black girdle on, and nobody knows it), and suddenly I felt a pain in my lower gut. I was usually an amazingly healthy person, and this hurt. In fact, I went to the doctor the next day, and he said he thought I had a fissure in my colon. I was horrified. How could my body do this to me? I was in a stressful job, I had just left a stressful marriage, I had two small kids, I was "living with a man" in a proper St. Louis neighborhood, I was working through my rage phase, and I was still involved in civil rights. Why would my body attack me now?

I went home and thought about it. If I had a fissure in my colon, it was letting the shit out into the rest of my system. I was shitting myself. (Isn't interpretation grand? At that stage of my learning, I *needed* that interpretation. Now, I know that it is simply enough to listen to my body and listen to what I need to do and that interpretation is interesting and essentially meaningless.) The next day I went in and resigned.

For some time, my workshops for women had been going very well. They were always full, and I was being asked to do more and more. Also many women were asking to see me privately in therapy. Many who asked to see me had been in therapy for years and in the workshops shared what was happening to them in their therapy situations and that they didn't know where to turn. There were no "feminist" therapists around. At least I was trying to develop a theory about what was going on with women and was working on my own issues. This seemed better to them.

Some of these women had been working with therapists who had been initially helpful to them, even saved their lives, they felt, and then they had come up against a steel-reinforced wall when they began to deal with what it meant to be a woman in this society. At the time, I felt intuitively that the issues these women were struggling with in therapy were not just related to the content of being a woman but also to the *way* the therapy was being done and how the process of it perpetuated the dominant system even when it was done by a woman who focused on women's issues. I feel much clearer about this issue now and will discuss it in detail later.

One woman in one of my workshops was particularly insightful about this issue. She stated that she loved and respected her analyst and that he had "saved her life" (probably *she* did) when she was in a terrible depression, but for the last five (count them, five) years, she had been uncomfortable with her therapy and had not wanted to hurt him by leaving. (It's important to take care of our therapists.) She also wanted to believe that *he was workable.* She shared that she felt, somehow, that the very way therapy was done was part of the problem with which she was struggling. She had to lie down, not facing her analyst, and talk while he sat behind her, nonparticipatory and "objective." She said all of this was symbolic of her role in society and what she had always had to do, and she refused to do this anymore. She had a point.

Instead of treating her perception as legitimate and encouraging her to process her reaction, he only focused upon her reaction and what he called transference issues (feelings from old relationships projected upon him). She was *stuck.* He refused to look at his training as integrated into a sick, sexist system that was built on the belief that transference was core. She asked to see me, and after only two or three sessions, we both agreed that she did not need any more therapy. Women like this were pouring into my life.

So with much fear and trembling, I went into private practice. I shared an office with a friend and in a short time had a full practice. There were no licensing laws in Missouri at that time, and I was covered for insurance, and so I began.

At first, I had a terrible time charging fees and felt an unbelievable pressure to produce, because people were actually *paying me*. I don't know whether this is true for others, but it certainly was for me. I realized how much more freedom I felt working for an institution. My salary from the hospital gave me the license not to have to produce. On my own, my training that I should know what to do, have all the answers, and be able to make wise and insightful input came galloping to the fore. Although I genuinely cared for my clients, I also was under the illusion that somehow my caring for them would make them well. This, I believe, harks back to my training in Christianity that love heals all and is enough. (There was, as I look back, some slight confusion between my love and God's love.) All of this, of course, I would now see as being tainted by relationship addiction and codependence.

Now I still go back to the two big decisions that I made during this time. First, I decided that I would not do anything that I was not excited about. I would not accept any speech, do any workshop, or work with any client in whom I was not interested and about whom I was not excited. If I did not feel an important connection with a client, I would refer him or her on ("objectivity" was losing its grip on me). Also, I would not do anything for ego, prestige, or money inasmuch as I was able to be aware and "clear" about my motives. If something was unclear for me, I would "wait with" my decision or turn it down. I still operate out of this commitment, and it has served me well. It has something to do with "right living" and integrity for me. Of course, at the time, I was terrified. I thought my kids and I would starve, and yet it seemed like another of those "soul" issues. Because of this decision, I never hustle, I only go where I am invited, I do not cultivate referrals, I only have people on my mailing list who have asked to be on it, and my books have mostly sold by word of mouth. This was an important decision for me. Of course, when I did the things I was excited about, I did them well, I always had plenty to do, and I always had the money I needed. I now see this as similar to the "attraction rather than promotion" philosophy of the Twelve-Step program of Alcoholics Anonymous.

The other decision was equally difficult. I had since married Bob Schaef, and we both worked full time. One of my rage attacks erupted around this issue. We had a college student living with us, and one day after work I was standing at the kitchen sink peeling carrots. I was tired, but the kids were hungry and dinner needed to be fixed. I looked outside, and the college student and Bob were playing in the yard and relaxing. We had all worked all day, and I was still working. Carrots and carrot peeler were thrown in the sink, and I went out and sat on the porch swing (could this be the beginning of recovery from my care-aholism and my relationship addiction?). One by one, everyone came up and asked when dinner would be ready. "When you help fix it," I snarled. My husband's reply was, "When you make as much money as I do, I'll do an equal amount of housework." (He was a Ph.D. in psychology, was head of the psychology department at the state hospital, and taught at the university.) I tucked that one away for future reference.

Anyway, back to the decision. One day when I was consulting with Her Majesty's Royal Commission on the Role and Status of Women in Canada (I *loved* the title), I was talking about feminism, rights, practice and preaching, and I suddenly realized that I was not practicing what I was preaching.

I had the freedom to not do any job I didn't want to do because Bob *felt* that he bore the financial responsibility for the family. I could not control what he put on himself, and I also did not need to contribute to it. So when I came home from Canada, I announced that from here on out I was going to be *equal*. I would take responsibility for half the expenses of the family even if I had to do something I didn't like. I know that not every woman can do that, and for me the decision to do it was very important at that point in my development. I had come from feed sack dresses as a child to contributing my share to the family, and I was doing it on a competence model. I never had to do work I resented (I feel very grateful for that), and I was willing to do the work necessary to be equal. All my life, I have done whatever work needed to be done, and I don't do much "categorizing" or "judging" of work. I guess I really believe in the nobility of all work, now that I think of it. It's the compensation that's so unfair. Anyway, I have never done anything *for* the compensation. I have always just done my work. That's been enough.

As an aside, I do have to add that at the point where I was making more money than Bob, I really had to bite my tongue not to tell him to get in the kitchen. Unfortunately, when we react to that addictive system, it is always a lose-lose situation. If I go along with it, I lose. If I fight it, I lose. If it *wins*, I lose. If I become like it and try to win with its strategies, I lose. All I can do is live my own process.

After I was "launched" in private practice, I also continued to speak at women's groups, run workshops, consult with organizations and corporations, and focus on women's issues. My rage phase lasted about two years, and I did lose some things that were very important to me during that time. My family hung in with me, but I lost some friends and I lost some professional contacts. At the point where I decided that I could no longer put up with sexist behavior coming at me (it's a wonder I even thought I could stay in this culture), one of the sad things that happened to me was a very painful experience with NTL. I had been asked to be senior staff at a personal growth workshop. I was to be the only woman on the staff, and my husband was to be junior staff. I was excited with the possibilities. (Now, I would know better than to put myself in such a situation without the support of another woman and senior staff when my husband was junior staff, but that is after years of recovery from my addictive patterns. My disease of relationship addiction often took the form of "I can handle this.")

The first day of staff planning for the workshop did not go well. One of the other senior staff members did not let me complete *one sentence* during the entire day of planning. I was livid. (Today, I would consider him a gift, do my process work with whatever he was triggering in me, and then talk it over with him if I needed to or thought it was worth the time and effort.) At that point, I was still in my rage phase. I carefully sat across from him at dinner and with the control of a lioness about to pounce, announced that this was war. I told him that he had not let me finish one sentence during the planning and that this had happened for the last time. I was not going to put up with this. With quiet fury, we looked at each other across the table, and the rest of the staff dissolved into catatonia. The workshop, amazingly, went well, but the staff was in total chaos. Some staff members felt they had to take sides (a clear indicator of an addictive situation); some were terrified; some just disappeared. One consultant to the staff who really liked me took me for a walk and said, "Anne, won't you just try to seduce me? I don't mean that we have to do anything, but I *don't know how to relate to you*." I told him that he was going to have to learn some new ways to relate to women and kept on course. My "mentor" from

NTL "dropped by" and lovingly told me that he understood the situation, and I would have to do what I had to do. We even had visits from the national staff—nothing changed. As is common in many situations like this, the woman was eliminated. I was never asked to do anything else for NTL, which was very, very painful for me. I loved the work with NTL. I loved the people. I had lost something very important to me, *and* I felt my soul was still intact.

During this period, my husband was recruited to head up a private psychological clinic in a town outside St. Louis. It was a fairly heavily populated area, but the only real mental health providers were two psychiatrists who wanted to set up a private mental health clinic where they could refer people who needed long-term therapy. The operation sounded a little "fishy" to me (as in conflict of interest), but the offer was to Bob and not to me. They made him an offer he felt he could not refuse, so he left the St. Louis State Hospital and began to lay the groundwork for setting up a clinic. At that point, there was only one staff person at the clinic, and he was a social worker who was also a part owner. The place was to be run like one big happy family.

Bob, being a smart administrator, began to pull in a top-notch staff. Almost all of them were Ph.D.s. He asked me if I was willing to work part-time and carry the children's and adolescent services because of the many contacts I had from my work with the state of Missouri and the state of Illinois. This is an example where my relationship addiction clearly was more active than my common sense. I knew that I did not like the setup, and through my previous work I had heard some pretty negative feedback about these two psychiatrists, especially about one of them. And I wanted to be a good wife (I knew this job was important for Bob. It was the first time he had ventured out of "the system"). I knew I could handle the work and bring in some referrals, I was *only* going to work there part-time, he *needed* me, the clients needed *me*, and *I could handle it* (the rallying cry of the relationship addict)—so I accepted the position.

Again, the work was okay. I started seeing some adults in therapy and did evaluations. Unfortunately, the more I worked there, the more I learned about the owners. I longed for Bob's ability not to get hung up on "issues" and just do the work. That approach seemed completely foreign to me and my disposition. The setup was that we were all to come to a board meeting once a month and then, at the largess of one of the owners, taken for a grand meal at one of the excellent local Italian restaurants owned by "friends." I *hated* these soirées, and yet I went.

At one of the board meetings, we discussed a contract with an agency that worked almost exclusively in a black area of a nearby city. The agency was suggesting a good contract, and the board voted to act on it. It was in my area of expertise, so they consulted me. I could handle the work, but I thought if we were going to be working with a significant number of blacks, we should have a black on our staff as he or she could do a better job (by that time I had learned about my inherent racism and knew that I could be compassionate and sympathetic, but I could not really know what it meant to be black). I had a black colleague that I knew would be interested. The owners replied that having a black staff member would be "out of the question." We could do occasional evaluations of the black kids at the clinic (although they hoped that I would be able to do most of them at the referring agency), but we could not have a black person coming and going on a regular basis at our clinic because it would offend the basically white neighborhood. Unfortunately, my husband caught my eye as my mouth fell open, and he signaled me to keep quiet. On the ride to the restaurant he asked me please to back off and keep my mouth shut. He agreed with me in principle but knew that I wasn't very diplomatic. I never have been.

After a few months, I began to see some of the women who needed therapy since I was the only woman on the staff at that point and Bob understood that it was important that they be seen by a woman. Most of these women had been hospitalized by the psychiatrists before we saw them, and most were on drugs. As I read their records, I began to discover that many (too many) had received one or two series of shock treatments while they had been hospitalized *regardless of their diagnosis.* I could not believe (and didn't want to believe) what I was reading. This "discovery" was closely followed by one of our board meetings. At the dinner afterward, some of the staff were asking me about some of the "research" I had been doing about women, women in therapy, and feminist therapy for a paper I was preparing for APA (the American Psychological Association). I was getting some "loving teasing" by some of my colleagues about my intensity about this topic.

We then settled into a discussion of some of the interesting information that I was gathering, and suddenly one of the psychiatrists went berserk. He stood up, banged a spoon on the table, and shouted that women were bitches; they were just like his ex-wife, who had almost ruined him financially when they were divorced, and they deserved whatever they got. I knew he had been drinking, but I also remember the charts of all those women who had been "treated" with electroshock. In one of those moments of blinding clarity, I remembered my psychodrama training about the feelings engendered when someone stands on a chair and looks down on you—he was short, and I had very high heels on—so I stood up, towering over him, and calmly started quoting statistics from the papers I had been reading. He went nuts (a clinical term). He fired me on the spot and told me that I was not even allowed to come back to terminate my clients. I looked brave and confident, but the bottom fell out of my stomach and I felt shaky. There was a heavy moment of silence, and then Bob Schaef stood up and said that he was also resigning and that I *would* come in to terminate with my clients. Then, one by one, all the staff members stood up and resigned except the original social worker who was also part owner. I had never been so proud of Bob in my life. He was not a "cause" person, and at that moment he was a brave person.

While I was struggling with whether to go through the effort to bring ethics charges against this psychiatrist, I heard that he had had some kind of "breakdown" and was taking a long rest. I had my hands full with my own problems and did not follow up.

We had two kids, we had just had a contract accepted on another house, and our income had just been decreased by two-thirds. It seemed that we had been given an unusual opportunity. We had a choice to see where we wanted to live and what we wanted to do.

I still had my private practice. The agencies who had been working through the private clinic had come in through me and wanted to work with me. There was no clause in my contract that said I could not take my clients with me, so I thought we were okay. We went off to the APA convention with Bob unemployed and me fired and had a wonderful time. Again, when I had not trusted my intuition and followed my process, I had to deal with intensely negative consequences. It was embarrassing to say I had been fired, but it was not uncommon in feminist circles at that time. Frankly, I was getting pretty tired of the system.

Bob was twelve years older than I, and he had worked all his life and never taken a sabbatical. I suggested that I support the family, that we try to pay off any old debts, and that we take the year and see what we wanted to do. He could travel to various parts of the country and check out possibilities. We put the word out to our professional contacts around the country, and Bob designed one of his famous charts.

We generated every variable we could think of, from climate, housing, schools, to professional contacts. He felt that he needed to go somewhere where he could fit into a professional group, and I felt that I would do my work anywhere, so that was fine with me.

I was sad at the thought of leaving my friends and my practice in St. Louis, but I have always felt that life should not be "lived by default." We had not really made an active choice to be there. We just ended up there. I do trust the process, and I know that "trusting the process" also means making active choices about our lives. We needed to explore the possibilities and trust what was right for us. Magically, we were able to get out of the contract on the house and not even lose our deposit, so we were free to go. After much exploration, we decided to move to Colorado. When we got to Colorado, I was to get my year off. That never happened.

Shortly after we moved to Colorado, I received a call from one of my former clients, whose husband had committed suicide. I now realize that he was a sex addict (I didn't know about those things then), and she was certainly in a relationship addiction with him. Part of their joint disease was for him to take sexually explicit photographs of her. Sadistically, he had carefully recorded his dying process on a tape recorder for her and hidden his "photographs." She was completely devastated by his suicide and needed help.

Working with women, I had developed the completely unusual practice of introducing clients in the waiting room and even suggesting that they get acquainted and form support networks. This particular client had been in group workshops, so I asked if she wanted me to alert the network (community). She heaved a sigh of relief, and I got on the phone. In less than two hours, a group of women were with her, and she had constant support until the apartment was completely gone over and everything was disposed of. The community that I had left behind had been created with me as the hub, but it did not need me to function. I was relieved to be dispensable. In reflecting on this call, I realized that I had been setting the stage for a community focus for some time.

After a few months in Colorado, it became clear that our marriage was shaky, and I decided that I'd better see about going back to work so I could support myself and my family. I was loving being at home in the mountains, having time with my kids, and doing what I wanted when I wanted. It was the first time since I was a kid that I was not working at all, and I loved it.

I did not have a license in Colorado, so I met with the then head of the Colorado Psychological Association to explore my options. I have to say that I was not too eager to go back into an "institutional" job if I could possibly avoid it.

The president of the Colorado Psychological Association was very nice when he told me that I had more training and more experience than many of the people practicing in Colorado and that my credentials were excellent but there was no way I could practice psychology in Colorado without a Ph.D. I couldn't believe it. In Missouri I could be "grandfathered" in, but that was not possible in Colorado. We even discussed my moving back to Missouri, "getting grandfathered in," and then transferring my license. That wouldn't work. There was no way for me to practice the profession I had, at that point, been working in for fifteen years and I knew I was good at. However, he said I could work under Bob's license and supervision if Bob was willing to cover me and if I did not call myself a psychologist. I had been a "psychologist" for fifteen years, had completed all the requirements for a Ph.D. except the dissertation, and could not for the life of me see how a dissertation could make me a better psychotherapist, but I could no longer be a psychologist.

By this point in my development, I identified myself as a feminist therapist anyway, so being a "psychologist" did not seem important. Bob agreed to cover my practice for insurance purposes, so I started seeing clients, became a member of the staff at Evergreen Institute (which was Denver's version of Esalen), and started running groups with Bob. Soon, I had a full practice.

Some Difficult Years

When I first arrived in Colorado, I set about trying to establish the kind of professional support system I had had in Missouri and New York. I have never found that to be possible. It may well have something to do with where I am in my life, but instead of professionally supportive colleagues as I had in New York and Missouri, I have found competition, trashing, backbiting, and attacks. Over the last eighteen years, I have learned not to expect (nor did I get) professional support in Colorado. This turn of events has been very shocking for me and has been a constant source of pain. That I have had to look for my support and stimulation elsewhere has saddened me. Periodically, I venture out and try to find new areas of support in the professional community, but I have been attacked because of differing theoretical positions so many times that I am overcautious now.

As I have reflected on this painful rejection by the professional community in Colorado and my inability to find people with whom I could relate professionally, I have been through several levels of awareness. First, there is the pain and sadness. In Missouri, almost all our social life and relationships were with other professionals in the field. We would spend hours talking about new approaches, techniques, and theories. I could not find these kinds of relationships in Colorado, and this experience was isolating and painful. Not only did I not find support, I was often viciously attacked and was often confused as to the real reason behind these attacks. I have always felt a great deal of pain about this rejection. However, as I have been writing this book, I have wondered if I would have had the awareness and courage to move away from and beyond the field of psychotherapy in which I was trained if I had been welcomed into the bosom of the professional community in Colorado. Had I not been forced to find another community of support (the radical feminists), would I have had the need and the strength to stand over and against everything I had been taught as a psychotherapist? I don't know. More about all this later.

I expected to find the same kind of feminist support in Colorado that I had enjoyed in Missouri. Feminist therapy had become a way of life for me, and I was hungry to build networks again. There may have been some people I missed, but my experience was that when I mentioned feminist therapy, this was a new idea to most people in Colorado. Consequently, I was often asked to speak on the subject and received calls and inquiries from persons in the feminist community. The professional community was amazingly silent. At the grass-roots level, I became known as a resource to the feminist and the gay and lesbian community, and my practice moved in that direction. I did continue to do workshops and speaking throughout the United States and Canada, and I kept in touch with what was going on in various parts of the country. Some churches and campus ministries invited me to consult with them, but compared to my work in Missouri, I felt lonely professionally.

In my work with Evergreen Institute, I was able to do encounter groups and personal growth groups and to keep my connection with the human potential movement and humanistic psychology, but generally, I was getting bored with what I now consider "technique-oriented" approaches.

Because of the ideas and theory I was developing in my talks and in workshops, I received many requests from people who wanted to train with me and who wanted to learn from me. These requests were flattering, confusing, and frustrating. It was nice that people wanted to learn from me, and I couldn't imagine what they wanted to learn. I had no idea how to go about meeting these needs.

Somewhere in this process, my marriage was coming to an end. I knew when I married my husband that he was a man of affairs and I was his fourth wife. He always struggled with himself, and down deep he was a wonderful person. He later told me that he knew that I would never let him destroy me, and he felt that his other wives had. I knew that too. I also was heavily into my relationship addiction with him, and I now believe was trained into relationship addiction in my work. I believed "hanging in" was love, and I believed the good therapist was one who would always be there for clients. As I look back, I think I believed that if my clients (and my husband) just had someone who would be there, someone they could count on, who loved them, that they would heal. Certainly my training had taught me this, and I was conscientious and caring. (I have come to realize how arrogant and self-centered this approach is. People have to heal themselves.) I also did not realize that I was practicing an addictive disease that was inherent in the helping professions. Fortunately (or unfortunately), I was a "good therapist." I now believe that being a "good therapist" in the traditional sense is practicing a disease.

Although Bob and I were deciding to separate, because we had already paid for our trip, we decided to go to the APA convention in Hawaii and take our two children with us. This was not my first experience on a flight chartered by psychologists, and it certainly was to be my last. I have *never* had a more embarrassing experience. These esteemed healers of people fought, screamed, got drunk, hit each other, and generally behaved in such a way that I was embarrassed to be a member of the group. Yet, there was nothing presented at the convention about alcoholism or addictions. The presenters were full of "scientific research projects," "growth groups," and new types of "techniques."

Coming back from Hawaii, Bob joined those who became stinking drunk. We had to get a policeman to restrain him so we could get out of the airport, and the children and I spent the night with a friend. That night he chopped up the front door, my desk, and my car with an ax. His psychiatrist said that he'd had an infantile rage like a baby whose bottle had been taken away—so much for psychodynamic interpretations of alcoholic rages. No one seemed to notice that he was drunk. No one seemed to care that he had a progressive, fatal disease that was in its chronic stages.

A few weeks later, I began to put some pieces together, and because of my training in alcoholism as an "organic" problem (medical), I noticed that Bob seemed to be having a terrible time with his memory, and unless he was prematurely senile (which seemed unlikely), he might be alcoholic. I asked to go see his psychiatrist with him, to which he quickly agreed, and I put forth my theory that Bob might be an alcoholic (a good relationship addict's intervention, but at least it was an intervention). His psychiatrist turned to him and said, "Bob, do you drink too much?" (Dracula, do you like blood?) And, of course, Bob said, "No, I don't think so." (He used to drive home at night with a coffee mug in his hand. In my good denial state, I thought it was coffee. It was vodka.) Then his psychiatrist made a typical statement. "Well, Bob, lay off the booze for a month or two, and if you can do that, we'll know you're not an alcoholic." Case dismissed. I believe there was a possibility that Bob would have gone to treatment and our family might even have had a chance if his alcoholism could have been named at that point. We'll never know. He never had the experience of recovery.

This is not "holy" Anne pointing the finger here. I am sad that happened. I know that at that very time, I was seeing many people in my practice who were suffering from various forms of addiction, and I also did not know enough to name them.

I continued to work in my private practice and do my research about women. Now I had half the income and all the same expenses except one less mouth to feed and one less car to support. I had seen how angry, bitter, and mean Bob's previous wife had become when he did not pay child support, and I refused to do that to myself. I could handle it. Besides, either way was a lose-lose. At least I respected myself enough not to want to harass him when I knew that it would not work anyway.

I continued to live in the mountains and support my family. An ex-nun who needed "time off" moved in to help with child care, and we lived in the mountains until the bridge washed out and the road washed out and all of us had to walk miles to get in and out.

In good relationship addiction fashion, I kept checking back with Bob periodically to see if he was all right—that is, to see if he was "well" so we could get back together.

One weekend, Bob and I had decided to spend some time together to "see how it went." We had a really easy, intimate time together. Both of us decided that we wanted to be together more, but he had promised to take the son of his new "girlfriend" fishing. Because we had a pond that he had stocked with fish at our place and we were getting along so well, he asked if he couldn't just bring them up to our place, and then he would take them home and come back. As a good relationship addict, I, of course, said, yes. I could handle it. I even went down to the pond, took some snacks, and invited them up to the house to use the bathroom if they needed to. Later, Bob came up and asked if I would be willing to drive them down to the road in the Jeep; they were tired and had to walk because the bridge was out. Of course, I said of course. When I got down to the pond in the Jeep, I noticed that his "girlfriend" had a little jade pendant on a chain around her neck. Now to most people that wouldn't mean much, but to me it meant instant *rage*. Bob and I had studied jade together and had learned a lot about its spiritual and symbolic meaning in the East. Early in our relationship, we had bought a few pieces that we were able to get inexpensively, and we always were on the lookout for pieces of jade that we could give each other on special occasions. Romantically, jade was the symbol of our relationship. Clearly, this was something that Bob had given her, and she obviously wanted me to see it. I was furious.

To help the situation along, because I had a regular CJ5 Jeep, we put the kids in the back, and because I was driving, Bob and his friend snuggled in the other seat. And, boy, did they snuggle! Like any good relationship addict who had pushed herself too far, I had reached my limit. When they started to get out of the car, I calmly reached over, grabbed the jade, snapped the chain, and tossed the jade into the woods. I then went down and turned the Jeep around and gunned it. They were standing in the road, screaming at me, telling me how crazy I was. I'm glad they jumped out of my way. I do not relate this story to brag. I relate it to demonstrate how crazy I had become in my disease and to show that a relationship addict can become just as insane as an alcoholic. It's the same disease.

When I got back to the house, I felt crazy and ashamed. What a fool I was! How silly I had looked! I knelt down in my bedroom, and I wailed and moaned. My friend came and sat beside me, and I did my first deep process that I recognize as such. I just went into the pain and shame, and these evolved into anger and rage, which I also went with.

By that time, my deep process was leading me; I was not leading it. I howled my pain and frustration, and my body convulsed with feelings. Suddenly I started laughing. I rolled on the floor laughing, what some people would call hysterically. I couldn't stop. That was followed by calm, and I felt great. My last piece (which was so funny) was realizing that I had ruined their evening. Bob wasn't with me, but I could sure bet they were *talking* about me. At that moment, it seemed very funny. The content of the deep process was not really that important. Experiencing it on such a deep level and trusting it was of immeasurable importance. The most important learning, which I could have never "figured out" in a million years and which is typical of deep process work, was that the door into the deep process had little or nothing to do with what the deep process was really about. I started with my pain, rage, and embarrassment about the afternoon, and my process was really about my fear of being crazy. After I did that process, at some level I felt that I had been to crazy and back and I didn't need to worry about that anymore, and I haven't.

Moving in New Directions

I mentioned earlier that people were asking to train with me and to study with me, so I offered to teach a class in my basement in Boulder about what I knew about Women's Reality, The Reactive Female System, The White Male System, The Emerging Female System, and Feminist Therapy. I charged a nominal fee, and that money was put into a special account to explore starting some kind of institute for feminist therapy or for some alternative to therapy as we knew it.

That decision plunged me into one of the most intense and traumatic periods of my life. The class was attended by therapists, counselors, clients, students, feminists, "straights," lesbians, and interested laypeople (many fit more than one category). The information about the class was spread by word of mouth (my old community psychology experience), and about fifty or so women came to the basement of my house to hear the ideas I had gathered and to share their own. Each week there were more than the week before. Just like the communities in Illinois, the feminist community in Denver/Boulder was small at that point, a few people played many different roles, and there was a lot of excitement and intensity with what we were doing. I have always been a "grass-roots person," and I liked the mixture of service providers, consumers, interested laypeople, and concerned feminists.

Out of this class, a cross section volunteered to generate ideas about starting some kind of feminist institute for an alternative to therapy. Because of the experiences of many in that group, it was clear that traditional therapy techniques and focus were not meeting the needs of these women, and, often, they had been harmful. Some therapists (especially women) were becoming aware of women's issues, but they were embedded in the same philosophy, science, and process of traditional therapy, and it was clear to that group of "planners" that a change in content or even awareness was not enough.

We met over a long period of time in that group, and there were some minor issues and power struggles, but, basically, we were building a loving and supportive community of people with divergent backgrounds and interests who shared very important convictions about feminism and the value and rights of women.

Just by chance, one of my physician friends told me of a grant that was being offered in creative projects in postsecondary education. He was going to apply to start an Indian medical school that would be a combination of Indian and Western medicine. I asked if he would mind if we applied also, and he said no and generously gave me the materials. It was less than two weeks before the deadline to apply.

Several of our group met to brainstorm ideas, and then two of us volunteered to put the grant together. I was terrified of writing, so we worked out a system of brainstorming ideas, my colleague writing, bringing it back to me for idea and content clarification, and then rewriting. Much to our surprise, we passed the first screening and were invited to submit a final proposal. Then the trouble began. Suddenly, everyone wanted in on the act, and everyone wanted to be in control. "Interested persons" came out of the woodwork. In our "feminist spirit of openness" we wanted to include whomever we could, and chaos ensued. I believe that we were caught in a typical feminist dualism—we did not want to be hierarchical, and we swung to little or no leadership. I was one of the leaders and not "the" leader and did not want to be "the" leader. The "Institute" was only one of the things I was doing in my life. In addition to raising my children and having my own personal relationships, I was continuing to evolve my own way of working with people that was unlike anything I had ever been taught. The approach was integrated into my personality, my feminist beliefs, my spiritual beliefs, my experience of community; it abandoned my training in psychodynamic, behavioral, and humanistic psychology and included all the facets of my life. I did not set out to develop a new approach to psychotherapy or move beyond psychotherapy. I was evolving beyond any place I had thus far been.

I also wanted to write my book, *Women's Reality,* and I had been invited to study with an Indian medicine man named Rolling Thunder. He had said to me, "you use a lot of Indian medicine in your work. You know a lot more than you use, and I can teach you more. Come to me when you are ready." His words touched something very deep in me, and, intuitively, I believed him to be right. I had grown up among native people, and my mother was an adopted Cherokee. There was something there for me. So what was I doing in the midst of these bickering women jockeying for control?

Right when I had almost had enough, the director of the granting agency called to say she was flying through Denver, and would I meet with her on her stopover? To this day, I am grateful that I took with me one of the Ph.D. psychologists who was on the planning committee for our proposed institute to verify what the director said. The funding director said that they were interested in our project, but they would not fund it unless I was willing to be the director. They felt that it needed *my* leadership. My relationship addiction, ego, and guilt kicked right in. These women had worked so hard on this, I couldn't let it just go down the tubes (here we see an example of the suffering grandiosity of relationship addiction or any addictive disease—I could save the ship, and how *grateful* everyone would be to me!) I decided that I could pick up on my own plans later, and I could devote enough time to help the institute get on its feet and then turn it over to someone else or some other group. I said that I would be willing to be director (pure disease). I did say, however, that I would only be willing to be a half-time director, as I wanted to continue my private practice and the workshops and speaking that I was doing. Everyone agreed, we were given the grant, and we launched into the process of trying to develop The Women's Institute of Alternative Psychotherapy (WIAP), which would be a freestanding, accredited, alternative graduate program in clinical psychology.

This institute was based on two major beliefs: (1) that there was no adequate therapy model for women—all models having been designed by men—and (2) that the traditional training of the psychotherapist actually trained *out* those aspects of a person that were the most healing, with a corollary that the longer or greater the training, the more essential aspects were trained out. In the beginning, I only had the glimmer of an idea that a "Women's Institute of Alternative Psychotherapy" is an oxymoron, not unlike the terms *feminist therapy* or *military intelligence.* I also began to sense that we were really moving beyond the very *concept* of psychotherapy.

We encountered resistance, but not from the sectors we had expected. The accrediting boards, other educational institutions, government agencies, and even the men were either supportive or they ignored us. The resistance (and it was vocal, violent, and vicious) came from women psychologists and from radical Marxist feminists. But, again, I am getting ahead of my story.

I want to describe here the process we experienced in WIAP for three major reasons: (1) the process and issues raised in this experience are key to the work I was developing, (2) I believe the issues we struggled with and much of the ensuing insanity are similar to those disrupting other women's organizations and any organizations that are trying to present a new paradigm, and (3) I want to exorcise the demons from this experience and publicly state my experience and contribution to the issues.

At the next meeting, I was accused of being power-hungry and of lying about the grant. I couldn't believe my ears. Luckily, I had a witness for my interaction with the granting agency. Then I was accused of taking too much salary. Again, I was shocked. The funding agency had a formula for salaries of grant directors based on a percentage of their earnings and earning capacity so that good people would be attracted to become project directors. If I had taken what the agency suggested, there would not have been enough left to do what we wanted to do, so I took the salary of a quarter-time person and really worked an equivalent of three-quarters to full time (no disease here). Our meetings became an awful barrage of mud-slinging and defensiveness. Finally, some of the most violent members of the group walked out (to attack from the outside, as it turned out later), and those of us who were left tried to pick up the pieces. I believe that out of the remnants, we developed a tender, caring, supportive, close-knit community. We were ragged and battered, and we were "hanging in." (As I look back, I'm not sure if that was bad or good.)

We set about our tasks. We developed a board and gathered together a faculty of Ph.D. women psychologists from all parts of the country, straight and lesbian, and from a mixture of racial and ethnic groups. We began taking the appropriate steps in the accrediting process, and we started an embryo organization of alternative graduate programs in psychology. We designed and developed an alternative, external degree program that was quite innovative at the time and was praised by many educators. In the second year, after having designed entrance requirements and procedures, we started processing applications, and there were many of them. Occasionally a man would wander in or out, and we basically had an entirely female organization.

In order to spread the word about what we were trying to do and to meet what we thought was an existing need, we decided to sponsor the First International Feminist Therapy Conference. We were a very small operation. We had a part-time director (me), a full-time administrative secretary, and one other staff person. We rented a basement office from one of our friends and later worked out of an office in the Boulderado Hotel. Our money was going into projects, telephone, faculty travel, and salaries, and we were not spending anything on frills. Our first grant was for about $50,000. We had a grant for two years and no other sources of income. This was a labor of love, and we were all volunteers. I will never forget that conference as long as I live, and I am not sure that I have recovered from it to this day.

Because we were not capable of handling the logistics of a conference with our limited staff time, we worked out an arrangement with the conference planning office at the University of Colorado. We had a large group of volunteers working on the conference and an elaborate exchange system of volunteer time for conference fees. We tried to keep the cost down as much as possible by arranging for inexpensive meals on campus and making housing arrangements for those who could not afford hotels, motels, or dorms at the university. We all put up attendees in our homes.

We invited a range of keynote speakers and had a large variety of workshops. The conference was exploratory in nature; there was no one, agreed-upon point of view. All of our WIAP community was excited and exhilarated because we were doing something new and the response was much more than we had anticipated in our wildest dreams.

A short time before the conference, an event occurred that would shape our lives for years to come. A woman none of us had ever seen before (and we thought we knew most of the "feminist" community) arrived in our office one day, announced that she worked for a local feminist newspaper, and said she wanted to talk to a woman on the staff. I later learned that her approach went something like this: "We are both lesbians, and we can trust each other. I have a great speaker from the East who is one of the leaders in feminist therapy. She is really good, and she is willing to come. You say this is a national or international conference, and you don't have any speakers from the East." The setup was that getting this speaker on the program (which was already at the printers, but could, in all *fairness*, be changed) became, for our staff member, a personal act of honor and of lesbians supporting one another. I sensed the tension. It was true that we had no one from the East, and this "important feminist therapist" (whom none of us had heard of) was willing to come without pay (we weren't paying anyone). I was easy. I did not want to undercut our staff member. I consulted some of the other planners and then said, "Okay." Then came round two.

At that point our new "friend" came back and said that her speaker would like to change her speaking time. Up until then, we had three keynote speakers on the program, one on Friday evening, one on Saturday evening, and one at Sunday noon. I had been trained as a conference designer in NTL and thought that we had a pretty good design. In our minds, the three keynote speakers were all equal. None was more important than the others, and no time slot more important than any other.

Because I was the director of the sponsoring agency and we all believed that I could get the conference started off on a positive, high-energy note, I was to give the Friday night opening address, welcoming all who had come and presenting material from my as not-yet-published book, *Women's Reality*. My talk was to be followed by an outstanding multimedia presentation by a group of women from Arizona. We put our "new speaker" in on Saturday morning, the only logical place.

Our new "friend" told us that her "friend" was not a "morning person" and would like very much to change places with me. I felt uneasy about this, but I wanted to be "nice" (my disease, and not trusting my intuition), and, above all, I didn't want to look unreasonable, self-centered, or controlling (my disease), so I said, "Of course, no problem." Her topic was to be something like "The Development of Feminist Therapy." It sounded like a good title.

When the time for the conference arrived, the staff and membership of WIAP were like little kids. We had planned a great program (we thought); the turnout was terrific; people had come from all over the United States and Canada, plus one foreign country. We had arranged for audio and video recordings of most events, we were getting press coverage, and we had a photographer on hand. We could relax and let our long hours of work and planning come to fruition.

There was a flurry of energy the night of the opening session. I was so proud I tingled with excitement. Several of our board and members welcomed the participants, and then I got up to add my welcome, and warmly, with a great feeling of sisterhood, introduced our first speaker. She took the microphone and stood up and announced that her topic was "The Development of Feminist Therapy *Under Capitalism*." I was in a state of shock. It had never occurred to any of us that another feminist would *lie* to us. I felt like my guts had been ripped out.

She then launched into a half-hour tirade against WIAP and how it exploited women, how the conference was making money off of women (our budget was planned on the number of people we anticipated, and we budgeted to break even. Because more came than we expected, we did make some money, which we put back in WIAP and supplemented our grant. Suddenly, there was something *wrong* with a women's organization making money), how there were no minorities or poor women there (we had gone out of our way to invite minorities, we had an elaborate system of trades and exchanges, and no one was turned away because of lack of money), and generally how awful we were.

After I recovered from the initial shock, I was furious, overwhelmed, and paralyzed. How in the world could I say anything and not be the bad guy? The violence and the dishonest accusations had a familiar ring, but I really was still pretty innocent.

Immediately, I thought of our staff person who had arranged all this. My first thoughts were, "Where is she? I'll kill her!" (And I am sure at that moment I meant it—violence always breeds violence.) These were old SDS (Students for a Democratic Society) tactics, but I had really never encountered anything like this in the women's movement. None of us had. I would now think of it as addictive functioning and know that the confusion and the dishonesty are part of the addictive system, and that trying to make sense out of this kind of behavior just exacerbates the problem.

With blood in my eye, I went in search of our staff member, and when I found her, she was weeping. She looked at me and wailed, "I didn't know. I didn't know." I realized she too had been used.

After her scheduled hour for speaking, our "featured speaker" continued to rant on and on. When I intervened and told her her time was up, some of her "colleagues" started shouting and screaming accusations and threats. One I especially remember was that I was taking the money from the conference and going to Hawaii for a vacation. I was, indeed, going to Hawaii after the conference and was planning to start work on my much-delayed first book, *Women's Reality*. I had scraped together every penny for that trip myself.

Here we had an auditorium full of women who had just arrived at the First International Feminist Therapy Conference, and the very first session was turning into a brawl. We had expensive multimedia people standing by to launch into the presentation (we had to hire them from the university and pay them by the hour), and the first speaker refused to relinquish the microphone. I wanted to be, but there was no way to be, "nice" in this situation. I physically wrestled the microphone away from the speaker and asked the group what they wanted to do. The overwhelming response was to go on with the program as planned. We tried to pull the rest of the conference out of the fire, and most of the attendees seemed to think it was a good conference. Afterward, the board, the staff, and the membership of WIAP were all sick. We felt as if we had been poisoned. The entire experience of trying to get that organization off the ground turned out to be a replication of this conference. (I still feel sick and fearful as I write this.)

One nationally known feminist decided that WIAP would be a good power base for her and decided to oust me and take it over. She nearly bankrupted us by charging all her long-distance phone calls to our number. Luckily, the phone company handled that one.

There was much hullabaloo from the licensed women psychologists about the fact that I did not have a license or a Ph.D. I was an administrator for WIAP—all our faculty had Ph.D.s and were licensed. The attacks were vicious and slanderous. A list of several false accusations presented as facts were circulated about me, and even today I occasionally have to deal with them. I was repeatedly reported to the Colorado Board of Psychological Examiners and each time exonerated. I reached a point where I was ready to sue the board and those calling for the investigations. The board agreed that I was being harassed and refused to do any more "investigations."

One psychic told me that I was being attacked by a coven of fascists from the same soul group as Hitler, and, at the time, it certainly made sense to me.

I learned the meaning of being "trashed."[3] My ideology was never attacked; my character was attacked. Not only was I rejected, isolated, and ostracized, but anyone who had anything to do with me was treated the same way. That's trashing. I began to feel that the best way to care for the people I loved was to stay away from them lest they get hurt by the fallout. I felt contaminated, yet I didn't believe that I had done anything wrong. I was open to looking at anything I was doing wrong, but the accusations seemed crazy.

Several times when I was invited to speak at a large university, the sponsoring group would be told that I was unethical,[4] I wasn't licensed (true, but what speaker has to be licensed?), that I represented myself as having my Ph.D. and didn't (not true, at the time I frequently used *not* having it to get my point across that psychotherapy training often trained *out* of us those aspects of ourselves that were most healing). I have since completed my doctorate but have chosen not to practice psychotherapy or to be licensed. Once at the University of Wisconsin in Madison, the campus ministry received a call from a woman who threatened to disrupt the meeting and cause a scene if they did not cancel my speech. The woman who had invited me panicked, but luckily one of the other staff members had dealt with these tactics in the 1960s with the SDS. He called the legal counselor for the university and was informed that if he or I canceled because of these threats, it would be considered forcing a breach of contract and the caller, a licensed Ph.D. psychologist, could be sued. At the event, he had people in the audience equipped with hidden cameras and tape recorders. It's not easy to be a relaxed speaker under circumstances like that, but I must say it does produce a certain creative tension.[5]

I still feel haunted by this stuff. Only a few months ago, one of my attackers told the director of an agency in Boulder that she shouldn't have anything to do with me because I was unethical. I asked the director what she did with the information, and she said that she didn't trust the woman who had said it so she assumed it was untrue.

Those few years of WIAP seemed like a century. There are many more stories to tell, some of them equally as horrible, but why? I am convinced that one of the persons we took into our ranks was a CIA agent (we later found out that she had been involved in the demise of several "feminist" ventures). I never thought we were important enough for all this attention, but we got it.

What I now realize about WIAP is that we were really trying to present a new paradigm. We called it an emerging Female System. We made the mistake of trying to stay in the old therapy paradigm and get acceptance in and recognition by clinical psychology when what we really were doing was moving into a new concept entirely, one that was not congruent with mechanistic science or therapy.

Eventually, we met with our funding agency and discussed all that was going on. The funding agency said that they liked what we were doing, but they thought some of the women we had stirred up were really crazy; they were afraid that they would go to Capitol Hill and create an uproar that would threaten some of their other programs. I agreed. I thought they were funding some very exciting projects, and we all were exhausted. We folded our tents and went home.

For years, I have tried to understand what that horrible process was all about. Clearly, I was into my relationship addiction and my "nice girl" in not turning down the job as director at the very beginning. This also turned out to be one of the most horrendous whacks on the head that I have ever received for not trusting my own process and doing what I needed to do at the time.

I recognize that my relationship addiction, just like any other addiction, is progressive and fatal, and it was affecting every aspect of my life. Because of my own addictive process, I was not able to spot the characteristics of the addictive process in our attackers or in myself, nor to avoid entering into the resultant insanity.

I have never felt so battered or beaten up in my life. I used to be afraid to come home from out of town because I never knew what new disaster would be awaiting me. My stomach was always in a knot, and I dreaded to hear the phone ring. I could see my health and my sanity deteriorating, and I felt trapped in the situation. This was my bottom.

I have tried to learn as much as I could from those experiences with WIAP and with the barrage that came at me from the "feminist psychologists." Even when I was going through these experiences, I kept asking myself three questions: What am I learning from this? What is this preparing me for? How am I contributing to this mess? At some basic level, I have always believed that we are active participants in our lives—I don't mean this as blame but that the decisions we make in the great and the small do affect us. In addition, we are acted upon by our society and our surroundings, and we do not control the universe. I have found that most theories of human behavior jump from seeing us as having no influence in our lives and being victims to our "creating our own reality." I know that bad things happen to me sometimes, *and* I am not a "victim" (though, I admit, during the WIAP years I sometimes slipped into that role), and I also know that I do not completely "create my own reality." I see both of those positions as part of the thinking of the addictive system.

I also know that during those years I was heavily into my disease of relationship addiction. I was taking care of others (the therapist syndrome), I wanted to "make things all right," and I often felt insecure and on shaky ground.

Paradoxically, I was in touch with a growing inner knowing and a growing trust of my process and my perceptions. I had the feeling of "breaking new ground," and in some perverse way, the constant barrage that I was enduring threw me back on myself. I had to explore myself, and I had to trust myself while trying to be open to input from any source.

Up until this time, my experience with women who called themselves "feminists" had been nothing but positive. Whenever I met a feminist, I always felt open and eager to be friendly. Now I was encountering a group of women who were *mean* and, as far as I could tell, didn't even like women or "females." I needed to regroup and rethink things.

There were two other areas in which I was starting to rethink "feminist therapy." My vision of feminist therapy had been to listen, to support, to accept, and to honor and be open to feelings, whatever they were and whenever they came up. It certainly was not my role to tell women how to be women or what kind of women they should be. I had trouble enough knowing what was good for me, much less knowing what was good for others. If a woman came in feeling bad about herself, describing herself as "a piece of shit," I encouraged her to stay with that feeling and see where it took her. I discovered that what came up for each woman was very individual, and because I had no theory to back me up, I just stayed with whatever came up. (This has proved to be absolutely essential in the evolution of the work I do now.)

In my practice, I had been getting "dropouts" from other kinds of more traditional therapy. Now I was getting "dropouts" from feminist therapy. Now I was discovering that many "feminist" therapists had agendas for women, too. For instance, a woman would see a "feminist" therapist and say, "I feel like a piece of shit," and the "feminist" therapist would say or somehow communicate, "You are *not* a piece of shit. You are a wonderful, beautiful, powerful human being." When I spoke with women who had been through sessions like these, the feelings they reported from those sessions were, "Wrong again. I'd better play the game."

I began to see that as a group, feminists had changed the *content* of therapy but not the process. They were just as ready to tell women what they should be and try to "direct" them into these "shoulds" as the old therapy models were. The process of therapy in the "new therapies" was based on the same models and the same mechanistic-empirical assumptions.

I could see that some of the problems that we had with WIAP were that, in more ways than we had realized, we were really breaking with the accepted tradition with what we were doing. We were not only talking about changing the content of therapy, we wanted to change the scientific, theoretical assumptions about therapy. We wanted to change what therapy was. We were really talking about a new system. We were moving beyond therapy. One of our guiding statements in trying to form WIAP was that "we believed that traditional graduate training trained *out* of people most of the attributes that make them healers."

On reflection, I could see that one of our big mistakes with WIAP was that we had not carefully articulated our assumptions and philosophy. It was difficult for us to do that, because we did not fully know what they were. Much of our philosophy emanated from the material in *Women's Reality,* which many of us were living out as the book was being written. As I look back, almost all of the people with whom we had trouble internally and externally had not lived the development of this philosophy. We did not realize until much later how "radical" what we were evolving was and how much not only what we thought but the way we functioned came out of a model that was not White Male System and was not Addictive System and was not part of the prevalent scientific model. No one was talking about "the new paradigm" or "postmodern" ideas then, at least in our circles. We were not starting with the ideas, we were starting with the practice and trying to deal with what came up in a way that was congruent with our being, our values, and our inner integrity—one step at a time.

In retrospect, my "isolation" from the professional community and "psychology" was probably essential to my developing my own way. I had been involved in the evolution of enough "maverick" approaches to therapy that had since become part of the mainstream that developing a new approach out of my feminism, my civil rights involvement, and my "community" background did not seem like something new to me. In fact, it was not something that I ever thought about or set out to do. I was exploring what worked, and what I was doing seemed to work. The people who were working with me were getting better, and the women were actually processing through old hurts and healing. The material that came up was sometimes new and shocking to me, it was often intense, and it was never overwhelming. Even when processes became filled with rage and were loud, I was aware that the women were doing what they needed to do, and I stayed with their process.

At times, I was filled with gratitude toward my mother, who had a nice, healthy "Irish temper." I fondly say that when I was a kid, we often scraped our dinner off the kitchen wall. When my mother got angry, she threw something. We went through a lot of sets of dishes when I was growing up. The good thing about my mother's anger was that she rarely directed it *at* anybody, and after she "blew," it was all over. My mother never had niggling, hanging-on, picking-at anger. As a consequence, I did not believe that anger was dangerous.

During this period, there was a time when people referred women to me to do "rage work" or "rage-reduction therapy" (their term, not mine), and I worked a lot with anger. Early on, I felt that I had to "control" the situation, I had to "elicit" the anger with some technique or another. I "knew" that it was good to get it out, and I "knew" what people needed. Gradually, all those assumptions fell away, and I realized that not only were they not helpful, they were part of the problem and they were perpetuating the problem.

For a while, I believed that it was "helpful" to have people bring in props for their rage work. I had a garage that I had turned into a "rage room." It was sort of padded, and the windows were protected. The only rules were that you could not hurt yourself or destroy the rage room, and you did not have to clean up your own mess. Women had done enough cleaning up after themselves and others. My clients were quite creative in their "props." (Sometimes I had to bite my tongue, but it was their stuff and their rage, not mine.) One woman whose father was a "big" Eastern analyst brought in pictures of her parents, a set of dishes they had given her as a wedding present (which she *hated*), and a piece of art of the kind she hated but they liked. She set up the pictures and art and threw the dishes at them, screaming some very colorful language.

Another client, who was a nun and had been principal of several Catholic schools (also had attended them), brought in several wooden school desks and a hatchet. (Actually, she was quite a sight arriving with these desks sticking out of her car.) Her process was not loud or explosive. One by one she quietly and with great concentration chopped the desks into little pieces, mumbling all the while. When she had finished all but two, she said she was done. I asked, "What about the others?" "I'll leave them," she said. "Perhaps someone else can use them."

I feel it is important to say here that I was surrounded by therapists who were doing primal scream, whose clients looked like the watches in a Salvador Dalí painting as they waited in the waiting room, people who were lying across the laps of people sitting knee to knee and tickling and poking them until they "broke down their resistance" (all done with licensed and certified psychologists or psychiatrists). What I was doing seemed tame in comparison. It was a time of experimentation and "new techniques," and I also had a social concern and a huge amount of caring underlying what I was doing. I found it easy to genuinely "love" my clients, and I still do. I truly believe that knowing how to love clearly and simply is one of my gifts. It is not something I *try* to do or believe is *right* to do. It just is. Now, I believe that it comes out of my deep awareness of oneness and feelings of being one with the universe.

At one point, because of what was coming up from the women who were attending my workshops in Colorado and in other parts of the country, I decided that women who were out in the world needed safe places to heal and that a weekend workshop could not really even touch the tip of the iceberg. I decided to do a month-long workshop for women. I did three of these, three consecutive summers, in Colorado. These were powerful experiences for all of us who were involved. I brought in a co-facilitator I valued and trusted who worked in Gestalt. In addition, I brought in a variety of "resource people" to present new ideas and experiences to the group. We had a body worker available, and I invited men and women who made input on aikido, psychic phenomena, women's issues, "The Journey of the Female Hero,"[6] nutrition, and other topics. We had at least one guest speaker a week and sometimes more. The rest of the time was spent sharing our stories, exploring ourselves, doing deep process work, and being in nature. These were important workshops for me and for those who attended.

Progressively, I saw how the work that I was doing was different from everything I had been taught or trained to do. My path was diverging more and more from the philosophy and form of psychotherapy as

I had known it. People started telling me that I needed to give a *name* to the kind of work that I was doing. After a while, I started calling it Process Therapy. Then I discovered that there were lots of people saying that they were doing "process therapy," "process work," or working with "the process." At the same time, I would try to describe what I was doing, and people would say to me, "You and so-and-so are doing the same thing." I eagerly started attending workshops being conducted by other people to see what they were doing and to see if we were doing the same thing. I found that we were *not* doing the same thing at all. I decided to call what I was doing Living Process Therapy (I very soon dropped the term *therapy*) to distinguish it from work that involved many elements with which I was not comfortable, such as interpretation, breathing exercises, and other techniques.

After those three years of doing the one-month "Intensives," I decided to try other kinds of Intensives. During the final days of the last month-long Intensive, I experienced another one of those "pivot points" from which my life took off in a new direction, but which was a logical movement from where I had been and to where I was going.

The month together was coming to a close, and the participants and staff decided to go out and have a special meal to celebrate before we went our separate ways. I do not remember feeling ill or over-stressed before we went. In fact, I was in a mood to celebrate. By the time our main course came, I was feeling very strange—almost in an "altered state"—and I noticed that I started to give my food away when it arrived (I have no idea "why," and that is what happened). Suddenly, I slumped over my meal, and I was *gone.* I want to point out here that what I am now going to report is my *experience.* I know it was real, I don't question it, and I don't completely understand it. (But, then, there are lots of things I don't completely understand.)

I felt as though I were falling through levels of consciousness. I "came in" to what seemed like a village in the Andes getting ready for a celebration, which I associated with the opening scene from the musical *Brigadoon.* Clearly, "they" were preparing for some kind of festival. It was apparent that I did not just "drop in" like Superman. I was already there and already "participating." I had just not been conscious of it. The thought went through my mind (or somewhere), "I better look around and see who I know here." Right at that point, one of the women sitting next to me shouted, "Anne, are you all right?" It seemed that I heard it from far away, and I felt my whole soul sigh, and I said to myself, wistfully, "I'd better go back. I'm not finished yet."

The people around me thought I was dead. When I came to, a person in the restaurant trained in CPR checked me for orientation (I was foggy) and checked my vital signs. He said that my heart rate was "real slow," but it was strong. I was rushed to the hospital and checked into the emergency room. They didn't really know what to do with me. They asked me if I was using drugs. I never have been into cigarettes, drugs, or alcohol. I don't even use aspirin more than once a year or so.

Immediately after this experience I consulted several people, including my physician, my psychic friend, an Indian medicine man, a chiropractor who had learned acupuncture in China, and a Spanish curandera. Their responses were all a variation on the same theme. It appears that my vagus nerve had fired, my heart had stopped, and I had experienced a near-death, out-of-body experience. I had not read anything about any of these phenomena, so I had only my experience to rely upon.

It was clear to me that I had been somewhere else. I was terribly curious. Where had I been? What was it about? I was afraid that some part of my being was so "curious" that it might take over my conscious awareness and I would "go" "there" and not get back. For a while, I continued to have the experience of "leaving my body." Often, it was triggered by eating out. Even my kids would notice it. We would be sitting there, and they would suddenly say, "There goes Mom!" My internal experience was one of standing upright and slowly moving (floating?) backward down a long tunnel. Getting up and walking around, preferably in the sunshine, seemed to help the most. The experiences were never frightening. My inability to "control" them was. I began to focus upon my heart rate, biofeedback, and regulating my heartbeat, and after a few months these "episodes" did not recur.

The important result of this experience was that during that first episode when I was "away," somewhere deep in my being I made the vow and commitment, "If you decide to go back, you have to be completely honest, and you can't let anything just 'go by' from now on." Even as I write this, I am not feeling that I have the right words, and yet, I knew that I must plumb the depths of living out of my own process, being as honest as I was capable of being, and leading out of my own being. I needed to see what I saw, know what I knew, and share that.

Facing Addictions

I had seen myself as a very honest person, yet I knew that the subtlety of my dishonesty was seated in the imbalance of not caring for myself and taking care of others. I began at home. I stopped taking care of (not caring *for)* the adults in my household. At that point, I was living in a household of women and children. I can now see that my relationship addiction was not only killing me, it was not at all good for those around me. I have since learned that when I take care of others, it is not always kind. In fact, it usually is not kind. I am often feeding my own ego and making myself indispensable.

Part of the blindness and confusion of the addictive disease is that I *thought* I was being kind, loving, caring, and a good family member when I took responsibility for others, when I picked up the financial responsibility, when I tried to make it all right to others when someone in our family did not follow through on a commitment, or when Ijust tried to keep it all together and "make things work right." I also realized that my professional training had taught me that I was responsible for others. After my "heart stopped," I began a concentrated effort to take care of myself and be as honest as I could about everything.

It was about five months later that we "discovered" that one of our housemates was an alcoholic. I believe that there are two reasons this discovery took such a long time. One was because we did not have a "drinking" household. We rarely drank. It was not a focus or even much of an interest in the house (I did later learn that "partying" was not unusual when I was on out-of-town trips). Second, a couple of us in the household were "professionals" and thought we "knew" something about alcoholism—no one was ever "drunk" (she was on a "dry drunk" most of the time), so it did not even occur to us that one of us was an alcoholic. We did not consider it and rule it out; we did not even *consider* it. Even with the current raised consciousness about drugs and alcohol, I still find this to be true among professionals who have an "intellectual" knowledge of addictions. Often, addiction in its many forms is just not seen.

My intervention on our family member was quite something. I now know that interventions need to be planned, that they are not confrontations, that you need to gather with those who are affected by the disease, and that interventions are times of expressing our caring for the person, sharing how the disease is affecting our lives and clearly stating our limits with consequences for which we are willing to follow through.

This intervention wasn't quite like that. One day she was coming into the bathroom as I was coming out and (figuring I had the advantage), I looked her right in the eye and said, *"I think you're an alcoholic!"* Squarely gazing back at me, she said, *"I think you're right."*

Well, I had no idea what to do next. Everyone knows that when confronted with the disease, an alcoholic always denies it. I was stunned. I was the one coming out of the bathroom, but clearly I was caught with my pants down.

I quickly called friends in Minnesota (what I then considered the addiction and incest recovery capital of the world), and they said, "Treatment." "Ah, yes, treatment." I asked, "Where's the best?" "Hazelden." "Hazelden it is, then," I said. She had no insurance, and as a household, we were just making it. I was supporting two children as a single parent. However, my philosophy about money has always been this: Get clear on what's important and what you *have* to do and then find a way to do it. I have always believed that the practical should be in the service of the important. So we got the money together, and she went to Hazelden (and she later paid me back). Interestingly enough, as I had done with my former husband, what I had zeroed in on was her lack of memory, an organic aspect of alcoholism.

In true "clinical" fashion, I started reading anything I could get my hands on about alcoholism. This was before we really had any general awareness about addictions, and most of what I read was pretty useless. Of course, I didn't start with the "Big Book" of Alcoholics Anonymous because "that was for alcoholics" and I wasn't one. Besides, I was a trained clinician. I wanted to *understand* alcoholism so I could be helpful (and on top of it). I was willing to study it and even develop theories about it. I just was not willing to be *in* it.

One of the first things I learned from my reading was that "the family is usually resistant to the alcoholic's recovering and will try to sabotage the treatment." Well, I sure wasn't going to do that. I was determined to be *cooperative*. I was too educated, open-minded, self-aware, fair, and enlightened—might we even say "perfect"—to be resistant. I made up my mind to cooperate, and not only was I going to cooperate, but everyone in my house was going to cooperate. We were not going to be like "the others" in the books I was reading. We had no investment in our "family member's" disease. We only wanted good for her and would cooperate in whatever way possible. Of course, none of the rest of us had a disease. We only wanted to do the right thing.

In my contacts with Hazelden, I was told that I was as sick as our family member was. "Okay, I would accept that." (I didn't really believe it. Wasn't I working, functioning, keeping the family together, and even doing some very innovative work?) I was told that I had a disease and needed treatment. "Treatment, you say? Okay." (Can you believe it? After all I've done, they are zeroing in on *me*?) "All of you need to come into treatment." "Everybody?" "Yes, everyone connected with the alcoholic is affected by this disease." They all said, "Okay."

So I rounded up the whole household, my kids, my daughter's boyfriend, my ex-husband, (I was *sure* he needed to come), my secretary, her kids (obviously they had been affected). Several of my clients asked if they could come (clearly they had been "infected," too), and I said, "Sure." So we had quite a bunch. In fact, there were so many of us that no treatment center would take us. We hired our own family counselor from a treatment center (she asked if her daughter could join the group since she had not been through treatment—"Of course"), and off we went to have our treatment (as we were supposed to do). We learned some important things, but at that point in the evolution of treatment for family members, we learned more about alcoholism than we did about our respective diseases. But *we were cooperative.*

Of course, at Hazelden and in our treatment experience, the Twelve-Step program was stressed. Frankly, I had many misgivings about Twelve-Step programs. I knew exactly what Twelve-Step programs were and I even (quite open-mindedly) recommended them to my clients on rare occasions. Clearly, Twelve-Step programs were for people who could not make it on their own and were not in control of their lives, and this did not include me. I was doing okay.

From a rational, "scientific" perspective, I could see that the Twelve-Step programs often became a substitute addiction, with addicts becoming emotionally and psychologically dependent upon them. Of course, they were a better dependency than alcohol or drugs, so I supported them.

Also, it looked to me like Twelve-Step programs just took over people's lives. They became their church, their social group, their therapeutic group, and so on. I *saw* them taking over people's lives. I was willing to be cooperative, but *I was not willing to turn my life over to anyone or anything.* I was willing to be cooperative, but I was not willing to be dependent on anything, even a Twelve-Step program.

After our family member went through treatment and spent an eternity in a halfway house, she came home. I can remember once when she was in the halfway house when I was home alone with the kids for a few days. I noticed that we were all tiptoeing around the house and talking in whispers. I had the feeling that I was always looking over my shoulder and waiting for something. Suddenly, I realized that I was looking over my shoulder to see where the next "whack" was coming from. When one lives in an addictive family, chaos, confusion, and psychological "battering" are par for the course. They are the norm. I realized that we were all experiencing their absence, and we did not know what to do. It was the "absence of" that we were responding to.

When our family member came home, things were worse than ever. We had spent all that money and gone to all that trouble, and everything wasn't "fixed." What a disappointment. What an *infuriating* disappointment! When she didn't have the support of her alcohol to take the edge off, all those feelings were hanging right out there.

After a while, when things got tense, I would find myself saying, "Why don't you go to a meeting?" (I never considered that *I* could go to a meeting, even though Al-Anon had been suggested to me. I had, however, bought the concept of meetings.)

Our family member would go off to meetings, and she would *come back better.* I couldn't *figure out* why she came back better. As a scientific, intellectually curious, and open-minded person, I decided to start going to meetings as a research project, to see why they worked. I almost died of smoke inhalation, but I believed that there was something there worth understanding.

I began to see that I could not identify with alcoholism at all, but I sure did understand relationship addiction. I began to look at relationship addiction as a model for my understanding of addiction. I could see that addictive relationships were the norm for the society, and everybody had probably been in at least one, some time or another. Here was a vehicle for me to begin to understand my own addictions.

During this period, I continued to focus my attention on learning about addictions. I spoke about what I was learning, and I began asking for information wherever I went. I found that once the word was out, alcoholics and other kinds of addicts were coming out of the woodwork.

After I went through treatment, I sat down and carefully went over my client load, reviewing their symptoms and psychological functioning. I unearthed five alcohol and drug addicts I had been seeing in long-term psychologically oriented psychotherapy. (I didn't even know to look for adult children of alcoholics, codependents, and subtler kinds of addictions at that point.) I believe that not knowing enough to zero in on addictions was not uncommon for psychotherapists fifteen years ago, and still isn't.

Out of the Old, Into the New

In the meantime, I was continuing to do my Living Process work. I found myself being more comfortable with the deep process work that participants in my workshops and support groups were doing. I bought more pillows and spent less time "talking" during Intensives. I progressively dropped "exercises" and "input sessions" from the Intensives and found that I was getting much more astute in picking up when a deep process was coming up and in just encouraging people to sit with their process.

I began to see that not only did I often not know where a person was going, I frequently did not even know what was going on with her or him. Furthermore, I didn't *need* to know. Again, it was like a gynecologist interfering with a birth. If I just stayed out of the way and stayed with people, being totally present to their process, they would do what they needed to do. Really, all I had to do was see that they did not hurt themselves or anyone else. When I had first started doing deep process work, I was more vigorously encouraging, believing somehow that I was an active and necessary part of the process.

As I talked more about deep processes and shared my experience and my learning, I could see that doing my own deep process work was the most important factor in my understanding deep process work. I also saw that many people had spontaneously had deep processes and thought they were going crazy. I began to see that deep process work was a normal state for the human organism and that it was a way of healing old wounds and completing unfinished life processes that is inherent in the human organism (at least those of the Western mechanistic scientific world). I saw that because most of us had not been process-parented and had grown up in a repressive, controlling society that had not helped us process and deal with events as they happened, and also because we probably did not have the insight, strength, and support to deal with these things when they happened, we all had unfinished, aborted, pushed-down processes rumbling around in us, waiting to come up and be processed through. Whenever we have even the semblance of a safe place and let go of some of our illusion of control, up they come. Usually, at these times, we have feared that we are "losing it."

Also, during this time, I was aware of my civil rights and feminist consciousness that demanded that I work with people in a way that did not force them into the dominant culture, that I respect their personal, racial, cultural, sexual, and gender differences. I realized that this conviction demanded more of me than rhetoric. My actions and *what* I did or did not do had to fit with what I said. I became aware of a growing congruence in myself and a desperate need for that congruence.

Even though I was in private practice, I believed that it was important that no one be turned away from the therapy they needed if they couldn't pay. I saw many clients who could not pay at all. Sometimes, clients would barter for their therapy. I had come from a bartering society (rural America) and believed it was important for people to pay their way when they could. When I was growing up, I had heard of many doctors who had accepted chickens or a bag of apples in payment for their services.

During these years, I saw many struggling women artists in therapy and was traded more art than I could possibly squeeze into my house. I always insisted that they set the value on their work, just as I did on mine. Frequently, I did not charge the going rate because I often felt that the going rate was unethical for me. I always charged what felt comfortable for me and did not referent this outside myself. For some, I developed an approach of "guaranteeing my work." Many women came to me when they were just coming out of a divorce, had never worked for an income, or had not worked outside the home for many years while they raised children, and had no self-confidence. Whether they had money or not, many probably didn't even feel that they were *worthy* of having money spent on themselves for therapy. With these women, I made a deal. "You need to do some work. Do your work with me, and when you have done your work and feel more confident and find a job worthy of you, pay me." I'm still getting checks from some of these women.

My work in the various movements had convinced me how subtle the training into this system is and how difficult it is to see our blind spots. I knew that my perceptions and interpretations had to be colored by who and what I was and what my background and training had been. I even saw feminist therapists imposing their views upon clients. I knew that as far as I was capable, I did not want to do that, although, as I look back, I realize I was doing much more analyzing and interpreting than I could now comfortably do.

There was, however, a feeling among all of us (clients, groups, participants at Intensives) that we were involved in something new, something important, and that we were in it together somehow. Therapy was often just mucking around in personal dynamics; what we were doing was beyond that. It was in some vague way related to healing the society and the planet.

Many of us were working inside and outside at the same time, and we were somehow all leaders and participants in this process. For those who did not feel this way, that was all right, too. There really was tremendous freedom for people to do what they needed to do, and that took many forms.

As I quit fighting my awareness of my own relationship addiction and broke through my denial about being a relationship addict (and codependent), I began to see how the way I was trained to be a therapist was, in itself, training to be a relationship addict (or codependent). I was trained to believe that I was responsible for my clients, that I should be able to diagnose them and know what was wrong with them and what they needed, that I should know what would help them get well and do it, that if anything happened (like suicide) it was in some way my fault, and so on and so on and so on.

I gradually became aware of how disrespectful all these beliefs were and how disempowering they were. I also began to see why psychotherapists burned out and were often exhausted. We were practicing the disease of codependency in our work; the way our work was structured *was* the disease of codependency. I not only had to do my recovery on a personal level, I had to do it on a professional level.

By this time, I was beginning to see that society functions as an addict and that we are all involved in one addiction or another. I was seeing that what I had called the White Male System and the Reactive Female System were not two different systems but the same system and mutually supported and needed one another. Also, what I had called the White Male System was really the Addictive System, and what I had called the Reactive Female System was really the enabler or relationship addict (codependent). The helping professions are to the Addictive Society what the enabler/relationship addict is to the alcoholic; the helping professions (the way we have them structured) enable an addictive society. And, like every good enabler/relationship addict, we really mean well, but we nonetheless perpetuate the addiction of the society and keep it limping along so it won't "bottom out," just as the enabler does with the alcoholic. If we are to do the work we want to do in the helping professions, we are going to have to take a look at everything we do, why we do it, and what the theory and assumptions are behind it.

Concurrent with all this work, I began to glean an understanding that shifted my whole perception. I started to see that it was not possible to understand addictions intellectually and that trying to do that was part of my denial system. Thinking and understanding just were not enough. I saw that the people who had the most thorough understanding about addictions were the recovering addicts themselves, and if I really wanted to understand this disease, I had to work a recovery program. Abstract awareness and goodwill were not enough. Recovery demanded participation. I had to work the program and participate in my own recovery to "grok" this disease.[7] Finally, I began my own recovery in earnest. I started working the Twelve-Step program of Alcoholics Anonymous for my relationship addiction.

This next part is difficult for me to communicate. As I simultaneously began to Live in Process more and more, to do my deep process work whenever I needed to, and to do my own personal recovery, I found myself internally making a system or paradigm shift. This was not something I set out to do. This system shift was a by-product of my doing my work, one step at a time. I began to see my world very differently and experience myself in it very differently. I began to develop an uncanny ability to name the addictive process whenever I saw it and, at the same time, to avoid participation in it. I was able to stay with my own process, my own sobriety, my own spirituality, and feel serene most of the time. As I traveled around the United States and Europe, lecturing and doing workshops, I could immediately spot those people who were in recovery, and I knew that in their solar plexi, they knew what I was talking about. There seemed to be a growing number of people who had shifted their consciousness and were seeing the world through different lenses. My experience was that these were usually people who were actively in recovery from addictions.

I experienced my recovery work as very complementary to my Living in Process and deep process work and began to see how they were interrelated. Not only were they interrelated, they were mutually necessary processes for full recovery.

I took a new look at spirituality for myself. I had long separated religion and spirituality, knowing they were not the same. I knew that the Twelve-Step program is a spiritually based program and I was no longer hung up on the sexism in the wording of the program or their suggested prayers. I knew that my "spirituality" had always been important to me, and I had always had a connection with it. Then I moved to a new level. When I am Living in Process, everything I do is spiritual. There is no separate "spirituality" in me. I am spirituality. Spirituality and process are the same. I began to see that my process is God, that God is more than my process, and when I am living my process, I am one with what we call God.

I began to focus upon recovery (the Twelve-Step program) *and* the process work in my profession. As I did this, I began to see a significant change occurring in the way I worked and the way I lived my life. These facets of my life became progressively more integrated until there was no real separation between my living and working. Everything I did easily flowed as the process of my life, and everything was spiritual or the Living Process. In the living of my life and work, "why" and "understanding" became less and less important.

During these years, I was invited to speak and do some workshops in Germany. Recognizing that everybody's process work is unique, it was still an amazing discovery to see how similar the deep process work that came up in the German participants was to what I watched in people in the United States. The difference in language and culture didn't matter. When given a safe place to emerge, the deep processes looked and sounded similar. The content of the deep process work often differed, but the *process* of the deep process was the same.

I began to introduce information about addictions and Living in Process in all my work. Slowly, I began to be less and less content with doing a private practice. My work seemed to be involving more and more travel, and I finally decided that it was time for me to give up being a therapist.

This giving-up process took about two years and was not an easy one for me. Long ago, I had established my professional identity as a psychotherapist, and even though more and more of my income came from speaking engagements and workshops, in my gut my support for myself and my family had always come from the therapy practice. I felt as though I was jumping off into the abyss. Still, I was more and more aware of trusting my process and living my process from my clean and sober self, and I knew that this was the direction I needed to go. I loved my clients and I loved seeing them and I found myself progressively bored with individual sessions. Because I was putting the focus less and less on me, and I saw how much more we could learn from one another in groups, I opted to quit doing individual therapy and any therapy, itself, completely. I have never regretted this decision.

Also, during this period, so many people had asked to train with me that I sent out an announcement and said I was willing to do a year-long "training group." I limited the first training group to people in the health care professions.

A New Paradigm Emerges

During the first year of the "Training," I realized that everyone was in this year to do his or her own work, and I really was not "training" them to do anything, and the training was for living their lives, so I decided to open it up to people who wanted to face their addictive process, do their deep process work, and learn to Live in Process. Sometimes, I think of it now as an alternative to addiction treatment or therapy that comes out of a very different scientific model, and it's quite a lot less expensive than either. Also, because the group as a whole only meet three times in the year, I am not the center of focus, and people who train with me have to live their lives in their normal settings, work in local Twelve-Step groups, and do their life process. The exciting thing is that this way of being with people feels very congruent, and those who participate really get amazingly more fully alive in a short period of time. Living in Process work is much more effective than any therapy I have ever seen.

The prerequisites for doing the Training Year are being alive and having attended an Intensive so we know the person and the person knows what this work is really about, experientially. I used to say that one Intensive saved six months to a year of psychotherapy. Now, I no longer believe in psychotherapy, as such. I do still believe that the Intensives are very powerful, and they are a good way to determine whether or not the Training Year is appropriate.

Since the early seventies, I have made many changes in the deep process facilitation that I do. We have evolved to a point where there is no need for any exercises, techniques, or gimmicks. As we gather, check in, and share our stories, the deep processes that have been bubbling around in people begin to come up. We just stay with these people and this deep process. Trainees, staff, and participants all do our own work when it comes up, and all of us share our struggle with our addictions and our recovery process. There is no agenda and no "right way to do it." We do not set out to be kind and loving, and we have found that as people are as honest as they can be, this creates an atmosphere of honesty and safety. We do this not by telling people we are honest or that the situation is safe but by being honest ourselves and by sharing ourselves. If a person doesn't feel safe, that's okay, too. What can she or he learn from that? Whatever comes up, the question is, What can I learn from this?

I think of deep process facilitation as being like midwifery. We are present, it is not our show, and we are there encouraging people to stay in touch with themselves and see for themselves what they need. People who have observed and experienced deep process facilitation say it is the most respectful work they have ever seen.

In the seventies, I had been calling the work I was doing Living Process Therapy, and some of the people who had trained with me then called themselves Living Process Therapists. There were a growing number of people who had trained with me, and Living Process Therapy was now becoming a discipline in and of itself, yet it had still not "gone public." When I became clear that I could no longer accept the models out of which all psychotherapy comes (based on mechanistic, reductive science), I decided that I was no longer comfortable calling myself a therapist of any kind. This was not an easy decision. I had given up a private practice as a therapist. Giving up the belief that the work I was doing had anything to do with therapy as I had known it shook me to my foundations. This was not a "decision" that I "made" and then was done with it. This was a process of coming to know that I had made this decision. It took me almost six months to come to this knowing after I had the first awareness that I needed to address this issue in myself. Fortunately, by this stage in my work with myself, I knew to trust the process and not try to control the outcome (often easier said than done), and more and more I felt my life guided by my inner process when I had the wisdom to listen to it.

By this time, I had the clear inner awareness that "therapy" was based upon a worldview and scientific philosophy that prohibited its being able to accomplish what it existed to do. I also knew that it would have been easier just to have this awareness and keep it to myself. Announcing that I was no longer a therapist and that I no longer considered the work that I was teaching to be therapy was not an easy decision. Yet, I came to believe that I needed to do this for my own integrity and sobriety.

Some of the people who did the Training with me did it as professional training to learn a new technique. This was a major source of my income. What would the effect on my income be if I no longer was training in "therapy"? I had no real category or language to talk about what I was doing (Living Process Facilitation, maybe?). Where did what I was doing "fit"? Was it therapy, counseling, education, religion, psychology, medicine, psychiatry? No! In a world so very much bound by categories, was my decision condemning the work I was doing to oblivion? Maybe. What about insurance and third-party payments? Was I willing to give up that option? Yes! I hated to deal with insurance companies, and, in keeping the costs of what I do reasonable and being willing to work out an endless variety of payment plans, I knew I could feel comfortable with my decision. My experience was that insurance payments were pretty random anyway and getting more unpredictable by the minute, so I welcomed the idea of not having to deal with insurance companies. I was beginning to see that there might be another "up" side to this decision, along with maintaining my own integrity and sobriety.

What if the people who trained with me refused to make this change? Ah, a tough question. I could try to demand that they did, knowing full well that I could not control what others did with my decision.

After living with this decision for some time, I decided to write a newsletter to the network of people who had trained with me and share my process and my decision and belief that what we were doing was *not* therapy. I presented my process and decision and let it go, asking those in my network to explore this issue in themselves and *do what felt right to them*. Some have shifted. Some have not. Their decisions about this have nothing to do with what I felt was right for me, and vice versa.

What a relief for me was the decision that what I am doing is not "therapy" and the process of the decision. I felt a great burden lift, as it always does when I trust my process and am in integrity with it.

I realized that because I was not doing "therapy," the rules and regulations, which were based on a system that I now considered insane and demanding addiction, no longer applied. Just like the Indian medicine women and men I knew, I was working out of a different paradigm. Frankly, the paradigm I was working from had more in common with that of Indian medicine than it did with the American Psychological Association. Another relief. Slowly my work and beliefs and philosophy were becoming more and more congruent. One of the best process facilitators we had in the network was a man who was dyslexic, had never gone to college, and was an artist and a carpenter. The more we developed this work, we saw that there was sometimes an inverse relationship between education in the helping professions and being a good Living Process facilitator.

In order to develop this work, I had to be willing constantly to challenge my assumptions, my truths, what I had been taught was "right," how I had been taught things "had" to be done, and the ethics and belief systems I had learned. I prayed for guidance, asked for feedback, sought to stay in integrity with myself, worked my recovery program, did my deep process work, and trusted my process.

As the work I was doing came more and more into its own, I saw healing that I had never imagined possible taking place before my eyes, and *I was not necessary for it to happen.* I could help facilitate a setting and support the healing, and what was happening in the individuals who came to the Intensives and Training sessions was healing in ways I had never dreamed possible. I came to see that the human organism does, indeed, have an inherent inner process for healing whatever experiences have occurred in living life. At some metalevel, the issue is not *what* has happened to each of us. The issue is owning it, claiming it, and letting our inner process take what avenue of healing it dictates. I saw healing that could never have come about through intellectual insight and understanding. I was appalled with the memories and body awareness of incest and early sexual abuse that came up in people when they did their deep process work. I began to see that the training that told me to have guarded expectations for healing in certain categories of people was off base and severely limited. First, it was crazy to have expectations of any kind, and second, the healing that was possible seemed more and more related to willingness and ability to do one's work than to diagnosis—yet another "god" attribute, prediction, taken away. I could see myself knowing less and less and having more and more wisdom.

I saw people in their deep process work (never manipulated, controlled, or brought about by us) touch memories of early incest, violent abuse, and/or sadistic, sexual, cult experiences and work through these experiences, integrate them, and move to living their lives in ways I had never thought possible. All this would happen during a Training Year during which they met three times with their Training group and me, attended peer Regionals approximately once a month, came to occasional Intensives during the year, attended Twelve-Step meetings of their choice, and did their own work at home, asking another Trainee, a family member, or a friend to sit with them.

What excites me so much about this work is that it is truly consistent with a paradigm shift *and it works.* It is opening doors to healing that I never thought possible, and it is so simple and easy on the facilitator. I never have the experience of burnout and exhaustion that I had when I was a "psychotherapist." I don't have to know what is going on; I don't have to have the answers; I don't have to be in control (or think I am). I only have to be present and participate by sharing what is going on with me.

As I said earlier, my relationship addiction recovery process has been key in its interaction with my professional work and how I came to view my work. In my recovery process, I came to see that addictions are much more than specific ingestive or process addictions (see *When Society Becomes an Addict*).[8] I saw that addictions are integrated into the society, that the society itself functions as an active addict, that all of us have learned this addictive process, which is the norm for the society, in our families, institutions, and society as a whole. This addictive process is based on illusion and requires us to disown our own reality in order to fit into an illusionary paradigm or worldview.

I also came to know that because this addictive process is the foundation for our society, none of us escapes it (it is only the arrogance of our disease that makes us *think* we do), and each of us needs to face up to this addictive process and the form it takes in each of us. We need to face the *specific* addictions *and* the underlying addictive process. I realized that if we are not actively in recovery ourselves (a participatory model), we *are* the problem. I came to have tremendous respect for the wisdom of Alcoholics Anonymous, which calls this disease "cunning, baffling, powerful . . . and patient." This is a tricky disease, and those who think they have it conquered or think they are not affected by it (or afflicted with it) are probably in denial. (These are strong words, and they have come to be true for me.) My own personal recovery process became more and more important to me and was central to my life.

When I was on a publicity tour for *When Society Becomes an Addict*, I had an experience that later proved very important to me and to the evolution of my process. I had been asked to be on a one-hour radio talk show to discuss the book. When I arrived at the studio, the host told me that there was a psychiatrist who was the head of a chemical dependency unit in a large Boston area hospital who insisted on being on the show with me. I was flattered.

Now let me quickly say a little about the kind of person I was. When I watched the movie *Easy Rider,* at the very end when the men in the pickup truck had shot the one biker and were turning around, I believed they were coming back to help. (Naïveté and gullibility are characteristics of a relationship addict.) So, of course I was thrilled that he wanted to be on the show with me. I assumed he had had a great breakthrough while reading *When Society Becomes an Addict* and wanted to say so on the air.

He hated the book, and he seemed to hate me. It was one of my first conscious experiences with what I now call a fundamentalist scientist. Nothing or no one can be as violent, dogmatic, or emotional as a fundamentalist scientist.

Years ago, I had noted that the scientific method was nothing but a religious belief system. As I have written in *Women's Reality,* the reaction to that statement was so violent that I kept my mouth shut about that observation for over twenty-five years.

Like any other religious fanatic, a fundamentalist, dogmatic scientist firmly believes that the only true access to truth must come through their procedures and belief system. Anyone who has had any contact with a fundamentalist religious fanatic knows the syndrome, whether the fanatic is Christian, Muslim, scientific, or political. Regardless of the content, the process is one of closed-mindedness, violence, discounting, righteousness, and superiority.

Being an innocent in this situation, I approached this man receptive and eager for dialogue. For openers, he said that he thought this book was dangerous. I took that as a compliment and thanked him. He said that it wasn't scientific, and I again took this as a compliment, if he meant it was not approached from a mechanistic scientific paradigm, and again thanked him.

I believe the work that I do is very scientific—if science is open-mindedness, exploration, and the kind of science we find in native cultures, thermodynamics, or the new science. I believe that we can have a science that is participatory, as Morris Berman has suggested, and is based upon the basic wholeness of the universe.[9] This kind of science is not reductionist, it is expansive.

Anyway, I tried to find something, anything, in common with this man. Early on, we had both mentioned the Twelve-Step program of Alcoholics Anonymous as a good program. I thought perhaps we could find some area of rapprochement and pull the show out of the ashes, so I tried to go back to the Twelve-Step program. "Well, at least we both agree that the Twelve-Step program of A.A. is the best tool to use for addictions," I said. "I didn't say that," he snapped. "What did you say?" I asked. "I said that it is a good program for those who cannot afford anything better." Needless to say, at that point I gave up the hope of communicating with him.

At this stage in the development of my ideas, I desperately wanted support and recognition from professional colleagues. I had been in this position before, many times. When I was involved in civil rights, I wanted racial bigots to listen and be open-minded. When I was preparing the material for *Women's Reality,* I wanted to be heard and accepted by the White Male System. Here I was again. I had learned so much from listening to other addicts and doing my own recovery. I wanted those fully entrenched in what I was calling the Addictive System to hear and value what I was saying. Not only did I want them to hear and validate me, I wanted them to agree with me.

During each of those phases of coming to understand a system that was not in keeping with the dominant system and trying to articulate my learning to the dominant system, a little voice inside me whispered, "What is this experience preparing me for?" Each time, I could not imagine any situation that could be more horrendous or more difficult than the one I was in at the time.

Well, I think I have found it. I have never run up against a more sacred cow than the science based upon Descartes and Newton. This reductionist, mechanistic science permeates all of Western thinking. All of our social, political, religious, healing, scientific, and economic structures are built on this limited scientific belief system.

I had been playing around with the idea that in order fully to understand what I was delving into, I had to dig deeper into the "science" on which psychotherapy was based. This fanatic psychiatrist was the gift that convinced me that I was right.

As I worked with alcoholics and did my own recovery, I became more and more convinced that traditional psychology, psychotherapy, psychiatry, counseling, ministry, and religion really were not helpful in treating addictions and often exacerbated the problems (giving drugs to treat alcoholism and thus developing another chemical dependency, for instance). I was also beginning to see that these very same disciplines were not very useful with the traditional "psychological" problems that one finds described in the *Diagnostic Manual III*.[10] In fact, I was toying with the idea that many of the categories found in the *DSM III* fit much more readily under the rubric of addiction and codependence, and working with them with the tools of the Twelve-Step program and the deep process work not only was cheaper and easier, it was more effective.

Maybe the reason the professions had systematically ignored addiction and/or had been so ineffectual in treating addiction was that they came out of a model that itself subtly supported addiction and was based upon addiction. I now believe this to be true.

I started getting mail from "fans" who had read my books or heard me speak. When I was feeling very insecure about writing about my ideas, I gathered these letters (hundreds of them), and I was going to dedicate one whole section of this book for publication of these letters that support my observations. When I quit listening to the trained experts and listened to the "nonexpert" experts who were struggling with the problems they were facing, I discovered that I, too, could be a participatory expert.

I feel more secure in what I have to say about these ideas now, and I do want to quote a few of the letters to share some of the information that was coming to me and influencing my thinking because I believe the real experts are the people themselves.

The letters supported a range of ideas I was developing. Some of them verbalized the need to take a new look at psychotherapy and the way it was practiced. For example, C.D. from Maine wrote,

> I met an addictions counselor at a brunch yesterday, and I was almost shocked at some of the things that came out of her mouth. I know that you are right—with all my heart I know that you are right. What she said sounded so grandiose in the sense of the therapist being the one to decide when and under what conditions a patient would "get into deep work." I said to her that what she was describing sounded very controlling and manipulative to me and arrogant too. She'd just returned to the mental health field after a two-year burnout period and had relocated to Maine. She also kept talking about helping her sick patients get well

and then when they were well they might not need so much direction. It made my skin crawl. I could really feel how disrespectful her approach is to her clients. Thank God I don't ever have to work in a mental health agency.

Some were amusing, opinionated, and thought-provoking, like this one from California:

RE: *When Society Becomes an Addict*
Hi Anne,

Hey, what's this! a book about society/psychology with no big fat (macho, role-playing, authoritarian) flaws. The mountain is really a mountain again, hurray!

Ya know, those addicted to guilt and raised on rape want to play games that create more guilt, that can be blamed/projected on "the other," to keep a bit of certainty, a little control/power over, never having to face their inner real self. So what's new?

On your idea that schizophrenia is simply a point on the continuum of society's programmed thinking—quite correct. I see in the personal history of the "insane" I know some point where authority and authoritarian thinking—control control control—was shoved too hard down their throat, and they took it very seriously, tried to be the best possible performer they could for the Master and the Man, took the thing to its logical conclusion—insanity. Many have super-developed one of society's acceptable delusions, like there being a holy ghost, which leaves you haunted, ripe for paranoia and voices. Also lots of "schizoids" are, they claim, directed by the Master, which is the epitome of internalizing hierarchical patriarchy.

I have a low threshold into the unconscious, so mental illness is all too explicable. I'd really rather not know, be able to forget. Ever look up and out when you're submerged in a swimming pool? People above look like actors on a stage. Seeing from down deep, you just can't believe that most are living in a daydream, that nothing matters to them about their inner real selves, that having at least one delusion about something is the norm, especially for those who are supposed to be "somebody." There is no humor (unless you're lucky or have mad humor), like being a radical, fundamentalist Christian, who himself is insane. Society accepts the Christian because his hierarchical ideology is simply a "mystified"—obscured—mirroring version of patri-archy, with it's hero worship, follow-the-leader role model.

Ya know, it's all the hocus-pocus ideas that the psy-chotherapists carry that stop them from seeing any of this. The biggest problem I find most of the time, when attempt-ing to discuss what schizophrenia is, is the "shrink's" un-willingness to give up her/his role as the authority, which demands that one not ever really help anyone, 'cause you'd hafta help yourself—face your very own pain and guilt and love—simultaneously. Might leave ya singing "The Real Love Blues."

Enough!

Thank you for the Lincoln Logs. I was stumbling on that. I could see that the preacher man had to lust to judge it, that you gotta think you're better than others (not just like all the rest) to get depressed over your worthlessness, but—you're good!

"Left-brain" emotion of panic—great idea. I've certainly been there. Half of all thinking is inspired by a controlled panic when one/society is addicted to fear.

Hey, in your next book: (1) "Dig yourself, as you would have others dig you!" (2) "To live outside authoritarian think-ing's grip you must be honest—with yourself." (3) "Lighten up, fool!" (now that's en-lighten-ment). (4) "Engage your feelings—that's the spiritual." (5) "Love beats this thinking shit!" (6) "Learn to forget."

Well, I've probably put you to sleep.

Thanks, B.K.

Some were touching and heart-wrenching, like that of M.D. from Iowa, who wrote on 16 June 1987:

This is a letter which I feel a need to write. I want to take the risk: to communicate me, to thank you, to congratulate us on the recovery process. And to share. I am aware of wish-ing to protect myself from disclosing any true feelings because they are still codependent and adult child–like. I feel ashamed I still process them. I am grateful for your books. They help clarify. I also feel envy and a twinge of resentment. I too write, about the same issues. And I have tried to get the enclosed article published. From submitting it to *Ms.*, to imploring Ellen Goodman of the Boston *Globe*, to do something with it—because it needs to be heard: like your books.

I do not like that I still need the external ego-boost/validation which I believe publication will bring. At the same time, though, I have grown. For I am grateful that finally someone who knows is being heard!

I also feel sadness and regret, anger and hurt. Reading books by you brings back many painful memories.

I began my journey via psychotherapy in Denver. I worked with a then leading woman psychologist whom I know you know. And I am just now, over ten years later, beginning to work through my anger toward her ignorance of 1976 and society's need to fragment and categorize.

I knew then I was struggling with addiction and disability. All types. I was also painfully conscious of my reality as a woman seeking autonomy in a male-dominated society, and of the psychiatric genocide which perpetuated my dis-ease.

My psychotherapist became my demigod, second only to Dilaudid, barbiturates, and alcohol.

And as I screamed, "I am not: organic brain syndrome, borderline personality disorder, acute schizophrenic reaction," I reached out for the only solutions I knew worked. Addiction. Time and time again I became traumatized by inappropriate hospitalizations while being victimized by the *DSM III.* But that didn't stop the suicide attempts, nor the institutionalizations, nor the egocentricity, nor the using.

I finally left Denver Aug. '80 for hometown Sioux City, bottomed out at 62 pounds and 10,000 mg. a day. When I was a year plus sober, I returned to Denver to visit only to discover that I had been a major psychiatric controversy within the psychiatric community. That didn't help me to overcome my already extreme attitude of "terminal uniqueness."

While in Denver, then later in recovery, I tried to communicate to the "professionals" what some of us had been beginning to realize in the early '70s—what your books tell. No one wanted to hear. Especially from a bona fide nut.

For a while I traversed the road of sobriety. It hurt. I stayed in self-pity and in condemnation of self and others. Yet my journey has led me to sobriety and more recently to recovery.

Nor has it been externally fruitless, even though I am not now employed. Along the way I obtained a master of science degree in counseling and vocational rehabilitation and have just been certified as a substance abuse counselor.

Currently I am trying to market myself as a consultant and yet I sense I am being called back West—perhaps to train with you at some point.

Some, like the next two, share the failure of therapy and traditional models:

> Another note—I continue to understand the role that my many years of therapy have played in my efforts to try to heal: in the last two deep processes I have had, I have struck upon material that I had intellectually covered in psychotherapy. I immediately moved out of my feelings to my mind, cutting these processes short. The impact of this has felt like a kind of sterilization to me. Enough said.
>
> G.G.

> I have struggled with depression all my life—I am fifty-one years old, and have been in therapy off and on for over twelve years. Since I have been working the Twelve-Step program my life has become more and more positive. My depressive episodes, which lasted months at a time, now are only three or four hours at the most, and certainly by the next day my mood has usually lifted. When I first heard you say that "depression is a gift" that really amazed and excited me, and now I am learning not to fight it, to explore its presence instead.
>
> I date the beginning of my Recovery from my first meeting in Nar-Anon, in April, 1987. I now attend Al-Anon and O.A. meetings as well, and use the daily literature from E.A.!
>
> I am aware I am still very much in early recovery, just beginning to move from the intellectual to the emotional understanding of the program really.
>
> C.H.

The next three letters indict the mental health system and what happens to therapist and client alike in this system:

> I feel kind of like I did when I first started the program (almost nine years ago). Back then I was hopeful and I believed in the program. I was enthusiastic and I worked a pretty good program. About five years ago, I went into ther-

apy. When I look back, I feel like I was in a big slip. Therapy was a fix for me. I received good information while in therapy, it was a place for me to relieve the pressure and tension I had from operating out of my disease, but I didn't feel serene and I knew there was something missing. Also, during my years of therapy, I went to meetings, called my sponsor, "kind of, sometimes, maybe" "worked" my steps, and to some degree, I was coping. However, I was not recovering.

I don't feel judgmental about my therapy. Rather, I feel finished with it and I am looking back at that piece of my life. While looking back, I am aware that I feel like I was in relapse. I also feel accepting and believe that I am (and was) at the place that I needed to be at the time. Also, I know that I learn from my slips and I know that I learned from this time in my life.

I feel different today. I see a difference in my program today. I can read the promises and see how some are coming true for me. I am trusting my H.P. [Higher Power] and the program. And I am working the steps, one day at a time. Nowadays, I am sharing my program, before, I was sharing information that I knew about the program. I feel serene. I know that no problem is too big for me to handle. Probably because I am not trying to handle them by myself. I am doing my footwork and leaving the results to my H.P. *And it works!!! And I like this!!!*

R.R.

I have just finished rereading your book *When Society Becomes an Addict* for the third time and have recommended it to several friends in my Al-Anon group. I believe this is the single most helpful and enlightening work I've ever read (and I'm an ex–high school English teacher, and read a lot). I would like to share with you some of the insights and synthesis of ideas I've been getting and some of my own experiences, especially as they relate to the statements you make on pp. 60–61 about stinkin' thinkin' and possible connections between addictive systems and schizophrenia.

I am forty-nine, married twenty-eight years, mother of three adult sons, myself an adult child of an alcoholic father. My mother's two siblings were both alcoholics, as were both of her grandfathers. My mother's extended family, from which my role models came, was full of extremely controlling, capable, judgmental, loyal women. I also fit that pattern and was a "perfect" child and only child in an alcoholic family.

My husband, an M.D., is the youngest of three children from an anti-drinking, fundamentalist religious family. His older brother has been identifiable as a workaholic from age fifteen. Phobias, depression, and obsessive-compulsive behaviors abound in his extended family. All members of my and my children's generations are college graduates—no suicides or psychiatric hospitalizations on either side until Rick—

Rick is our middle son, age twenty-three. Cigarettes at eight years (and still smokin'), pot and alcohol repeatedly sneaked at a friend's house at ten years, possible LSD trip at ten . . . daily pot smoking by age fourteen (As & Bs in ninth grade, Ds & Fs in tenth grade)—he added LSD twice a week and regular drinking by tenth grade—dropped out of school that year.

By age sixteen he was living with his girlfriend, whose brother dealt coke. Rick was certainly drinking alcoholically by then, large amounts, drunk alone, according to her. At age seventeen, he injected MDA for the first time and had a psychotic break—psych ward—Haldol—the first of many rounds. He lasted ten days at an adolescent drug treatment center.

In the six years that followed, he chalked up five more stays in psych wards and three treatment centers. At age nineteen he stayed dry for one year and in that year had no psychotic break (on no meds), made up all high school credits, took his first semester at U.W. and made the dean's list. (!) Next semester he went back to using, went on an acid binge, and became psychotic again. He has had three different psychiatrists and every major label in DSM III—manic-depressive, schizophrenic, and schizo-affective. In June he voluntarily committed himself to three months at DePaul-Milwaukee Dual Diagnosis program, but left after five weeks because the staff psychiatrist refused to discontinue his Haldol. He is back in Madison, in his own apartment, continues sober and in A.A. at present. He has had many attempts at sobriety, A.A. attendance, a sponsor, N.A. meetings, but nearly constant relapsing. Some of his biggest acid binges have occurred while he was an outpatient on high doses of Prolixin.

I have obsessively hung on to remembering "what happened when" despite constant urging from my family and psychiatrists that "it would be better for me if I forgot." Your section on forgetfulness in an addictive system showed me that it would be better for *them* if I forgot. I would then stay fearful and confused, and dependent on psychiatrists to help me deal with my life—a pattern I spent many years in with no help.

My son's addictive behavior began many years before his psychotic break. And my codependent, controlling behavior began years before he was born. He was raised in a conscientious, hyper-responsible, upper-middle-class doctor's family, which was also coercive, controlling, dishonest, and full of "crazy-making" communications. His older and younger brothers are sane, workaholic high achievers. Our oldest son is in addition a smoker, a Phi Beta Kappa, an obsessive student, has had a hand-washing compulsion since age eleven, has been on lithium in the past for hypo-manic depressive states, has been through a phobia clinic, uses a depression light in Wisconsin winters, and from age eighteen to twenty-two injected cocaine every weekend. He successfully stopped using coke four years ago, but obviously is working full tilt at half a dozen other addictions.

No psychiatrist has ever taken a patient or family history for Rick, though I have tried many times to give one. In reading your book, I began to understand that in traditional psychiatric explanations and labels for behaviors, it is usually in the psychiatrist's best interests and the family's best interests and society's best interests to be sure *not* to find addictions and addictive systems fueling crazy behaviors. Psychiatrists know they can't control crazy alcoholic behavior. Calling a piece of crazy thinking schizophrenic gives the psychiatrist the illusion that he is looking at a disease he *can* control—despite the really abysmal track record. I believe the family often prefers to label a member schizophrenic rather than label the whole family coercive, dishonest, and unnurturing. And like the addictive family, our society is frankly relieved to find a fairly powerless and confused individual on whom it can focus a lot of judging, caretaking, and controlling.

These insights come from your book plus two years of hard Al-Anon work, but mostly they come from a newly found spiritual growth which is showing me that it is safe for me to admit my contribution to the addictive family Rick grew up in—a spiritual growth in which admitting my behavior is part of changing it. Statements about my past codependent behaviors no longer feel like an anchor keeping me stuck in guilt—they now feel like passing thru a door, a way of dropping those behaviors.

In your book you say, "See what you see and know what you know." This is something I know from the sixty or so people I have met in Al-Anon. I know of about fourteen families in which either the chemically addicted member is also labeled schizophrenic, or the family member labeled schizophrenic is a teenager of an undiagnosed, but very sick alcoholic parent or parents. Obviously, the diagnosis of schizophrenia benefits the psychiatrist; he solves a puzzle and gets a patient to control with meds. And the label benefits the alcoholic parent; his or her addiction can continue unconfronted. In fact, the hysteria surrounding a diagnosis of schizophrenia practically guarantees that something as ordinary as drinking and being emotionally unavailable or controlling will go unnoticed for years.

I recently came across a book by Thomas Szasz, a psychiatrist himself, who contends that while the behaviors associated with schizophrenia have been around a long time, before the term was coined in 1911 by two psychiatrists, those behaviors were attributed to a variety of diseases—syphilis and alcoholism foremost—that the term schizophrenia collected together, in part, some behaviors previously associated with alcoholism. It seems to me that this new term accomplished at least two things. It invented a disease which had to be treated only by a psychiatrist; any G.P. with a streak of masochism can decide to treat alcoholics. And it took the identification of "alcohol-induced" off those particular behaviors, thus enabling the alcoholism to avoid detection. It seems to me that the introduction of the term *schizophrenia* took society one step back from identifying alcoholism and one step deeper into addiction.

I would be very interested in communicating with you or anyone you know who is looking at possible connections between addictions and classic mental illness diagnoses, as well as possible misnaming of mental illness diagnoses in an addictive culture. Challenging current and traditional labels is not likely to come from professionals who have a strong economic and career advantage from these very labels. But the bottom line is always the same: Is the patient getting better? If not, why not?

Again, thank you for your book. It has given me the courage to trust my memories, my gut, and my instincts, in the face of nearly constant discounting from family and professionals. Your book has given me the ability to believe that there is more than one "true" way to look at the same reality, and that we may recognize the truth by its power to set us free.

Later, the writer of this letter (who wishes to remain anonymous) added this postscript:

P.S. Ten months after I wrote the above letter, I stopped drinking and started going to A.A. meetings. When I wrote the bit about "the hysteria surrounding a diagnosis of schizophrenia practically guarantees that something as ordinary as drinking and being emotionally unavailable . . . will go unnoticed," I had no idea how true it really was, or how close to home. I was still so focused on Rick's drinking and drug use that I literally did not see the wine glass in my own hand. Also, I was a controlled, maintenance alcoholic, and simply needed to learn more about the disease of addiction. I needed to reach the awareness that my controlling my drinking was not a solution; it was the proof that I had a problem. At present, I continue to live sober, one day at a time, and attend A.A. and Al-Anon regularly, and so does Rick.

The next letter is from a man who asked to be identified by his "recovery name," Chumly:

I just finished reading your book *Co-dependence: Misunderstood/Mistreated*. I was amazed and yet enlightened and angered. I am now ready for major changes in my life. After I relate my story to you, maybe I can help make changes happen in the codependency field.

To start with. I am being treated for alcohol and drug addiction. I go to A.A. meetings and few N.A. meetings. I tend to go to the A.A. meetings more because I am more comfortable there, plus the fact that it seems more and more people go to these meetings (A.A. meetings), announcing that they are cross addicted.

I also have been going to a drug and alcohol treatment center; Mr. C is my counselor—feel free to call for veri-fication—and has been helpful in helping me cope with my codependency problem. So much for background. This is where my codependency nightmare begins. On January 1, 1990, I attempted suicide. It stemmed from: a relationship in which I was, taking time off from work so I could take care of her children, get her to college, and be indispens-able. Also I was going thru a divorce and was angered because I am happy to end the marriage, but my wife was out with another man. I was not with a date on New Years Eve, my relationship was in deep trouble with this girl, and I was feeling angry and alone. Looking back, I had spent the New Years with my daughter, whose relationship with me was about nil for six months. Here I was, should have been content to be with my daughter, and I decided to kill myself. I felt I wasn't worth anything because I did not have a physical or real relationship with a woman. This is a mess in a nutshell. I got in touch with A.A. the next day. Went to a meeting and was told I relapsed. I got in contact with Mr. C. I just went thru a codependency, more or less introduc-tion course, class, and I and Mr. C. decided that perhaps [a CD rehab] would be of help. This was of course upon the approval of the insurance company. Still with me? This is where your book opened my eyes after I ended my nightmare.

The insurance company informs Mr. C. and I that I must go to M. Counseling Center for an evaluation. I see a Mr. D. for ten minutes, after waiting for almost an hour in the wait-ing room. He asks me how I feel. I tell him I'm agitated and depressed and told him about my January first incident. This is about ten days after the attempt. Mr. D. goes to the M. counseling psychiatrist, a foreign doctor I had a hard time understanding. This doctor says I have to go to the [mental health ward]. I was panicked. I did not think I was mentally ill. I made them call Mr. C., and Mr. C. explained that it was just an evaluation for my depression. Calmer, I apologized to the doctor and Mr. D. for my behavior and checked myself in for a three-day evaluation. I stressed I had a CD problem and wanted a CD rehab, preferably in [state of choice]. Twelve days later I am still in the [mental health ward], why? When I got there a Dr. W. heard my story for about five minutes and said, "I want you to take these drugs for depression." I refused. I told him I was only in for an evaluation. I had a drug problem. I had tried to kill myself with prescription drugs and I had a CD problem and wanted to go to the CD program in [state of choice]. The doctor said he could do nothing for me unless I decided to take the drugs. For the next three days he kept trying to push the drugs on me. The insurance company said that unless I took the drugs they could not do anything for me. I was threatened that I would be sent to a mental hospital in [place] if I did not take this medicine. The insurance company refused any type of rehab. Finally after Dr. C. sent an evaluator from M. Counseling, and an arbitrator came in to hear my case, I was assigned to go to [medical center]—feel free to call.

During all this I felt I lost trust in A.A., N.A., the mental health profession, and I told Dr. C. that if I got out, the way I felt I would be either drunk or dead before the week was out. I was promised, once again by my insurance company and the doctor, that I was going to a rehab with a codependency program. I was taken to the rehab by ambulance from the hospital. I arrived only to find that there was no CD program. The girl that admitted me said, "codependency program? I'm not sure. We must have it. *All rehabs have it, don't they?*" I thought I lost my mind. When they assigned me my therapist, I asked her point-blank for her qualifications. She said she had attended a few classes, but it was not her field. I decided to work on my drug and alcohol problem with her. I talked to [another counselor], my savior, she was qualified in CD and admitted that there was no CD program there but she would try to help me. She, a psychologist—I believe—also ran the floor I was on. She gave me books to read and we spent about a half hour a day if time allowed. I saw my D & A therapist twice, and we just never hit it off. I think it was due to my frustration and I intimidated her by asking for her qualifications. During my self-study course, a lot of things were happening to me inside. My CD relationship folded. The girl I did everything for informed me she could not see or talk to me because she was afraid people would get the wrong idea. I was confused about this. What it boiled down to, she had gotten herself a lover and new friend—I was out. This, piled on with inner feelings coming to the surface, I became depressed and was put on a suicide watch.

This happened after I was there for about ten days, at [place], I talked to a different doctor, and she, I forget her name, was real helpful. I was even considering taking these anti-depressant drugs. Thank God she did not give them to me or I would not be writing to you.

Well! I am under the impression that I will be here at [place] for twenty-eight days. My feelings are open. I learned there is no CD program, and not an adolescent program, adults and adolescents are mixed! The insurance companies (and because of the dishonesty of the mental health people in this area), instead of saying we cannot help these people, send them to a place where they can be helped, these good-intentioned people say, "We got them so let's keep them and give them a band aid." Sound familiar?

After fourteen days, the insurance company says, I'm cured, "Let him go!" [My counselor] explains I just got off of a suicide watch, I was not ready, and I needed two more weeks. She said she was informed if I needed the extra time it would be approved. The insurance company [name] mentions maybe I need a mental health hospital, *again!* The discharge process begins, I fight. I am afraid and confused. [My counselor] and the doctor that helped me get me an extra week. By this time all I can do is shut down. I start building walls to prepare myself for discharge.

I was supposed to go back to M. Counseling and see Dr. D. again. I refused. I believed he knew nothing of my problem, and my trust was shattered. I arrived home and did a great deal of hiding. My car was totaled while I was in the hospital and I got that taken care of. I wanted to quit work, I refused to go to A.A. meetings because the girl I lost was active in the program and we went to the same meetings. For one week I was petrified I would meet her and I would end up being controlled by her again. Meaning I would be back controlling etc. . . . If I had those anti-depressant drugs it would have been all over.

Finally I made an appointment with Mr. C. Mr. C. gave me a CD meeting to go to. I went. After that, I read Earnie Larsen's *Stage II Recovery* [my counselor] gave me, and I finally understood what he meant. CD was my missing piece in my addiction. Thank you Earnie and you too Anne.

I am still angered by what happened to me. I contacted a lawyer and I want people to be aware of insurance companies and how I was treated so it won't happen to anyone else. I talked to [an attorney]. My divorce is coming to a close and we will work on this next [CD]. What your book did for me was take the edge off my anger. I realized that it is just pure ignorance in the insurance and in the mental health field itself.

I hope I expressed myself clearly enough. If you have any questions please write or call. I went to [name] college and studied psychology and minored in education. I went four years and earned close to 120 credits. My drug addiction ended my schooling about five years ago. I am thinking about resuming, and if I can get myself in a better space, maybe I can help others like me. I guess being a CD type helping others would be a good field for me. I agree that the dangers, as outlined in your book are real. I want to enter this type of therapy for myself and others. Presently I am a factory worker. Nineteen years. I never thought I could be anything better than that. Now, maybe, a little hope. I was a union steward, but that is another CD story.

Thank you for spending the time reading this. If it wasn't for you and other caring persons in the CD field, like Mr. C. and [my counselor], I'm sure there would be a lot of lost and deceased people claimed by this addiction.

Enclosed is a report that you may or may not find interesting. It is my aftercare plan. Note I wrote, "I feel I'm not ready to leave this facility because I did not complete the program." With your book I feel I finally began a program.

Some are the concerns of therapists who themselves are in recovery:

I thank you for your seminal works on codependency. They are exciting, trail-blazing works. I believe your reconceptualization of the mental health/addictive processes field is crucial. I have been struggling with what I now call my primary codependency for many years, under other names in the mental health field, and made "progress" but missed the codependency completely until recently. I am convinced, from my own experience, that most of us in these fields are unrecovered codependents who have minimal knowledge of the addictive/codependency processes.

My own awareness that I was uncomfortable in "therapizing" others until I had a better handle on a route out has kept me in neuropsychology.

I deeply desire to work with a group of other professionals who also acknowledge their primary codependency
and wish to work toward recovery. I haven't found such a
group here. I was very interested in your mention of your
"trainees," and would like to meet you and learn more
about what this involves.

I am grateful for your works: what you are saying about
society, the women's movement, mental health, and individual growth/spirituality is, in my opinion, at the core of
many of the ills the human population of this planet must
confront if we are going to survive. This can be done only by
becoming more fully human (as opposed to dehumanized).

A.A.

I want to tell you about a process that came up for me two
days ago. I started out feeling my pain about my relationship illusions and had the knowing that the pain of my illusions is so much more painful than the reality that (in my
disease) I seek to avoid. Then, my process took me into
another level of knowing my anguish and rage about Therapy. I saw therapists ripping into people and tearing out
their hearts. I saw Therapists holding hearts in their hands;
squeezing, molding, puncturing, pawing. The people's
hearts remained attached to their bodies by only a few frag-
ile threads, and their spirits faded the longer they had contact with the Therapist. (I also know that the spirit of the
therapist also fades the longer he/she is in the profession—
as it is.) I experienced the words of therapy as slime that
covers the body, suffocating life. It all seems so big to me
Anne.

M.M.

And here are four who are truly beginning their recovery and
healing in a workable paradigm and have taken the time to share their
learning with me:

I have remembered, in reviewing my friendships of the
past, that my role in friendships has always been to be the
good listener, always available for a friend in need. I always
was available, it seemed, because I didn't run around in
cliques. I spend time alone. This happened when I was
twelve and my family moved from the town in which I was
born; it was hard to fit in and I was shy or quiet and didn't

seek friends, I took whoever showed interest in me. Most of the persons I would spend time with sought me out when they were in need and went off playing with others when they didn't feel like crying or being taken care of. I have had this same uncanny ability in choosing husbands. I know that I chose my husbands to keep my disease going and my stash filled. I always realized after the fact that I wasn't so-and-so's best friend, as I had always allowed myself to believe. I often felt as if I had been used and let down. To this day one of my big bogey men is that I will be forgotten. As I see the intricacies of it all, I am totally amazed. How I thought I had gotten over all of that. Well, I've changed and much is still the same. Today, I am looking around at how I keep my distance from intimate friendships. I have liked the control of being the listener, I discovered. I see the parallels of this stuff in my relationships with my clients. I no longer want to play that game. I don't want to play games at all.

So, my work, my business changes. I can no longer give people what they want in the old way of guessing at their expectation and thinking that their wanting something means that I must supply it. I question my motives these days. I know how slick my disease is. I was feeling aware of being full of exhaustion around work, lots of new client inquiries and no time for them. Feeling frustrated and not knowing why. One day I found myself looking at a list of my clients' names and realizing how few of them were actually in a recovery program. It seems that I was still in old client mold with many of them and feeling drained. I know that I cannot afford to be my clients' answer machine; that would assume that I have the answers for them and I know that I don't. So, what do I do? I realize that I don't want people to walk away from an experience with me feeling that I didn't have what they wanted. So many persons are not only willing to give me that kind of power, they are begging me to tell them what to do. I wish I never took them up on their offers and sometimes I do. Time for amends. Well, I have tried to come clean with some, and I wonder if they even know what I am talking about. I marvel at how people hear what they want to hear, it often does not even matter what I say. So, I glimpse the importance of being present, and I pray for that. I used to do groups to teach people about process and show them how it looks so they could imitate it I guess. What I often created was my clients feeling expectations from me, and I hate to know that that was the case. I have spent much time sharing what I know about my own recovery and what I have learned in working with you, and I feel good about that. Yet, that old good listener and direction giver has been there too. I no longer feel a *cause* to teach about process. And, I feel naked and vulnerable. I don't know what happens next.

Anonymous

Your books have helped me to make sense of things I have felt all my life, but never had validation for, although I have been in recovery as an Adult Child from an alcoholic family for about a year and a half. It has been during this time that I finally have begun to understand myself, and to fit many pieces into place of a very obscure puzzle, which was my family experience. Your books are helping me to understand the pieces that were still missing. I had long suspected as I have grown into health, that the problem was larger than just a syndrome involving a few specific persons within a family system, unconnected to the rest of the world. As a nurse, and especially working as a nurse in psychiatry, I feel the impact of those co-professionals who would benefit from recovery but who continue to deny their need for it. Daily, subtly, I hear the message still that I am not seeing what I am seeing or feeling what I am feeling. Fortunately, I think in some ways I learned to ignore that message long ago, and to refuse to completely buy into the addictive system. I am interested in process therapy, and learning as much as I can about it, because I know it works.

S.W.S., RN

Referring to my interest in what you call "the living process": Today I believe like you that there is a disease process that underlies both alcoholism and codependence; and I do it out of my different experiences. I am involved in the CD field both as an actively recovering codependent and a personnel counselor. I am a graduated social worker. Since five years I am also involved in developing and implementing an alcohol/drug program in a big organization.

When I read your book for the very first time in summer 1986 I was in Chicago, where I took part in a course of twelve weeks in Alcoholism/Substance Abuse Orientation at Parkside Medical Services Corporation. In connection with that stay I also got the opportunity to study Employee Assistance Programming for three weeks at the Summer School of Alcohol Studies, Rutgers University. The year before I visited the Hazelden Family Center, where I took part in the Family Program.

All this new knowledge has helped me to perceive the complex of addiction in a way that I had not imagined when I first entered into my own recovery in summer 1984 and with help of the Twelve-Step program. And nevertheless, I did not understand to the full what you meant by the underlying disease process until last summer after I had slipped back once more into the addictive process and at the cost of my health. Thanks to the program, Al-Anon friends, and your book I did ask for help, and this time I felt, deep in my guts, what addiction is about. This new knowledge urges me on. Therefore I will ask if you still train people in living process—and if so, on which conditions would it be possible for me as a foreigner to take part in your training program or other alternatives you may suggest.

A.B.

Due to an incredible stroke of luck, I bought your book *Co-dependence*, and realized after I read it, that your work *named* things for me which were previously a collection of sadnesses; vague depressions are ghosts, impossible to pin down. Then I bought your book *When Society Becomes an Addict* and so many new ways of seeing our world presented themselves. For me, your work reminds me of those children's puzzles that are quite ordinary at first glance and then reveal monkeys in trees or pussycats in the breakfast cereal and the picture never quite looks the same again. I am looking for your book *Women's Reality* with great enthusiasm; for some reason, this book is hard to find

I am an adult child of an alcoholic, a member of a family that was dysfunctional in many ways. (My brother was physically handicapped also.) The result of such chaos in my youth was a person whose need for control was overwhelming—and I never knew what was wrong, only that I was overcome with grief, always, for everything. I went to four or so psychologists without relief, thinking my problems began in a difficult marriage or that they were the result of my bearing a son who inherited my brother's fatal illness, but these things were mere window-trimmings, obscuring the real devil of addiction—addiction, just like your book says, to worry, to depression, addiction to control.

Lucky again, I found Al-Anon for Adult Children and I am working very hard on my recovery. I am a writer who was so beset by worry that I was unable to work on more than "fluff" pieces for the newspapers. Since joining Al-Anon seven months ago I have been able to feel better for the first time in my life and as a result, my work improved and I have a literary agent and a contract for my first book.

C.O., a NY writer

Some may think I have gone overboard in quoting others here. I don't think so. The wisdom of the work I am doing comes from listening—really listening—to others, hearing what they are saying and not saying and then putting this information together in a way that makes sense to me. This process, by definition, demands that I listen carefully to the feedback I get and rethink and relearn when necessary. The work in this book does not come from some disembodied laboratory experiment or some cerebral theorizing. All of the work I am doing comes from the grass roots, from the mouths and souls of those who are having the experiences. Of course, that includes my experience—reflecting upon, getting response to, and sitting with my experience. I am part of the experience of others, and they are part of mine. As I remove the layers of my addictions and my addictive process, I am increasingly aware of that connection.

Participating, Healing, Recovering, and Living in Process—It All Comes Together

I began to know inside me what it meant to live out of my own process (spirituality) and to put my sobriety (spirituality, process) first. Personally and professionally, I asked myself more and more often, Will this threaten my sobriety (spirituality, process)? If it does, I just cannot do it. As I began to live more and more out of my sobriety and really respect my process (spirituality), I was clearer and clearer about habits and behaviors that threw me back into the addictive disease or my addictive process. I began to see that putting my sobriety first meant that I had to be willing to let go of anything that threatened it. This sounds harsh, and in Twelve-Step circles, we often hear that we have to be willing to let go of anything—spouses, children, home, work, money, prestige—anything that threatens our sobriety. We have to be willing to go to any lengths.

Slowly, I gained a new knowing of what it meant to put my sobriety first. I had to "fly by the seat of my pants" a lot. I had to live a life of faith. I had to be willing to let go of anything that interfered with my living this way.

I discovered that the key was *willingness*. If I was *willing* to let something go, I probably wouldn't have to, because that willingness helped me move to a place where my sobriety wasn't threatened. Then I had to be very careful of my little addictive thinking process, which went something like this: "I have to be willing to let go of anything that threatens my sobriety. But if I'm *willing* to let go of something, it then isn't threatening my sobriety, so I can hold on to it." Logical—and diseased—thinking. I was becoming familiar with how cunning, baffling, powerful, and patient the disease is and how tricky. If I was truly willing to put my sobriety first, I had to be genuinely willing to let go of anything, and I couldn't fake it or bargain with it. I could see the similarity between this "turning it over" and letting go of attachments and the "unattachment" that we hear of in so many spiritual paths, especially in Eastern religions.

However, one of the major differences that I was seeing between putting my sobriety first and "unattachment" was that the former was a process and the latter was often done as a control mechanism.

As I was busily working on my recovery from my relationship addiction, I began to see the connection between my disease and the work I had chosen. I do not believe, as some writers are saying, that I simply chose my profession out of my disease. I believe it is more complex than that. As I said earlier about our philosophy in trying to start WIAP, we believed that the educational process for training psychotherapists not only did not provide adequate training for working with a range of people, it actually trained *out* of us many of those qualities that were healing and could facilitate recovery.

My relationship addiction (codependence) contributed to my wanting to take care of people, wanting to be "helpful," wanting to be indispensable, wanting to be liked, to my willingness to "take care of" my patients to my own detriment, to my subtle "caring" controlling, and to my willingness to use techniques, interpretations, and exercises to help people get where I thought they needed to go.

My training exacerbated all of the above and, springing from a scientific worldview, also added the "myth of objectivity," a legitimizing of and demand for control, and a set of ethics that were based upon the myth of objectivity and control. I saw that these ethics were geared to controlling the very problems the ethics had set in motion. As I realized that many, if not all, of the therapeutic practices I had been taught were developed to adjust the client to an addictive system, I also began to understand that my use of them was a threat to my own sobriety.

About this time in my own work, an estranged wife of a man who was doing my Training Program reported me to the ethics committee, accusing me of a sexual relationship with her husband. This was a horrible experience for me and, again, proved to be a very important piece of my learning (when the student is ready, the teacher appears).

I was approached as if I were guilty until proven innocent. Because I was innocent, I initially thought I could easily say just that and be exonerated—not so easy. I was sent a long list of questions to answer, most of which took the tone of "When did you stop beating your wife?"

I got scared. I asked a lawyer who had gone through the Training with me for help, and I decided to try to stand up for what I believed and for myself. My lawyer was horrified with the process. Not only was I guilty until proven innocent, not only was I set up to be dishonest to survive, but I was also told that because I had been accused, I was not allowed to drop my membership in the APA (a voluntary professional organization). My lawyer questioned the legality of this, but in a process that feels more like a witch hunt than a legal process, legality seemed irrelevant.

I spent one year of my life and ten thousand dollars defending myself against something I didn't do. Finally, my lawyer suggested that no one had asked the man if we had had a sexual relationship. When asked, he signed an affidavit that we had not. To the credit of the APA ethics committee, I have to say that they found me "not guilty."

However, this incident was not the end of the issue for me.

In the process of defending myself, I needed to study the ethics of the American Psychological Association word for word. I was *horrified* with what I found, This group's entire ethics were based upon the myth of objectivity,

Belief in the myth of objectivity and holding that as a value has set up a scientific worldview that tells us the only valid information comes from being "objective." This view so permeates our society that we have systematized cutting ourselves off from our feelings and our internal information systems. The most effective means of that cutting off are addictions. We have developed a societal system that only values information that is disembodied. We have developed a societal system in which addictions are not only supported by the society, they are required. If we were aware of our feelings and in touch with our internal information systems, we could not live the way we are living. Recovery from addictions makes us more aware of our feelings, knowing, and intuition. I saw that the ethics of the APA were based upon the necessity of treating the therapist and the client as machines to be manipulated, controlled, and "fixed." I started to see the relationship between the ethics we were taught as professionals and the sexual acting out of therapists.

The therapeutic relationship cannot be treated like a scientific experiment. Yet that is the way it has been set up. In that setup, ethics are based upon the illusion of control (self-control and external controls), threats, and the fear of punishment. I have seen that any system that is based upon the illusion of control is, by definition, an addictive system. No wonder the APA felt so comfortable to me when I was in my disease. It was familiar.

I started to see that the ethics do not actually help the psychotherapist with this intimate relationship, because there is no *real* philosophy of accepting and working through the feelings that come up *as* they come up. The therapy model is one that is based upon the belief that the person who is most helpful is the person who is the most expert and has it all together. In this model, not to have it together is a crime. (One should be able to manage through *control.*) It is a model based upon the illusion of perfection, which is, again, part of the addictive system. In a nonparticipatory, objective model, it is impossible to let feelings come up and work on them without being bad and incompetent.

I realized that in continuing to be a member of the APA, I had turned my life over to a group of men and women with whom I strongly disagreed, whose ethics I thought were unethical, and whose philosophy and theory I was slowly coming to believe were not only destructive for individuals, they were destructive to the planet. I saw that it was not without reason that psychology and the association were so well integrated in an addictive society and it was not without reason that I had quit going to conventions and participating some years ago. I dropped my membership.

There was another important learning that came to me out of this process. Several years before I was "investigated," I had realized that I had progressively little in common with APA and I probably should drop my membership—and I didn't. As I have done my recovery work and live my process more and more, I have discovered that my intuition is usually right and needs to be listened to. When I don't listen to my intuition, I usually get in trouble. This is true especially if I am aware of what I should do even though I don't know why. When I don't pay attention to my intuition the first time, I usually get another chance, and the tuition I have to pay for the learning is usually directly proportionate to my stubbornness, illusion of control, and denial. The tuition was high on this one, and the learnings were many and great.

Also, as I progressed in my own recovery, I came to know that when I slipped into dishonesty, control, manipulation, dualism, defensiveness, judgment, "objectivity," self-centeredness, perfectionism, or any number of other addictive behaviors, I not only was disrespectful to other people, I threatened my sobriety.

I began to see that "setting goals" was a form of control. I began to see that thinking I knew what a person needed or even where they were or what was going on with them was disrespectful and a form of control. I began to see that my subtle forms of "interpretation" were disrespectful and doing the client's work for him or her, which in itself is a form of disrespect. I was catching on to the myriad subtle little ways that I threw in "suggestions," "interpretations," "I remember whens," "I wonder ifs," and so on. More disrespect! I acknowledged how that behavior was trained into my very bones. It was now clear to me that not only did these behaviors threaten my own sobriety, they were grossly disrespectful of others and the participants in our Intensives and Training Programs.

Unfortunately, I was very good at these subtle "inputs." I happen to be very intuitive and very present. This gives me the ability to pick up on nuances, inferences, body language, and even intuitive thoughts and feelings. People paid me well to do that. These were the very skills that had made me a good psychotherapist. People wanted me to do their work for them, take care of them, and give them their fix. Every addict wants a quick fix, whether it is a drug fix or a psychological fix. I began to see that what I had learned in my training was usually to give clients a fix. Slowly, I began to become increasingly uncomfortable whenever I gave people their "fix." I saw the depth of the disrespect.

I began to see the innumerable theories and the "reasons" why things happen in psychology and the frequent and often exciting interpretations that we have developed as mental exercises. I began to see interpretation and intellectual insight as akin to trying to make a baby by masturbating. It could be fun, it could be exciting, it could even be true, but it just couldn't produce a baby (healing and recovery). In fact, these behaviors on the part of the therapist seemed to feed into the dependency and denial system of the addictive system; they were an insidious way of keeping people dependent and therefore a part of the addictive system.

I could see how far I had ranged from my original professional roots and how uncomfortable I had begun to feel with psychotherapists who came out of a scientific model that I now felt was obsolete. It was clear that although the insight, awareness, and positive experience that comes during psychotherapy offer some relief, at a metalevel psychotherapy and psychology only exacerbate the problems they are designed to solve.

I began to see that in the work I was doing I had my finger on the pulse of something really *big*. The people with whom I was participating in recovery and Living in Process were showing signs of health I had never seen before in all the experiences I'd had with all the experts. The people with whom I associated were beginning to claim and take responsibility for their lives in a way I found extraordinary, and many were beginning to go through and heal from intense, unconscious, buried experiences such as early incest and sexual religious cult experiences that truly amazed me. I felt I had a leash on an inter-city train and there was no stopping where this work was going.

In our deep process facilitation and in the structure and process of the Intensives, we became more and more aware of the subtleties of manipulation and control in the things we did and found ourselves dropping more and more behaviors that we now saw to be controlling, keeping people in their rational, logical (left) brain, and contributing to the addictive process. We could no longer participate in the subtle behaviors of "the addictive system."

During this period, I also became aware of a growing uneasiness with the techniques and exercises that I saw developing in the recovery field. When I first became involved in my own recovery and the field of recovery, I was impressed that most of the "counselors" in the field were themselves recovering people and their main "credentials" were that they owned the disease in themselves and they were recovering from it. This was a new model for the helping professions. This was a "participatory" model. I liked it. I was intrigued by it, and I sensed that there was something of great importance in this model. The people in the field were not trying to develop a new model. They were trying to recover and share their "experience, strength, and hope." They were not "objective." They were participatory. This made more sense to me than anything I had learned in graduate school, my internship, or my training. I sensed that this was revolutionary in the helping professions. I began to see a whole new movement developing that could influence the helping professions in a way that was needed. Then, I began to see the helping professions—especially medicine and psychology—not only try to get on the bandwagon—because there was suddenly big money and a lot of prestige in treating addictions (political figures, including president's wives, movie stars, and athletes were all coming out as addicts)—but I also saw them acting out of an addictive paradigm, trying to manipulate and control the field and keep this "out-of-control" movement under their jurisdiction through such maneuvers as credentialing, licensing facilities, and demanding further education of people who had been working in the field as "participatory experts" (a traditional tactic in the helping professions). I was seeing the disease trying to take control of the disease, and the very way it was doing it *was* the disease.

Treatment centers were medicating, "techniquing," and interpreting up the wazoo. They gave lip service to the Twelve-Step program of Alcoholics Anonymous, but fewer and fewer of their staff members were really working a Twelve-Step program and truly in recovery.

More and more psychotherapists in private practice were becoming instant "experts" on codependency and addiction. I saw a field that I had hoped and believed could offer a needed new paradigm and approach to healing (a participatory approach) being absorbed by the pseudopodic ego of the old paradigm.

The participatory "experts" (those who were themselves recovering) began externally referenting and looked to the established professions for legitimation. The established professions continued to operate out of a scientific paradigm of control, manipulation, solutions, fixes, and dishonesty (internal and external). They were not allowing themselves to be impacted by a paradigm that had the potential to more adequately support the healing they wanted to do than the one out of which they were operating. I continued to witness how seductive the old paradigm was in myself and in others.

I saw more and more clearly that when I was tempted, during someone's deep process, to touch them or hold them (which some of them would have liked and which would probably have stopped their deep process and brought it under "control"), it was an indication that something was being triggered in me. I was wanting to "get busy" in their process in order to avoid my own process or my own feelings. I saw that when I was tempted to make an interpretation, it sometimes was because I enjoyed the adulation and the dependence. Being an astute interpreter had made a place for me. I was indispensable. Being indispensable took care of my disease process. I also saw that when I kept my mouth shut, the other person came to her or his own insight, and often it had a "twist" on it that could only have come from inside that person. I saw how interpretations are often rational and logical to the interpreter but may have nothing to do with what is going on in the person who is being interpreted.

I also began to see that I was not winning any popularity contests by *not* interpreting, not doing exercises, and not giving fixes. At one point, when I was doing workshops in Europe, I slipped into the slough of despair. I since have called it my "imperfect vessel routine."

Many of the people who work with me in Europe have trained with and worked with some American psychotherapists. There was one, in particular, whose work just preceded mine in Europe. Almost everyone who was working with me at that time was or had been working with this therapist.

A part of me enviously looked upon the way this person was "worshiped," the eagerness for the techniques, the clonelike behavior, the way this person was treated like royalty and waited on hand and foot, and I was jealous. I was not willing to do what this therapist did or work in the same way, but sometimes I thought all that adulation would be nice.

As I struggled with my own feelings, I wept—not for myself, but for the work I was doing. I believe very strongly that this work is important and that it may well even be the next step in the evolution of working with people, and I felt (and still often feel) so inadequate to be the one to teach it. In my own deep process work that day, I found myself saying, "I'm not good enough. If this work needs to be done, why didn't 'they' choose someone who was smarter, nicer, more articulate, better educated, and who didn't come out of poverty. It would be better if the person who is teaching this new way were a man, an M.D., came from an influential family, traveled in the 'right' circles (whatever they are), came from the East Coast, and basically was someone other than who I am." I really got into "Oh, woe is me" (not for myself, but for this work). I could hear my relationship addiction calling to me like the Sirens: "It's okay to give people a fix; it's okay to let people be dependent upon you; it's okay to be dependent upon your clients and let them take care of you." I know that I could teach a bag of techniques with one hand tied behind my back; then those training with me would happily take them and impose the same techniques upon their clients and preserve their "immortality" and mine. Everyone would love it. I knew that I could teach these "techniques" and not have to be completely present and not have to do my own work along with everyone else. The German Trainees almost fainted the first time they saw me do my deep process work. They were accustomed to the "professor" being an *authority*. Some of the Trainees in Germany only wanted to learn about facilitating deep process work and to learn to Live in Process. They did not want to look at their addictions and their addictive process. They would have liked me more if I had only focused on the process work and left the addictive "stuff" alone. They didn't "love" me when I confronted their addictions.

I felt that I was letting this important work down. I was an "imperfect vessel." I just did not have the right "personality" or skill to be able to give this work the proper forum. I was depressed.

I went for a walk with one of my friends and tried to articulate my hopelessness. She said, "You're right. I don't know why people aren't falling all over you. All you are doing is offering them the opportunity to change their entire lives. You aren't offering a technique they can take home. You are not encouraging or even allowing them to be dependent upon you. You are offering them the opportunity to face their addictions and to live their own lives. I don't know why they aren't falling all over you. All you are saying is 'Change your whole life.'" I had to laugh.

Even though I envied some of the "easy times" that I observed gurus enjoying, I didn't want to be one. I had watched gurus and had concluded that "guru-itis" is a fatal disease. Even my "nemesis" in Germany was drained by the caretaking and being taken care of. I did not want any part of that. Even if it all looked great on the other side of the fence, I didn't want to crawl over that fence.

Though I still questioned the wisdom of the "powers that be" in choosing me to do this work (for, by now, I was truly Living my Process and turning my "life and will" over on a regular moment-to-moment basis), as I stayed with my despair I came to the place where I just could let myself settle in and do this work, following wherever my process would lead me with it. I did not need to promote or push it, and I also needed to be ready to walk through the doors that were open to me. I began to think of Living in Process as like the old biblical passage, "Behold I stand at the door and knock." I think our addictions occlude our awareness so much that we not only don't hear the knock, we don't even know there's a door there to walk through. The more I experienced recovery, the more I realized that not only did I not have to saw holes in steel-reinforced concrete walls, I could hear the gentle knocks and see the doors. I did not have to push this work, nor did I need to block it. I only had to do my work, trust my process, and trust *the* process. I could truly trust "attraction, not promotion" as I always had in my work.

I began to accept that I *was* the perfect person to do this teaching. I would not be the perfect person to do someone else's teaching. My being a hillbilly, being close to the earth, being a woman and recognizing and respecting the processes of the body, being involved in civil rights and feminism, my confronting my addictions and being in recovery—all were playing their part in who I was and how I saw things. This work was my work; it had evolved out of my process.

In *When Society Becomes an Addict*, I wrote that the universe is like a puzzle and each of us is a part of that puzzle. No one else has the same genes, the same chromosomes, or the same experiences. No one else can take our place in the puzzle. We live in a time when so many of us are cut off from ourselves by our addictions. When we are not in touch with ourselves, when we desperately try to live a life that either we or someone else has designed, then there is no way we can take our place in the puzzle. This means that there are a lot of holes in the universe, in the hologram that is the universe, in the holomovement. As each of us recovers from our addictions, does our deep process work, and learns again to live our process, the universe can become whole again. No one else can know what our process is. Only we can find that out.

For over twenty-five years, I have been participating in developing the Living Process work and combining this work with the Twelve-Step program and recovery. Thousands of people have attended my Living Process Intensives in the United States, Canada, Germany, Austria, Sweden, Australia, and New Zealand. For ten years, I have been conducting year-long Training groups in the United States and Europe and this year have been asked to start a year-long Training group in New Zealand.

Until now, I have not written about what I actually do. I am not really sure why. What I do know is that now I am ready to present these ideas and this work to those who are ready to hear about them.

For the last several years, most of my time has been spent with people who are seriously working on their recovery from addictions, who are trying to be honest, and who are attempting to do their deep process work and Live in Process. I have become progressively more aware that I feel uncomfortable with those who are not willing to do their own work. In fact, I find it foolish to trust people who aren't doing their work.

I have a network of people throughout the world who are doing this work, and these are my family and friends, my colleagues, and my support system. I also have found that I spend an increasing amount of time with native people throughout the world—American Indians, Hawaiians, Maoris, the Australian aboriginals. I have been drawn to the writings of black, Maori, American Indian, Hawaiian, and other ethnic authors, as well as women authors, to the point that I read little or nothing from "mainstream America." The writings of native people and women are so close to what I have been learning about Living in Process that they feel supportive and comfortable to me. I am tired of fighting and confronting the dominant system. I want to live in a way that is healing and healthy for myself and those around me.

Recently, I had an experience that was a strong motivator to get this book written and get on with this important work. I was invited to be a guest member at a gathering of "important" psychiatrists, scientists, and thinkers to discuss addictions. I was thrilled to have been invited and especially eager for dialogue with one of the scientists, whose work in physics, I believe, parallels mine in the helping professions.

As the meeting time approached, I became increasingly uneasy with the list of participants, their disciplines (heavy loading of psychiatrists from the East), the tone of the preconference mailings, and the fact that out of the twenty-some of us who were gathering to discuss addictions, there were only two of us (both women) who admitted to having any addictions and only three or four who had any real experience working with addictions. Even though my intuition said, "Don't go," I went anyway (ego? stubbornness? denial?). What an awful experience!

Here were a group of professionals who were not confronting their own addictive processes or doing their own deep process work.

I realized that I had not been in a situation like that for many, many years. It was a group of "good" people, wanting to do "good" things, operating out of a system I now recognized as violent and destructive. I felt as though I was tossed into a situation in which everyone was saying and doing the "right" things, and this denial was a thin covering over a subtle violence that absolutely terrified me. I had met people like this when I was in the civil rights movement and the women's movement, and I felt frightened of them. At least in those instances, I had the "rightness" of a movement to back me up. Now, I had nothing but the voice of a recovering addict and a challenge to the religion of their scientific worldview.

I saw, in living color, how truly violent interpretation and projection were. I saw how violent and judgmental professionalism is. I got a tiny glimpse of what it must be like to be an American Indian, an aboriginal from Australia, a Hawaiian, or a Maori and come up against this addictive, scientific worldview.

I am grateful for the experience, as it impressed upon me what so many people who go for help experience. I still feel the terror I felt there at times, and I'm glad I left.

A few weeks later, I was invited to be an honored guest at an American Indian Science and Engineering Society conference. The contrast between these two gatherings was powerful. There were over 2500 people at the AISES meeting and it was held in downtown Buffalo, New York, but it was so human and humane. There were no drugs or alcohol at that meeting. Everyone agreed that American Indian families and communities had been so devastated by drugs and alcohol that there was no need for it at the conference. Can you imagine a meeting of that size with no one in the bars?

At every meeting at that gathering, in one way or another, we were reminded or knowledge was shared with us that (1) everything that we do has to be respectful of and in the service of Grandmother Earth, (2) that the honor of one is the honor of all, and (3) that we are all brothers and sisters and one with all people, with all creatures, with the planet, and with all creation.

I felt I had been given a healing experience. The two experiences provided a glaring contrast of systems. The system at the "scientific" meeting exposed the naked violence of the addictive system in action. There was a belief that their consensual (almost) assumptions *were* reality, the only reality. By contrast, the Native American conference honored the uniqueness *and* connectedness of each of us and all of us.

I had come full circle from *Women's Reality,* and the stakes were very high. Will the helping professions continue to operate out of an addictive worldview that enables an addictive society and the possible destruction of the planet?

We have an opportunity to move into a philosophy and worldview that truly supports and facilitates healing. I think I have made some important steps in bringing that possibility into operation. I am now ready to present this approach for response.

The inner soul
Is buried by the outer shells
And further smothered by
Conformity to physical beauty
That the culture dictates.

Attempts to break through
These layers of shells
Is accompanied by ridicule,
Criticism and personal attacks.

Children are permitted, at times,
To express their inner souls
But soon the family and
Education train them
to conform, to regurgitate
The party theme.

The measure of maturity is
Determined by this conformity
So the so-called productive years
Reflect what others have dictated.

The successes achieved are tangible items
Like dollars, besting your rival and
Climbing the ruthless ladder.

The soul becomes atrophied
At times of crises and illness
Crying out for some recognition
For some connection with
Other fellow inhabitants.

At times this is accomplished
But for a fleeting moment
For when the crisis or illness is over
Once again, the soul retreats to its niche
Hibernating until the next crisis occurs.

So the culture prevails
Dictating to us, who accept
With various degrees of resistance
What is expected of us.

GOLDIE D. IVENER

Part II

Introduction to Living Process and Deep Process Work

In Part I, I attempted to share my own development in the work I do, share why I can no longer identify myself with the field of psychotherapy, why I call myself a recovering psychotherapist, and why I have developed a way of working that is an alternative to what now exists or, as I see it, that is beyond psychotherapy.

In Part II, I want to share how I work and what I have learned from working the way I do. Although I will approach this section from a perspective of what I *do* and how I actually participate in the Intensives and Trainings that I do, it will be important to remember that there are three intertwining concepts and processes to keep in mind. These processes are: (1) Living in Process (or the Living Process System), (2) confronting and healing the addictive process, and (3) deep process work and facilitation.

The Living Process System

I see the Living Process System as a paradigm or worldview in and of itself. I do not believe it is a new system. It is a system that we have always known and have tried to submerge and give up so that we could make ourselves fit into the addictive system, which is based upon a very simplistic, mechanistic, reductionist science. Rediscovering this system is not something we have to try to do. It naturally emerges when we confront and recover from our addictions and addictive process and do our deep process work.

I will not explore the Living Process System thoroughly in this book because it is a much broader topic. The scope of this book focuses more narrowly on the helping professions and, specifically, on moving beyond psychotherapy. I am planning another major work, *Living in Process*, that will include a range of issues, such as parenting, spirituality, and living and health, examined from a Living in Process perspective. I do hope, for now, that the reader can see that deep process work and recovery from addictions are more than techniques and need to be seen from the perspective of a much larger system or paradigmatic worldview.

Confronting and Healing the Addictive Process

I have come to believe that we live in an addictive society and that everyone in this culture who comes out of this particular current pervasive worldview has been taught the addictive process. The addictive process is learned, and it can therefore be unlearned. It is much bigger than the chemical addictions. Genetic and physiological factors may account for the *choice* of addiction but not the underlying addictive process (which is learned in the society). The addictive process is a disease of the body, mind, and spirit. This is not to imply that because we call it a disease medicine and/or psychiatry are the best modalities for treatment. In fact, it is my experience that both medicine and psychiatry have been woefully inadequate in working with addictions, so inadequate as to be almost useless.

Medicine can help relieve some of the physical effects of the addictive process, and I question strongly the role of medicine in enabling the addictive process. For example, medicine often heroically rushes in to try to save people from the consequences of their indulging in their addiction (smoking, drinking, overworking, or overeating) while steadfastly refusing to confront the addictive process as the root cause of the disease. When we see these behaviors in the family, we call them enabling and destructive to the possible recovery of the addict. Yet, one way to look at much of medicine (as it is now practiced) is as the systematized enabling of addictions, as what allows and supports addicts to continue to use until their deterioration is so far progressed that there is no hope of physical recovery. In not being informed about the addictive process and in not confronting it as a primary cause of illness and dysfunction, medicine and the other helping professions have become the systemic enablers to an addictive society—they have taken the edge off just enough so that the society can indulge in and play with its addictive process. The field of psychotherapy has been especially guilty in this respect.

A disease has an onset and a progression, and unless there is some sort of intervention or change, it will result in death. To say something is a disease does not necessarily imply that the medical model as we know it is the best or appropriate response to it. When we have a disease of the body, mind, and spirit such as we have in addictions, new methods and new approaches are called for that are far beyond anything we have thus far developed in psychology and medicine.

When a disease process is learned and integrated into the society, it is very difficult to separate out that disease process from the reality of the society, because they appear to be one and the same. This is one of the major tasks of early recovery. We often hear people say, "I have a disease. I am not my disease." People need to learn to separate themselves from this disease process while admitting to having it.

One of the reasons recovery is so difficult is that addiction is part of the society in which we live. This society *demands* addiction to fit into it, and everything around us invites us back into the addictive process when we are trying to recover from it.

My experience is that the best tools we have for dealing with addiction are the Twelve-Step program of Alcoholics Anonymous and the variations of that program that have been developed out of need.

I do not think the Twelve-Step program is perfect. There are problems with language, concepts of God, sexism, and any number of issues, but when one can transcend the problems and actually focus on the program, the Twelve-Step program works with the addictive process. I discovered in my recovery that part of my fighting and picking at the specifics of the program was, indeed, practicing my disease. As long as I could focus on "objectively" (really emotionally) identifying what was wrong with *it*, I could use that process to avoid looking at myself. This is a technique I learned well in my graduate training that I now identify as part of the addictive process. I have learned to take what's there for me and leave the rest.

One of the major limitations that I have found with the Twelve-Step program is that it is really not designed to deal with feelings and deep processes as they come up. Of course, I have found that most therapies and medical psychiatric approaches are not able to deal with feelings and deep processes as they come up, either.

As we begin to let go of our addictions, one of the most obvious things that begins to happen is that we start to have *feelings*— all kinds of feelings—and old, submerged, hidden deep processes begin to come up. In fact, one of the major functions of addictions is to keep us out of touch with our feelings, our awareness, and our deep processes.

Deep Process

As I said earlier, it is obvious that because we were not raised in a process environment and because we were not process-parented, all of us have unfinished deep processes rumbling around inside of us. Also, I believe that things happen to us as infants and children that are unfinished because we just do not have the strength, maturity, awareness, or integration to deal with these unresolved processes. Yet, we have inside us a built-in process to help us work through and resolve these old issues. As long as they are rumbling around inside us, we have to expend energy to keep them at bay. One of the ways our inner being (process) "loves" us is that it keeps these old processes alive and waiting inside us until we are ready and in a safe place (internally and externally) to work them through. Our inner process will, however, push us to work them through. Frequently, I believe, not only psychological but physical and spiritual diseases are caused by holding down and avoiding these festering processes. We have seen phenomenal "cures" as people have done their deep process work.

One of the major functions of addiction is to keep these deep processes at bay so we don't have the opportunity to heal. To me, one of the most miraculous aspects of the human organism is that when we stop trying to control, we have this marvelous internal mechanism on alert just waiting for healing.

Deep process is not catharsis; it is not relief; it is not just getting feelings out. It is much more than any of these and includes all of them. Many technique-oriented therapies have focused upon catharsis or getting feelings out, and this has given some relief, *and*, ultimately, these processes did not get finished.

Throughout this section, I will elaborate more fully on deep processes and deep process work. Suffice it to say now that as far as I have been able to investigate, the work I am describing here is unlike any other that is currently being done.

In order to give a perspective for this section, I want to share a diagram that has been helpful in representing the process of recovery and paradigm shift.

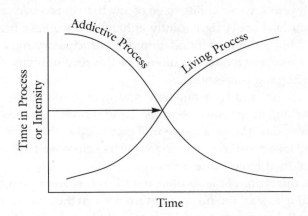

Before we begin our recovery, most of our time and energy are spent in our addiction. In fact, we often have become so detached from and nonparticipatory in our lives that we have no memory or recognition that we have (or are) a Living Process. This is true of many people in our society. It is no wonder that we can participate in some of the behaviors that we do, because we have used our addictions to completely cut ourselves off from our inner guidance and the awareness that we are one with all things. As we do our recovery and begin to live more in process, this awareness returns.

This residing in the addictive process is one of the reasons anyone working with people on any level should have a thorough knowledge of addiction and experience with recovery. For me, this means that anyone setting themselves up to facilitate anyone else must themselves be actively in a recovery program and have a good strong recovery. I have come to recognize that this is especially important for those of us in the helping professions, because our very training has been training into codependency and relationship addiction, not only with respect to our own clients but also in relation to the entire society. Again, it is my experience that the best tool we have for recovery is the Twelve-Step program of Alcoholics Anonymous and its satellite programs, (and why wouldn't one want to have the very best?).

When people sincerely want to heal and grow into who they are, this, by necessity, means being ready to confront their addictions and their learned addictive process. Otherwise, their work just becomes the temporary "fix" that subtly supports their disease and keeps them adjusted to an addictive society.

Needless to say, our ability to be of any help in recovery and have any wisdom to share is significantly enhanced if we have been there ourselves. This is the very foundation of a participatory model of science, and a recovery model has offered us this revolutionary opportunity in the helping professions.

So, early on, much of our time and energy has to be spent in actively working on our own recovery. Early recovery for most people is two to five years. (Most of us are well grounded in this addictive system.) It will take most of us two to five years before we have an actual *experience* of the Living Process System.

To me, this is one of the absolute miracles of recovery. So many people are willing to start on the path toward it when they have absolutely no experiential memory of what it is like. (I like to believe that somewhere down deep in the brain we remember what it is like to live our life in process, completely in tune with the process of the universe [God?]).

The first time a Living Process breaks through our addictive process, it scares us to death. We have a sudden moment of clarity, serenity, oneness with the universe—and it terrifies us. We stop (maybe), and we say, "What was that?" It goes through our consciousness like a meteorite and we say, "My heavens. What was that?" As we continue our recovery, these seconds become minutes, hours, days, even months and years—all, probably, with occasional forays back into the addictive process. That is why the diagram shows the addictive process curve approaching but not crossing the axis. My experience is that it never completely goes away; it's always there waiting—cunning, baffling, powerful, and patient.

Our recovery work makes our Living Process and our deep process work more available to us. Our deep processes present themselves more and more for us to work on. As we do our recovery, and do our deep process work, we begin to make a shift into a Living Process System. This shift is not something we plan and try to bring about—in fact, if we do that we stay firmly stuck in the control mechanisms of the addictive system. This systems shift or paradigm shift is not something we maneuver or control. It is a by-product of our doing our work.

By necessity, these two processes, confronting and recovering from the addictive process and learning to Live in Process, must both happen and must happen simultaneously.

132

As Diane Fassel has said in her speeches about organizational transformation, "There is no transformation [Living Process] without recovery." So many disciplines and techniques (psychology, religion, medicine, New Age spiritualities, organizational consultation, even Eastern paths) have wanted to bring about transformation without facing addiction—their own and the addiction embedded in the society. This is why so many have failed or only offered what has turned out to be partial "fixes" that ultimately perpetuate the addictive process.

Conversely, there can be no recovery unless one is willing to make a complete paradigm or system shift (no recovery without transformation). This has always been what spirituality has asked of us, but as spirituality has become systematized into religion in an addictive system, nothing short of the willingness to shift completely and go where our process takes us (that is, to live a life of faith) really works. Luckily, our process will not push us or force us to be someplace we are not really ready to be, although it does not always feel this way. I have found this consideration on the part of our inner process (God?) always to be there.

I have come to think of my inner process as God or what I used to call God, with whom I am one. God is more than my inner process. I have come to understand God as my process and the process of the universe, and when I am truly living out of my inner process, I am one with God.

When I am still enmeshed in and operating out of my addictive process, I cannot live my process. Wanting a quick fix or a quick transformation without facing my addictive process will not work. Wanting to recover without being willing to change my life will not work. There is no recovery without transformation, and there is no transformation without recovery. The two processes, by necessity, go together and paradoxically are the same.

At our Intensives and Trainings we pay attention to both these processes simultaneously as they present themselves. We do not try to elicit or control them. We deal with what comes up. Given this background information, I will go on to describe how we function at Intensives and Trainings and how we are present to deep process work.

Doing Living Process Work

The bulk of the work that I do is in four-day or nine-day Intensive workshops and in the year-long Training groups. I occasionally give speeches or one-day workshops about this work; they are, of necessity, input sessions about the work. They are not Living in Process. Because I grew up professionally in the heyday of the human potential movement, I was accustomed to believing that short, structured experiences or experiential learning and/or demonstrations were superior to lecture and input sessions. I have come full circle on that belief. I have come to feel that this deep process work is not appropriate to do in demonstrations or in one-day workshops. It is so powerful and so deep that it almost always triggers work in other people.

Also, because the very nature of a Living Process philosophy is that this work cannot and should not be controlled, elicited, or manipulated, it would be antithetical to the work itself to set up a situation in which either I elicited, or someone was expected to go into, a deep process.

To really learn about and experience deep process work, one has to be at an Intensive. And being there, I believe, indicates at least some willingness to try Living in Process and with that to be confrontive of one's addictive process and be open to doing the deep process work as it comes up. I believe the experience of an Intensive starts long before coming and lingers long after leaving, so I want to say something about the process of getting to an Intensive.

People learn about the Intensives by asking to be on our mailing list. I have never advertised, and I have never solicited business. Long before I knew of the phrase from A.A., I believed in attraction and not promotion. I only go where I am asked, and I don't hustle.

People who have asked to be on our mailing list receive a brochure every year with my international schedule on it. This brochure has an application form in it. Also, people can request information directly from my office. If the Intensive is full, we start a waiting list.

Approximately one month before the Intensive, participants receive a letter that addresses travel, climate, what to bring, how to get there, and so on, along with a list of other participants, Trainees, and staff for information and ride-sharing purposes.

In the past, these letters generated a great deal of pre-Intensive process and probably still do. For example, I used to do Women's Wilderness Intensives in the Boundary Waters in Minnesota, and when the letter arrived stating that people were to come with tents, sleeping bags, flashlights, and their own roll of toilet paper because there were no indoor toilet or bathing facilities, some people's "Intensive process" started right then. (I later learned that some of my detractors were spreading the rumor that I was running nude groups because women were bathing in the lake—one does these things in the wilderness, and also in Europe—and lying out on the rocks. At home or away, I am personally more comfortable bathing in the nude. These experiences triggered a lot of work about bodies, sexuality, and so on, which was very important for those doing their work.) We do not try to elicit specific responses, and the setting in which Intensives are held always is part of the process. The issue is not to find the "perfect" setting to elicit what "needs" to be elicited. The issue of Living in Process is to deal with whatever comes up in relation to the setting, the group, or whatever, because it is part of the process.

In my National Training Laboratory encounter group, group process, and training in individual therapy, we believed that we could manipulate and control the group into feeling what we wanted them to feel and what we thought they should feel. How arrogant.

What I do know is that I like to be in nature and I like to work and spend my time in beautiful and, to me, healing natural settings. I find it easier to be in touch with my process in nature, and I stay healthier when my workplace is in nature. This is not true of everyone (some people are, at least initially, terrified of nature), and it is for me, so that's where I work. More and more, this work will be centered in a magnificent 110-year-old hot springs hotel in Boulder, Montana. The waters and the setting are very healing, and it is located in a beautiful valley that is guarded and sheltered on both sides by mountains. The American Indians used to call the place Peace Valley because tribes gathered there to be healed and would not participate in any traditional hostilities in this valley.

Arriving at an Intensive is very casual. There is usually a sign-up sheet, and people are asked to find a room and get comfortable. We usually have our first meeting around 7:30 P.M. on the first day. Clearly, the Intensive has begun before the first meeting.

Staff, Trainees, and Participants

I usually try to limit the number of participants at an Intensive to twenty-five people. This group can include former Trainees and people who have previously been to Intensives. It always has what we euphemistically, with tongue-in-cheek, call "process virgins." In addition to myself, we will have from ten to twenty Trainees who are at different stages in their recovery and usually a person who has trained with me and has been working on his or her recovery and Living in

Process for some time and who often runs Intensives and groups. We always have a high ratio of those who are part of the Training group to participants. This is important for many reasons. When people do deep process work, it is very good to have a facilitator to sit with them. Also, since everyone participating does his or her own work and deep processes when we are there, it is good to have plenty of facilitators, although anyone can facilitate.

Over time, I have also realized that one of the reasons that this process works so well at the Intensives and at the Training is because we have a range of people at different levels and different stages of their recovery and their ability to Live in Process. I think it would be much more difficult (in fact I *know* it from experience) for people to try to feel secure with deep process work if they weren't seeing it all around them. Sometimes, some of the Trainees are doing their deep processes before the Intensives even start, as they come ready to "pop." We have lost a few people who found themselves surrounded by deep process work before they began to feel and understand what it was all about, and also before they had the experience that people actually live through their deep process work and even seem to come out the better for it.

I must admit that when we have a Trainee processing through gory cult experiences at the first session, I have had a feeling of "Oh my God, what will the newcomers *think?*" but that is only my impression management cropping up. I deal with the feelings, turn them over, and let go—trusting the process. I want to say right away that whatever feelings, awareness of addictive functioning, or learning that I, or any other of the facilitators, have are shared with the group at check-in.

We practice what we preach to the best of our ability, assuming and assuring that we are all on this road together. Over the years, I have noticed a change in me and what I share. Before I really started my recovery as a psychotherapist in earnest, I would always share an "awareness" that I thought others needed to hear, one that was brilliant, or one that made me look good. I have become somewhat less arrogant and controlling (progress, not perfection), and I now am more likely to share what I am currently aware of or working on to the best of my ability. It's an occupational hazard to try to be "wise." The more I do this work, the more I learn that what I really have to offer are my struggles with my addictive process, my deep process work, and my Living in Process. Letting go of the illusion of a power imbalance between a "leader" and "others" is something I have been practicing for many years and is absolutely essential in a participatory system. This is really what civil rights, feminism, and the new paradigm mean to me. Oppression occurs whenever we set up a power imbalance. Full disclosure and participation on the part of the facilitators dissolves the illusion of a power imbalance.

We frequently have present another person I want to mention. At most Intensives and Trainings, we have a massage person who has been through at least one Training Year and who offers massages at a reasonable fee. I know that these massage people are all good because I ask them to give me a massage before I agree for them to work on others. If they give *me* a good one, I assume they are good with others (and there has to be some advantage to being the person who schedules these events). I enjoy getting a massage during an Intensive, and like everything else at an Intensive, it's a choice.

The First Session

At the first session, I welcome people (I am almost always really glad to start an Intensive. I like to meet the new people, and I look forward to an atmosphere where we can do our work. If I am tired, don't feel good, resent having to start when we are starting, I always say so and share where I am and what's going on with me.) We usually handle a few logistics: make sure everyone has a room, ask if there are special needs, review necessary rules for the site, and then have the massage person say a few words and send around a list for people to sign up for massages. She describes the type of massage she does and usually asks people to indicate any special problems and/or needs: if they have a feel for when they might want a massage (beginning, middle, or late in the week), if they like massage early in the morning or late in the evening, if they prefer being worked on during breaks or during group. She invites people to keep checking in with her if their needs change as the Intensive progresses. In general, she is inviting people to get in touch with their own process, see what they need, and ask for it, all key elements of living our process. Anyone else in the group can throw in anything they want at that time. This may include such things as organizing groups to cook or eat together, special excursions for the times off, room changes, and so forth. The Trainees, those who have been to Intensives, and the other facilitators are usually quite assertive in sharing their needs and information. Again, there is the possibility of modeling.

Following that, I usually do a general sketch-out of the schedule. I have to laugh now as I think of how rigid and controlling I was when I first started doing Intensives. Of course, then it was what we all had been trained to do, and we thought it was "professional" and provided "structure." It also was very draining and contributed to burnout in group leaders. I shudder to remember how exhausting all that illusion of control was.

I tell the group that our daily schedule is flexible and usually runs something like this: We usually have a time for Twelve-Step group meetings at 9:00 in the morning. It is up to those who want and need the groups to set up the kind of meetings they want. There are usually announcements for A.A., Al-Anon, and Overeaters Anonymous, and lately we have more people wanting Sex and Love Addicts Anonymous, Relationship Addicts Anonymous, Self-Abusers Anonymous, Workaholics Anonymous, Debtor's Anonymous, and Survivors of Incest Anonymous. The Twelve-Step groups that are popular differ from Intensive to Intensive, depending upon the wants and needs of the group. The Twelve-Step groups at Intensives are usually open groups, and I invite persons who are not familiar with or have limited experience with a variety of programs to try out the meetings. I stress that the meetings are available, and each person has the choice of what they do.

The whole group meets around 10:00 when the Twelve-Step meetings are finished and usually meets until around 12:30 or 1:00 P.M. Then we take a break of two and a half to three hours for lunch. We come back around 3:30 or 4:00 and meet until 6:00 or 7:00 P.M., when we usually break for the evening. Depending on the needs of the group, we may have a shorter session in the afternoon and then a short evening session.

I usually stress that this is not a marathon, and I do not believe that there is a direct correlation between their learning and the number of hours spent in the group. As a matter of fact, some of their most important learning may be outside the group. In learning about Living in Process, *everything* is an opportunity to learn about ourselves and to learn to trust our process. For example, learning how to deal with a snoring roommate or a messy kitchen or with feelings that come up while we are waiting for the bathroom may all be important.

I emphasize that one of the most important skills of learning to Live in Process is *noticing*—noticing when you are tired, noticing when you are hungry, noticing when you need to go to the bathroom, noticing when you need time alone, noticing how you get your addictive fixes. I encourage people to notice during the Intensive.

The last thing that I mention is that during the long Intensives, we usually take one or two evenings off and one full afternoon and evening, or sometimes a full day. I suggest a day, and we usually check to see if that seems okay, with the possibility of renegotiating it if necessary as the Intensive gains momentum.

There is something that I must add here to give a flavor of this beginning time. This process is never cut-and-dried and matter-of-fact. I tend to have a lot of energy and to be quite funny. Also, I came from a family where teasing is very loving and is a form of loving, so I tease people. Some have difficulty with this teasing, but I know it is loving and it's who I am. Anyway, we all laugh a lot, especially at our own disease and what A.A. calls character defects. There is an atmosphere of being open to laugh at ourselves and each other. There is a lot of spontaneous humor and laughter at Intensives. This is one of the things I really love about the Intensives and Training sessions. We experience laughing at ourselves and with each other. After all, getting serious about our problems is a sure sign of problems.

Following this short introduction and dealing with logistics, we "check in." I ask everyone to share their names, where they are from, why they came, their hopes and expectations for the Intensive, and anything else that they feel is important to share at this time. Some share a lot, some share very little, and some may opt not to share at all at that point. It's up to the individual. Some of the group may ask for clarification or more information, and no one has to answer or give more. Everyone is encouraged to stay in touch with themselves and see what they have to learn from their feelings and reactions. These Intensives are the most honest and least controlling or judgmental groups I have ever experienced. I believe this is not because we set an agenda to be honest, nonjudgmental, or noncontrolling. I believe this atmosphere emerges because we are all doing our own work as sincerely and fully as we can. When we do check-ins, everyone has (and usually utilizes) the opportunity to check in. This means that participants, Trainees, facilitators, and I all check in about who we are, where we are in our lives, any recent deep processes we have had, our struggles with our addictive process and our recovery, and how we are feeling about being there. This is not done as a technique. Each of us does this because we value our process. If I am tired, I say so. If I resent being there, I say so. If something is going on in my life, I say so. If I have had a foray into or a new insight about my addictive process, I say so. This level of sharing is usually true for everyone there, to the best of our ability.

We usually only just touch the tip of the iceberg of checking in on the first evening. We only meet until we start getting tired as a group. The first session runs for about two to two and a half hours, and, depending on the group, it may be longer or shorter. Before we close, I again encourage people to get in touch with themselves and their needs. Many arrive completely exhausted, having attempted to arrange and organize their entire lives before coming to the Intensive.

If I have not done so before, I usually say something about the setting. Often we meet in places that have a much higher altitude than most are accustomed to, so I often give some information about altitude sickness—what it feels like, what to notice—and I suggest things like getting more rest, easing into exercise, and drinking extra liquids. Sometimes I need to mention local animal issues like how to deal with moose, rattlesnakes, mosquitoes, and so forth. We close by seeing which Twelve-Step groups are meeting where in the morning, and I am off to bed. I usually see that I take very good care of myself during Intensives. This means that I try to get plenty of alone time, rest, and exercise. This supports my being very present to the group and to myself.

The room we meet in is usually big and is usually a mess. We have mattresses and pillows all over the place. I prefer to sit in a sand chair, myself, and others bring various kinds of beach chairs and camping or canoe chairs. The important issue is that we have space for the group and mattresses and places for people to do their deep process work while the group continues. This sometimes takes on the atmosphere of a six-ring circus, *and* it all seems to work out. I have long since learned that there is no perfect way to set up or do a group. It's like life. One just has to be open to whatever comes up and deal with it. I have discovered that this approach is often frightening to some people initially, especially people who do not know how to do this kind of work. It does, however, offer all of us the opportunity to deal with our illusion of control and certainly mobilizes control issues. Again, this mobilization is not "designed" in, it is a result of what happens.

I mention this specifically because I believe it is a very good example of the paradigm out of which I am working as an alternative to the traditional mechanistic, scientific paradigm on which "therapy" is usually modeled. Therapy is modeled after a scientific experiment that removes one from life as much as possible so as to control as many "variables" as possible and provide as pure a situation as possible. Working out of a Living in Process paradigm means that we are dealing with life. We are dealing with the process of life as it occurs right then, right now. As with life, we need to be open to whatever emerges, notice it, and deal with whatever that means for us. Safety comes from responding and "dealing with." Safety is not based upon the illusion of control.

Making Input

After all of us have done our initial check-in, I make some input into the group. Although it was not consciously designed, I now realize that it is very important that the first real information the group gets, other than logistics, comes from the group itself (the check-in). By this action, and not just by words, we all have said that our learning comes from ourselves and from one another. Initially, I started out with short check-ins so I could know who was there and because I believed checking in would help people get there, and, most of all, because I really like check-ins and am truly interested in what is said. I learn so much.

Many people, however, come with the belief that I am some kind of guru and that I will be orchestrating "fixes" for them. This is their expectation based on their previous experience. I am not the center of the Intensives. The group is not the center of learning. Everything and everyone is important. Our ability to model that belief has evolved.

I usually start the "input" session with the information that I give at the beginning of this section, focusing upon (1) the Living Process System, (2) confronting our addictive process, and (3) deep process work. It is important for the reader to remember that by the time I make this input at an Intensive, the people who are new have already experienced all three in the day or days that we have been doing the initial check-in. We often say "the Intensives are a safe place for *you*, and they are *not* a safe place for your disease."

Much is shared during check-ins that sets the tone for Intensive. For example, one Trainee has written this about his check-in at his Regional group:

> I got confronted by [two former Trainees] (and then by just about everyone else) at our last Regional. [The two

former Trainees] have been participating with us, and I'm grateful to have the additional people around, since our "core" is only about four people (five when John's around). I got into my disease during my check-in. I thought I was sharing feelings, but it was the same old circular thinking and self-abusive fears that drove me into Training in the first place. It was no fun being confronted like that, and I am confused now because some of the assumptions I've made about myself are being challenged. I was also encouraged to check out S.A. [Sex Addicts Anonymous], and called my A.A. sponsor right after the Regional. He had told me that he knew some people in S.A.—turns out he's in it himself! How's that for getting what you need? I told him I wanted an interview, and haven't called him since—that was almost three weeks ago. I am waffling on giving up masturbation— and so I guess I'll say here and now that I will call my sponsor before I go home for Christmas and set up an interview. There, now I'm committed. I have been doing some first-step work on my sex addiction; i.e., I am noticing how my energy changes when it switches on. I notice how I sexualize so many situations. I bought a magazine for Adult Children because there was an S.A. article in it, with a twenty-one-question self-test. I got "yes" on probably fifteen of them. Groan. Well, I've not felt "at home" in A.A., so maybe this is a door I need to open.

M.J.

We are very aware of the temptation to interpret during check-ins. Often, we own up to having made an interpretation or to being tempted to make one, or we may ask someone to check out if they are making one. I have come to believe that there is just no role for interpretations in this work. Most interpretations are either projections or so theory-bound as to be completely useless. At most times, I find that interpretations are really arrogant and disrespectful. They almost always throw people into defensiveness and resistance. No theory can possibly cover the intricacies of the individual. Most theories, if not all, are built upon elaborate thinking patterns that I have come to call Thinking Addiction, and they actively keep us stuck in the addictive system. A former Trainee says it much better than I could:

> We all have a wall, and mine is not where yours is. His is not where hers is. No one can say who is not doing enough,

or what is right for another. I do not know anything about anyone else. I know exactly nothing of who another being is or what they need. Any interpretation to that effect would be past presumption, beyond arrogance. It would be assuming the responsibility of a god. Yet how quick I am to judge, even knowing my severely limited perspective into the soul of another. The challenge and the battle is purely personal, entirely internal in each and every spirit. The external results are obvious in behavior, attitude, and actions. The awareness of this concept is an invitation to personal responsibility. Ours to accept or deny. And then it begins.

J.

Throughout the check-in, people who are new to Intensives can observe the facilitators and me participate in our struggle with our disease. They can observe and participate as we do our deep process work (noticing what our work brings up for them, helping to make sure there are enough pillows, etc.). So by the time I make input, I often can and do use material from the present group to illustrate the points I am making. I do not have a set routine about what I say, and what I say during the Intensives almost always includes what I will share here.

I think it is important to say many times in many ways that deep process work is only a part of Living in Process. People are so accustomed to the therapy or the psychological "fix" that I want to stress that deep process work is not a technique. It only can really occur in conjunction with confronting our addictions and learning to Live in Process. As we begin to shed our addictions and recover from our addictive process, we begin to be more aware of our unfinished deep processes. As we learn to Live in Process, our deep processes come up more. As we do our deep process work, we confront our addictions and learn to Live in Process. This work is not linear.

Sometimes at an Intensive, the group and I take a strong hand in confronting addictions and may even do a planned or an unplanned intervention during the Intensive. We intervened on a woman at one Intensive, and when the Intensive was over, we left not knowing whether the intervention had had any effect or not. A year later I received the following letter from her:

I have been taking a few moments to reflect over the last year and I wanted to take time to let you know how very

143

grateful I am to you for your wisdom and insight into my addiction. When I was at your Intensive last December at Womanspace, you suggested to me that I check out going to Sierra Tucson for inpatient treatment. You told me you saw me as being desperate and that I was playing Russian roulette with my life. I didn't see any of that at the time (however, there were a lot of things I didn't see), but somehow I was able to find just enough honesty and courage to commit to going to Sierra. That turned out to be the most precious gift I could have ever received. God truly did for me what I wasn't able to do for myself. When I came to the Intensive, I was only able to see the problems that my former husband was "causing" in my life. I had no concept of my own addiction or responsibility for the "awful" things that kept happening to me. During my stay at Sierra I was able to see and own that I am an alcoholic. That was a biggie for me. I have since realized the lengths I have gone to in hiding that from my friends and family and, more to the point, from me. After I left Sierra I went to a recovery home in Tustin, California. I stayed there three months as a resident and one month as a staff person. During that time, I was really able to accept my own responsibility for the chaos and the unmanageability in my life. I had learned to perfect the victim role throughout the years. What a shock it was to find out people hadn't done anything to me that I hadn't allowed to happen. I came back to Tucson last June and decided to make this home for a while. The spirituality here is overwhelming and inspires me each day. I received my first-year medallion last Tuesday night, and I can honestly say I have never been happier in my life. God has also given me another miracle this Christmas; my former husband has also started a journey into recovery now. He has come out to Tucson to go to Sierra and has thirty days clean and sober. It has been wonderful to watch the changes and the growth begin. Well, I know this is just the beginning, Anne, but it sure has been wonderful so far. I sometimes stop and remember how this all started coming together for me and I think of you; I wish I could reach out and hug you. Please know that in spirit my love surrounds you. Thank you for helping save my life!

S.J.

From what she shared, there was no doubt that her former husband had a problem with drugs and was doing all sorts of "awful" things. Granted, but that was not the issue at hand. She was a substance user, and the addiction that was killing her the fastest at that time was her relationship addiction. She needed to address both. The group shared their experience with her, which helped her to do that. There was no doubt that she was in a crisis situation, and it is very difficult to see our addiction when we are in it. The group did an intervention.

Sometimes people just get a taste of the important interaction between Living in Process and facing addictions, and they go on from there. One of the Trainees wrote these words after a Training session:

> I felt from the first day of our facilitators training (this title now seems odd to me, but I lack a good substitute) that there is something beyond our immediate conversations about addictions and recovery, and is tied directly to the sense of "process" about which we talk so much. (I will add that "process" also seems sadly lacking as a descriptor, yet I lack an appropriate name for what this is.) I sense that once having broken the dam holding back my addictions, that there is an endless flood of possibilities. I see my addiction to food, and my addictive behavior in my relationships with family (and others—I am a relationship addict . . . confession!) and I see myself as a music addict, in that I listen to music to alter my mood. . . . From here, it seems that there is an endless list of behaviors which I/we do which alters our state of being . . . so what lies beyond, or within, all of this? . . . Again, I have no name for it, but my sense is that all of these things are the *same*. When I express my sense of joy and aliveness at being in our family of trainees, I recognize that I am engaging in almost none of my addictive behaviors . . . the being alive *is* the process for me, which is different from, perhaps the opposite of, the addictive behavior. . . . I feel "clean" somehow. The work on each addiction is important, and the realizations associated with each addiction are important, and I have a profound sense of these all being woven together into a gauze which in some ways is the very essence of our living. . . . Somehow the work on one addiction *is* the work on another, is the work on another, is the work on another. Perhaps when I/we use the word *process* we are simply naming that which is this gauze, yet I am obviously struggling to "see" a heart beating beneath these words.
> "H."

Clearly, we all struggle to find words for new concepts and new experiences. I constantly struggle to find words. It's hard. Often, I feel that I am trying to describe a new system in the language of the old system or I am falling into jargon, which I hate. There is no doubt that we have developed a language at the Intensives and in the Training that attempts to convey and communicate our experience. Sometimes our experience is so different from those experiences we have had in the system in which we have grown up that new terms are important.

Given the struggle, I will proceed with the kind of input I make at the beginning of the Intensives and hope for the best.

Doing Deep Process Work

As I have said, deep process work is only one small part of Living in Process, *and* it is a necessary and important part. Because we do not live in a culture that respects and facilitates our processes as children, because few (if any) of us have been process-parented, because as children we don't have the internal or external tools adequately to process what happens to us, because we have been raised to believe in controlling or denying our internal processes (through addictions and other methods of control), and because we have tried to fit in, most of us carry many unfinished, aborted, pushed-down processes inside of us that are rumbling around, waiting to be healed and integrated. I have been astounded with the loving way our inner being has kept these sometimes huge and sometimes very tiny processes alive in us so we will have the opportunity to allow them and learn from our experiences in this life. I often say that in a Living Process System, there is no judgment. Nothing is either good or bad. At some metalevel, it doesn't matter whether we have been raped, beaten, overindulged, spoiled, abandoned. The issue is, ultimately, What do we have to learn from these experiences, and what do we have to do to work through the processes that present themselves to us to become whole? Our inner process has preserved these fragments so we can deal with them when we are ready.

I tend to think of these deep processes as what Freud was referring to when he talked about the "boiling cauldron of the unconscious,"[1] Of course, I believe that he was afraid of deep processes (he was, after all, an addict) and tried to keep them under control. I do not believe that talking will ever suffice for our deep process.

Our deep process has to include feelings, and it goes much beyond feelings. Deep process work is not just catharsis or the expression of feelings. Deep processes have a life of their own, and it often takes a while to be willing to let go of control enough to actually go through a deep process.

Most of us have had deep processes come up in our lives; we usually thought we were becoming hysterical or "losing it." We have been taught to fear and mistrust our deep process, yet they offer us a level of healing that I have never seen take place in any other way.

Doors

There are many doors into our deep processes. Remember how sometimes a song just keeps running through your mind over and over? That may mean that you have a deep process that is ready to come up. There was a woman at one Intensive who had a very profound, very quiet process that started with a song.

We had a Wilderness Intensive at a youth camp in Indiana that was a pure Tom Sawyer land. Every bend in the trail held a tree house, a swinging bridge, or a rustic rope course. It was wonderful. (So were the bugs, snakes, and cicadas!) Outside the dining hall and meeting room, the owner had strung up a number of hammocks between the trees.

This woman was lying in one of the hammocks during the break and gently swinging. As she lay there, a song came into her mind. She was surprised at first and then decided just to "stay with" the song and see where it took her. She just kept humming the song, and she suddenly remembered the age she was when this song was popular.

Almost immediately, she began to have some body memories, and, very calmly, she suddenly remembered that her father had molested her during that time in her life. She was astounded with this memory because it had been completely repressed until that moment, and as she quietly lay there, tears of relief streamed down her face, because so many seemingly unrelated pieces of her life fell together at that point.

She lay there for a while, just waiting to see if there were any other parts of this process. Nothing more came to her except that she felt peaceful, so she got up and came in to the group and shared her deep process. She was glowing.

This deep process is a good example of many aspects of our deep process. The woman was led into her deep process by a song, which is not unusual, and the process that came up had little or nothing to do with the door into it. Frequently, the door into a deep process is just that—a door. It has nothing to do with what the process is really about. This is very common in deep process work, and, I believe, is one of the loving ways our inner process "tricks" and bypasses our logical and rational mind, getting us to a level where we can heal. We tend to be so controlling that we would do everything we could to avoid our process if we knew what was coming. The part of our mind that our process bypasses is not supposed to have emotion, but it does. It has one primal, undeveloped, unsophisticated emotion, and that emotion is panic—panic at what it perceives to be the loss of its illusion of control.

In addition, I believe that no one has ever healed in his or her logical mind. No one has ever healed from "understanding" something. Yet, much of our psychotherapy is built on the belief that if we just *understand* something, we will be all right.

Another universal process learning that we get from this woman's work is that no two people have the same reaction to the same experience. We have whole areas of psychology built on the belief that *if* this (incest, for example) happened to you, *then* this, this, and this are true. In deep process work, I have not found this belief to be valid. We have developed these "if-then" theories, which are too simplistic to be applied to the human organism, so that the professionals can believe they are the experts, hold the power, and be essential. Working the way I do with people now has taught me how little I know and how little I need to know. All I have to do is be present and available to a person's deep process, and that process will put the scattered pieces together in the way that particular being needs them put together. No one but that person can know what they are and how they should go together. Even they don't know until they have finished their deep process.

This deep process was not loud, raging, excruciating, or intense as so many are, especially for an incest memory. It was quiet, simple, and peaceful. All deep processes are different. Perhaps a better way to put it is to say that each deep process is unique, and everyone's processes are unique. To give people batakas and tell them to get their rage out or to have them face a chair and talk to a dead parent may temporarily give them some illusory relief, but this is *not* deep process work, which has to follow its own unique course and cannot be programmed according to predetermined prescriptive procedures.

Another door into our deep process may be the times when we are watching a movie or just listening to someone talk and tears start to well up. That may be an indication that a deep process is coming up. Sometimes, we are just aware of feelings: feeling sad, feeling angry, feeling alone. That's probably a deep process coming up.

Doors to deep processes take other forms too. You know how sometimes we wake up in the morning and we just feel grouchy? Someone says good morning, and we want to bite their head off. That could be a clue that we have a deep process near the surface that is ready to come up.

Another door to a deep process can be remembering people we haven't heard from or seen in a long time. Suddenly they just pop into our mind and seem to keep popping in and out for a while. As I said earlier, often the door into the process has little or nothing to do with what the process is about, and when we open ourselves to noticing these "doors," and take some time out and wait with our process, frequently we finish something that has been waiting around to be worked through.

Much of traditional psychotherapy has been built on the belief that there is some logical relationship between these doors and the issue we are confronting. I have found that rarely to be true. Think how much time and energy we put into trying to analyze and make sense out of a Freudian slip, when it just may be a door into a deep process that has nothing to do with the content of the slip.

A dream, also, may be a door into a deep process, and I have found that some dreams are a working through of a deep process themselves. Often, when we have a significant dream, it will leave a residue of a feeling or an awareness. Frequently, if we just stretch out and make ourselves comfortable and stay with the feelings or awareness, that will lead us into our deep process. The dream may just have been a door to the deep work that was ready to be done. Here's how a former Trainee, B.H., describes it:

> Dream time—I just love to receive dreams, which I do only infrequently—or remember infrequently.
>
> I was in the backseat of a car at a four-way stop in the country. The car turned right and crested a hill. As it did, I looked over my shoulder and saw a child standing at the intersection alone. I yelled, "Stop, let me out! That kid has no sense of direction." The car left as I walked back to the child and took her hand. End of dream. The dream left a strange and powerful feeling with me. Of course, I gave in some to the temptation to interpret and in sitting with the

feeling from this dream I am learning not to do this. What I notice about my behavior since the dream speaks more loudly to me than any left-brain guesses. I notice I say no to whatever I don't want to do with great frequency. I seem to be considering my wants and needs daily. I play some everyday—this from a workaholic! I purchased a couple pairs of purple socks and purple shoes—which I just love wearing. I sit almost daily with the feeling from this dream. I know that kid is part of me and I am including her in now.

I do not believe that dream analysis has any value other than keeping us away from our deep process work and feeding our intellectualizing and thinking addiction. I have never seen anyone really *heal* from interpreting a dream. It can, however, be helpful to focus on and stay with our dreams. Again, I think dream analysis is similar to masturbation. It can be fun and interesting, it can keep us occupied, it can result in a lot of speculative books and keep a lot of people in business, but ultimately it does not heal, and it supports an addictive process.

In working with people's processes that are triggered by dreams or start in dreams, I have come to believe that there is no real universal symbolism in dreams and that we have imposed that concept upon our dreams because they are actually the closest conscious access that we have to our deep process. Like our deep process, our dreams bypass our conscious mind and try to get us dealing directly with our inner process. I see dreams as just one more attempt on the part of our inner process to allow us to break through to the work we need to do and to heal.

I cannot say often enough how impressed I have become with the ingenuity and creativity of our inner process and how, in spite of our innumerable addictive cover-ups, our inner process attempts to offer us every possible opportunity to heal. How deaf we are to our inner being, sometimes.

There are two other doors into our inner process that I want to mention just briefly. One experience I have had with my deep process is that sometimes in my mind or in my "mind's eye," I will just have an image. It may be a tree or a room I knew as a child. It may be a situation or a setting. The temptation always is to try to *figure out* what these images mean. At best, that approach is counterproductive. If I just take some time out and "wait with" the image, frequently some feelings will come up, and the process will take me where I need to go.

The last door I want to mention is depression. Frequently, depression is a door or an invitation into our deep process. When we recognize that depression is there for a reason and we let ourselves go into it, it often leads us to a deep process that may have nothing to do with depression. One of the things I was never taught in graduate school is that joy and depression are alike. They are both processes, and the process is the same. The content is just different. The major difference between them is how we treat them.

We are always seeking joy, and when we see it coming, we say, "That's it! Come on! I want to hold onto you forever!" Joy says, "Ah, she's heard me. No need to hang around." With depression, when we see it coming we say, "Oh, no! There it comes again! Go away! I don't want to have anything to do with you!" So depression says, "(Sigh.) Here we go again. I'm going to have to get bigger and bigger so she will notice me." It moves around and keeps trying to find a way in. It taps us on the shoulder. "Over here." It gets behind us. "Back here." And it continues this process until we finally get the learning.

Joy and depression are the same from a process perspective. They will come, and they will go. Each has something to teach us, and they will be back. It is only when we fight them that they have to become so overpowering. Many clinicians believe that they must be in *control.* Their philosophy is built on control, and they don't have the courage or the skills to stay with a person and his or her deep process work, so they resort to a treatment (usually harmful to the body) to *control* the depression. Since I have been doing this work, I have seen people move through heavy depressions, learn from them, and heal.

Often, depression is a natural response to some hidden process and life experience. For example, one Trainee writes,

> I think it's interesting that there are seven men in my Regional. A lot of my rage work I did with my therapist was centered around men and my sexual abuse issues. Now there are a lot of issues around my mother—a lot of anger and rage—and who should facilitate me but a man—very gentle and sensitive—it's all a miracle how this works. It's becoming clearer how strong my disease is and how it has blocked my memory more than anything, and I'm sure the shock treatment added to it. What continually amazes me is the wrenching letting go of these fusions I have with people and things—including my therapist, my son, my stepfather,

the man I lived with—and the last heavy letting go was at the Regional and was letting go of my grandfather. What's coming up now is this fusion I feel I have with my mother, and I feel that my fusion with her has a lot to do with my memory loss. Every time I go through one of these letting go processes—it's like death, like a little child has died—it's so wrenching and painful. The daily emotional abuse from my mother feels like the core of my issues—even more so than the sexual abuse! I guess only time will tell—my processes will tell! I'm so thankful for this process work and can imagine why they put me down as being hysterical when I was in the hospital when I was sixteen—who wouldn't be hysterical over all these traumas. God, how primitive we have been in our attempts to "heal," not only thirty-four years ago, but two years ago when a recovery center wanted to put me in a lockup ward to do rage work!

I plan to go back east this spring and visit all the places of my childhood—where I was raped, where the incest took place, where I tried to commit suicide, and the hospital where I received the shock treatment. I know I need to do this in order to heal and possibly regain my memory. My mother very angrily gave me some addresses and has refused to talk to me anymore about the past—so it's up to me—god, I'm scared and excited at the prospects of reconnecting with my memory of long ago—because the beauty of it is in my poetry and my photography.

N.F.

I think her letter is an example of going into rage and depression and coming out the other side.

It's important to remember that these doors into deep process are just that, doors, and we have to be willing to go where the deep process takes us, because there are no road signs and no guarantees.

Readiness for Deep Processes

My experience is that no deep process will come up unless we are ready for it; I have never seen a deep process come up that the person was not ready for. We may not *think* we are ready. We may not *feel* we are ready, and we are.

For example, when we get depressed or we start to get agitated or overwhelmed by feelings, that's our inner process telling us that there is something deep inside us that is ready to come up and be healed. The very fact that it is surfacing (we used to think of these situations as "losing it") is an indication that we have reached a level of maturity, strength, insight, awareness, growth, and integration that will enable us to deal with and integrate whatever comes up.

This trust in our deep process is very difficult to have until we have had the experience of doing our deep process work for some time, and I do think it is important to remember. However, doing deep process work does not mean that we set it up as a task to be accomplished. If we try to do that, we are back in the same old control paradigm. If we feel resistant to our process, honor the resistance and see what comes up. If we feel stuck, honor the "stuckness" and see where it takes us. If we feel fear, honor the fear.

I have always said that blocking our process and forcing our process are just opposite ends of the same continuum. They are both based on control. It is so tempting to try to control our deep work and make it happen or make it *not* happen. One of the men in the Training shared his awareness about this issue:

> One of my learnings during this time was that I wasn't doing anything to *make* it (deep process) happen. I have spent time in the past trying to figure out how to let (get) my process going—which I knew I had trapped just below the surface and which, if the right tool could be found, I could release. There were even times that I would eat (or, more likely, not eat) before an evening group session because I thought it might have an effect on my process.
>
> At any rate, what was different for me in Colorado was simply that I was able to be *willing* to be with myself and not be manipulative or try to run away. What happened with that seemed like a gift—freely given and freely received. I will take credit for many of the ways in which I acted out of my commitments to not direct or isolate, and I really feel good about having done these things—like naming my addictions when they came up and working the steps around them, experiencing the sunrise on the hill behind the dining hall when I woke up on the second morning and realized that I was not connected to God and my own spirituality and like simply moving to the center of the room when I would rather have been an observer hanging out on the edge (a familiar place for me).
>
> The things that "I did" are all things that I have done in the past (couple of years). I also know that I have been

willing to be present with my process in the past and that I have experienced a lot of healing as a result. I have not experienced it so deeply or for so long, however. I am realizing now, as I write this, that an important part of what I have been experiencing is the progressiveness of recovery. I am really grateful that addiction is not the only thing that is progressive.

D.W.

If we don't "get" a deep process that is ready to be worked, we will get another chance. I think of our inner process as very conservation-minded. It recycles our garbage, and recycles our garbage, and recycles our garbage. If we don't get it the first time around, we get another chance, and then another, until the deep process gets through to us. Again, I think of this recycling as "caring."

Unfortunately, each time our deep process recycles it does it with more force, until it gets our attention. I have come to believe that the intensity of the "whack" alongside the head we have to get is directly proportional to the strength of our stubbornness, our control, and our denial. We are the ones who set up the need for the intensity, and often our addictions are the cause and the vehicle for the "whack."

Deep Process Work Cannot Be Programmed

People often come to Intensives with preconceived notions, learned in therapy, about what deep process work is. Initially, with these people, there will be a tendency to have an agenda and to force their work in a form that is familiar to them. This is not deep process work as we know it.

For example, at one Intensive, a man arrived with an agenda that his therapist had given him: "If you don't do a rebirthing at that Intensive, we will do it on Monday when you get home." This kind of statement is antithetical to deep process work.

Deep process work will come up when the person is ready to handle this specific piece and when the inner being is at a point where it is ready to integrate what is coming up. The deep process work cannot fit the program of the person or the person's therapist. Often, the role of the therapist has been dualistic. They either block or force deep processes.

The techniques and tools that therapists use are, in my experience, very misleading. They are misleading in that frequently the material they elicit is true and valid and needs to be worked on. Unfortunately, using techniques to elicit this material often does more harm than good and entrenches the client more firmly in the addictive relationship between therapist and client. In the first place, the client looks to the therapist for a quick "fix" as a "junkie" (psychological junkies exist, too) would do, and the therapist willingly obliges, seeing her or his job as one of knowing and being able to give clients what they need. In this way, the client not only becomes dependent upon the therapist, the client becomes dependent upon the technique. Subtly, but importantly, the therapist agrees to do the client's work for the client.

Even more important, when material is "elicited" like this, it is not integrated into the inner process of the client, so the awareness of the material not only becomes useless, it can become destructive. Our inner process has an internal timing device that monitors our awareness, maturity, and strength and sends us information (doors) to notice when something is ready to be worked on and has the greatest probability of being integrated for healing. When we preempt that process, we not only are playing God, we are psychologically raping the client.

The more I do this Living Process work, the more horror I feel at the horrendous violence I see in psychotherapy practiced by people who are genuinely caring and who mean well. I know that I have been one of those people, because we were trained to believe we had to be in control and have the power; this book is one of my amends to my former clients. I also have to say that from early in my training, I rejected the assumed power imbalance expected in psychotherapy and for over thirty years have been developing a new model for healing.

Let me give an example of one of my recent experiences with a woman who had been violated by a technique suggested by a very well meaning therapist. This was a woman who came to one of the Intensives I did in Germany. I noticed her immediately when she walked into the room. She looked like a shell, and her *entire* body language manifested depression, yet her eyes were darting from side to side, she had quick, jerky movements, she never seemed to be able to get comfortable, and she was constantly agitated. Back in my clinical days, I would have immediately labeled her as an agitated depression and thought of ways to "calm her down" (which, because of my training, I would have believed that she needed).

I decided to keep an eye on her and wait with her. Her check-in was very short and cursory, somewhat like name, rank, and serial number, with little information about herself. No one asked for more, which I believe was wise.

She was very quiet during the first few days of the Intensive, watching carefully. I must say, my impression of this woman was that she was like a wounded bird or a frightened animal, and while people were supportive of her, they gave her a lot of space and opportunity to find her own way in the group.

On the last day of the Intensive, *she hit the mats.* She did some of the deepest and most intense rage work I have ever seen. This deep work lasted for almost two hours. Her facilitator stayed with her, and others jumped up to assist with pillows and mattresses when needed. She was really into it.

After she had finished her work, she was encouraged by her facilitator to stay with herself for as long as she needed, and it took her a long time to "come back."

When she was ready, she shared with the group. This woman had been working with a therapist, a man whom she trusted a great deal and who had been very helpful to her. Over a year before, because of her symptoms and patterns, this therapist decided that she had been sexually molested at an early age. She had no memories or awareness of this having happened, and she trusted her therapist.

He suggested that he hypnotize her to access this material. She was willing because of her confidence in him, so they agreed to use the technique. Now, one of the defenses for the use of hypnosis has been that no one could be hypnotized unless he or she agreed. It has also been asserted that the client would not carry out any suggestions that did not fit with his or her basic value system (even though that might create considerable distress). I find it amazing how we have developed such airtight rationales to support our violent procedures and techniques.

In any case, he hypnotized her, and, lo and behold, she *had* been sexually assaulted orally by her father (which is much more common than we once believed). Her therapist was right. Unfortunately, she was not ready to hear, deal with, and integrate this material, so it had a disastrous effect upon her life. She became profoundly depressed. (It is my experience that depression often is a cover for rage, but that's for the person to find out, not for me to interpret, because it is not always so.) She was no longer able to work and had to quit her job. She could not care for her family adequately, and her relationship with her husband and her family deteriorated. When she came to the Intensive, she felt quite desperate.

As she shared her work, she said that in her deep process she was full of rage, and her rage was focused toward those who had raped her. She became aware, in her deep work, that she felt she had been raped twice, once by her father and once by her therapist. Her father had raped her physically. Her therapist had raped her psychologically and spiritually—with the best of intentions. The change in this woman's appearance was striking as she shared her work. She seemed at peace. Not only had her deep process work helped her resolve the issues that were "up" for her, the group had respected her Living Process. This meant that she could take her own time and that her own process was respected. If she had left without doing that piece of deep work, that would have been all right, too, because she would have had an experience of respect for her process and her timing. Her process was respected on many levels.

Psychotherapists have become victims of their own worldview, belief system, and disease. Co-dependents/relationship addicts always have to be indispensable. One of the major ways we make ourselves indispensable is by giving "fixes." Unfortunately, the fixes may foster dependency and may kill the person being "fixed."

Deep process work cannot be programmed, nor should it be.

There Is No "Right" Way to Do Deep Process Work

Deep process work is unique to the person and to the specific processes that are coming up. There is no set form for deep process work. Some people believe that unless they are down on the mats flailing around and emitting huge noises, they have not really done a "good" deep process. Deep process has many forms, and no one form is more real or better than any other. Whenever we try to determine the form our (or someone else's) deep process will take, we are exhibiting a major characteristic (character defect) of addiction, the illusion of control.

Certainly, many deep processes do invoke an intense outpouring, and the person can be quite active, even requiring "helpers" to hold pillows and keep the person safe so they can give full vent to what is coming up without having to split themselves between doing their deep process work and simultaneously monitoring their own safety. Still, even when they are active, deep processes can take different forms, one from another, and even one deep process itself can have different forms from start to finish.

One of the deep processes I had a few years ago illustrates this point very well. For years, I have worked with the church in various capacities. I had at one time or another worked with every major and many (considered) minor denominations of the Protestant church. I had worked with the Catholic church, and I had worked with Buddhists and with New Age spiritual groups. I had always believed that the church could be "the Church," and, of course, in my arrogance, I believed that I knew what that was and that I could help bring it about. After many years of laboring under this belief, I began to see that my relationship with the church was just like my relationship with my ex-husband. I was an enabler and a relationship addict, and I was also relating to an active addict. I was working with a national church group that certainly helped me with this awareness. At that stage of my recovery from relationship addiction, I was clear that I could not maintain my sobriety and continue to work with the church. I decided to stop working with all forms of the church for a while, aware that I might never go back. After making that decision in the spring, I moved into a slow grieving process.

I had been involved with the church in many ways and for a long time. Yet, I was not at a stage in my own recovery where I could escape being affected by and critical of the hypocrisy, dishonesty, and judgment I observed in the church. I was beginning to experience what "going to any length" for my sobriety really meant.

I had expected that this decision to let go of my relationship with the church might trigger an intense deep process—and it didn't. For many months, I was aware of this low, underlying, rumbling-around depression and grieving. It just seemed to go on and on. At times, I was tempted to try to "trigger" something to get it over with, or to ignore it. Luckily, I had been doing this work long enough that I did neither of these. I just "noticed" it and respected it.

The following January or February, almost a year later, I was facilitating a Nine-Day Intensive for women. As the women in that group checked in and shared their stories, almost every woman had some kind of horror story to relate about her encounter with the church. I listened to one woman after another tell of bringing her gentle, innocent spirituality to the church and then relate her experience of being spiritually battered and violated by the church. I myself felt battered with the information. After hearing these kinds of stories from almost every woman there and being aware of a growing tension and a rising rage in my body, I "hit the mats."

The initial phase of my process was rage. I was just furious. How could the church justify this behavior? How dare it batter and control people's spirituality? After I had raged and howled with pain and frustration, my deep process work shifted. I found myself sitting quietly, slowly shaking my head from side to side, and saying, "How could you? How could you?" I was aware of a quiet, deep throbbing feeling of betrayal and disbelief. How easy it would have been to try to interpret and analyze that feeling, but I knew enough just to stay with it and let it be. I wept and wept. After I had wept and howled with my pain for some time, I was on my knees with my head in my hands. When the wailing and crying subsided, I sat back on my heels and then lay down on my back to rest a while and see if my process was finished. As I lay there, I was aware of my hand on my head and my index finger rubbing in a circle on my forehead on the place some people call the "third eye." I have come to know that a process is not finished when there is still something going on in the body, so I "noticed" what my hand was doing and just stayed with the awareness.

Suddenly, I had a flash: "This is my spirituality. It is right here in the middle of my forehead, and it has always been here. It was there long before the church, and it is *mine*. The church has tried to convince me that I needed the church to have my spirituality in order to make itself indispensable. But, I have always had it. I am a spiritual being." I suddenly "knew" this at the root of my being.

I have never felt such relief. My whole being sighed as I quietly lay back on the pillow. As I lay there, I was sure I was finished, and then I became aware of something in my body. I was lying on my back with my left foot on the floor and my left knee in the air. My right ankle was resting on my left knee with my right knee in the air, and my right foot was fretfully tap-tapping in space. I became aware of my foot, and what flashed through my mind was, "This position is not very ladylike, and prophets don't have to be ladylike." I roared with laughter. I thought this idea was one of the funniest things I had heard in years. I rolled all over the floor in peals of laughter. I couldn't stop laughing. Pretty soon most of the group, including my facilitator, were laughing with me, although they had no idea what it was about. I laughed until my body was finished (very important), then I stopped and rested, checking myself out to see if I was finished. I seemed to be, so then I shared my process with my facilitator. After that process, I noticed that my grieving of my loss of my relationship with the church was finished. All I had to do was trust my process, and it would feed me what I needed when I needed it. I had only to "notice" and let the deep process do its work.

This deep process illustrates how the "door" into the deep work is almost always not what it is really about. The "door" into this work was my grieving over my perceived loss of the church and the anger I had over what I had seen the church do to others. What came out was a deep awareness of my spirituality and the importance of working out of *my* spirituality.

I believe that this deep process is also a good example of a process taking many forms, with every piece of it being as important as any other. We must never get it into our minds that one kind of process is the "right" process or that there is a "right" way of doing deep process work. Our deep process requires a profound level of trust from us. We must trust wherever the deep process takes us—or, if we don't trust it, see what we have to learn from that. Sometimes our deep process may be being unable to do our deep process. We need to respect and trust that, too. This deep process is also a good example of "waiting with" a deep process until it is ready, not blocking it, not forcing it—allowing it.

Our Deep Process Has Surprises and Humor

The above process illustrates the fun and sense of humor I have come to believe our deep process has. Often, in even the most tragic of deep processes, there may be little infusions of humor and laughter. A person may go into a deep process about their experience of incest and end up roaring about how silly their perpetrator was.

I have found in most of my deep processes that there is a little "twist" at the end that always "sets the hook," as we would say in fishing, and often that set is funny. I have come to respect these little "twists" in our deep process work as one of the ways our deep work bypasses and undermines our logical, rational brain. These twists are almost always something that we could not have "figured out." They make a lot of sense, and they are not logical and rational.

For example, the "prophets don't have to be ladies" piece was just what I needed to finish my grieving about the church and go ahead and do my work with my spirituality intact. That deep process was a very profound process for me.

160

Finishing a Deep Process

For many people, having the respect for themselves and the faith to finish a deep process is very difficult. Many people do not feel that they deserve the time they need to complete a process, or they think it is their responsibility to take care of the facilitator, and they shut off their process.

Any deep process that is shut off or blocked will just have to be done again. Each deep process is a piece in and of itself. Although I am more comfortable with feelings than many, I am aware of how many deep processes I blocked and aborted when I was operating out of a psychotherapy model.

Recently, I was in a highly prestigious group with psychiatrists and psychologists. During a period of sharing in the group, one of the psychiatrists began to cry over some extremely painful experiences. It was very clear to me that he was going into a deep process, but I had been carefully told that I was not to try to "control" the meeting. (That meant I was not to do anything that I knew how to do.)

I sat and watched the other psychiatrists hold their breaths until he quickly got himself under "control" (another opportunity missed). It was clear to me that their theory had no other way to handle this than to see it as a loss of control. When he got himself under control, almost everyone heaved a sigh of relief and spent some time congratulating themselves on how safe the group was, as evidenced by the fact that their colleague could "show feelings." I left the group shortly after that.

I have to admit that before I learned about deep process work, I let people feel a few feelings, cry a few tears, and express a little anger, and then we both congratulated ourselves and moved on. (That kind of ignorance of deep process work on my part is another reason I need to make amends with this book.)

Psychological, medical, and psychiatric therapies just block, shut off, or attempt to control our deep processes, aborting the very built-in means we have inside us to facilitate healing. Luckily for us, the process just goes underground and recycles, and the next time it comes up, it does so with more force.

As I have worked with psychotics and psychotic processes, I have come to think of psychosis as just speeded up, intensified deep processes. I have also noticed that schizophrenic thinking and addictive thinking appear to be on the same continuum.

Doing this deep process work has forever altered the way I see people and the way I choose to work.

Deep Process Comes in Waves

I think of deep process work as very similar to the natural process of birthing. Deep process, like birthing, comes in waves. People who don't understand about deep process work frequently cut off a person's deep process after a few waves. As I have already mentioned, this is an occupational hazard among the helping professions. When we first come into our deep processes, we may come in very gently or we may plunge right in. Either way, deep processes come in waves. We will have a shallow wave, and then a rest, another wave and then a rest, then one a little deeper, and then a rest.

Just as in birthing, it is important that the facilitator does not try to rush or control the process. A good facilitator is an attendant *to* the process. As people do their work of each deep process, they move deeper and deeper into the process. There will be a place—often intense—where it looks like they are all the way in. Then, they will come out of the process in progressively shallower waves, with rest phases in between.

In the workshops I have attended with people who said they were doing "process" work, I have seen many therapists cut off and abort processes by touching, hugging, asking a question, making an interpretation, or some other means. This is usually done with great "caring and concern," and my perception is that the therapist is often afraid of the deep process and needs to feel "in control."

The time coming out of a process is just as important as the time going into a process, and the rest periods are an integral part of the process. The process itself is a whole. If that whole is not respected, that "piece" has to be done again. I believe this is the reason we see people going over and over the same material in psychotherapy. They may even have some good understanding of the problem, but they never have completed the healing process of the deep process, and this is where real healing takes place.

I am truly grateful to all the good teachers I have had on the way to learning to do this work, not the least of whom was Fritz Perls. Gestalt work and many other of the humanistic psychologies have had their finger on this work, but they just never have gone far enough. When Fritz facilitated a person, that person would often go into what was at least similar to a deep process. Frequently, when the person would get what seemed to be "all the way into" the process, Fritz would rush in and make an often brilliant comment (he would never have called these "comments" an interpretation, and now, for the most part, I would) and stop the process. As a result, in early Gestalt, people never got an opportunity to deliver the afterbirth. *And* they never got to complete the process. Sometimes, I have an image of our inner healing process trying by every conceivable means to get around the helpers we have selected.

In order to complete our processes, we need to "wait with" our process—especially be willing to wait with our rests and our pauses and not let ourselves or anyone else shut off our processes. Of course, we may have some of our most significant learning in seeing how we and others shut off our process. It's really important not to get into right and wrong and leave ourselves open to all possible learning and options in Living Process work.

The following is an excerpt from a letter from a former Trainee, a therapist herself, who wanted to experience the work of a well-known therapist who uses the family sculpting techniques developed by Virginia Satir. I think the last paragraph speaks eloquently for some of what happens when deep processes are aborted:

> There's a lot I want to say about my experience with [this famous therapist], and I am still sorting. I learned a lot—not the least of which was that I could/can stay open to whatever learnings are to come when what I am observing seemed to me to sometimes be abusive therapy (not so much by [the therapist], but from the group "facilitators"). The visual impact of psychodrama and sculpting was very powerful for me *and* everywhere I looked there was some kind of control. I am pondering whether using sculpting can be used with process, and I'm seeing how it feels. The control was intense around only allowing one person to work at a time, and during the entire day of the psychodrama no one was "allowed" to do any "processing" until the next day, which was set aside for "group work." You get my drift regarding control. I was really clear with myself before I went that I would stay out of my judgmentalism and the distancing that creates for me, so I looked for "What is happening here? What kind of healing is happening?" What I came away with is that some kind of healing takes place and that I am grateful to have found Process work.

I was very aware that the peacefulness I feel about both my recovery and about my work spoke on its own about the value of Process Living. What I have also been experiencing is the "fallout" from not being able to deep process several times during the workshop when deep stuff wanted to express. So I have spent the past two and a half weeks not feeling particularly wonderful physically and also knowing that I needed to get back to (and so far couldn't) my unfinished processes. That has now happened (yesterday afternoon to be specific), and I feel much better. I kept thinking about the difference between the way I felt when I returned from the Co-Dependence Intensive last winter—clean and open and as though the wind could blow through me as well as carry me along, in short, absolutely fabulous —and how blocked up and unfinished I felt now.

Anonymous

When We Can't Do Our Deep Processes

Many times we cannot do our deep process work at the time it comes up. When I have not been taking good care of myself or not paying attention to my deep processes, one of the favorite loving "tricks" of my deep process is to try to push up a deep process at a most inopportune time, such as during major speeches to large audiences.

I'll just be chugging along, sharing information that is important to me, and suddenly my tears will well up. I usually stay with them for a while, and then I say to my deep process, "I hear you, and I'll get back to you as soon as I can. I promise."

My experience is that the deep process that is ready to be worked will subside and wait until later. This means that when I go back to my hotel room, I don't turn on the TV, get on the phone, or run out to get something to eat. I stretch out on the bed and wait with my process. If I don't do this (in other words, if I lie to it), it will get me, and usually in a setting that is even more inconvenient. My deep process has a life of its own, and it is also me.

Sounds in Deep Process Work

Sounds are very important in deep process work. Most of us have been told to be quiet all our lives. We not only have had our angry, hurt, mourning, sad sounds shushed; we have been told to shut off our excitement, our joy, our squeals of laughter, the sounds that come with our energy, and our life noises. What child who has been taken to church has not somehow been given the message that God does not like noise, even happy noise, and that we need to keep quiet?

As children, we learn to protect our parents from our pain and the sounds of our pain. We learned that to cry out our sounds was not to be a "big girl" or a "big boy." Unlike many indigenous groups, we rarely have cultural outlets for grief, mourning, or joy and excitement. We have not made our sounds.

I used to think of our sounds in our deep process as our primitive language. This is a language that dips far below our cultural differences. It is known to all of us. At an Intensive, when a woman is howling out her rage about what has happened to her as a woman, everyone knows what she is saying. When a man is huddled up in a little ball, whimpering and obviously trying to protect himself, everyone knows what he is saying.

In fact, I have found it amazing how easy it is to facilitate process work in another country where I don't even understand the language—because the language of our deep processes is the same. I may not even be able to put what I am hearing into words, and I *know* what I am hearing. I may not even be able to articulate what the sounds were that I made in my own deep process, and I *know* what they said to me.

As I have been with more deep process work, I have moved to a new level of understanding sounds. As I have seen people work and seen them letting their sounds out, I have come to envision our sounds like huge nets with large grappling hooks on them. As we move through our sounds, these nets move through our bodies, hooking the pockets of poisons and pulling them out of our bodies. So many people look clear, fresh, and cleaned out after their deep process work. Some people have actually reported physical healing after their deep process work. I have come to wonder how much dis-ease is really just blocked, aborted deep processes.

We had a man who came to Intensives who was from a very large ranch in the West that comprised thousands of acres. According to him, his father was an alcoholic and his mother was what we would call a raging codependent or relationship addict. This man was an only child. His only close companions were his animals, toward whom his father often had violent rages. His most frequent survival technique was to be *quiet*. He spoke softly, he tried to disappear into the woodwork, and he never made sounds, even in his deep process work. After some time of doing process work and listening to others' deep processes, he began to make *his* sounds. Whenever he went into a painful process, these little "squeaks" would come out of him. Then he really began to "make his sounds." He squeaked in his sleep, he squeaked when he was sitting quietly, and the most amazing thing was that he squeaked when he was talking. I have yet to be able to figure out how he did this or to be able to reproduce it. Usually, he seemed to have no awareness of his little sounds. Yet, when his sounds decided to come, they just kept coming. I have no idea whether they ever got any bigger or whether he still is making little noises; they seemed very important at the time.

Just as in any other aspect of deep process work, it is important not to block and not to force our sounds. There are always some eager people who, when they hear that sounds are important, try to force their sounds. Yet, even then there is no right or wrong. When we try to force our sounds, we have a great opportunity to learn about our control issues.

Breathing in Deep Process Work

I have always been aware of the importance of breathing in deep process work, and my understanding of my role and the way I perform it as a facilitator has changed immensely over the years. I continue to be embarrassed when I realize how controlling I was when I first started doing this work in the 1960s. I am amazed with how far I have come, and I am sure that I will be just as embarrassed with where I am now when I look back ten years from now.

When I first started doing deep process facilitation, I used to hover very close to the person working, reminding them to breathe. I somehow had the notion that their breath and their *deep* breath was the way to "get to" their feelings. Obviously, as I was trained to believe, I knew best for them, and I knew how to get what they needed (how embarrassing to see this in print).

Early on, I was also concerned about hyperventilation. I asked the facilitators to keep a close eye on people, and when they started to hyperventilate, to tell them to breathe deeply. Over years of facilitating deep process work, we have become much less active as facilitators and, I am happy to say, much less directive. Always, when I think I know just how deep process should be done, something or someone comes along and helps me see that not knowing is a preferred state for a process facilitator.

Let me illustrate with a deep process that challenged my views of the dangers of hyperventilation. I was facilitating the deep process of a young physician at a Men's Intensive. This man was a very strong and a very gentle man who had never really done any deep process work before. Early in the Intensive, he started crying, and I quickly moved in to sit with him. He cried and wailed for a long time, and then he moved into a type of short puffing breathing. Immediately, my brain kicked in that he was going to hyperventilate, *but* something in my intuition said, "Wait this one out," so I just sat with him. His breathing became shorter and faster, until it very much had the tempo of an old steam freight train going up a hill (I had to admit that my mind flashed on the story "The Little Engine That Could"). When he reached the peak, he let out a huge burst of breath and fell back in a heap. He was quiet for a very long time, and then he began whimpering softly and started tentatively reaching out. Then he just held himself and quietly cried and cried, rocking himself. (Of course, I had *no* idea of what was going on.) After a while he just lay there peacefully.

When he opened his eyes, he was glowing and seemed to be both with himself and beyond himself. As he shared his process with us, we all cried and were touched. He shared that he had started just feeling sad, and he had just let himself feel that sadness. (He had been talking about his young wife who had been in a mental hospital for many years—a door?) As his tears came, his body took over, and that's when the strange breathing pattern "just seemed to happen." When that breathing pattern stopped with the burst of air (he later said that there was *no* sense of hyperventilation), he found himself in a different time and a different space. It was winter, and he was standing looking out the window at a naked baby lying in the snow. At first he was transfixed, and then he realized that the baby was he and that the baby was dying—*he* was dying. He felt himself rush out and grab the baby. He held it and rocked it and assured it that even though it was almost dead, he would not let it die. He and the baby were separate, and they were also one and the same. He came out of that deep process knowing that he would live—that he would live his own life. We all believed him, and he has.

I came out of that process feeling the awe of this work and aware of the sanctity of it and of how grateful I am to have the opportunity to be a part of it.

I also came away from that deep process with new ideas about hyperventilation and how much control I had been taught I needed to exert. I believe that if I had interfered with that process, he probably would not have had the process he had. He might have had another—equally as important—and, down deep, I doubt it. Of course, we'll never know.

However, I do believe that it is important to observe or be aware of breath in deep process work, and occasionally we may need to intervene. Another example will illustrate that point.

One of our best deep process facilitators was an old dog I had named Bubber. He often sat in on groups and went to Intensives. We had a person who had just moved into our household who had little or no knowledge of deep process work. One day one of our neighbors who was a Trainee (that's why she had become a neighbor) came up in a terrible state and asked for someone to sit with her while she did her work. This woman was an alcoholic, a bulimic, an anorexic, a recovering nicotine and relationship addict, and a self-abuser, and she had cancer. The new member of our household was terrified to sit with her and she was the only one around, so she agreed to try (never facilitate someone when you don't feel right about it—facilitators are people, too).

At one point during her process, the woman began to hold her breath. The woman sitting with her sat there trying not to interfere with her process, watching the woman's fingernails turn black. This woman was self-abusive and self-destructive enough that, in her deep process, she just might have been able to go too far. I know as a facilitator I would not have risked it, and neither did Bubber.

He jumped up—jumped right on her middle and licked her face. She gasped and came back. He again took his position of watching.

When I get uncomfortable with someone's process, I intervene. Luckily, I know they will get another chance at it. Also, I have been observing deep process facilitation long enough that I rarely get uncomfortable, and I still do keep an eye on people's breathing. Sometimes, I will remind them to breathe. I definitely will not try to force their process with breathing techniques. I find that disrespectful and violent.

Checking in After a Process

I have come to believe that it is very important to check in after a deep process. This is one of the ways that we "fix" our experience and give it language and concepts, which human beings seem to need.

Usually, the person doing the deep process first shares the experience of the process with his or her facilitator. I have found that listening is very important at this point. I may ask some clarifying questions; mostly I listen. I then usually ask the person if she or he is ready for any response. If they say no, I don't give it. If they say yes, I share what I *noticed* during the deep work and any responses or associations that are mine.

Basically, the same process happens in the group. I do think it is important in and of itself to share deep processes with the group, *and* if a person does not want to or need to, that's all right too.

In the group response and associations the group usually calls attention to responses that sound to them like interpretation, and they ask people giving these responses to check out what's going on with them. Responses and associations should be just that—responses and associations. I believe it is imperative not to interfere with the person's experience of her or his own process. Giving associations or responses is giving information. Interpretation and projections are another matter.

Deep Process Facilitation

Deep process facilitation is a skill that comes with training and experience. Usually, this training and experience are necessary in order to unlearn what we have been taught. Frequently, those in the helping professions and highly educated persons like lawyers, physicians, college professors, and so forth have the worst time. I think this is largely because they believe that they should and do know something.

The idea of training facilitators is not new. Freud long ago set up the model that the people who are to be analysts need to be analyzed. Unfortunately, he had the right idea and the wrong modality. As Jeffrey Masson so ably points out in *Final Analysis*,[2] not only does the model not work, but those who are training in the model of psychoanalysis do not follow the model.

Good process facilitators have to be willing to face and confront their addictive process and, if they are "helpers," be willing to see how what they have been trained to do is perpetuating the addictive disease. Notice that I said "be willing." They have to be on the way, they do not have to have arrived. One of the reasons I believe that good recovery is so critical is that the addictive process has played such a subtle role in the shaping of helpers. As I said earlier, we are often trained out of what is really healing in us.

Also, good process facilitators have to be *present*. We cannot be in our heads trying to figure out what's going on, trying to control the situation, or not wanting to be there. Nor can we be clear in our facilitation if we ourselves have a deep process emerging that needs our attention. I consider one measure of a good recovery to be the ability to say no to a request to facilitate someone when you know you just could not be present.

Good facilitators are not perfect, and they don't have it all together. They do their own work; they know that there will be times when they can't be present, they can identify those times, and they have the self-respect and respect for others not to sit with someone at those times.

SAFETY. The prime functions of the facilitator are to keep a person safe and to be present. Often, a person doing deep process work becomes quite active, as in, for example, a rage process. It is critical that persons in deep process be safe to do their work. Frequently, a process is so deep and the individual is so involved in the process that he or she has little awareness of their physical surroundings. This kind of focus is usually necessary to do the work that needs to be done. It is important that a person doing work not have to split his or her attention.

This safety issue is one of the reasons I quit doing individual work. I could see deep processes coming up, and I knew that I could not, alone, provide the safety needed for persons to do their work. I became increasingly aware that my office itself was not safe for deep process work. Most offices where "therapy" is done are not safe for deep process work. Also, I recognized that individual work is antithetical to Living in Process. The individual model gives the therapist too much power and cannot model participation and a leveling of power the way a group can.

Before I quit seeing individual clients, one of the ways I tried to cope with this issue was to call together a group of people to be present with the client who needed to do deep work. I did this several times with a Vietnam vet who had enormous amounts of pain and rage. I usually asked people who knew and cared about the person. In the case of the Vietnam vet, I invited some men who had met him at a Men's Intensive, other clients who knew him, and my teenage son, who had met him and had come to be friends with him. It was a powerful experience for all of us.

I cannot emphasize too strongly the critical need for safety in deep process work. At one of the Intensives, one of the facilitators was not really present in her facilitating, and we all learned a lot about the need for safety. The woman who was doing her process work was a very strong woman who was dealing with a lot of rage. At one point, she stood up and was flinging herself from side to side. The people holding the pillows and mattresses were doing everything they could to contain her, but she was powerful and she was *big.* The facilitator did not stop this process, but let it continue. Just as I was about to intervene, on one wild fling, she threw herself between two mattresses and hit her head on a brick fireplace. I was concerned that she had a concussion, and we whisked her off to the hospital to be checked. Luckily, she didn't.

When we processed this incident, her facilitator said that she was uneasy, but she didn't want to interfere with the woman's process. I pointed out that she probably would have another crack (no pun intended) at a process, but that it was terribly difficult to facilitate the process of a dead person. Safety is of utmost importance!

Another learning to be pointed out here is that it is absolutely necessary for facilitators to trust their intuition and awareness. The facilitator just mentioned was getting uneasy, but she did not trust herself and she did not listen to herself. Instead, she let her thinking mind and her theory interfere, with almost disastrous results.

TOUCHING. It is not within the scope of this book to do facilitator training. I wanted to introduce deep process work and say a few things about facilitation. Still, I do want to say something about touching during someone's deep process.

In general, I do not touch during a deep process. Touching someone who is in a deep process can often stop the process. If I feel tempted to touch someone during a deep process, I need to stop, go inside, and see what is getting triggered in me. Usually, my *need* to touch is related to something in me that I want to avoid. By touching, I not only shut off the other person's process that is triggering mine, I shut off my own process. Also, I sometimes discover that I am getting frightened or for some reason want to keep the other person's process "under control" (or my illusion of control), and that is part of the disease of the relationship-addicted psychotherapist. I have seen many psychotherapists do this under the guise of caring or hugging. My perception is that touching is often used as a control mechanism. Now that I have more confidence in a person's deep process and my ability to be with it, I find less need to touch.

Sometimes during a deep process, the person who is doing it will ask to be touched or held. Each situation is unique, and, in general, I ask people to stay with what they are feeling and see what comes. Often the issue is not offering a "fix." By staying with their feelings without being touched, people discover that they have what they need to deal with whatever is coming up. This process learning may turn out to be as important or more so than the content of the particular process.

Of course, this is not a hard-and-fast rule. Little, if anything, is in Living Process work. I was facilitating a woman and, at one point, she seemed rather stuck where she was in her process. As I watched her, I had this strong urge to touch her between her left shoulder blade and her spine. I checked myself out carefully, and I felt pretty clear, so I gently touched her there with a couple of fingers. She suddenly went very deep into a pain process that was very intense. I hoped I had not done something wrong.

Later, she asked me, "How did you know?" "How did I know *what?*" I asked. "How did you know I'd had a very traumatic and painful injury right in that spot?" I hadn't.

Good facilitation is simple, and it is a lot more than meets the eye. Anyone can facilitate, and there are many skills to being a good facilitator.

A SACRED TRUST.   Almost always, I feel very honored to have the opportunity to sit with someone during a deep process. I learn so much, and it is powerful to be witness to such intense healing. I often say to the Trainees that I think of deep process facilitation as a sacred trust.

Deep-process facilitation is not a job, it is not a skill, it is not a technique, and it is not a profession. It is an honor. When I have the privilege of sitting with someone, I am usually blessed. As one former Trainee says,

> I have heard you talk often about process work being sacred work and have not understood/known what that meant. Today I believe that I have a knowing/understanding of what that means to me. I was with [a woman] while she was doing her work in group a few weeks ago and realized that all I was, was an overseer. Only there to provide a safe space and minimally more.

> Also during [her] process I was able to finally put words
> to why I have been so uncomfortable with "rebirthing." It
> feels like they have taken something sacred (i.e., process)
> and made it into a technique. I also know that that is why I
> was so angry as a kid when I sat in temple and watched the
> hypocrisy occurring . . . that they were taking something
> so sacred (i.e., spirituality) and making it into a technique
> (i.e., religion).

Being a witness to true healing and realizing that we don't control it—
nor do we have to—is truly powerful.

Final Thoughts About Deep Process Work

DEEP PROCESS WORK IS FAMILIAR.   Deep process work is probably not
new to any of us. Most of us have deep processes as infants and as children. Unfortunately, part of parenting has been to train us out of deep
processes.

Many of us know about deep process work, because we have
done it, and, yet, usually we have not been allowed or have not
allowed ourselves to go all the way through a deep process so that it
gets finished. Often in the past when we started a deep process, we
scared ourselves and others to death. Also, we frequently felt or were
told that we were hysterical or "losing it." Needless to say, few of us
have been encouraged to do our deep work.

THE PARADOX OF KNOWING AND NOT KNOWING.   One of the exciting and
also scary aspects of deep process work is the knowing and not knowing. We frequently describe the Training group as a "group in search of
a rule." When many people come to the Intensives to learn to do deep
process work, they believe that if they just learn what to say and what
to do, then they will be all right. One of the men who recently attended
an Intensive says what I am trying to say better than I can:

> I expected a shock from the experience [at the Big Sky
> Intensive] and in a sense that is what happened. In my
> attempt to control, I planned in advance what I wanted to
> accomplish at the lodge. I was sure I'd get a big jump for-
> ward in my recovery from my disease if I could only get an
> understanding of the goings-on by asking a bunch of left-
> brained questions. My confusion, much of which I believe
> was a result of years of misdiagnosis and mistreatment, has

taught me to question everything. I've always been able to learn by questioning and it seemed the logical approach. What now seems to catch me off guard is what I learn by being quiet, waiting and noticing. And I do it, in a sense, alone. Questioning is still important, though I can see how it kept me stuck in my disease in my psychiatrist's office. I'm glad that I finally questioned myself about what I was actually getting in therapy . . . any questions?

I'm struggling with the awareness that I'm powerless. I see how my long-term attempts to control have caused me pain and kept me from enjoying my life. To deal with it I've tried substance abuse, isolation, denial, and psychotherapy, to name a few. I'm exhausted from running away afraid, pushing it down, and trying to cover my tracks with work, pity, or something else. I'm tired of living in my past while worrying about my future, and always focusing on the negative aspects of both. I want to learn how not to keep beating myself up.

One of the more amusing stories we share in the Living Process Network is about a Training group who desperately needed a rule. I was a little late getting to one of the Training sessions, and when I arrived, the group excitedly told me that they had discovered a "rule." "What is it?" I asked. "When you sit with someone, call them by the right name."

This was the first meeting of a new Training group, and they really did not know each other very well. One of the women in the group had gone into a deep process, and one of the other new Trainees had dared to sit with her, desperately asking everyone around what her name was. He was given the wrong name, and he used it. At a lull in the process, she had corrected him. He felt terrible but was sure he had discovered a rule that, in some way for him, saved the day.

After he shared this insight about a "rule," the woman he had facilitated spoke up and said that she was not sure that she agreed. She had always felt like she was invisible and not being called by the right name had been facilitative to her process.

In a Living Process System, we are always learning about what we know, what we don't know, and paradox. Living this way is not always easy, and it is certainly living.

One woman wrote me some interesting thoughts about knowing:

I learned a lot about what I know and what I don't know. Example: I have thought that I know what will happen if I do such and such *and* I don't know that at all. That kind of illusion of knowing has stopped me in my tracks many times. While at Lynn's I did some deep process work that was about incest. Some of my resistance to knowing that I had been incested by my father was knowing (or so I thought) I wouldn't be free to pursue relationships with men or that then I couldn't love my father anymore. During this deep work, I was able to own that my father had incested me and to know deep inside that that doesn't mean I didn't/don't love my dad. I also feel a bit more open to relationships with men. On the other hand, I have denied and minimized what I do know way inside. What has been feeling very significant is that I am letting myself know those things more and more. I remember that one of the things I would hear other people say about your speeches/your books, etc., was that you articulated what they knew and didn't have the words for. I couldn't really relate to that. I chalked my different perception to my knowing you more through Intensives and the Training Year. This year when I heard you (speak in my town) I did know more what you were saying from my own experience—it was not abstract anymore. I feel more and more alive; even though a lot of times I feel a lot of sadness at seeing things as they are, I feel joy because I am feeling/I am alive! This knowing is such a paradox; on some level I don't know anything and on another level, I know as much *as I am willing to know what I know!*

M.G.

The paradox is not always easy, and it certainly is more in keeping with the universe than our simplistic linear or cause-and-effect thinking. Another woman puts it differently:

What I have loved learning the most lately is how little intellectualizing I have to do around all this. Ever since October in Hemet I have been aware of a need to let go of so much that I "know," and relearn my life through entirely different channels.

Part of Living in Process is seeing what we see and knowing what we know, which is not always easy. Several women have written to me about integrating their deep process work into their lives. One describes it this way:

I am also deeply aware of the invitation into my disease this latest incest memory . . . has given me. On Saturday morning I ran my car through a yield sign into another car and damaged the whole front end of my car, plus the other's rear fender. I can only say that I was not in my body, and it took until midafternoon to get some sense of reconnection. I feel as if this all happened in a dream. I feel so disconnected at times, more a nightmare than a dream. This latest information about being raped by my uncle is so overwhelming, I move in and out of denial, belief, anger, numbness. What brings me back to myself is the acceptance that "it makes sense." On my drive home from Montana (I drove alone and took four days), I stayed overnight with the aunt that has always been my other parent. After hours of talking to her about this period in my life, asking questions and skirting the issue, I decided to tell her about what her two brothers did to me. She was shocked, and she believed me. I guess there is little difference in telling her now or telling her twenty-seven years ago, although who knows what my life would have become if I had not known the extended silence of my life. I am certainly better equipped to live with this rape now than I was twenty-seven years ago. I do want to heal.

She goes on to say this:

I experienced a significant deep process those last few days in Montana, a process that allowed me to see that I can allow myself another training year with you, Anne. Since I was operating that last week as a twelve-year-old girl with a thirty-nine-year-old woman standing up for me and choosing to live differently this time, I really felt my higher power giving me the "courage to change the things I can." In my checkout I was operating in the chaos I felt so often in a family with nine children and no tools for getting my needs met. When another year of training was offered I could not think past rushing into the first training session in September and the immediate expense that I needed to discuss with [my husband]. When I asked you for an option of joining a weekly process group in Minneapolis, little did I know at the time how important it was for me to ask for that space. My deep process was finally triggered on Thursday afternoon.

This process led me into taking huge gulps of air and crying not to be suffocated. "I want to breathe!!" I couldn't get enough air! I got in touch with the extent of the abuse I've experienced, from thinking my mother wanted to kill me in the crib, to my dad taking a leather strap after me, two uncles who sexually abused and raped me, my older brother and sister telling me to just keep quiet, don't cause trouble, my husband in a drunken rage kicking me and cracking my rib. Even the kitchen at Mountain Lodge entered in there! I was pushing it all away. I felt despair, "Why?!" I felt rage. "Why!!" And I felt how little trust I had for two parents who I thought wanted to "kill" me, who would *tell* me what I was going to do next with my life, whether it was getting a job or going away to college. I was offered no choices. In being *told* to take the training year again I felt trapped into abuse by people I didn't trust, even though I know these "people" (my parents, the training group) love me. In my process I actually felt how hard I have fought for my life and how trapped I felt with no options. And I could see how my addictive process will also kill me. So what do I let go of?

Anne, giving me the space of an *option* to a second year of training gave me an element of control of my own life that allowed me to enter into the confusion I needed to work through the paradox of letting go.

Another woman writes about struggling with some of the same issues:

I came back from the . . . Intensive with so many new understandings. Some have been very scary and almost more than I care to know—finally I have begun to look at what has really happened with both my eyes open to look at it. This has been very hard for me, even excruciating at times. At times I have just looked at it very, very fast and then turned away again. . . . I have been thinking lately of the saying "We are as sick as our secrets" and knowing that somehow I needed to begin speaking again, out loud, about what I now remember. I had a hard enough time doing that at the Intensive; it's even harder here. Sometimes I have to say it first with my hands before I can let the words go out into the open air. Again and again, my body has been helping me, showing me the way each step. I realize that I am totally dependent upon my body and the Process. I am very glad when I can recognize this and turn it all over.

When I left the Intensive, one of my fears was that I would "lose it," lose feelings of calm, contentment, trust, the knowing of how to listen to my body, the ability to let go and truly turn it over to my Process. . . . One of the things I've done since then is begun to cook for myself—good, real meals—I saw clearly that this was really important for me. I also have tried very hard not to deny everything I learned during my deep process work. I *know* denying it makes me sick. And I pray. If not "unceasingly," then at least frequently! I have prayed thanks over and over and over again, sometimes to remind myself of how much I have to be thankful of, and oftentimes because I just *feel* very grateful. This is my life-rope now. Always this guidance and calm center is there for me, and I'm really glad because I surely do need it.

Sometimes the information we are given in our deep process *is* excruciating, and sometimes it *is* difficult to integrate into our daily lives, yet there seems to be something to what Jesus said, "Ye shall know the truth and the truth shall make you free."

I include the following letter because it is a good example of the unbelievably painful experiences you can have and still heal:

I feel a need to tell you what my deep processing has revealed to me—sometimes I can trust that it is the truth and other times it feels so unbelievable—too crazy. It is as though my sister and brother grew up in a different family—their reality is not even close to mine—then I feel like I'm crazy—that all this came from my imagination. My process revealed that sexual abuse—violent and sadistic abuse—began when I was an infant—I never felt loved by my mother so any attention, affection—from my father— was all I had. Our mother died when I was a child. She was sick and suffering long before that, so she was, as I remember her, unavailable—just not there for me. My brother was born two years after me—the family's Christ Child—a son —a process was triggered when [one of the Trainees] went down [to do his work] in September. People were so concerned—saying things like—that war experience must have been a terrible secret to carry around with *no one* wanting to hear or listen to it—you must have felt so alone with that secret—and then so many people were there for him when he went down—I had to leave—I went outside and cried—I felt so ashamed of my feelings—it felt like he was my brother—in pain—and I envied and resented all those people caring about his pain—I felt like no one has ever wanted to hear my secret—it was just too crazy—in the telling—I have had therapists block me—one told me—are you sure you're not just trying to torture yourself with this? She couldn't stand hearing my story—another therapist tried to get me to release the pain with cybernetics—and other techniques from a training school in the East—"I'll help you release the pain—but don't *feel* it and you don't need to tell me the details" was the message I got.

This is what my process has revealed to me . . . my father was a sadistic sexual addict—He taught me that I was a sex object—there to serve his needs. I was the object he needed and despised at the same time. He got off on my pain—my powerlessness, my terror, and my humiliation—I became totally absorbed into his reality—and very codependent with him—caught up in his disease. My hate, my love and sex were all tangled up—at one point, I would feel very powerful—and at another, very powerless. I felt I should protect him and somehow find a way to help him stop— Well, I'm no longer protecting him—he was very sick and I got very sick—and I'm still enraged that that little girl never had a fighting chance to escape from his madness.

C.L.

She goes on to delineate some of his sadistic sexual abuse of her and I will spare us the details. However, the details are important to her and powerful for her to claim as her past. Paradoxically, as she lets herself remember and work through these memories *as they come up*, she regains her life. When these memories are suppressed or forced up, she does not have access to her life to live.

It is key that a facilitator not have an agenda for a person in process, because memories as painful as these can only be integrated when our inner being is ready to handle them.

DEEP PROCESS TRANSCENDS TIME AND SPACE.   I have often had the experience of deep process work that transcended time and space. Some years ago, if someone had said that to me, I would have been skeptical, at best.

Still, I have seen people during deep processes be a thirty-five-year-old man in a room at an Intensive, and also be an infant in a crib. Both realities are present, and both are very real. The sounds and movements are of the infant, and the body is of a grown man. Experiences like this are quite common in deep process work. There seems to be a collapsing of the time-space continuum, and I have come more and more to know from my own experience with deep process work that time is not linear and it may well be possible to change our past. This changing of the past will not happen if we are *trying* to change the past, and by going through the feelings that are present right here, right now, it is possible to alter what we thought was real, alter our experience of it, and alter its effect on us. We cannot, however, predetermine the direction of that change. We have only to take a leap of faith and trust the outcome.

It is another paradox that, after doing all this hard work and going through these difficult processes, we seem to look and feel better. In fact, some people seem to look younger and younger as they do their work. At one point in developing this work, I was discussing my need to drop the word *therapy* in my work with the German Trainees. "Then what will we call it?" they asked. "You know how Germany is. We have to have a category for everything."

"I know," said one. "We could call it a Schönheit farm, a beauty farm. People get prettier, younger, and healthier. Isn't that what's supposed to happen at a beauty farm?" Frankly, I tried a beauty farm once, and this Living in Process works better.

THE PROCESS OF THE PROCESS. No discussion of the Living Process System and deep process work would be complete without mentioning the importance of the process of the process.

Most psychotherapies and most psychological approaches, and consequently most people, are most concerned about *content*. If a person touches an incest memory, immediately we want to know *content*: who, when, how, why? We have become hooked on content because we have developed helping professions that are hooked on understanding.

Often, in deep process work, it is the process of the process that is important and is where the real learning takes place. When we get hooked on content, we may miss the process learning altogether. Let me give a short example to illustrate what I am saying.

Several years ago, we had a man in the Training group who had a master's degree in business from Harvard. Obviously, he was very intelligent, and he also had a lot of unfinished processes moving around inside him. He desperately wanted to understand himself and get his life figured out. He spent most of his time thinking, intellectualizing, and generally using his very good brain.

His deep process would have nothing to do with all his intellectual acuity (I said that our deep processes had a sense of humor). Whenever a deep process would come up, he would eagerly "hit the mats." For over a year there was no content to his deep work. He would go through the feelings, and no pictures, no images, would come. It is to his credit that he continued to do his deep process work. At the point where he had completely given up believing that he would ever get any content, and had finally given up on his desperate need to *understand*, he began to have images in his deep work. There is only one thing more stubborn than we are—our Living Process.

Again, I want to reiterate that deep process work is only a small part of Living in Process. Living in Process is a whole way of life, and doing deep process work is part of making a shift into a way of being that is far more life-giving and life-sustaining than any system we have thus far developed. If we lived in a Living Process System, we probably would not have that much deep process work to do.

A woman in the Training group expresses this interplay of facing addictions and learning to Live in Process very well:

> I have been working with [a former Trainee] for over four years now as she has helped me in adjusting to the breakup of my thirty-year marriage. I worked with her individually first, and for the last two years have been in the Process group that she and [another former Trainee] have co-facilitated. In addition I have attended Al-Anon regularly during these same years as well as O.A. about a year. All of the growth and support that came as a result of this has been invaluable to me. First I survived, then found myself developing and growing in ways I never imagined possible. Then I began to realize that what I was not able to do was to work through the grief of the loss of this relationship—not necessarily of what it was, but of what I wanted it to be. Feelings of betrayal are strong, along with some bitterness that my life is not, and will not be, what I had expected and planned for. This is one of the major things I hope to deal with while in Training.
>
> Other concerns I have are my own—apart from this particular relationship. I feel I have made much progress in my recovery from codependence, and also agree with you that using the term *codependence* may make it easier to not take responsibility for one's own problems and growth needs. I found that even as I grew in the Al-Anon program,

I developed other addictive behaviors, such as overeating. I feel right now that food is my substance of choice to "reward" myself. Also in my uncertainty regarding my capability of being totally responsible for myself I feel that I have to explore the issues of work and money. After reading your last book and being involved in some S.L.A.A. [Sex and Love Addicts Anonymous] meetings at the last Intensive, I want to explore these areas, realizing that relationship (and/or sex) issues exist for me. I think they played a part in the selection of my mate as well as how the relationship developed and its eventual dissolution. What has happened can't be changed, but understanding can hopefully make acceptance easier and also allow me to be involved in healthier relationships in the future.

J.B.

We cannot transform without recovery, and recovery cannot happen without transformation.

The following is a letter written by a man in his sixties after he completed the Training in Germany:

Since 1975 I had gone through a lot of therapies, for I did not feel capable of living. The last therapy I had was with R.K. I got over some difficulties, so that I was at least able to do my job. I was functioning more or less. But I did not come to live. I had no feeling of self-worth. I ran down myself; I pointedly punished myself—or I was arrogant. I felt my own failure, in vain made great efforts, and unconsciously reproached the people in my surroundings for this failure. I was suffering very much from the feeling that people disliked me. Soon I knew that the reasons were to be found in myself. So, I tried to control me and the others. This led to a vicious circle. I was not present. I could not feel.

Due to the deep process work and the philosophy I got to know through you, fundamentally new aspects came into my life. This became obvious in the first year of training. I noticed that my relation with people was changing, and this was quite obviously due to the fact that changes took place in myself. I could let go of my attempts to control me and my effect on others. You had advised me to work the first three "steps"; with these steps I started again and again. In February, 1988, in the Men's Intensive in Boulder, I consciously experienced for the first time that people simply accepted and loved me. I was deeply moved.

You did not try to change me through manipulation. You accepted me lovingly, as I was, even with my disease. You let me stew in my own juice, until sometimes this and sometimes the other was done. In this way, I always found something new myself.

I learned to differentiate when I am present and when I am not; I can remember that you said this was one of the beginnings of recovery. I learned to endure it when I was not capable of feeling, and then I was glad that my frozen feelings were thawing now and then and more and more often.

I recognized how pernicious it is to be a good nice boy. I came to learn that the responsibility for what I am and feel lies nowhere else than with me. Above all I learned what responsibility is: That taking the responsibility for my life does not mean to punish myself for my life, my essence, but that with this responsibility I accept me and my life, and thus own it.

It is not always necessary to take the same route to transformation and recovery, and I was impressed with the grasp the following young man had of the Living Process work I am doing:

A little about myself. I started drinking when I was twelve. By the time I was thirty-six I was unable to control alcohol. It is the typical story I am sure you have heard many times in many ways.

It has been nineteen months since I stopped drinking. When I quit I did not go to A.A. or any other conventional therapy.

I have been a serious student of Buddhist meditation and J. Krishnamurti since I was about nineteen. When it became absolutely clear to me that I had to stop drinking I was too scared to go to conventional therapy or A.A. or even trust my Buddhist friends and teachers. Most of my drinking companions were refugees from A.A. and various treatment centers.

I did two things. First, I began to take good care of the body, good diet and exercise. Second, I began to meditate in a different manner than I had been taught, instead of directing attention to a specific object (tunnel vision) such as breathing. For example, I would sit still and let attention go to whatever was distracting me at the moment, whether it was thoughts, feelings, emotions, sensations, and give complete attention or completely embrace whatever it was with each breath, without reacting. For example, if I desired a drink I would embrace the desire without repressing the desire (control) or acting out the desire by drinking or whatever (also control).

I began to trust this process completely because the more I did it, the freer and happier I felt, the more I realized I could turn to this process, which I secretly named the wisdom of attention process, whenever something was distracting or bothering me instead of turning to drink or other processes or substances which are unhealthy, including meditation teachers.

What excites me the most is I feel what you found is not another therapy technique or spiritual technique, but simply that if we quit distracting ourselves from our own living process and begin to get in touch with it, simply allow it to be, it will guide us and eventually reveal everything to us. I feel this process is authentic or true selfhood. Any technique for therapy or meditation is an imposition on the process of authentic selfhood, therefore becomes part of the disease.

I wanted to share these ideas and some of my process with you and let you know your work has touched me.

W.M.

I was very touched by this letter and this man's feeling for the Living Process work. The most exciting thing about this work is that it works. People do not just become adjusted to a sick system. They become healed, and being healed means that they have the opportunity fully to live their life.

The work I am presenting here goes way beyond psychotherapy as we have known it to a "postmodern"[3] approach to being. It is "of" a new paradigm. New scientific awareness is ushering in the potentiality for the human species to embrace its rightful place as part of the planet and part of the universe with a wisdom that is old, yet new. We do not have to give up technology in order to move into the twenty-first century. We need to recognize that the approach to truth that technology has represented can no longer be seen as the only approach to truth. Indeed, this approach cannot be seen as a valid approach to any truth other than mechanistic truth, and the planet and people are not machines.

I believe this work goes far beyond therapy and recovery, as we have known both. It offers the real possibility of healing and a genuine system shift.

Overview of the Intensives and Training

The Intensives and Training Year are not psychotherapy, nor are they built on the scientific model out of which psychotherapy comes. The model of healing, if there is one, is a community model. Everyone who is at an Intensive or Training is participating and working on and sharing his or her own issues. There is no support for a power differential, and if people initially try to put the Trainees or other facilitators on a pedestal or defer to them, that usually breaks down as we all share and do our deep process work.

In a community model, we are all living and working together, and the Intensives and especially the Training are integrated into our lives. The model is not one of isolation from life in which everything is manipulated to be an "ideal, perfect" situation. Every Intensive and Training session is different, what happens at either is what happens, and we deal openly with what happens. There are no "secret" staff meetings to decide how to deal with a problem. Everything is dealt with in the group, and everyone is encouraged to bring gripes, complaints, attractions, observations, or anything else back to the group. The power is in the group, and the power is also in the individual as we stress that some of the most important learning may not take place in the group.

Most of the learning comes from people in the group sharing their deep process work, sharing their struggles with their addictions, sharing their stories, sharing their awarenesses, and responding and sharing with one another. Anyone in the group can and does make comments along the way or after and responses to everyone's sharing always prove rich and powerful. Any of us in the group may point out examples of the addictive process or Living in Process as we hear them in the sharing.

Most people report that the Intensives are the safest and most respectful places they have ever been. This is not because we *try* to make them safe and respectful. It is because all there are striving to be as honest as they can be, all are participating, and no one is trying to manipulate the group, individuals, or the setting. The Intensives are just like life. They are what is, and we deal with what's there. When one "contrives" to make a setting safe or "protect" the participants, the end result is that they do not trust themselves, and themselves, after all, is what they have.

Interestingly enough, these process groups rarely get into the group processes that I learned that all groups experience (power plays, coalitions, subgroups, "hump the leader," and so forth). When they do, we all know that we are dealing with an addictive process, and it is confronted as such. Many people have said, "I am safe here. My disease is not."

As I have said, during Intensives and Training sessions, everyone is supported in the fine art of "noticing." People are supported in whatever they need to do: rest, go for walks, not come to group, not go to Twelve-Step meetings, leave the Intensive. They are supported in beginning to choose themselves as their main point of reference. The group will meet when it meets. If they want to be in it, fine. If not, that's fine too. They have the opportunity to see what they need and are encouraged to act on it. The issue is the learning, not what's right or wrong. Even when people decide to leave Intensives, they are encouraged to learn what they need to from that experience (or not—as they choose).

I usually only give one input session with the previously mentioned information about the addictive process and deep process work. Sometimes, I will share most of this information at one time, and sometimes I will only give a little input at the opening session and then make comments as issues come up in the group or as people share their deep process work. How and when I make the input depends upon the group, how I feel, what happens in the group, and what seems to be needed at each point in the group. Instead of following my old training, which led me to believe that I could schedule and design what I wanted to happen in the group and what I wanted people to learn, now I am myself, do my own work, stay present to myself and the group, and live in the moment. I am much less exhausted and realize that my taking responsibility for others was not respectful of them or of myself. This work has been so much more healthy for me and, I believe, shows more respect for others than any kind of therapy work I have ever seen. This kind of work is good for me, and it is good for others. The community focus breaks down feelings of isolation and also, without attempting to control anyone or anything, all of us are ushered into participation in a holomovement universe. All of us, without trying to do it, find ourselves beginning to operate out of a different paradigm.

In the final section, I will explore some of the theoretical and scientific issues that need to be addressed to understand where we have been, where we are, and where we have the opportunity to go in healing in a new scientific paradigm.

Part III

The Scientific Paradigm, Psychotherapy, and the Living Process Paradigm

In Part I, I shared my own rise and demise as a psychotherapist, my journey from excited, hopeful anticipation and faith as a young psychotherapist, to burnout and confusion, to recovery and belief that people really can heal but not with the models we have developed, which have arisen out of a mechanistic, scientific worldview.

In Part II, I explored an alternative to psychotherapy as we know it. It is a model that is more congruent with my experience and my beliefs and that I believe is supported by postmodern scientific theories and discoveries. I have shared in detail the work that has emerged out of individuals courageously facing their addictive process and attempting to be true to their own life process, fully participating in their lives and in all life. I have suggested that when one gives up one's addictions and confronts one's underlying addictive process, the deep processes that have been masked by the addictions begin to emerge, and I have discussed why I think the models that psychotherapy has developed to work with those deep processes are not only not helpful, they are usually harmful.

This is not to say that some people have not been helped by psychotherapy. They have. I am even sure that I, indeed, helped some clients. To be sure, I cared deeply about them and utilized everything I had been taught to facilitate their healing. Yet as I look back, I was, by necessity, doomed to the frustration of Sisyphus because without a doubt the model out of which I was coming made it impossible for my clients and me to accomplish what we wanted and needed. I believe that at some very deep, perhaps preconscious level, every therapist knows this and that is why they are always seeking some new technique, some new approach. We all meant, and mean, well. We just did not have the theory and tools at our disposal to do what we knew needed to be done. Because the worldview out of which we were operating was presented to us as reality in our training, we really had no place to turn, except to our own niggling feelings of discomfort and uneasiness. Out of desperation, doing my own work, and trusting my perceptions, I have evolved the kind of work that I presented in Part II.

Now we are ready for the tough part. I will try to present and clarify the theoretical assumptions that have been the foundation of modern psychotherapy and the scientific worldview on which these assumptions are based. I firmly believe that if we presume what is only a worldview to be truth and reality, and/or if the assumptions of that worldview are not articulated and understood, we become slaves to it.

I do not pretend to be an authority on the history and philosophy of science. There are much greater minds than mine writing on the current paradigm shift in our scientific worldview. Many theoretical physicists, philosophers, and historians are presenting learned books, articles, and papers on the topic of what is most often called the "postmodern scientific worldview."[1] In addition, there are writers decrying the use of psychotherapy and citing the harm it can cause.[2] However, I find some of the books on the history and philosophy of science very tedious to read (and I encounter huge blocks of hostility when I ask the people who train with me to read them). Thus, it seems to me, this information is not so easily accessed by the general public. One has to care a lot even to try to understand these issues, and most people do not have the energy to care that much.

In this third section, I will try to make the important understandable. First of all, I deeply believe that those who go for help need to know and understand the assumptions that underlie not only *what* the professionals they see think but *how* they think and how they *operate*. Unless these assumptions are clearly understood and articulated, we can never hope to be free of them or heal from them when we need to.

Many New Age and/or "holistic" approaches, for example, have changed the *content* of their thinking. They talk about holism, spirituality, the environment, and many concerns that seem to encompass a postmodern paradigm. Yet, when they actually work with people, I find that their *behavior* and their techniques continue to come out of a mechanistic cause-and-effect paradigm that is subtly based upon the illusion of control.

Also, I believe that the professionals need clearly to understand the scientific and theoretical assumptions out of which they function. Most people who go into clinical work have little or no interest in the science and the theory behind what they are learning. They set themselves up like mechanics. They want to learn the techniques of how to "fix," get their "mechanics' license," and begin work. I do not want to sound cold and hard-hearted here. From my own experience and my experience with others in the healing professions, I know that we all have great concern for those with whom we work. Yet, the profession itself has set up a system that moves more and more toward procedures, tools, and techniques and toward training technicians who can be certified as tested for specific skills. Values, concerns, spirituality, love, and caring all have taken a backseat to the illusion of objectivity and "skills."

So, even though I know that there is much I do not understand about modernist and postmodernist science and its relationship to psychology and psychotherapy, I want to share what I *do* know and understand. I have learned from my previous books that when I put forth my truth as I at present understand it, some people want to listen. I have loved science and I have loved the field of psychotherapy, and I know that my basic commitment to science and to life is to be open-minded, to challenge dogmatism and rigidity when I see it in myself and others, and to trust myself when I know that something is wrong.

So little true healing has been brought about through the work of psychotherapists that we must conclude that something has been seriously wrong with the field of psychology and psychotherapy and with the helping professions in general. I believe I have found an important piece in understanding the "what and why" of the puzzle, and I want to present my current understanding in this final section.

Are Helpers Helpful?

I have devoted an entire section to telling my story as a psychotherapist; I certainly do not need to repeat that here. I do, however, want to focus upon a specific thread that forced me to look deeper and deeper into the history and philosophy of science. That thread is codependence.

Initially, codependents were roughly defined as family members of an alcoholic. Then the definition broadened. We saw the same syndrome in dysfunctional families with no alcoholic. Then we began to define codependents as anyone who lived with, worked with, or had an ongoing relationship with an alcoholic or addict. Because I was consulting with treatment centers and working with drug and alcohol abuse counselors, I could see that this *definition* applied to counselors who worked with alcoholics or other kinds of addicts and that I should be alert to Al-Anon or codependence issues in those with whom I was consulting. I was also observing the same sorts of behaviors, attitudes, and assumptions in those working with addicts that I observed in addicts' family members, and I could see some counselors and therapists "feeding off" the disease in their clients, just as I had seen this in the most well-meaning family members.

Simultaneously with these observations, I became convinced that addiction was much more widespread than I had ever previously imagined. I began to consider that most (probably all) counselors and therapists could be considered codependents by this definition because they were probably all working with active addicts, in numbers far greater than they realized. It is not surprising that this was not a popular idea with some therapists, yet I also found an amazing number who were open to exploring the concept. As I look back, I can see that there was another significant thread developing in my personal life that very much affected my professional life.

In my personal life, I was working very hard on my own recovery. I could see that the Twelve-Step groups of Alcoholics Anonymous worked, and I accepted the information and recommendations of others attending meetings who seemed to "have what I wanted" (while there were many psychotherapists I liked, I did not see many who had the aliveness and serenity that I wanted for myself). I began to heal. As a result of my healing, or in spite of my healing, or unrelated to my healing (I tend to think it is the first, but that may be my need to think I am in control!), my family began to heal. As a family, we have been through codependency treatment twice, and we have worked hard.

During this period, Dr. Diane Fassel and I wrote *The Addictive Organization*.[3] Since the publication of that book, thousands of people have spoken or written to us about their recovery and what has happened to them in their addictive organizations as a result of their personal recovery. Their words differ, and the stories are essentially the same. They go like this: "I'm an addict [alcoholic, workaholic—whatever kind of addict, it doesn't matter]. I am in recovery and I feel good about my recovery. It's going well. My life has really improved and I basically feel happy. Because of my recovery and, I believe, the changes in me, my family is changing. We are all actually getting better. *But . . .* I am not sure that I can maintain my sobriety and continue to work in my addictive workplace. If I really put my sobriety first, I cannot continue to work where I do." Often, I suggest to these people that they attend Al-Anon, with the workplace as the addict in their lives.

As I talked with people about their sobriety and what they needed to do to stay healthy, I found some interesting phenomena emerging. As people get healthier, they are no longer able to support the level of pathology that is present in their workplace. One of two things usually happens. As the individuals get healthier than the system in which they work, they either leave and start their own entrepreneurial efforts, or they get fired. They cannot stay and remain sober, and the workplace cannot tolerate persons who no longer support the pathology of the organization. In addition, recovery often brings about a real systems clash within individuals, within families, within organizations, and within societal systems. The recovering person has to move on and keep growing. Nonrecovering systems seek to maintain the status quo as a closed system; they are static.

At first, I only looked at this phenomenon from the perspective of the pathology of the workplace. Recently, I have begun also to look at it in terms of the individual in recovery. When we reach a certain level in recovery, we have to look at the *way* we do our work and see if the way we do our work threatens our sobriety.

Imagine my surprise when I realized that my personal recovery also had led me on a path that required professional recovery; I no longer had the ability to be or to identify with being a psychotherapist. I had come to a place where I had to leave the field of psychotherapy as I knew it. Since then, I have called myself a recovering psychotherapist (as in recovering from having been a psychotherapist, *not* a psychotherapist in recovery). My personal and professional paths have been parallel and intertwined.

When I reached the awareness that because they worked with addicts (again, probably many more than they knew), those therapists who were not themselves active addicts were probably codependents (and maybe both), I began to look at the field of psychotherapy as a whole. I was somewhat horrified when I realized that the entire field of psychotherapy was *training into the disease of codependence.* We are trained to believe that it is our *responsibility* to know what is going on with our clients and what needs to be done about it. This is exactly the belief and behavior of the nonrecovering codependent.

We have been trained to believe that we should be able to use our training and knowledge to *control and manipulate* clients in order to get them to do, see, or feel what we, with our greater knowledge and understanding, know is good for them. This is what codependents do. Everything they do is "for your own good."

We were also taught that the clients could not tolerate honesty, and we should feed them only such information about themselves (which we, of course, had) as they could handle. The "information" we were told to keep secret from them was, in fact, *our* perceptions, *our* interpretations, and *our* theories about them. We were taught systematic *dishonesty*, which is part of the addictive system.

We were taught that it was all right to use *techniques, exercises,* or *wise leads* to pull out of people information that we knew and believed would be helpful for them and that, as professionals, we should know how and when to do that. Only recently have I fully understood the *violence* of this behavior: it truly rapes their souls, their beings, and their processes.

We were taught that *dependency* upon us (at a certain level, of course) was inevitable and helpful and that it was our responsibility to control the level. Of course, we were also going to be financially (and I believe, in most cases, emotionally) dependent upon the client, but that was glossed over. However it was dealt with, therapy set up a situation of *mutual* dependency, but only one direction of dependency was recognized.

Finally, we were supposed to have the knowledge to *interpret* the other person based, of course, upon our knowledge and theory, which gave us an accepted position of "rightness." Every codependent (relationship addict) will recognize this one immediately. We were to set ourselves up as a *power base,* if for no other reason than we knew more about the clients than they did about us (and, we thought, about themselves). Part of our power base was that we were supposed to be perfect and a model of health. Whether we chose the field because of our disease (Wounded Healer) or our choice of field caused our disease is a moot point (and we will see later why simple cause-and-effect ways of thinking are part of the problem). There is probably an interactive relationship between the two with many more factors, including our religious upbringing, being relevant.

As I write the above statements, most therapists and former clients will immediately say, "That's too extreme," or, "That's not my experience." However, I would encourage you to keep an open mind and explore the subtleties of the issues I have raised.

It was only a short leap to begin to see the society as the addict and the helping professions as the enablers/codependents. The role of the enabler/codependent is to pick up the pieces just enough to keep things going so that the addict doesn't hit bottom and doesn't have to face his or her addiction. The codependent "protects the supply" of the addict, thereby establishing an important and necessary place for themselves. Of course, this role robs the addict of the possibility of the rewards of recovery, because recovery is really not possible unless one admits the disease. Are the helping professions in some way taking the pressure off just enough so that the society does not have to face its addictive process? It makes sense to me.

In the process of pondering all these questions, I began to look at scientific paradigms and at the scientific paradigm in which psychology has placed itself and out of which it comes.

As is often the case, a book came into my life that was just what I needed to read at the time: Morris Berman's *The Reenchantment of the World*.[4] Berman uses the terms "a participatory and a non-participatory science." His thesis is that we have developed a nonparticipatory scientific worldview that is entropic and destroying the planet. He stresses that we need to develop a participatory scientific worldview. One of the major differences I sensed between professional colleagues and recovering people was that professional people tried to remain aloof (perfect, expert) and be objective, whereas recovering people knew that they had to become fully involved and participatory to recover.

Berman had stated that in order to remain "non-participatory," one had to remove oneself from oneself and make the self object to be observed and manipulated and one had to remove oneself from the other and make the "other" (other people, animals, nature, the planet, the universe) object to be observed and manipulated. We had removed ourselves (or tried to) from the universe and therefore were attempting to play God! I quickly recognized that this kind of removal of the self from the self and from the universe was exactly what addictions did. We use addictions to shut us off from awareness, from our knowing, and from ourselves and all others. In reading Berman's description of a nonparticipatory science, I was reading the description of an addict.

I was also acutely aware that the cornerstone of my training in psychology had been what I call the myth of objectivity. The good therapist was the one who was perfect and who remained perfectly objective (assuming both were possible). The good therapist was one who could remain aloof and detached and manipulate the client the way an experimenter does a rat. Given that many approaches have tried to counteract this belief (Rogerian, humanistic therapies, even feminist therapy), still, at a deeper level, most have maintained that to be scientific in the form of this definition of objectivity is good.

I then began to realize that I needed to go back to the history and philosophy of the science in which I had been trained to fully understand what this scientific model meant to me personally and professionally. Could it be that when I was being my absolute best in the model I had for being a therapist that I was actually exacerbating my disease and that of the client? I now believe so.

I have spent several years studying scientific paradigms and relating this material to my work and my own personal recovery. This search has been rewarding and difficult at times. Could I throw out a particular scientific paradigm and not have to throw out science? I wasn't sure. I had loved science and had fun with it. Yet, the most basic tenets of the science that I had learned from my father were exploration and open-mindedness, and I did not see much of this in the mechanistic empiricism that governed psychology and the helping professions.

I will try to share the understanding I have about mechanistic, reductionist, linear, empirical science and hope that this understanding at least provides a step along the way in your journey.

Setting the Scene

In this section, I present some of the theoretical issues that underlie the assumptions we make about why we work with people and the way we work with people. As I stated earlier, I have come to believe that there is little more dangerous than unstated assumptions and that this is especially true in the world as we know it today.

We live in a time of major expansion for the Western, modernist scientific worldview. This is a time when indigenous knowledge and non-Western philosophies and worldviews are facing the grave possibility of extinction. Paradoxically, we are also facing a time when this modernist scientific worldview may well be reaching entropy, the turning upon itself and devouring of itself. I choose to call this particular scientific system an addictive system because it is one that requires addiction in order to survive in it and support it. Unfortunately, like any addiction, *this worldview absorbs positive attributes like love and then presents them as if they were its own, feeding off of nonaddictive energy and, at the same time, seeking to overpower and destroy it.* Again paradoxically, perhaps because there is a God or a Living Process System that seeks not to let us implode ourselves, *this addictive system has within it the path to heal it or the path to force us into a system shift.* Regardless of what we call this addictive system, whether we call it modernist, mechanistic science, consumerism, Western religions, capitalism, socialism, communism, Western thought, or simply reality as seen by a small but growing segment of the world, we need to articulate assumptions so we can be free to make choices.

In order to change, we have to be able to understand what we are doing and why we are doing it. We need to see that psychotherapy is progressively a one-party system of healing. We need to see that the very form of healing that we have embraced in the helping professions is political and that its politics support and exacerbate the problems of this dominant system.

In this section, I will attempt to make scientific assumptions understandable and show how alternatives that are in keeping with a paradigm that more accurately reflects a potentially healthy universe are not only urgently needed, they are absolutely essential.

The Existing Scientific Paradigm

> Our myths and legends tell us that you white people,
> centuries ago, decided to go the way of science and
> technology. It's going to destroy the planet. Our job is
> to protect the planet. We only hope that you realize
> what is happening before it's too late.
>
> *Reuben Kelly,*
> *Australian aboriginal elder*

In order to understand the society in which we live and the assumptions we make about life, it is necessary to understand the scientific worldview around which modern Western society is structured.

The science that is commonly accepted as science, according to the British physicist David Bohm, is based upon a "worldview that physics provided from the sixteenth through the nineteenth centuries."[5] "This approach has assumed that nature could be thoroughly understood and brought under control by means of the systematic development of scientific knowledge through observation, experiment, and rational thought."[6]

In scholarly circles this science is called "modernist" scientific thought, or Newtonian physics (although some doubt that we can truly blame Newton for the state we are in). Griffin would call this a mechanistic, reductionist science. From my reading, I would add the adjectives *empirical, linear, objective,* and *rational.*[7] Now, let's break down those concepts so they make sense.

Empiricism

Empiricism is based upon things that can be dealt with empirically.[8] Reality is defined by that which can be observed, measured, predicted, controlled, and repeated. From an empirical perspective, the only way that truth can be approached is through measurement and numbers. If empiricism is pushed to its extreme, anything that cannot be measured or documented by numbers does not exist and therefore, also by definition, is not "true." Reliance upon the belief in empiricism also leads to proof by measurement and control as the only legitimate definition of "science." Recalling the example that I gave earlier of my experience with a Boston psychiatrist on a radio show during the book tour for *When Society Becomes an Addict,* you will remember that his chief objection to my book was that it wasn't "scientific." Basically, he disagreed with what I was saying, but that would not be a strong enough damning of the book. Then, too, in empirical circles personal observations, feelings, or opinions have no validity. Thus, he believed that if he just said that I was not scientific, with his concept of science resting upon measurement and empiricism, then those who heard him could logically assume that what I was saying was "logically" invalid. Of course, this criterion would make invalid the majority of books that are published and the majority of what is taught in our institutions of higher learning.

Empiricism is dependent upon the experimental method and sees the experimental method as the only avenue to truth. Berman paraphrases Newton's saying, "I have measured, that is enough."[9] Because empirical knowledge has popularly come to mean knowledge that is dependent upon controlled laboratory procedures, the knowledge gained through empirical research is necessarily restricted. For this approach to be accepted as the only avenue to "truth" leaves us in a confused state indeed. My experience is that the test of empirical truth is used politically more often than it is scientifically, especially in the social sciences.[10] Frequently, when an emotional, political, or ideological issue is at stake, the ultimate argument offered to dismiss someone has been that his or her information is not "scientific," usually meaning empirically based. Griffin has made a good point about this issue. He says, "Any activity called *science* and any conclusions properly called *scientific* must, first, be based on an overriding concern to discover truth."[11] Other concerns will, of course, play a role but the concern for truth must be overriding, or the activity and its results would be better called by another name, such as *ideology*, or *propaganda*, or *politics*.[12]

Given that the quest for truth and observation is basic to what is scientific, one could even argue that the information I had in *When Society Becomes an Addict* was, indeed, scientific. However, I doubt that calling it scientific makes it more "true."

Mechanistic Thinking

A mechanistic science sees the universe and everything in it as a huge machine that probably, at the time of the "big bang," was launched into motion and continues to function as a machine with mechanical parts. In a mechanistic scientific worldview, everything is seen as a machine and can be understood as a machine. Plants are machines, animals are machines, nature is a machine, humans are machines, and the universe is a machine. If we understand the mechanics, we understand the entity. This view of the universe leaves no room for anything other than mechanical functioning. At some basic level, people are seen as just like cars. If something is wrong, you find out what it is and you fix it. Western medicine has grown out of the theory of the body as a machine. Modern psychology was developed upon the assumption that the human being could best be understood as a machine. Both would probably decry these statements, and, at best, say that they are too simplistic, yet that's the very problem, isn't it? Seeing the world as a machine is too simplistic.

A mechanistic model of science limits us to a simplistic cause-and-effect approach to ourselves and our universe. Very simply put, the belief is that if we push here, the effect will be seen repeatedly and predictably over there. For example, if you have certain genes, you will be an alcoholic. The genes are the *cause* for the alcoholism. If you experienced sexual abuse as a child, then you will show this, this, and this characteristic as an adult. Fortunately (or unfortunately, as the case may be) this doesn't always happen. We are really not that predictable, and we do not fit a mechanical model very well. When something does not fit these assumptions, the belief has not been that the *model* is not valid, the belief has been that we just do not have enough information.

Following through on the mechanical model, if we know the cause and we know the effect, then the experts (the mechanics) should know what to do to "fix" whatever needs to be fixed. A simplistic, linear cause-and-effect mentality may work well with the physical world—though not always; ask anyone who has built a house—and it is limited to only some aspects of the physical plane. To use a mechanical model to try to reach universal truth sounds preposterous, yet we have built an entire civilization on the belief that the universe is a machine.

It is interesting that Berman notes, "Newton made the Cartesian worldview tenable by falsifying all of its details. In other words, although Descartes' facts were wrong and his theories not supportable, the central Cartesian outlook—that the world is a vast machine of matter and motion obeying mathematical laws—was thoroughly validated by Newton's work."[13] Berman had previously stated that Newton had analyzed Descartes' propositions about the natural world step by step and demonstrated their falsity.[14] Such is the politics of science. It is not unusual in the history of science that even when the facts do not support the theory, the scientist is often wedded to the theory.[15]

Fortunately for us and for the planet, we and the material world, even machines, do not operate only as machines.

Reductionism

Reductionism, as I understand it, very simply means that to understand something thoroughly, one must reduce it down to the smallest possible parts, its most elemental state, and then it is understandable. As Frederick Ferr has said, "To know what a thing really is, in terms of this ideal [modernist science], would be to know as much as possible about the parts that comprise it."[16] This suggests that when we know that water is composed of hydrogen and oxygen, and hydrogen and oxygen are composed of electrons, neutrons, and protons, and so forth, then we understand water. Reductionism, as I have often said, assumes that if we want to understand cat, we kill the cat and dissect it. Then we understand cat.

This reductionist approach to science suggests that analysis of the parts is sufficient for understanding and that understanding is all that is necessary for healing or getting the proper fix. I find it astounding that when we know there are so many possibilities for error in a simple mechanical machine, we continue to believe that the human being can be reduced to its basic parts and be understood. The reductionist belief system suggests that the problem is not in the methodology of reductionism. The problem, if one accepts that there is one, does not lie with the construct or the methodology; the problem lies in the fact that we have just not perfected our instruments to the point where they can accurately break down and measure the component parts. How much of psychotherapy has been based upon tearing down and then rebuilding according to the value system of the therapist?

For example, I know of a woman who, with the help of her therapist, "reduced herself" to fourteen "inner" children, each of whom had its own teddy bear. Then, again with the help of her therapist, she needed to kill some of them off, so she ended up with extra teddy bears and, as far as I know, with the same set of problems with which she began.[17]

Reductionism can certainly be helpful for fixing our cars, but it has not proved very helpful in facilitating our understanding of ourselves, our world, or the relationships therein.

Linear Science and Logic

A linear science assumes that all movement is in one direction or in a direction that moves like a straight line. It assumes that causal relationships are linear, simple geometric, mathematical terms. A linear science assumes that X causes Y, which causes Z, which causes something else. A linear science divides the planet up into acres, tracts, squares, and rectangles, and assumes these are the best forms of division, even on a spherical planet.[18]

The form of logic on which linear science is based is very simplistic, often ignoring the complexities of mind and reality. Linear science cannot deal well with vortexes, spirals, or multidirectionality. Linear science does not understand or encourage multivariate thinking processes or nonlinear reality. Linear thinking does not lend itself to understanding wholeness.

The Myth of Objectivity

In a non-participatory scientific worldview, it is necessary to remove oneself from participating fully in one's life and the life around one. This attempt has resulted in what I call "the myth of objectivity."

A laboratory-based scientific worldview is built on the illusion that it is possible to remove oneself from oneself and from the situation or, at least, to set up "controls" to limit the influence of the self on the situation. Western culture has given great credence to the myth of objectivity. There is a belief that the person who is most objective is the most correct. This belief, of course, is underwritten by the belief that it is possible *and* desirable to be objective. Objectivity is almost always set up as a polar opposite to feeling or emotion in a dualistic fashion, and objectivity is *always* superior to subjectivity or feeling.[19]

Being objective has been so valued in this society that it has been held up as being almost an elite state of being.

I have been especially fascinated with the role that the myth of objectivity has played in the development of the modernist scientific Western culture and the relationship of this development to the progressive prevalence of addictions.

Anyone who has worked with a broad range of addicts knows that the basic purpose and result of addictions is to put us out of touch with ourselves. Addictions shut off the awareness of feelings and generally keep the addict shut off from internal processes and information (which basically are not recognized as existing in a modernist scientific world). Addictions shut off our internal information system. It is our body and bodily awareness, for example, that tell us when we are being lied to or manipulated. These messages do not start with our brains. They begin in our bodies, usually in our solar plexus, and then move to our brain. If we don't know when we are being lied to, we are easily manipulated. Our bodies tell us when we know something is wrong or is unethical for us. When we are out of touch with that information, we are able to perform acts that are not in keeping with our basic belief systems. In fact, when we are laboring under the myth of objectivity, we are not aware of our oneness with all things and our inner relationships with everything on the planet. We are non-participatory with ourselves and our environment and thus can and do exploit both.

Addictions are not only *supported* by a system that comes out of a non-participatory worldview, they are *demanded* by it. The pain of the estrangement from one's place in the universe needs to be assuaged, and nothing assuages better than addictions. It is no wonder that so many people see the Twelve-Step program of Alcoholics Anonymous as the best program for recovery, because its support of self-defined spirituality reconnects a person with his or her own universe. If one really works that program, one has to take ownership of all aspects of one's life and become participatory in one's universe. I wonder, for example, if what Griffin calls the epistemological meaning of objectivity (a "good" aspect of objectivity) is what recovering addicts would call being sober—that is, being clear and not projecting the addictive "distortion" into the situation. Has, then, the real meaning of objectivity been distorted by an addictive, mechanistic, society?

Given the above, it is not surprising that the "scientists" who are interested in addiction are critical of and threatened by the Twelve-Step program of Alcoholics Anonymous and all its spin-offs. With a vowed intention of not being political or advertising (attraction, not promotion) and not entering into debate, its very existence has become a threat to those who wish to cling to a non-participatory scientific worldview. At the same time, I find it fascinating that a bunch of high level physicists and philosophers (at the top of the scale of influence in the society) and a bunch of recovering addicts (often at the bottom of the scale of influence) are taking the leadership in a major shift in consciousness that is currently happening globally. The scientists and the philosophers are talking about the paradigm shift, and the addicts are *doing* it. Seeing myself in both camps, I present this book as a way of *talking* about doing it.

Rational Science

The concept of a rational science implies an inherent mind-body split, with the mind providing superior information to that from the body on all counts. A rational science certainly adheres to the old adage, "I think, therefore I am," and adds to it, "I measure, therefore I can predict and control."

Rational Science/Scientific Bias

The concept of a rational science[20] is almost always linked with the concepts of "logical" and "linear." I have found that many things in the modernist scientific world are very logical and very rational, they just do not make any sense, especially with respect to my experience. Of course, experience is subjective, not objective, and therefore not measurable or amenable to the rigors of modernist science, so by definition it does not really exist.

I recently read the accounts of three scientists who dismissed their own experience out of their need to adhere to their own scientific bias. One was Newton who, as I have already cited, accepted Descartes' propositions even though he, himself, had proved them wrong in his own system.

Another is an example offered by Griffin in recounting the behavior of a physicist named John Taylor. He relates, "After studying several people who he [Taylor] had come to believe had psychokinetic power to bend metal without touching it, he published a book entitled *Superminds*, complete with supporting photographs. However, after deciding later that no explanation was to be found for psychokinetic effects within the scientific worldview, he wrote a second book called *Science and the Supernatural* in which he declared that no such event can occur. . . . He concluded that all such reports must be due to hallucination, trickery, credulity, the fear of death, and the like."[21] Griffin continues, "Taylor concludes by castigating himself and other scientists for having seriously investigated phenomena which their scientific education should indicate are impossible."[22] So much for open-mindedness.

Basically, this attitude has evolved into a need to deny our own experience and our own perception in order to fit into an ideology. It is all very logical and rational. It just does not make much sense.

The third example involves Albert Einstein. Brian Swimme tells the story of Einstein's development of his field equations (laws governing the universe). He relates that Einstein was alarmed that his calculations indicated that the universe was expanding (a theory now accepted). This theory made no sense in a Newtonian "static" universe. Einstein was so stunned that, according to Swimme, "To avoid these alarming implications, Einstein altered his equations to eliminate their predictions."[23] Objectivity and rational, logical thinking seem to defer to beliefs, even in the best of scientists.

Now that we have defined the terms that define the modernist scientific worldview, I would like to delve deeper into some of the implications of these ideas.

The Language of Science

One of the traditional ways of trying to maintain power and control is through the use of language. The more specialized a language becomes, the more it is accessible to only a few. In fact, one might look carefully at the correlation between accessibility of information and participation in a modernist worldview. Most of the great world teachers (including religious teachers) have tried to put their writing and teaching into the simplest language possible to make it available to those who would hear.

When I was doing the reading that I needed to do to try to understand the postmodernist science intellectually (I felt that I already had an intuitive understanding of it from my experience), I noticed an interesting difference between a mechanistic approach and a postmodern approach. In a rational, mechanistic approach, one gets an idea and then tries to understand it (through experimentation), and in a postmodern approach, one understands something and then tries to get an idea about it. I was also appalled at how difficult it was to read some of the writings on the philosophy of science that were published as popular books. Wading through some of the information was a formidable task. At times, I almost felt that I needed a translator, and I was trained in the sciences (the "pure" sciences). In fact, as I mentioned earlier, when I suggested that some of the people who train with me read some of these materials, they complained bitterly and asked me to translate the information and make sense out of it. If the purpose of modernist science is to understand nature, why isn't the understanding of nature accessible?

Ursula Le Guin, one of my favorite writers, made some relevant comments in a speech she gave at her alma mater, Bryn Mawr, in 1986: "People crave objectivity because to be subjective is to be embodied, to be a body, vulnerable, violable."[24] It sounds a bit like what I mentioned about the role of shutting off awareness in seeking to be objective.

In another part of the same speech, she talks about language:

> It began to develop when printing made written language common rather than rare, 500 years ago or so, and with electronic processing and copying it continues to develop and proliferate so powerfully, so dominatingly, that many

believe this dialect—the expository and particularly the scientific discourse—is the *highest* form of language, the true language, of which all other uses of words are primitive vestiges.

And it is indeed. Newton's *Principia* was written in it in Latin, and Descartes wrote Latin and French in it establishing some of its basic vocabulary, and Kant wrote German in it, and Marx, Darwin, Freud, Boas, Foucault, all the great scientists and social thinkers wrote it. It is the language of thought that seeks objectivity.

I do not say it's the language of rational thought. Reason is a faculty far larger than mere objective thought. When either the political or the scientific discourse announces itself as the voice of reason, it is playing God, and should be spanked and stood in the corner. The essential gesture of the father tongue is not reasoning, but distancing—making a gap, a space, between the subject or self and the object or other. Enormous energy is generated by that rending, that forcing of a gap between Man and World. So the continuous growth of technology and science fuels itself; . . .[25]

Le Guin not only eloquently describes the effect of the use of language to control and confuse, she plumbs deeper to touch upon the very essence of language, scientific Western worldview language, to separate and remove us from our relatedness with ourselves and the other.

She also touches upon another issue. Jon Clark calls it "Macho Science." In his paper on the subject, Clark writes, "It helps me understand and remember the tenets of traditional, mechanistic science to think of it as 'Macho Science.' Macho science is method-oriented. It explores science only if they fit into a proven methodology."[26]

Clark likens his observation of the basic axioms of male sex-role training to what the psychologist Abraham Maslow delineates as "cognitive pathologies." "They include the need to control, fear of letting go, denial of doubt, the inflexible neurotic need to be tough, powerful, fearless, strong, severe, the inability to say 'I don't know' or 'I was wrong,' the need for immediate certainty, no indecision, the need to win approval and be part of a group, the need always to be rational, logical, analytic, intellectual, arrogance, megalomania, and grandiosity."[27]

This description fits much of what I described as the White Male System in *Women's Reality*. It is interesting to see the modernist mechanistic scientific model equated to male sex-role conditioning and the Addictive System. Clearly, there is a profound relationship between science as we know it and the issues that women and native people are raising about the destruction of the environment and the need to respect the earth and live *with* one another.

Brian Swimme formulates the dominant modernist scientific system as mechanistic, scientistic, dualistic, patriarchal, Eurocentric, anthropocentric, militaristic, and reductionistic.[28] This sounds right to me.

It seems to me that it has been very difficult for feminists to confront the role of modernist science when they confront patriarchy. In my perception, the issue has been especially confusing for many feminist therapists. Because they have the need to be accepted by and accepted into the fraternity of psychology and psychotherapy as science, they have tried to walk a careful line between confronting and criticizing the White Male System, and courting legitimacy from it. I will say more about this when I discuss psychotherapy, specifically. Unquestionably, the issues of male dominance and Western European dominance are intimately related to modernist science. It seems appropriate to move to an exploration of dualism in understanding mechanistic science and the role it plays in our everyday lives.

Dualism

Dualism is at the very core of the modernist worldview. In order to be rational, logical, and *objective*, especially objective as in the modernist worldview, it is necessary to distinguish between the self and the other. A dualism is established when we set up a self-other reality.

In her article "A Different Reality: Feminist Ontology," Caroline Whitbeck states, "Dualistic ontologies based on the opposition of self and other generate two related views of the person and of ethics: the patriarchal and that of individualism. The proponents of individualism or of patriarchy often argue for their view by attacking the other view, as though the only possibilities were variants of these two masculist viewpoints."[29]

In a previous book, I described dualism as one of the cornerstones of the addictive process and an addictive system.[30] I came to that conclusion by working with recovering addicts and working with my own addictive process. It was much later that I discovered that some writers (Griffin, Berman, Whitbeck, Harman)[31] were viewing dualism as one of the basic problems with modernist science.[32]

In *When Society Becomes an Addict*, I described the two basic reasons for dualism. First, dualism takes a very complex universe and breaks it down into this or that, thus feeding our illusion of control, and second, dualism keeps us stuck (a duality is static) so we don't have to or can't make decisions between two poles, neither one of which makes sense and both of which are oversimplified. Setting the world up in dualities keeps us static and feeds our illusion of control while, at the same time, it removes us from our participation in the world around us. All these issues are, of course, key in addiction.

When discussing dualism, I coined the term *Lincoln Logs* as a way of describing dualities that are the basic building blocks of our society and then pushed the concept to more personal issues. I used the dualistic Lincoln Log to describe sets of feeling behaviors that go together and are completely interdependent. One cannot give up one without giving up the other. They depend upon each other. Persons vacillate from one end to the other, and the only way to break free is to move to a third option. For example, we often see the dualism of niceness and dishonesty in relationship addicts. One cannot get honest without giving up "niceness," and one cannot give up niceness without getting more honest. They go together. The third option, which is necessary to get out of the dualism or jump off the Lincoln Log, is operating out of one's Living Process.

Whitbeck sees dualism as a key issue in the need for what she calls a "feminist ontology." She says, "The self/other opposition is at the heart of other dualistic opposition, such as theory/practice, culture/nature, spirit/matter, mind/body, human/divine, political/personal, public/private (or productive/reproductive), knower/known, lover/beloved, that figure so prominently in Western Thought."[33] She suggests the need for moving beyond these dualities for a "new view of the person and of ethics."

Griffin hits dualism hard when he says, "A reenchanted, liberating science will be fully developed only by people with a postmodern spirituality, in which dualisms that have made modern science such an ambiguous phenomenon have been transcended, and only in a society organized for the good of the planet as a whole."[34] Griffin further points out that one of the sociological motives for the church's embracing of the mechanist philosophy was that it created "an extreme dualism between the soul and nature and between God and the world," thus giving support to the church as the final authority on spirituality and a hierarchical view of society. "It also, by eliminating all feeling as well as divinity and creativity from nature, was intended (e.g., by Descartes, Boyle) to sanction the *uninhibited exploitation of nature for human ends, such as mining and vivisection*"[35] (emphasis mine).

When we set up dualism such as mind-body, we deny the possibility of their interacting. This, in turn, requires that we deny our own experience. So if divine and human cannot interact and nature and nurture are set up as opposites, unrelated and unrelating, we have set up a system that makes understanding ourselves, taking our place in the universe, and touching the divine almost impossible.

Modernist Science and God, the Church, and Spirituality

"I believed these experiences [in nature] because I had them, but my parents tried not to because they were Christians." This was expressed by an old Hawaiian kapuna as he related some of the profundity of his spiritual experiences in nature. As he spoke, he seemed constantly to labor under the science-superstition dualism he was taught in church.

Griffin says that "what is distinctive about 'modern' philosophy, theology, and art is that they revolve around numerous strategies for maintaining moral, religious, and aesthetic sensitivities while accepting the disenchanted worldview of modernity as adequate for science. These strategies have involved either rejecting modern science, ignoring it, supplementing it with talk of human values, or reducing its status to mere appearance." Griffin sees the disenchantment of nature as denying to nature "all subjectivity, all experience, all feeling," therefore completely disqualifying it as valid and important. He points out that when we cannot internalize natural things, we cannot internalize God. God to the founders of modern science was external to the world and "imposed motion and laws from without."[36]

Interestingly, Griffin sees the founders of modern mechanistic science as being steeped in supernaturalism, but fighting against a more "magical" worldview. Their beliefs left room for miracles, but nature, the material world, was mechanistic and followed the "laws" of science. I believe that one of the most important statements Griffin makes is that historically "the mechanistic view of nature was adopted less for empirical than for theological, sociological, and political reasons."[37]

From my reading, I had always assumed that the church had fallen prey to mechanistic science and basically had to adopt it or die. According to Griffin, it appears that Boyle, Newton, Descartes, and Locke saw mechanistic science as being proof of God and God's transcendency. In fact, Newton thought God was necessary to explain gravitation.

Subsequently, mechanism was used to defend the authority of the church and its doctrines. Rewards and punishments after death and the concept of an eternal soul required a supernatural God. "This idea was considered essential for the preservation of the socio-political order against those who were seeking a wider distribution of material goods and political enfranchisement."[38] The church hierarchy found particularly useful the biblical passage stating that rulers are appointed by God and should be obeyed (not overthrown). It appears that mechanistic science has been touted as the savior of humankind while putting power in the hands of the few and providing a rationale to exploit nature and those not in power.

Griffin also points out that another influence that affected science "was a desire to develop a 'masculine' science of nature in contrast with the 'feminine' or hermaphrodite science of the alchemists."[39] In the new "masculine" science, domination was the goal. Modernist science pressed further to a position where truth could only be achieved through its methods and God had to be proved empirically.

There is no one more fanatic than a fundamentalist scientist; a fundamentalist scientist could make a fundamentalist Christian look moderate. Taking a closer look at any fundamentalism, however, we see the same dogmatism, closed-mindedness, and closed system, and so a fundamentalist scientist is really not a scientist (a scientist is, by definition, open-minded), and yet there are many pseudoscientists, who have made a religion of science.

Every addict knows that addiction kills spirituality. Institutional religion tolerates addiction very well—maybe because addiction kills spirituality. That is why the spirituality component and the participatory component are important and necessary in the Twelve-Step program. The Twelve-Step program may be under such attack by the helping professions because it opens a door out of the scientific paradigm that the helping professions have made a religion and in which they have become completely enmeshed. As Bohm says, the "new secular order" on the seal of the United States was to bring nature under control under science.[40]

This discussion brings out another particularly interesting issue. This relates to the current interest in the "Goddess" and the "feminine" and bringing the feminine back into the world. It is very difficult for some who are trying to do this to see that they are still continuing in an old dualistic paradigm and therefore in a scientific worldview that perpetuates the existing system. As Whitbeck points out, "Too often the project of constructing a feminist view is confused with the project of simply offering the goodness or the primacy of the characteristics associated with what masculist dualistic thought views as 'the feminine principle,' or appropriate to the feminine gender, or arising from female biology."[41]

A feminist view cannot use the constructs and assumptions and processes of a "masculine" mechanistic worldview and hope to bring about a paradigm shift. Changing the content and adhering to the processes of the "old" science will not bring about the changes the feminists hope for. Whether God or Goddess, the concept is trapped in a mechanistic, dualistic model. An active spirituality is needed for the new paradigm, and that spirituality must again connect us with the oneness of all things. That connection is not possible with institutional religion as we now know it.

Political and Economic Issues of Science

I think that it is clear, from the preceding exploration, that science as we know it is not value free, that it has been used to support certain political and economic views, and that the same political and economic views have been used to support mechanistic science. As a poster advertising the London School of Economics states, "Economics and morality are closely connected." The question is, whose morality and what morality? The mechanistic science has spawned a political and economic system that is based upon the illusion of control; that demands addiction; that is exploiting nature, animals, and the planet; that has elevated and revered the masculine and denigrated the feminine; and that has separated us from our spirituality. It has espoused materialism and a belief system that separates us from nature and ourselves. It is not essential for us to let go of technical pursuits; we do need to let go of defining the world through technology.

The Results of the Mechanistic Science

Almost every author who is exploring the issue of the impact of mechanistic science in creating what is known as Western civilization offers dire warnings. Berman says, "To succeed in Western industrial society, it pays to behave mechanically, to ignore feelings and concentrate on appearance and behavior." He continues, "Pushed to the limit, the view that nature is mechanical and that the world is dead has only one of two possible outcomes: nuclear holocaust, or the ecological annihilation of the planet."[42]

In *The Reenchantment of the World*, Berman eloquently states, "The alienation and futility that characterized the perception of a handful of intellectuals at the beginning of the century have come to characterize the consciousness of the common man [*sic*] at its end. Jobs are stupefying, relationships vapid and transient, the arena of politics absurd. In the vacuum created by the collapse of traditional values, we have hysterical evangelical revivals."[43] And further, "What I am arguing is that the scientific worldview is *integral* to modernity, mass society, and the situation described above."[44] Berman says of *The Reenchantment of the World*, "it is a major premise of this book that because disenchantment is intrinsic to the scientific worldview, the modern epoch contained, from its inception, an inherent instability that severely limited its ability to sustain itself for more than a few centuries."[45]

Griffin states about the *new* science, "It rejects not science as such but only that scientism in which the data of the modern natural sciences are alone allowed to contribute to the construction of our worldview."[46] He states that modernist science seeks a certain type of truth that results in power over nature. I would question whether truth can truly be sought if the goal for it is preconceived.

At some point, all of us will be forced to look at the implications of a science that removes the human from the cosmos and looks at reality from a completely egocentric perspective. Brian Swimme states, "We have nothing compared to the massive accumulation of hate, fear, and arrogance that the intercontinental ballistic missiles, the third world debt, and the chemical toxins represents."[47]

From Bohm we hear this: "Clearly, during the twentieth century the basis of the modern mind (modernist science) has been dissolving, even in the midst of its greatest technological triumphs. The whole foundation is dissolving while the thing is flowering, as it were. This dissolution is characterized by a general sense of loss of a common meaning of life as a whole."[48] He follows this with, "A postmodern world must come into being before the modern world destroys itself so thoroughly that little can be done for a long time."[49]

These are dire words, indeed, and they are being written by one of the most respected theoretical physicists in the world. Bohm states that the mechanistic view of physics "remains the basis of the approach of most physicists and other scientists today. . . . The adherence to this program has been so successful as to threaten our very existence as well as to produce all sorts of other dangers, but, of course, success does not prove its truth. To a certain extent the reductionist picture is still an article of faith, and faith in the mechanistic reductionistic program still provides the motivation of most scientific enterprise, the faith that this approach can deal with everything. This is a counterpart of the religious faith that people had earlier which allowed them to do great things."[50] As stated earlier, a religious faith operating under the guise of science can be more than confusing; it can be downright dangerous. And, although it can allow us to do great things, vast destruction has occurred under the guise of faith.

Willis Harman, the founder of the Center for the Study of Social Policy at Stanford Research Institute and president of the Institute of Noetic Sciences, states quite clearly, *"Experienced reality does not conform to the 'reality' they taught us in science class; the 'scientific worldview' is not an adequate guide for living life or for managing a society."*[51]

This inadequate scientific worldview has not had to be taught. It permeates every aspect of our society and what we have been lead to believe is "reality." Many voices are trying to sound the clarion call: like the old Australian aboriginal (a man named Reuben Kelly) who told me that "the science and technology that white people have opted for is going to destroy the planet. We hope you realize it before it is too late." So many people want to change a few things, but remain under the blessing of the accepted worldview. This position, I believe, can generally describe most of the New Age, feminist therapy, and anti-addiction and codependency groups.

As the above authors emphasize, the changes that must occur must affect every aspect of our lives and being, our thinking, and the planet as a whole. Harman says it eloquently, "We are seeing, I believe, indications of a 'new heresy' that is challenging modern secular authority at a level as profound as the 'scientific heresy' challenged the ecclesiastical authority in the seventeenth century. If so, this means that *the postmodern world will be as different from the modern world as the modern world has been from the world of the Middle Ages."* He goes on to say, "It is not immediately apparent how thoroughgoing a change this implies."[52] It certainly is big enough that massive entrenchment in the old worldview has already begun in spite of the evidence about deterioration from the microscopic to the global level.

In order to understand the role that psychology has played in the old paradigm, it will be necessary to explore the assumptions and issues of psychology as a whole and examine how psychology has accepted and tried to gain acceptance by fitting into the modernist scientific worldview.

The Mechanistic Paradigm and Psychology

He uses statistics as a drunken man uses lamp-posts,
for support rather than illumination.

Andrew Lang

Modern psychology has tried hard to be a science and to be accepted among the sciences. To be accepted as a science, as modernist science is defined, a field must accept the beliefs and assumptions described in the last section: that is, accept that reality is only what can be proved empirically, use the methodology of mechanistic science with which to experiment and define truth, and deny or ignore any information that does not match that scientific paradigm.

As Dane Rudhyar says, "What is now taught as psychology in universities are the various attempts classified in a number of schools to use the scientific method of observation, generalization, system-building, experimentation, and testing in order to interpret a specific type of phenomena."[53]

Even those psychologists like Jung, Maslow, and the humanists, who were willing to explore subjectivity and introspection, tried to struggle with the issue of mechanistic science. They, like the transpersonal psychologists, have held onto empiricism and the methods of modern science. Rudhyar makes the point that "They *had* to do so in order not to set themselves off entirely from what now is considered the mainstream of Western civilization."[54]

Rudhyar gives a good summary of what needing acceptance means for modern psychology:

> Objectivity refers to what can be perceived by the senses
> and the modern instruments immensely extending the

214

scope of sense-perceptions. These perceptions, moreover, in order to be acceptable to science, have to be obtained under strict experimental conditions. They must be repeatable by any trained observer. They must also be measurable and definable in terms of some kind of activity that is of observable and recordable changes. Thus, the field of scientifically objective knowledge finds itself limited by these conditions. It may be so limited as to lose all meaning in some directions. As Einstein once said, the physicist comes to know more and more about less and less.[55]

There is no question but that psychology has seen itself, and has been seen, as the bastard child of the sciences. All the social sciences have suffered under this inferiority complex, and like all codependent hero children (a role in which psychology might easily see itself in the "family" of the sciences), it tries harder and harder to be accepted. When a person or a discipline needs acceptance, it becomes progressively rigid and rigorous in trying to do the right thing while becoming increasingly aware of its inadequacies. In this process, as Einstein observes about physics, the focus is more and more directed on the tiny details it can "prove," scientifically, and psychology becomes more and more divorced from human issues and larger-than-human issues. Psychology's need for acceptance by science and medicine has pushed it further and further from creative, innovative thinking, lest it face rejection. When a person or a discipline needs so desperately to be accepted, it will literally sell its soul to get in. I believe psychology in general, and the field of psychotherapy specifically, have done just this.

There are elements of psychology that have fought with every specific aspect of science related in the previous section, but, in the end, the need to be a science and to be accepted by that science has won out. For example, the feminists in psychology have questioned the patriarchal system and have fought for recognition of and support for women's rights to be women. The Broverman studies[56] (which in essence suggested that therapists defined healthy as what is "male" in the society and unhealthy as what is "female," and then tried to move women toward what was, in the eyes of the researchers, an unhealthy adjustment) caused quite a stir. Yet, feminist therapists, by rigidly accepting the assumptions of an outdated science, have continued to cling to the mechanistic notion of science and have opted for the kind of power and control that they have rebelled against in men, while still pressing to be "scientific."

In addition, feminists have decried the "power" position of the therapist and especially the power over women by male therapists or even female therapists. Yet, the majority of "feminists" who function in the mainstream of psychology have never really questioned the belief that a power differential is inevitable in psychotherapy. It certainly is inevitable in the psychotherapy based on a mechanistic model. Still, this is not the only model for working with people, and although feminist therapists have certainly lobbied for an alternative cultural model, they have continued to seek acceptance from a mechanistic model. They have changed the content and not the process, thereby perpetuating the very system they say they want to change.

The same conflict holds true for transpersonal psychology. Transpersonal psychology followed the wave of humanistic psychology and bravely introduced the intuitive, the spiritual, the power of consciousness, the parapsychological, and the paranormal, all necessary issues and important to explore. Then, it tried to make itself "legitimate" by using the tools, methodology, and assumptions of mechanistic science to prove the validity of these phenomena, which cannot really be studied by empirical methodology.

Slowly, those who are looking at scientific paradigms are beginning to see that even science is relative, that, as Griffin says, "our interpretations and even perceptions are conditioned by language, by culture in general, by the dominant worldview of the time, by personal (including unconscious) interests, and by interests based on race, gender, and social class—this recognition has led many to the conclusion that a worldview is wholly a construction or a projection, not at all a reflection or a discovery of the way things 'really' are."[57]

Psychology as a "science" has, at times, recognized that these influences exist but has firmly believed that they could be explained and accounted for with the proper external *controls*. In fact, psychology has consistently refused to recognize that psychology itself is "political," as every science is political.

Griffin further states, "Recognition that the scientific community seeks truth is fully compatible with the recognition that the truths it seeks are selected according to various interests and prejudices."[58] Basically, what we are seeing is that psychology has enmeshed itself in a scientific worldview that reveres and believes in the myth of objectivity (a limited view of "objectivity") and does not have the objectivity (as can, of course, be understood) to reflect upon its own assumptions. It continues to teach that empirical truth is the only "real" approach to

216

truth. Being purely empirical is an especially difficult task for psychology because much of what it attempts to study (emotion, feelings, interactions, values, perception and perceptions, and family patterns) are not really amenable to the procedures of mechanistic science. Essentially, psychology cannot be what it wants to be and do what it wants to do.

A mechanistic science can deal with external cause and effect upon the organism because this can be observed and manipulated, but it denies the existence of self-determination or "final causation," as some authors call it.[59] In a purely mechanistic science, we are determined only by the forces operating upon us externally. We are determined solely by our environment and only those forces in the environment that can be seen and measured with the tools of science. This approach to understanding works relatively well with mechanical, nonliving matter that can be manipulated in the laboratory (although tribal, indigenous people throughout the world would question that assumption), but it progressively breaks down as one moves to more and more complex organisms. As Griffin says, "This paradigm has been less successful yet with rats than with bacteria. . . . Finally, the method has been less successful yet with humans than with rats. The record of success at this level is so miserable that many scientists and philosophers of science refuse to think of the so-called social sciences or human sciences, such as psychology, sociology, economics, and political science, as sciences at all."[60]

Psychology has chosen a difficult task for itself. It wants to be a science in order to be legitimate, and yet it cannot properly study what it wants to study with the tools of the science with which it aligns itself. Or, it can study what it can with the tools and assumptions available to it, and that will then be only a minuscule piece of what it now defines for itself as psychology.

Reductionism

Let us look at the issue of reductionism. The science of psychology has clearly accepted the concept of reductionism. It assumes that if we just break down the organism into more and more basic components, then we can reconstruct and understand the organism as a whole.

Rats, pigeons, mice—do any of us really believe that we can gain a clear understanding of how complex organisms function by studying a mouse? Do any of us really believe that we can understand the *mouse* by studying the mouse in the laboratory? Do any of us believe that we can run up and down the phylogenetic scale and understand the organisms along the way? All organisms are more than machines, but there is no place for that information in a mechanistic science. There is no place for ownership of self, responsibility, or self-determination in a science based on the mechanistic model. We can learn what we can learn in the laboratory, but is physics an adequate model for studying thoughts, feelings, perceptions, and motivation? I think not. At some very deep level, we have never seriously questioned the basic premises out of which psychology has risen. There is no place in the reductionist model to move beyond a mechanistic model of the human being or of the planet.

Reductionism in psychology has meant trying to reduce all functioning to a stimulus-response model. Although we have moved beyond simple behaviorism, it is still quite astonishing how the attitudes and actions of psychologists cling to simplistic behaviorist assumptions. For example, we are seeing a proliferation of this kind of thinking in the area of sexual abuse. Again and again, therapists have operated out of the belief that if this, this, and this happened to you, then this, this, and this will be true. I have found when I listen to individuals and their stories that they have very different and often surprising reactions to early sexual abuse. Frequently, the experience of the individual was not what the therapist's theory said it should be, and often the client's experience was one of being subtly pressured to affirm the therapist's theory rather than trust his or her own experience. It is a large leap from observing an experiment in a laboratory to predicting and controlling real-life experiences. Of course, the assumption is that if one could just *know* and *control* all the variables, prediction and control *should* be possible.

If we think of the human organism as a part of a grand whole that functions both individually with volition and purpose and also as part of the whole itself, reductionism seems irrelevant, at best.

Logic, Linear Science, and Knowing

Psychology has confused understanding and knowing. To understand something is to observe and analyze it as separate from the self (in an "objective" manner), and when the experimenter/observer believes he or she knows what makes it tick, then the object of the experiment is "understood." We do this in the laboratory, and we do it in the therapy session. The basis for this understanding is always linear thinking and logic—no real knowing is involved. Knowing is never just logical, rational, and linear. Knowing requires much more brain functioning and interaction with experience. Knowing involves the whole being and is *followed* by the rational brain, which gives it concepts and language. In understanding, the left brain leads. As I said earlier, linear, rational thinking can be very logical and still make no sense. Aristotelian logic can be a good philosophical exercise, but it does not work well with reality as experienced. How many psychological theories have been "logically" developed on minimal data, having absolutely no relationship to what is really going on? Jeffrey Masson gives a very good example of that process in his book *Final Analysis* when he impressively shares his conclusion that Freud rejected his own evidence in favor of his theory.[61] As is often true in psychology, the myth of objectivity is just that, a myth.

The Myth of Objectivity

I have already explained the lack of objectivity about being nonobjective in psychology. Accusations of "experimenter bias"[62] in the 1960s caused quite a furor in the academic halls of psychology, and it was amazing how quickly that furor subsided. However, the concern in psychology has been with the presence of or lack of objectivity, not with whether or not objectivity was even possible, much less desirable.

Many of the great discoveries of "modern science" (like penicillin and radium) have come about because of "accidents" or "intuitions." Yet, there continues to be almost a childlike belief in the possibility and the validity of objectivity. I question the impact that this almost religious belief in the myth of objectivity has upon the masses who have looked to psychology to define themselves and their world for them. Try as it might to be scientific and remain in the ivory tower, psychology has also sought to popularize itself and become indispensable in every crevice of our Western, mechanistically oriented world. What might have happened if it had followed the basic premise of science— to be open-minded? If the public knew that objectivity was only a myth and not really possible, would we have developed a worldview and a society that did not so completely require the anesthesia of addiction?

The Language of Psychology

Like all "sciences," psychology has tried to develop an elitist, specialized language. Again, I have always been suspicious of specialized language because it has been my observation that the great teachers of the world always have spoken in clear and simple terms. I believe that the height of my own love affair with the specialized language of psychology came in two phases.

The first was when I was in graduate school. I had been a pre-med student in undergraduate school, with heavy emphasis in the sciences. The graduate courses in experimental psychology and related areas were easy and fun for me. There was great pressure for me to go into the "true" psychology (experimental) and not waste myself on clinical. I have already related how my professor and adviser and my favorite professor from embryology and comparative anatomy even worked it out for me to have a special laboratory in the zoology building to do special joint research in conditioning of chick embryos in which I had induced "brain damage" at various stages in the development of the embryo. I was to study the learning curves from data gathered in a Skinner box. I had a wonderful time and worked long hours into the night and on weekends (one has to check one's embryos), *but it was all play.* I knew that what was serious for me was my work with people.

Yet, I learned the language. In my first year of graduate school, my lab partners were two men who had been clinicians for a long time. One was a white man who had been a jazz musician. He spent most of his time on his ham radio and did "psychology" for a living. The other was a black man who wanted to get a doctorate in psychology. He was a good clinician, and a doctorate in psychology was his ticket out of the racist world of the South in the 1950s. Neither was very interested in experimental psychology. Our deal was, I would set up the experiments and whiz through them (they were relatively simple compared to the physics and chemistry I had been through); they would take notes on what I shouted out; and then I would put the data together and whip out a preliminary report on the experiment. Their job was to get the materials and clean up. The language of "science" was easy for me at that time. I am grateful for having to write the lab reports, because after my trauma with writing in freshman composition, it was healing to do something that came so easily and quickly.

I progressed from writing lab reports to writing testing evaluation reports. I could knock those out in no time. All I had to do was describe my observations (in the correct language). No one asked me what they *meant*, because we all knew the same specialized language. (Of course, the use of specialized language is an easy way to maintain the illusion of power and control.)

Recently, a friend asked me to translate a series of testing reports that had been done on her son. It would have been easier to translate something from German. I could still do it, but I realized both how many of the concepts were based upon assumptions I no longer believed and what a closed system the language had set up. For some time, I have believed that if we can't talk in "normal" language, we probably don't really understand what we are talking about.

I have also become acutely aware of how language sets up support for a particular belief system. This poses a special problem for psychology. It wants to be obtuse enough to be accepted by the "pure" sciences, and it wants to influence the public (and maybe even make money as a "popular" psychology, although the purists frown terribly on making money). The psychologist who wants to communicate finds him or herself in much the same dilemma as the black person or the feminist, having to become fluent in at least two very disparate languages.

Psychology, philosophy, sociology, and theology all struggle with the same dilemma of wanting to share human truths but trying to do so in specialized languages. However, of all of these, psychology has the most investment in being seen as a science.

One last anecdote about the language of psychology: I had a dear friend who was a well-known artist with a dry, engaging, and socially perceptive sense of humor. His art always reflected his wit and simultaneously made an important public statement. He once did a carving of an empty-headed, empty-bodied person and called it "Westchester Man: no brains, no heart, no guts." One of his best shows was a series of three-dimensional prints of similar peoplelike creatures (like E.T.). He took his titles from articles in a journal of the American Psychological Association. One needed a dictionary to wade through the titles of his artwork. The show was a huge success.

Macho-Patriarchal Science of Psychology

Feelings, emotions, nature, relationships, interactions, caring, the soul, prejudice, healing, and even consciousness have all been assigned to the feminine by a patriarchal science. The science of psychology enters the issue of the masculinity of mechanistic science with the tension that its main field of study is what has been traditionally considered "the feminine." In psychology, all those attributes that are considered "feminine" (and the least understandable with mechanistic science) have been relegated to the less "scientific" aspects of psychology, such as clinical. Of course, clinical psychology stands in the same relation to "real" psychology as psychology stands in relation to the "real" sciences.

Still, the problem is bigger than that in psychology as science. As most feminists know, what has been considered "the feminine" by a male-dominated scientific worldview has always been denigrated. It is curious that what has been considered "the feminine" has also always been relatively impossible to study with the techniques of mechanistic science. I don't need to belabor that relationship, as others have already written about it. Whitbeck eloquently points out the importance of seeing that the use of the feminine-masculine dualism is irrelevant to the basic issues and a major part of the problem.[63] Yet this dualism is set up, when needed, to support a macho science. Still, there are issues women are raising that go much beyond traditional masculine-feminine values and are very much issues that focus upon the scientific worldview that psychology has chosen as its basis.

The real issue for women is not to challenge a system only on the basis of what it does to women. That is only the symptom. The real issue is to divorce ourselves enough from the system to understand the assumptions that result in discrimination and to stop supporting those assumptions. We cannot support a mechanistic scientific worldview and say that we support women's (human) rights and ultimate healing. Unfortunately, few "feminists" have made this connection or are willing to go that far.

This fallacy of masculine-feminine leads easily into a need to explore the forms that dualism takes in the field of psychology.

Dualism and God in Psychology

A basic dualism that is set up by the mechanistic scientific worldview is that between mind and matter. Obviously, the issue of mind, mind-body, and mind-matter is a legitimate and important area of focus for modern psychology.

Griffin states very clearly, "The main philosophical reason for rejecting the mechanistic, nonanimistic view of nature is that that view makes the relation between mind and matter problematic." He stresses that this is "due to the conjunction of a directly known fact, an apparent fact, and an inference. The *directly known fact* is that we have, or are, a mind, in the sense of a stream of experiences. [We know we are experiencing.] The *apparent fact* is that the mind and body seem to interact. . . . The *inference* is that the human body is composed of *things* [emphasis mine] that are devoid of experience."[64] In setting up two different sets of reality, there is no way philosophically to explain their interacting. Because the founders of this dualistic worldview were theists who believed in the supernatural, they just put God "out there," and whatever they could not explain by mechanics, they attributed to God.

This sets up a terrible dilemma for modern psychology. Only that which can be measured is real. "God" cannot be measured and therefore is not real. (I do remember a heated debate in the 1950s when I was in college, however. It seemed that some scientists had proved the existence of God mathematically. If we were in an expanding universe, then, inversely, it could be proven that at some point the universe did not exist—ground zero. Therefore, this proved the existence of God the Creator—at least.) If psychologists deny the existence of a force greater than ourselves, they cannot explain how nonphysical things such as ideas, values, thinking, and decisions can bring about change in the physical world.

Another problematic dualism that Griffin suggests is the implausible idea that "everything in the universe except human experience can be understood in physicalistic terms."[65] Yet, psychology has dedicated itself to understanding human experience in physical terms. Taken further, this means that because of the basic dualism of setting off human experience from the mechanistic world of other beings, psychology is not only incapable of studying the human organism with its methodology, it cannot transfer knowledge gained in the reductionist study of lower organisms to higher organisms (the human), because they are set up in a dualistic science to be of another class. Or, as Berman put it, "Nonparticipating consciousness cannot 'see' participating consciousness any more than Cartesian analysis can 'see' artistic beauty."[66] Dualism in and of itself sets up an impossible task for the field of psychology. When what it wants to study cannot be studied by its procedures and assumptions, psychology becomes nonviable as a science.

Harman notes, "There was, many felt, something unnatural about a science that denied consciousness as a causal reality when everyday experience seemed to confirm again that any *decision* to act causes action."[67] According to the dualism between mind and body, not only is this not possible but in a dualistic science, it's not possible to study it. Harman does point out that there have been attempts "to bring in self-reports of subjective experience as primary data (e.g., introspection, phenomenalized approaches, and Gestalt psychology)," and they "have tended to be considered failures."[68]

Dualistic thinking seems to set up an impossible way of viewing the universe—good-bad, right-wrong, scientific-nonscientific, spiritual-nonspiritual, mind-body—which, in itself, ends up judging each dualism in a dualistic right-wrong fashion. A science cannot be open-minded when it sets up its world this way.

When a science sets up the dualism of human being–deity and only the human can be approached through its methodology, then it needs to deny any object or process that it cannot prove. Magic, enchantment, a living, connected universe with forces that cannot be "proved" are "unsafe" for the belief system.

Occasionally, we have a brave soul like William James, who wrote about the *Varieties of Religious Experience*, but even his work was based on observations of experience. Psychology has no place for forces that cannot be empirically "proved." This has meant that psychology has had to ignore and eliminate human experiences of spirituality, and because of the close linkage of mechanistic science and religion as it is expressed in the Christian church, there has been a sort of unspoken conspiracy to label all other spirituality as primitive and/or superstition. When it has not been trying to disclaim spirituality altogether, psychology has attempted to study religious experience or the experience of spirituality in the same way it has studied mental illness. In general, there has been an underlying denial in the people interested in the areas of spirituality and religion that their very existence is antithetical to psychology as a science. Many people in the fields of religion and psychology, and others with a similar focus, have failed to see how they have needed denial in order to continue trying to do what they do, and this has resulted in a kind of schizophrenia in these fields.

Rogers, for example, wrote a paper entitled "Toward a More Human Science of the Person." Speaking from the perspective of a humanistic psychologist, he voiced his concern when he noted, "Humanistic psychology has not had a deep or significant impact on mainstream psychology in the United States, as it exists in our universities and colleges. . . . I have been unable to find any humanistically oriented program of graduate study which has been approved by the American Psychological Association as a program leading to a doctorate in psychology. . . . I have been unable to find humanistically oriented internships which have APA approval."[69] He goes on to say that all this is "in spite of the fact that in the criteria for APA approval there is a definite place for non-laboratory research carried on in natural settings, and for non-experimental forms of research."[70]

If humanistic psychology were really let into the mainstream of psychology, psychology would have to change. Rogers wanted to gain acceptance by those whose worldview politically supports the exploitation of women and minorities, animals, nature, and the planet. Like many of us, Rogers wanted to stay in the old scientific "club" while suggesting we broaden the concept of research. He did say, however, "I have been one of those who, over the past several decades, have pointed out the need for new models of science more appropriate to human beings."[71] He did not have the benefit of new ideas in science that have been emerging in the last few years, *and* he was on the right track, *and* he, like many of us today when we call for a new scientific paradigm, stated, "But we felt like David challenging Goliath—a small voice of protest against a massive and solid system."[72] (It is still important to remember who won out in the David and Goliath story.)

The Results of the Political and Economic Issues of Psychology

We have explored how psychology has not gained acceptance among the sciences and has sought that acceptance. We have explored the hold that "being scientific" has on the culture and how the "scientific" has been used as a power base. We've explored how the very issues, processes, and interactions that psychology wants to study cannot adequately be dealt with using an empirical science.

We have pointed out the confusion and frustration generated by trying to study a phenomenon with tools that are inadequate for studying that phenomenon, and we have also pointed out the tenacity with which psychology is clinging to a scientific paradigm that simply will not work for it as a field of study.

We have also demonstrated that even science and the basic scientific paradigm that emerges is strongly influenced by the culture. We've also stated that the basic purpose of any science is to find truth, even if it means rejecting itself.

Why, then, is psychology so wedded to empirical science? The reasons must be political and economic. The intensity of emotion with which psychologists defend the old paradigm strongly suggest that we are not dealing with open-minded science here.

Historically, we have always seen that when an old cultural paradigm is dying and on the verge of collapse, there is a tendency to become more rigid in the old paradigm, to set up progressively stricter controls, and to try to kill off new ideas and dissenters through the use of the regulatory and legal arms of the culture. We are seeing this in the United States today (and in many other parts of the Western world). As the old paradigm is being challenged professionally, politically, and economically, the arm of regulation and control gets stronger and stronger.

Contrary to popular belief, the push to maintain the old scientific paradigm and the Western worldview is very emotional and is based on economics and politics. If this existing worldview falters, we will not be able economically and politically to exploit Third World countries, indigenous people, the animal kingdom, or nature. The existing worldview has permitted and supported rape on every level, and, unfortunately, psychology and the helping professions have contributed to that rape. Holding on to old ideas in the name of science is always, after all, violent.

Medicine focuses a great deal of its time and energy heroically trying to cover up for, maintain, and heal diseases that are a result of the very scientific system out of which it comes. For example, many of the illnesses that physicians treat are illnesses that are the direct result of the addictive use of food, alcohol, drugs, or work, or of medicine itself. Yet, the physicians rarely focus on or deal with the addictions. They try, mightily, to patch people up so they can continue to practice their addictive behavior.

We find the same issue in other illnesses. How much of cancer is related to a scientific/economic base that puts carcinogens in our air, our water, and our food? How much in these diseases is related to a scientific worldview that is comfortable with exploiting and contaminating nature for economic greed and control?

The same holds true for psychotherapy. How much of what is done in the field of psychotherapy is focused upon making a place for itself? If psychotherapy supports a disembodied scientific worldview that exploits and uses people, ignores the basic internal processes of people in deference to seeing them as machines that are only objects to be manipulated and acted upon externally, and participates in that

226

manipulation, is psychotherapy not, itself, a part of the problem? I believe it is.

The Helping Professions in an Addictive Society

The helping professions are, indeed, to the addictive society what the enabler, codependent is to the addict. The helping professions patch up just enough so that people can keep limping along and perpetuate a sick society. This is just the role the enabler plays with the alcoholic. Enablers interfere and support just enough so that alcoholics don't get a real opportunity to face the consequences of their addictive behavior, which would allow them the chance to experience their disease and the chance to change and experience recovery.

The "helping professions" are holding up, enabling, supporting just enough so that the system does not have the opportunity to see its destructiveness and to change. However, as with all addictions, an addictive system's disease is progressive and fatal. Enabling its survival is not kind.

The Mechanistic Scientific Paradigm and Psychotherapy

I truly believe that most of the people who go into
the helping professions genuinely want to be helpful
and healing.

Anne Wilson Schaef

Are psychologists and others in the helping professions
open to ask, Is the unspoken worldview that underlies
the assumptions in the way I practice my profession
perhaps, unwittingly, contributing to the very problems
that I am committed to help solve? If we are not open
to struggling with this question and articulating our
assumptions, we are, indeed, part of the problem.

Anne Wilson Schaef

In this section, I want to examine the mechanistic, reductionist, empirical model as it relates specifically to the practice of psychotherapy. There are many schools of psychotherapy, many approaches, and larger categories out of which these schools have grown such as psychoanalysis, behaviorism, humanistic psychology, and transpersonal psychology. Still, none of these various major movements in psychology has challenged the existent scientific worldview. All these movements in psychotherapy (except, perhaps, behaviorism) have tried to challenge parts of the mechanistic worldview while still trying to gain acceptance from and remain enveloped in this worldview. It is somewhat analogous to wanting to challenge our parents and their beliefs and still get an allowance from them and enjoy their life-style.

If fitting into the reductionist, empirical, mechanistic, scientific worldview is difficult for psychology as a whole, it is completely impossible for the field of psychotherapy, but psychotherapy continues to try. In so doing, it sets itself up to undermine the very goal it is trying to accomplish.

The Mechanistic Model of Psychotherapy

As much as many psychotherapists would probably like to disown it, the model for psychotherapy has been based upon the empirical scientific laboratory experiment. Whether we adhere to the psychoanalytic model or not, it was the beginning of modern psychology and the precursor of the modern field of psychotherapy. As psychotherapy has struggled to gain acceptance as "scientific," it has attempted to move further and further away from being an "art" to being a "science." Interestingly, I have found much more openness for my ideas among some European psychoanalysts (and some in America, too) than I find among psychologists. In Europe, medicine is still seen as an art, and psychiatry is not as mechanistically oriented as it is in the United States, although this is quickly changing as medicine and psychology become more rigid.

Objectivity

In the laboratory experiment, objectivity is very important. The "experimenter" is supposed to be uninvolved in the outcome and be able to maintain a lack of subjectivity (objectivity and subjectivity are always set up as a dualism; one is one or the other). The field of psychotherapy has dealt with the need for and belief in objectivity in many different ways. Freud tried to set up the ideal model for nonparticipation. He did not interact with his patients, and his interpretations were basically informed by his theory. This set up a consistent demand that the patient fit into his theory, and there are indications that he sometimes distorted the information from the client in order to achieve this fit. He did have the wisdom to allow the client to free-associate. However, all of the work was kept on a mental, analytical level, *and* the analyst was always in *control.*

Objectivity in the more modern therapies has sometimes taken the form of a benevolent, uninvolved "neutrality." Some have viewed this approach to objectivity as a "stoic sentry duty that will guard their patient's lonely ascent to autonomy."[73] Or as Lerner says,

> Moreover, for therapy to be treated as a "legitimate" and "scientific" enterprise, it had to go through a long struggle to achieve recognition. In that struggle, therapists had to represent their profession as fundamentally different from religions, political, and other ethically based approaches that deal with people's problems. So, they developed an ideology of "neutrality" . . . by which therapists must, above all else, avoid imposing their own views on clients. While this is fundamentally impossible—every interpreta- tion, every intervention, flows from a theory that is ulti- mately based upon beliefs about what is healthy behavior and what is not—it provides therapists with a good cover to avoid examining the ways in which they are in fact reinforc- ing the dominant worldview.[74]

Holding on to the myth of objectivity and trying to set up a human interaction in which one party is not really involved has set up an impossible situation for psychotherapy. The therapist must be caring and concerned and develop a model of a "healthy relationship" and at the same time be a scientist conducting a laboratory experiment in which the more uninvolved, neutral, and objective the therapist can be, the better it will be for the client.

As feminists and other women have long recognized, this "scien- tific" approach to therapy has set up an interaction that completely ignores the "female" experience and development that focuses upon relationships. Jon Clark says, "Macho science, especially in psychol- ogy, never listens, never experiences the 'subject' fully, never opens up and interrelates with the 'subject,' never admits that that interaction happens in any case and affects the results. The subject is to be manipulated in macho science." He goes on, "Macho science never admits to the importance of the psychological state of the scientist, never examines the process of science, never questions the goals of sci- ence. They are *prediction* and *control.* Period" (emphasis mine).[75] Unfortunately, many "feminist therapists" have completely bought this Macho science while espousing women's issues; as stated earlier, they have changed the content and not the process.

Objectivity is a myth, anyway, and in psychotherapy it is, like all myths, completely impossible. It is no wonder that psychotherapists sometimes feel schizophrenic and are often gradually reduced to a somewhat rote use of techniques, with accompanying burnout. In all fairness, I must say there are those who are aware that they are trying to find their own way in a model that cannot work.

The Laboratory Experiment

The laboratory experiment, in its simplest conceptualization, is based upon forming a hypothesis to be tested (or disproved, in the "purer" sense), establishing the dependent and the independent variables, manipulating those variables, predicting the outcome, and using those predictions for control.

As psychotherapy has tried to emulate mechanistic science, it has tried to gain acceptance by using the laboratory model, which, of course, is completely ludicrous in a therapy setting. Certainly behavior modification has come closest to the model of the scientific experiment, and even it has failed to have the kind of impact on individuals and the society it hoped it would have.

In the scientific or laboratory model, the human being has to be reduced to fit the operations of science. I suggest this assumption is absurdly infeasible.

There is also the issue of believing that it is possible to isolate the variables acting upon the person and to control some and manipulate others for the desired outcome. We have trusted diagnosis and fitting the client into the *Diagnostic Manual III* to define the variables for us. (Psychological testing, screening interviews, etc., have been used as a "sample" of behavior from which we can predict outcomes. They have been used to set up the laboratory experiment with the client.) Once the client has been diagnosed, a *scientifica-medica* model clicks in, and it is just a matter of manipulating certain variables and holding others constant to bring about the very simplistic cause-and-effect outcome.

All of this is based, of course, upon a science that sees the person as an object being acted upon by external forces. Mechanistic science has no place for volition, feelings, beliefs, values, will, self-determination, or spirituality—anything that originates or emanates from inside the person.[76]

Throughout the history of psychotherapy, various practitioners have focused upon particular aspects of psychotherapy and their usefulness for healing, but only recently have therapists themselves begun to look at and challenge the scientific worldview from which their discipline comes and call for radical changes. People are not machines, therapists cannot be "objective," and the therapy session can never approach a laboratory setting. This erroneous reliance upon a mechanistic scientific method severely limits the efficacy of therapy as we have designed it. In effect, we have set up therapy in such a way that it asks both the client and the therapist to deny their own reality in order to fit into the model.

Another aspect of the assumption that therapy can and should be a laboratory experiment is that because the "scientist" should be able to predict and control, the therapist is ultimately responsible for the client and the outcomes. Like the medical profession, the field of psychotherapy has set up a system in which the expert takes ultimate responsibility for the client. This, of course, is modeled on the "scientific" assumption that the experimenter can indeed predict and control. It creates an untenable situation and is ultimately destructive to both client and therapist. I will discuss later how these assumptions lead to dependency and maintenance of the client in a "victim" position.

I was interested to note that in the *Journal of Psychotherapy* Cherry and Gold wrote an article, based completely upon Freud's assumptions about the role of the therapist, in which the model of the laboratory experiment is evident. They write, "Therapist abstinence, anonymity, and neutrality were intended not only to create an open context into which a client could project fantasy and feelings but also to impose limitations on the *behavior and experience of the client*" (emphasis mine).[77]

The confusion in their article is typical of the confusion in the field. They stress regard for clients and their needs, but they do not recognize that the way this is played out in their model is that the therapist must be an experimenter/god, who can really be abstinent, anonymous, and neutral. They focus upon the needs of the clients but assume that those needs can be met with careful rules and controls. They fail to see that a control system is an addictive system and that the assumption of control by the therapist is destructive to the therapist and to the client. Throughout their article, Cherry and Gold assume that through techniques and interpretations, the good therapist can, indeed, control the situation. Moreover there is an assumption that it is the therapist who heals and controls the healing.

Frederick Franck has written a wonderful little monograph called "On the Criteria of Being Human." In it, he borrows from the work of Paul D. MacLean, M.D., chief of the Laboratory of Brain Evolution at the National Institutes of Health. As Franck develops his concept of what it means to be truly human, he discusses the functioning of the reptilian brain (important and necessary) as having the required information for "mating, breeding, flocking, foraging, hunting, hoarding, grooming, migrating, and fighting."[78] The reptilian brain is also adept at "greeting rituals and the etiquette of challenge, aggression, and submission. . . . The reptile brain even established routines and timetables for the activities of daily life: breakfast at eight, lunch at noon, followed by a siesta. . . . This lizard-snake-crocodile brain remains an integral part of our genetic coding, so that the patient on the couch may be bothered, even dominated, by her reptile within; the therapist no less."[79]

With the advent of the mammalian brain, the species takes a quantum leap. Franck notes that there is added nursing of the young, play, communication, and even group allegiance. Both Franck and MacLean speculate that some of our modern behaviors may, indeed, have their earliest antecedents in more primitive brain functions. For instance, "that the jurisprudence of our legal systems may well have its earliest antecedent in the reptilian brain's fidelity to precedent and ritual."[80] Could we, perhaps, even view the conservative reactionism with which psychology, psychiatry, and medicine respond to the concept of addiction as coming out of primitive brain functions?

We next developed the neocortex, and with it came "deductive reasoning, speech."[81] Franck describes the neocortex as "relentlessly logical, consistently 'rationalistic' in its operations. It is, however, also *devoid of all intuition and feeling*, so that one may suppose the neocortical computer has managed to devise all those remarkably clever and demoniacally cruel ways in which humans exploit, manipulate, illtreat, maim and kill their own species."[82]

As I read this description, I could not help but think that in spite of our best intentions, the way we have set up psychotherapy reflects this level of brain functioning. Franck goes on to say that we mistake this kind of functioning for *"a fully 'human brain.' For it is not yet human, it is at most pre-human, proto-human."*[83] He then asks the question, "Could it be this pre-human brain which in its feelingless arrogance is

232

steering our Spaceship Titanic on its collision course with the relentless iceberg of Reality?"[84]

To be fully human as Franck describes it means, *"the control by the genetically encoded pre-frontal capabilities over the—equally genetically encoded—reptilian and mammalian drives. In short: This control by the Specifically Human capabilities of empathy, compassion, foresight based on 'insight,' over the reptilian and mammalian impulses, I venture to characterize as THE HUMAN IMPERATIVE."* [85]

Does the view of science that we espouse and the psychotherapy we have developed out of that view keep us functioning at a subhuman level? I believe so. Is psychotherapy, the way we have constructed it, in essence trying to alleviate problems that, by its adherence to a mechanistic scientific worldview, it is helping to create and perpetuate? I believe so.

Does therapy, by the model out of which it operates, serve the function that most addictions serve, which is to increase our tolerance for insanity in the culture and in us? I believe so.

The Medicalization of Psychotherapy

While psychology in general has sought to gain acceptance in the scientific community, psychotherapy has sought to model itself after and gain acceptance in the medical establishment. We have used words like *patients* and *clients*. We have modeled the therapy hour on the medical appointment; we have diagnosed and prescribed (psychologically). We have sought to establish the same kind of licensing requirements and to control the profession with an increasingly strict "one-party code," like the field of medicine (which, frankly, is actually less rigid, recognizing chiropractic, osteopathy, and acupuncture but not psychic healers, kahunas, or herbalists). We have sought to be reimbursed by third-party payments and to establish ourselves as part of the field of mental health—but at what cost?

Just as psychology tries harder because of its lack of acceptance in the sciences, psychiatry, psychology, social work, counseling, and, yes, even religion, seek to gain approval and acceptance by the real science in the helping profession, medicine (which, ironically, when at its best is probably more an art than a science).

Arthur L. Kovacs wrote a rather chilling article in the *Psychotherapy Bulletin* about the implications of becoming involved in the "health" professions. He, too, uses the image of the *Titanic*, but his analogy is the field of clinical psychology and its push to be accepted as a health-care provider. (As one reads all these materials, it is impossible not to wonder where plain old simple human greed enters these issues.) Kovacs describes three historical "accidents," that have happened to the "discipline." The first, he says, was "when our society took the responsibility for intervening in the lives of those who exhibited deviant behavior away from the priesthood and placed it in the hands of physicians."[86] (This is the modernist scientific revolution.) The second was during World War II when "thousands of young psychologists were pressed into military service and wound up in the home of medicine as corpsmen, mental testers, and junior psychiatrists dealing with the emotional trauma and wreckage created by the stresses of war in the lives of military men. Those who trained and supervised the first generation of our pioneers were physicians and the *heuristics used to 'explain' the disturbance of conduct requiring attention were physicalistic and reductionistic*" [emphasis mine]. Kovacs suggests that the third accident "occurred in the 1950s when our founders elected first to secure licensure and then to battle—successfully—for recognition as eligible providers for the purpose of health insurance reimbursement." He continues, "We declared fully to ourselves, to policy makers, and to the nation at large that we, too, as we engaged in the practice of psychotherapy (and think about the very word 'psycho*therapy*' itself), were engaged in the 'health' business."[87] And we are now clamoring for hospital privileges and the limited ability to prescribe drugs. If we wanted to be physicians, why did we go into psychology? If we wanted to help people to heal, why have we gone into a profession that focuses on illness and scientific study and manipulation?

Kovacs makes a valid point that as insurance providers become more rigid in their guidelines, therapists will become more and more constricted as to what kind of "treatment" can be offered to what kind of "patient" and under what kind of circumstances. We will have the same unreasonable professional controls as physicians have set up for themselves.

We have wanted to be like medicine, and medicine has wanted to exert more and more power and control over everything that has to do with the human organism. All this is based upon a mechanistic model of control. And now the tail has begun to wag the tiger.

In Boulder, Colorado, there was an old woman who many saw as a psychic healer. She ran a health food store and would see people, free of charge, and often suggest herbs for healing. In the rare times when I was sick, I would frequently consult her along with my physician, my acupuncturist, and maybe even an Indian medicine man and a psychic medical physician I knew, if I felt *really* ill. I always weighed, compared, and contrasted what they said and took the advice that made the most sense in view of what I was feeling and experiencing.

Recently, a local physician brought charges against this woman for "practicing medicine without a license." He brought the charges because a patient had become "sick" from the herbs she had suggested. First of all, she was not practicing medicine, she was practicing healing. Second, the "illness" may have been a healing crisis that happens when we clear out toxins (including prescription medicines) from our bodies. Third, how much of his prescription medicine has actually harmed his patients?

If the medical profession in Hawaii ever tried to enforce this type of one-party medical fascism, the entire pluralist society there would rise up in arms. Every ethnic group listens to its own healers and practitioners as well as to Western medicine.

What psychotherapy has failed to see is that they have jumped on the bandwagon of acceptance from a one-party scientific system that does not really include them. They are trying to emulate the narrow ideology and control of medicine, but that position of medicine ultimately does not include them. Actually, medicine does not even really adequately include itself. They are like the kid that is willing to sell his soul to be included, but no one can be included who is willing to sell his soul. The medico-centric view of the world does not have room for a holographic scientific paradigm or the essence of being human, as Franck would say. (Let me be clear, here, that I am not *just* talking about the medical model. I am talking about the actual scientific belief [model] on which it is based.)

The medical model is based upon mechanics, techniques, and procedures and believes that real healing comes from the ability to define these mechanisms in finer and finer precision and do them *to* people. Inasmuch as psychotherapy has accepted this model, it is in an untenable position.

A few years ago, I had the privilege of being invited to speak at a conference on addictions in the USSR in Moscow. I was saddened to see that there were only two women speakers and even more saddened to see that so much of the conference focused upon brain physiology and biology. The other woman speaker was, however, a recovering person as well as being a psychiatrist and director of a large addictions treatment center in a metropolitan hospital. I was eager to hear her talk and entered it with a positive mind-set. After listening for a short time, I began to develop a feeling of uneasiness and a head-ache. Then I began to listen without my positive bias. What I heard was everything being defined in terms of medicine. People did not have physical, emotional, psychological, or spiritual problems. They had psychiatric or medical problems. I was hearing a medico-centric view of the universe. Like any self-centered addict, medicine has tried to define the world in terms of itself, what it has done, and what it can do. (When we do not see how our disease [of addiction] interacts with our profession, we tend to practice it in our profession and use our profession to block the possibility of full recovery.)

In trying to gain acceptance in the medico-centric view of the universe, psychotherapists put themselves at the mercy of a fascist dictator, an unlikely formula for success. Psychotherapists have acquiesced to a model that is antithetical to what we hope to accomplish. That is why, for some time, I have no longer been able to identify with psychology or psychotherapy.

Wounded Healers and Codependence in Psychotherapy

There has been a great interest in the last few years in the concept of the "wounded healer."[88] There has been a recognition that people who want to "help" people may not always want to do it for the healthiest of reasons. The irony in what has been written about this is in the assumption that psychotherapy can ever be just a job.

"For such people, their job is not merely a way to earn a living [old scientific, objective model]: it is the essence of their lives."[89] An addictive, mechanistically oriented society has little knowledge of the difference between a job and a vocation and little understanding of living out one's process in a holomovement universe.[90] In a mechanistic universe, everything is separate and static. Therefore, there is a belief that one can do a job and not really be "in" it or relating with it. This assumption just does not fit with our experienced reality.

Many of the observations of the less than perfect people in the Maeder article (that they are authoritarian, dependent on others, and have a self-image of benevolence, that they hope to vicariously help themselves and expect adulation)[91] are probably valid, especially in the mechanistic scientific model we have been describing. Also, it is important to remember that these people whom Maeder probably accurately describes as needy people are also people who are expected to be perfect. In fact, they come out of a model that says that the person who is most helpful is the person who is most perfect. This paradigm assumes that the person who is the most helpful is the person who is trained, knowledgeable, objective, and perfect. The best "helper" is someone who has no needs. Cherry and Gold assert that "what distinguishes the 'therapeutic encounter' from other relationships is the relatively exclusive concern with the needs of only one member of the dyad, the client."[92]

I agree that people cannot be helpful to another when they are so enmeshed in their issues that they can't possibly focus upon someone else. But haven't we set up a situation in which the ways that we attempt to deal with this issue are through denial, control, repression, rules, and the threat of punishment—all elements of an addictive system?

Cherry and Gold go on to say, "Most important, the frame [of psychotherapy] assists the therapists in placing the client's interest consistently above all other considerations."[93] This is a completely untenable situation, at best, and an active codependent position, at worst. And Cherry and Gold think this posture of the psychotherapist is good. How is it possible to "help" others heal when the healers are not taking care of themselves?

"Wounded Healers" does a good job of analyzing (and judging) the dynamics that go into becoming a healer. What the author fails to recognize is that this role is intimately related to addiction and is a systematized addictive/codependent role in our addictive society. Maeder does recognize that having "problems," in and of itself, is not necessarily "bad." "The danger occurs when the wounded healer has not resolved, or cannot *control* [emphasis mine] his own injury."[94] There is no recognition that the role of psychotherapist as it has been set up continues to feed and exacerbate the disease of relationship addiction and codependence and require *control*. The model itself trains the therapist into systematized codependence. When one focuses only upon analyzing the individual practitioner, one loses sight of the fact that even an individual who sought to recover could probably not do so in that systematized role.[95]

Joe Reid quotes Carol Farina as saying that wounding (of the professional) is synonymous with the term *codependency*. Reid defines codependency as "a condition where people put the needs of others before their own, to their own detriment."[96] Farina sees the focus of these unmet needs coming out in one basic form—*control*—the need to control relationships. Certainly the psychotherapy setup meets that criterion. Reid describes Farina's assertion, "For some therapists, control is so important that any contact with others outside the therapeutic session is shunned. Their insecurity has a chilling effect on all other personal relationships."[97] Could this be part of the cause of burnout and workaholism in psychotherapists? Add the pressure for control to the need to take complete responsibility for others' lives, and the result is exhaustion and burnout.

When we look at psychotherapy as the systematized training into and the practice of the disease of codependence, we need to look at several levels. First, as we have stated, psychotherapists often come from addictive, dysfunctional families. They tend to migrate to a profession where they can use the skills they learned at home and where those skills are valued. But there is more to it than this.

Because psychotherapists often come from addictive/dysfunctional families and are usually not in recovery (and frequently their families are not in recovery), they do not understand or know how to recognize addictive dysfunctions or healthy functioning. Dysfunction seems normal; hence, when they find themselves in a profession that systematizes codependent functioning, it seems normal. We tend to look at the dysfunction in the individuals, but we fail to look at the match with a dysfunctional profession. For example, codependents do not know the difference between love and control, so they choose a profession in which the two are fused. Codependents tend to focus upon others and get their validity from caretaking, so they choose a profession in which they get paid for it. Codependents thrive on other's dependency upon them. Therapists are trained to believe that it is their role to be in charge of the situation, to know what others need, to be able to know and interpret what is good for others, to know better than they do what is going on in a person and what will "fix" it, to be able to manipulate others in their "best interest," and to be responsible for others. The very structure and makeup of the profession has perpetuated this disease process.

Unfortunately, codependents tend to try to make themselves "God" or a Higher Power for other people, often believing that they can "love" them into health.

It is ironic how often the treatment for codependency is codependent itself. A brochure I recently received states, "Leaders will provide participants with assistance in:

* understanding the developmental causes of their disease,
* removing the obstacles that resulted in their developmental stuckness,
* becoming more fully aware of themselves and the addictive ways they respond to situations and people so that they can make better choices,
* exercising effective *control* [emphasis mine] over their own lives, and
* learning to develop and maintain interdependent relationships.[98]

These leaders certainly know what the participants need and how to get it.[99] This is admirable in a mechanistic cause-and-effect science mode. I question how much healing it offers.

Cermak lists these diagnostic criteria for codependence:

* Continual investment of self-esteem in the ability to influence or control feelings and behavior in oneself and others in the face of obvious adverse consequences,
* Assumption of responsibility for meeting others' needs to the exclusion of acknowledging one's own needs,
* Anxiety and boundary distortions in situations of intimacy and separation,
* Enmeshment in relationships with personality-disordered, drug-dependent, and impulse-disordered individuals,
* Exhibitions of any three or more of the following behaviors: constriction of emotions with or without concomitant dramatic outbursts; depression; hypervigilance; compulsions; anxiety; excessive reliance on denial; substance abuse; recurrent physical or sexual abuse; stress-related medical illness; or a primary relationship with an active substance abuser that lasts for at least two years without the individual seeking outside support.[100]

That certainly sounds like many psychotherapists to me. For example, in a recent article in the Kauai *Times* about a Kauai physician known as "Dr. Love," he says, "As a physician, I've learned how to manipulate the body with chemicals, currents, procedures—how to influence the biophysical entity that we are—and yet, as I did all that and watched the results, I was impressed that the power of love is much greater than the power of science. If I add love to the dimension of science, then a whole new dimension opens up in the response of the individual I'm with and in my understanding of myself. So I've just come to understand that above all else, what I can give to anyone is love."[101]

As I read this article, I thought of Cermak's criteria for codependence, ("Continual investment of self-esteem in the ability to influence or control feelings and behavior in oneself and others.")[102] It struck me that the New Age therapist had just added love to the scientifically controlled bag of tricks. Unfortunately, when one controls the giving of love, it's not love. Many New Age approaches have substituted loving "techniques" for authoritarian techniques, and both are still manipulative techniques. I think it is easy to see that the subtlety of the training into codependency of the psychotherapist is many-faceted. Even when we are trying to be most helpful, we do need to recognize that the role itself is part of a progressive disease that ultimately can be fatal to the therapist and the client. More about this later.

Can Psychotherapy as a Model Work?

Although I recognize that many people are helped by psychotherapy and that as a former psychotherapist, myself, I helped many people, I do not believe that the model of psychotherapy that is based upon mechanistic science can ultimately be helpful. I have come to think that in those rare instances in which psychotherapy is really healing, the Living Process System has managed to break through an ultimately destructive paradigm.

When I am giving lectures, I often demonstrate it this way: I make a fist with my left hand and then cover my left hand with my right hand. My left hand is almost completely covered with my right hand, and you can see it here and there because, of course, my right hand cannot completely cover over my left hand.

It is as if my left hand is the Living Process System that is completely covered over with the addictive system (my right hand). But, every once in a while, the Living Process System breaks through (I usually poke a finger up between the fingers of my right hand). This breaking through can be a real healing. Then, in one of the typical processes of the addictive system, the addictive system co-opts this experience and uses it to perpetuate itself. Because the addictive system does not recognize the existence of the Living Process System, whenever this living system breaks through, the addictive system uses it to justify and perpetuate itself.

This is like denigrating the characteristics that are typically seen as female (softness, caring, nurturance) and then using them to perpetuate the White Male System. It is similar to the way the relationship addict functions, which is to suffer with an addictive relationship and then, when asked why she or he stays in it, to say, "Yes, it is terrible. But I remember a time two years ago when for a few minutes we really communicated. Maybe that can happen again." We use the "breakthrough" to sustain the addiction.

When the healing of the Living Process System breaks through in therapy, it is used to support a model that is designed on the very worldview that makes real healing impossible.

Specific Problems with Psychotherapy

EXPLANATIONS AND UNDERSTANDING. Psychotherapy often relies upon explanations and understanding as a cure. There is a belief that if people just understand their dynamics and those of their family, they will be all right. As I said earlier, I have never seen anyone heal from understanding. Because most therapists have so little real understanding of addictions, psychological "whys" become one of the ways psychotherapy is used to perpetuate the addictive system. The focus upon the psychological understanding of what is going on is a way of staying where one is and not really having to face our addictions or our underlying deep processes. "Understandings" often give license to behave addictively. Recovery from addictions, by contrast, requires that one take full responsibility (ownership) for everything that we have done while in our disease. A common misconception among psychotherapists who are not knowledgeable about addiction and recovery is that saying that one has a disease over which one is powerless gets one off the hook. Nothing could be further from the truth. The Twelve-Step program of recovery requires that recovering persons own everything they did during their time in the disease, even during blackouts, and make amends wherever possible. And a proper amend may mean a commitment to a complete life change. I have found that psychological explanations are much more likely than recovery programs to give one an "excuse."

POWER ISSUES. Because of the way psychotherapy is set up with the "expert" who is "perfect" and the client who needs to be fixed, there is in this model a necessary power imbalance. Moreover, in a belief system that says that the expert should always be in control, the setup of a power imbalance is a given. Feminists and blacks have long decried this power imbalance, but often, as they have entered the field, members of both groups have unfortunately succumbed to the "given" in the model.

This model feeds dependency, and dependency will never ultimately be healing. Of course, there is a belief that out of dependency comes independence; I think that bears challenging in the model and in reality.

IMPOSSIBILITY OF DOING PSYCHOTHERAPY. Masson eloquently, if angrily, makes a case in *Against Therapy* for the impossibility of doing psychotherapy. He does not, however, challenge the scientific model on which it is based, but takes on various "schools" of psychotherapy and brilliantly demonstrates how they just will not work and how frequently they are dangerous. My first reading of his book *Against Therapy* was like a wandering back through the history of my own development as a psychotherapist. Many of the people mentioned were those with whom I had studied (or refused to learn from, like Rosen), but it was quite an experience to look at my own "brainwashing" and refusal to be brainwashed through Masson's eyes.

I was especially struck, in Masson's discussion of Hans Strupp, with Strupp's statement that "the therapist does not treat a disease or disorder but rather a human being who experiences more or less specific difficulties in his adjustment to life."[103] Often in psychotherapy circles we have heard that it is the *relationship* between the therapist and the client that is really healing, but a "scientist" does not have "relationships." Yet, psychotherapy is based upon a "science," and this attitude has spawned therapies (like reparenting) that believe that the therapist can "fix" what was not done "right" the first time by just doing it "right." Another mechanistic approach that also doesn't work.

FEMINIST THERAPY. Masson raises some important issues about the tendency for feminist therapy to fall into the same traps as other forms of therapy.[104] It clearly is not enough to change the focus from men to women and continue to do the same old things based upon the mechanistic scientific worldview. Feminism, I believe, is at its very core an attempt to deal with the mechanistic scientific worldview and its implications for all humanity, nature, the planet, and the universe.

Feminist therapists have not, for whatever reasons of their own, been willing to take on the scientific "club" that undergirds psychotherapy and be consistent with their beliefs. As I have said earlier, the most vicious attacks on me have come from what I consider elitist feminist therapists who wanted me to be under their control and to get into line (or mostly shut up and get out). I see their major concern as being one of making feminist therapy acceptable and accepted into the therapy establishment. There has been little or no genuine attempt to challenge the model on which therapy is based. I completely agree with Masson that "all the defects inherent in the various approaches examined in [*Against Therapy*] will seep, subtly or not so subtly, into 'feminist' therapy."[105]

As Mary Daly writes, "Behind the more obviously misogynistic presuppositions for patriarchal psychotherapy (e.g., 'penis envy' and blaming the mother) there is a more subtle agenda, which is difficult to uproot and which seems to be endemic to the therapeutic situation in its various forms."[106] I also agree with Daly when she says that "feminist therapy is inherently a contradiction in terms."[107]

PREVENTION AND POTENTIAL. In 1982, George Albee wrote an important paper, "Preventing Psychopathology and Promoting Human Potential."[108] In it, I believe, Albee anticipated what we are learning about the effects of an addictive society and the failure of psychotherapy to meet the needs of the society. Like many writers of that time, he did not question the mechanistic sciences or even the assumptions of psychotherapy, but he did describe the issues of psychology and suggested that psychology as we knew it then was ineffective in meeting the needs of the society.

In his abstract he says, "Primary prevention of mental and emotional disturbances emphasizes the reduction of unnecessary stress, including powerlessness, and the enhancement of social competence, self-esteem, and support networks."[109] I find it interesting to note that the characteristics that he lists are all found in recovery from addictions (in the Twelve-Step program of Alcoholics Anonymous, for instance, personal power is increased when one admits powerlessness over an addiction) and that community recovery was demonstrated when a Native American community in Canada confronted all of these issues in going from 100 percent addicted to 95 percent in recovery.[110]

He further states that the approach he suggests "argues that one-to-one psychotherapy is a hopeless approach because of the unbridgeable gap between the large numbers in need and the small numbers of helpers."[111] (Not to mention that one-to-one therapy as we know it exacerbates the problems on a societal level and cannot possibly meet the existent needs.) I find it fascinating that psychologists and other "helpers" continue to push for stricter and stricter licensing laws that, progressively, would force the public into one political and theoretical choice of provider, while those providers even now cannot meet the existing needs. It is apparent to me that in the present state of psychology, we are dealing with economic issues and issues of control (the illusion of control) and not with concern for the needs of the public. Clearly, a community model is needed.

Albee suggests, "Two strategies for resolving our shortfall make sense. The first is to find alternatives to the kind of one-to-one intervention that must be provided by a highly trained professional."[112] I find this interesting on several levels. One is that the only place that I see this really happening on a community level is among the Native Americans I just mentioned. They have mobilized themselves to deal with addiction, often with no "experts" present, and have realized that they have to go back to the roots by which Western mechanistic society has sought to deprive them of their heritage and, in that process, confront their addictions, regain their self-esteem, and develop new (old) paradigms.

Second, I am remembering a battered women's shelter that was the first in its community. It was initiated and put into operation by battered women whose credentials were that they, themselves, were battered women and were concerned. The local "feminist psychologists" managed to get the shelter closed down. They thought it should be run by trained professionals because there would be "counseling" going on. Some time later, it was again opened with those professionals on the board and getting a consulting fee. The issues in these instances seem to be more issues of control and economics than concern for providing services.

Albee goes on to say, "We need to develop mutual aid groups, to encourage and develop self-help programs, to encourage paraprofessional workers who want to get out into the community and use existing helping networks and support systems."[113] Even as I write this, I am aware of the furor that the self-help groups are at present causing in the professional community. Jacobs and Goodman wrote a strong article urging psychologists to try to make a place for themselves in the growing world of self-help. "Psychologists are urged to enhance the relevance of the profession by taking an early leadership role in these developments. If we psychologists do not play a significant part in this development, other professionals will, perhaps dropping our national relevance a notch."[114] Why do we need to exert leadership in an area in which we are ill informed and not needed? Just what are the issues here? It seems that greed, the illusion of control, and competition play a big role—all are characteristics of an addict.

Albee's other strategy is that we need to "put more efforts in the primary prevention. We must recognize the fact that no mass disorder affecting large numbers of human beings has ever been controlled or eliminated by attempts at treating each affected individual or by training enough professional as interventionists."[115] Albee suggests approaches that "involve the development of personal responsibility for health, life-style changes, and less stressful and more humane environments."[116] In short, he suggests that we make a paradigm shift and begin to think and live in different ways. This is exactly what happens when one confronts addictions and learns to Live in Process. Since I have been trying to develop new models, I have had more attempts by "professionals" to stop the work I am doing than at any other time in my life. The need for change may be there, but generally people attempt to make modifications within the old scientific paradigm rather than change it entirely, even when it is not working.

The consensus among those who are seriously looking at the efficacy of the psychotherapeutic model seems to be that it cannot work. Yet, as in any system that is undergoing radical changes, this causes some to hold on ever tighter to the old model. Again, as I have stated many times, the irony is that the true basis of science of any kind is open-mindedness. If one is not open-minded even about the assumptions of one's science, that is dogmatism.

Some Assumptions That Make Psychotherapy Untenable

There are many spoken and unspoken assumptions that contribute to the indefensibility of psychotherapy as a vehicle for healing:

* That the person best qualified to help is the expert and the most perfect.
* That people are the sum total of forces that have acted upon them.
* That defense mechanisms are necessary.
* That dual diagnosis is essential.

✳ That we need to get rid of negative feelings and replace them with good feelings.
✳ That theory is helpful in psychotherapy.
✳ That transference and countertransference are necessary elements for healing.

In this section, I will look at each of these in turn.

THAT THE PERSON BEST QUALIFIED TO HELP IS THE EXPERT AND THE MOST PERFECT. I have mentioned earlier the assumption that the person best qualified to help is the expert and the most perfect, and here I would like to point out what it does to the therapist and the client.

For the therapist, it sets up a situation in which impression management and denial are the name of the game. This has been one of the reasons it has been so difficult to get impaired professionals to go for help for addiction problems. The professional not only has to deal with the personal stigma but also with the professional assumption that to function as a professional she or he must be a model of health. Add to this that the profession is very judgmental about illness, especially addictions, and (with desperate protestations to the contrary) sees people with problems as "bad" or damaged and not capable of real health. This makes admission of the need for help almost impossible for professionals.

In the mental health model, the one who is most helpful is the one who is the picture of "health" on every level, and even if she or he isn't, the model militates against revealing that.

In the addiction model, however, the one who is most trusted is the one who can truthfully say, "I have been there" and knows the struggle back to health from personal experience and not just in the abstract. It is a participatory scientific model.

THAT PEOPLE ARE THE SUM TOTAL OF FORCES THAT HAVE ACTED UPON THEM. Because of the assumptions about the necessary imbalance of power in psychotherapy, combined with the mechanistic scientific assumptions that objects only interact externally on one another (that is what can be observed and measured), assumptions are made that persons are the sum total of forces that have acted upon them. There is no place for volition, will, motivation, choices, feelings, or intuition and their roles in the individual.

Because the scientific view on which therapy is based believes in dualism and that a person is either a victim or to blame, there is no place for a person to own choices and not be to blame. Therefore, psychotherapy has set up a model in which people are victims—victims of their parents, victims of their childhood, victims of their friends, their therapists, and their teachers. They are not responsible for their lives (as in the meaning "to own," not to cause and therefore blame). Ever so subtly, psychotherapy as we have set it up works toward keeping a person a victim and therefore dependent. Unfortunately, no person who remains a victim has ever healed. No victim has ever regained self-esteem. No victim fully functions.

It is important to recognize and remember that women are victims of a culture that devalues females. Yet, if a woman stays stuck there and does not move on to quit focusing upon the culture—knowing that only she can heal what is inside her—and does not begin to own the choices she has made and do whatever she needs to do to heal, she will never have self-esteem. Self-esteem does not come from someone else. It comes from confronting and working through the reality of our own lives. In my experience, the Twelve-Step program of A.A. does a much better job of facilitating this move toward self-esteem beyond victimization than does psychotherapy.

THAT DEFENSE MECHANISMS ARE NECESSARY. Freud assumed that defense mechanisms are a normal and necessary part of the human makeup. In the work that I have been doing in the new scientific paradigm (the Living Process System), and in recovery from addictions, I have not found this to be true. The presence of defense mechanisms often indicates that a person is operating out of their addictive process. Defense mechanisms are only normal and needed in an addictive system. In this and in many other instances, psychotherapy makes assumptions about "normal" being what is normal in an addictive society based upon the mechanistic scientific model. It is quite possible that defense mechanisms were developed to cope with an abnormal illusionary society.

THAT DUAL DIAGNOSIS IS ESSENTIAL. There has been a recent assumption that addictions and mental health diagnoses are different, with addictions being a reaction to underlying mental health problems. This assumption, of course, eliminates societal influences, keeps the mental health practitioner involved with addictions, and eliminates the awareness of the physiological dependence involved with chemical addiction. It is also important to note that hospitals get paid much more for psychiatric clients than they do for those carrying the sole diagnosis of addiction. Under the guise of clearer diagnosis, there are several political issues that are in play here. There is still an unstated assumption (backed by little or no evidence) that psychological or psychiatric illnesses are easier to treat, or are treated better, or that we know how to treat them and that we have been successful in treating them. Dual diagnosis maintains an archaic power base (stressed especially since addictions do not respond well to the usual medical or psychological approaches). There is more ease in attempting to treat mental illness (which requires a professional) than addictions. This is another example of trying to get the client to fit what we know how to do.

THAT WE NEED TO GET RID OF NEGATIVE FEELINGS AND REPLACE THEM WITH GOOD FEELINGS. The statement that we need to get rid of negative feelings and replace them with good feelings assumes, first of all, that the therapist knows what is "good" for the client. Second, it assumes that bad feelings are not good and should go away.

There are no such things as negative feelings. Feelings just *are*. They are there for information and for us to learn from. When we try to control them, we suffer. When we judge them, we suffer. As McMahon and Campbell say, "The denial of any aspect sharpens and preserves it, while its acceptance transforms it by bringing it within the process of the whole."[117]

THAT THEORY IS HELPFUL IN PSYCHOTHERAPY. When I was in graduate school, I was told that theory was absolutely necessary and the worst kind of a psychologist was an eclectic. I now understand that the reason an eclectic is so "bad" is that the scientific role of psychology is to test theories; if there is no theory, there is no laboratory.

However, I have observed that the role of theory is often harmful to psychotherapy and is one of the aspects of psychotherapy that is rarely challenged. I believe that theories often limit and control the perceptions of therapists, causing them not to hear or to dismiss information that does not support their theories. (I am reminded again of Masson's description of how Freud sought to dismiss what he was hearing about early childhood sexual abuse in order to support his theories.)[118] This ignoring of information is far too common in professional circles.

Psychotherapists do try to fit their clients into their theories. Unfortunately, when the client does not fit the theory, the client loses. Then, too, when the therapist is thinking about the theory and trying to fit the client into the theory, the therapist has really left the client. The therapist is so busy thinking that being present is not possible.

Too frequently, our theories are just plain wrong. They are logical and rational, but they sometimes just do not fit. For example, why do we always assume that the womb was a safe place? The deep process work does not support the idea that the womb was "safe." Yet, many theories assume the desire to return to the "safety" of the womb. Theories are, by necessity, what makes sense, for whatever reason, to the theory maker.

I once listened to two well-known therapists talk about the birth process and how all of life is really working out the birth process (I doubt it, from my experience). They asserted, for example, that infants born by cesarean section never really had to confront the birth process and because of this tend to be rather passive and, as adults, never really confront life. I was appalled at the mental masturbation that went into the generation of this discourse. I volunteered that I was born by cesarean, and I am the most confrontive person I know. Needless to say, they were not amused, and they quickly pointed out that there are always exceptions. As if to prove how theory can be destructive, I could see the audience was loving this theoretical discourse; they were mainlining it right to the brain, not even checking out what was true for them. As Eugene Gendlin notes, "Such concepts make all sorts of mischief because we tend to try to fit them without allowing ourselves the very different process of getting there."[119]

I have always said that theory should remain in the background to help us miss less and be less ignorant than we would otherwise be. Theories are good for science. I am not sure how good they are for healing. They do offer security to the practitioner. These concerns seem to be hark back to a statement from Gerald May: "I tried to make a God out of science; science seemed learnable, masterable, and controllable."[120] Personally, I have found more often than not that theory tends to interfere with awareness and healing.

THAT TRANSFERENCE AND COUNTERTRANSFERENCE ARE NECESSARY ELEMENTS FOR HEALING. Although many therapists no longer consciously subscribe to Freudian psychodynamic therapy, there are many assumptions of Freudian analysis that continue to linger. Probably one of the most tenacious is the notion of transference and countertransference and how necessary they are for healing.

In traditional psychoanalysis, according to Masson, "Transference refers to the feelings that a patient 'transfers' from an earlier important person (primarily in childhood and most commonly a parent) onto the person of the therapist. The behavior of the therapist is considered irrelevant to the origin of these feelings. They belong to the earlier figure and hence are considered to be *projections*."[121] Countertransference is the process in reverse, when the therapist projects old relationships onto the client.

In psychoanalytically oriented psychotherapy, transference (the client must look to the therapist as superior) must occur for therapy to take place. The skilled therapist then uses the transference or the power imbalance in the service of the therapy.

It has been my experience in working with people in recovery in a Living Process way that transference *and* countertransference are always indicators that someone has slipped into his or her addictive disease process. I have found that it is much better to deal with this process in a group (where the atmosphere tends to be more equal) than it was when I was a "therapist." When projections come at me, I always check them out with myself and the group. If I have a part in the projection and some responsibility for its existence, I then do my own work to get clear with the person putting out the projection. If scrutiny by the group and my own reflection indicates I have no part, then it is clear that the person "projecting" has left the present and has moved into the addictive process. Often, projection or transference occurs when a person is trying to avoid a deep process that is ready to come up. Because there is at least an attempt to have no power differential and I also participate as a member of the group, countertransference is really a moot point. When I project upon someone, it is transference or slipping into my addictive process, and the group has the responsibility to call me on it. It is also *my* responsibility to be aware as soon as I am able that I am in an addictive process and to move out of that by doing my own recovery work.

My major concerns about the whole transference-countertransference issue are that a power imbalance is set up and assumed and there is a belief that it is possible to use an addictive disease process in the service of healing.

In my work with addictions and recovery, knowing that we have moved into the addictive process and using the tools of recovery to move out is the way to deal with the addictive process. Using transference is like trying to use poison to get healthy. Freud, who was himself an addict, set up a system of staying in and using the addictive disease process to try to get healthy. This was at least partially, I believe, because this was all he knew. Psychotherapy has continued to utilize addictive disease processes to try to bring about healing, and they simply will not work.

Transference cannot be "used." It can best be confronted, giving the person the chance to see that she or he has left the present, is projecting, and has slipped into the addictive disease process. It is only helpful if the projections are rejected or not responded to (which happens in Twelve-Step meetings). This confrontation gives people the opportunity to look at themselves and the way they "practice their disease."

To try to "use" transference as a vehicle for healing and to assume it is *necessary* keeps everyone mired in an addictive system. Addictive behavior can be a door into possible healing. To try to use it and work with it can only result in confusion and staying stuck in the addictive system, which is what, I believe, has happened to the field of psychotherapy. Psychotherapy has been trying to use tools that, by default, make it unhealthy and untenable.

Is Psychotherapy Ultimately Harmful?

After the above explorations, this question of whether psychotherapy is ultimately harmful almost seems rhetorical, yet I do feel that it needs to be asked directly. There is a difference between something not working and its being harmful. It is not just the specifics of individual schools upon which we need to focus. It is the very worldview out of which therapy comes that in the last analysis makes the whole approach untenable. In this section I will ask five related questions: Is therapy harmful to the therapist? Is therapy harmful to the client? Does therapy create and maintain dependency? Is psychotherapy based upon control and manipulation? Do New Age healing techniques emulate the model of psychotherapy and therefore render themselves harmful?

IS THERAPY HARMFUL TO THE THERAPIST? The role of the therapist, as it has been set up, is ultimately not viable. The therapist is legally and professionally put in a position of being God, for example. The therapist is supposed to know exactly what the client needs and be able to control and protect the client. The therapist is not just an advocate for the client; ultimately, the therapist is responsible for the client's life.

We have set up a system based upon the illusion of control in which mere human beings are supposed to be gods, and we have set up a professional relationship that is modeled after a sick codependent relationship. In a recent article in the *Medical Tribune,* Ari Kiev discusses the "Tarasoff Decision."[122] In this case, a psychiatrist who felt bound by ethics of confidentiality was found guilty of not warning a potential victim of homicide before his client committed the murder. This is an especially clear instance of the systematized and systematically accepted practice of a disease that is progressive and fatal.

It is not surprising that we find so much exhaustion and burnout in the helping professions. There are indications that codependents living with an active addict tend to die younger than the addict. If our profession is the systematized practice of codependence, it is not surprising there is such a high level of burnout in helpers.

IS THERAPY HARMFUL TO THE CLIENT? As I implied earlier, it is my opinion that one of the reasons that psychotherapists go to so many workshops and training seminars is that they really want to help, and, down deep, they believe that what they know and what they are doing just is not working. Psychotherapists have become a group in search of a technique, trying to incorporate every technique that comes down the pike.

I have come to see techniques, exercises, and interpretations as the "stash" of the codependent relationship addict therapist. By calling this our "stash," I mean that we use techniques, exercises, and interpretations just as alcoholics use their hidden alcohol—to perpetuate our disease.

Therapists use these three "tools" to maintain a power base, to keep themselves in their illusion of control, to manipulate the process of the client, and to foster dependency. When clients arrive at information through the use of these three tools, what they learn is to trust the tools and the therapist and not, ultimately, to trust their own process. These tools also make the therapist indispensable and necessary for the understanding of oneself. As Jacquelyn Small states, "Our inner voice knows how to be happy now. It is the wisdom of the organism. But we may not be able to hear this voice so easily. *So we need tools and methods that take us inward*"(emphasis mine).[123]

I have found that it is the *therapist* who needs the tools and methods, not the client or participant. Participants need a safe atmosphere, which, for me, implies an honest, self-revealing atmosphere where all present are participating at a level comfortable to them. They need some information about deep processes, and they need to have someone sit with them when their deep processes come up. They do not need to have their deep processes wrenched out of them or interpreted for them.

I have come to think of techniques, tools, methods, whatever one wants to call them, as analogous to the use of forceps in a normal delivery. There is no doubt that, when forceps are used, you get a baby. Almost always, the processes that are "delivered by forceps" out of people through the use of techniques are "true." Yet, as in birthing the baby, the mother, the baby, and the birthing process are often damaged by the forceps. It is difficult to reject something when the information is "true." Still, if the timing is not compatible with the person's inner process, she or he may not be ready to deal with the content of the forced process. Even if the timing is right, people do not learn to trust their own process when processes are ripped out of them. In the long run, healing comes from learning to trust our own process and deal with our deep processes, whether a "professional" is present or not.

When I think about damage done through the use of techniques, tools, methods, and so on, I remember again the young woman from Germany whose story I recounted in the section entitled "Deep Process Work Cannot Be Programmed." The tool (hypnosis) was used by a therapist who wanted only the best for his client. The client trusted her therapist and wanted to heal. Assumptions and decisions were made by the therapist as to the efficacy of the timing in bringing her incest issues to her consciousness. Despite all the good intentions on both sides, the information forced up through hypnosis was devastating to the client, and she spent many months in a dysfunctional downward spiral. As she did her deep process work in the safety of the Intensive, she was able to work through the damage that was done to her by her father and by her well-meaning, technique-bound therapist.

I can almost hear some readers countering, "This is a rare case. People are usually helped by these tools." Allowing that this is a rather dramatic case, it has still been my experience that techniques are only a method of keeping the client under the control of the therapist and that these deep issues will come up naturally when the person is ready and in a place the person feels is safe. I believe techniques are very disrespectful and, I feel, actually harmful. Even when they are used as a "shortcut," they ultimately take people away from their own process, and it is only in respecting their own process that people truly learn to live. Indeed, it is our *belief* that we need techniques and practices to access ourselves or the divine that keeps us from ourselves and the divine.

"Techniques are born of efforts to change others," notes Michael Kerr in the *Atlantic Monthly*.[124] He continues, "Much of what is done in the name of helping others—getting others to 'express their feelings,' for example—reflects the inability of the 'helper' to tolerate his own anxiety."[125] I have found this to be very true of techniques. Therapists often pull out their techniques to keep the client happy, to prove that they know how to get to material that is not accessible to the client, to give the client a "fix" so he or she will keep coming back. As codependent relationship addicts they cannot tolerate waiting and need to "do" something and/or they "need" the dependency and/or they use the "technique" as an escape from having to be fully present.

Speaking about anxiety reduction, Kerr also states, "A number of therapeutic techniques have been developed to reduce chronic anxiety, including biofeedback, transcendental meditation, yoga, jogging, and other 'stress management' activities. These approaches are primarily designed not to increase the basic level of differentiation of self but to help people become more aware of the physiological manifestations of anxiety and to learn techniques of self-control and relaxation."[126] This, of course, enables the client to get the "fix" from the technique and continue the destructive behaviors in a society that lives for the fix and will not deal with the underlying issues. The therapist, through her or his techniques, becomes an enabler par excellence. Or as Efran and Lukens put it, "Clients want to be confronted, chided, shown startling demonstrations, and introduced to bold new conceptualizations and formulations. Otherwise, why not just stay home or continue talking to their usual cohorts?"[127]

In my own use of the "tools" or the "stash" of the psychotherapist, I have found interpretation to be the most difficult to give up. Probably the most important reason is that I tend to be very present and intuitive, hence, very good at interpretation. Clients loved it. I was always doing their work for them, and what I came up with always made such good sense. Yet, as Kerr says, "Conjecture about why a person says or does a particular thing immediately takes the observer out of a systems frame of reference."[128] Not only that, but though it may be perfectly logical, rational, reasonable, and true to theory, it may have absolutely nothing to do with what is really going on with the person, which may not be logical at all and yet make perfect sense. Interpretation often keeps people from doing their own deep process work, trusting their own process, and getting to the true issue, which almost never follows a logical, rational pattern. We have failed to recognize how violent it is to tell someone else what is *really* going on with them. Many therapy hours have been spent attempting to deal with the experience a child has when he or she says something like, "I'm feeling sad," and the parent says, "Oh no you're not." It is violent to tell someone else what he or she is thinking or feeling. We are just so used to it that it seems normal.

I have come to see interpretation as disrespectful and actually brutal. I again remember a recent experience of being at a workshop in a group composed mostly of analysts and analytic thinkers. I could not believe the *abusiveness* and *violence* I felt. The interpretations went beyond disrespect to violence. These were all good people, individually, but the group norm of interpretation was one of the most violent experiences I have had in many years. It is important to remember that benevolent dictators are still dictators.

A big part of my recovery as a psychotherapist has been the slow, and difficult at times, process of letting go of my very good interpretations. I now know that with their use, I was perpetuating a system I no longer consider to be viable. It also strikes me as very interesting that I have never seen interpretations used by elders in native cultures.

DOES THERAPY CREATE AND MAINTAIN DEPENDENCY? Any system that is built around dependency is an addictive system. Whether the issue is dependence, independence, or interdependence, the core focus is still dependency. Therapy is a system that is built on dependency. It is interesting to note that many therapists can only sustain dependency relationships. They can only depend upon or be depended upon. Much of the behavior we see in therapists and codependents is what we used to call counterdependency, which is acting independent and encouraging other's dependency in order to deny dependency needs in oneself. This is systematized in the field of psychotherapy.

No person can ever decide what another person needs to learn and needs to do. Many approaches to therapy are based on subtler and subtler levels of deciding what another person needs. No one can decide that we need to heal the child within, forgive our parents, experience our consciousness, or anything else. True healing has to come out of organic processes. Manipulations are always ultimately harmful.

Another important corollary of dependency is keeping people in a victim role. Jacquelyn Small put it nicely when she said, "We are never victims; we are co-creators."[129] Victims are acted upon. They are never co-creators of their lives. No victim ever gets well. Dependency creates victims. Once again, a scientific view that denies volition, by default, creates victims. We are not always to blame for what has happened to us, and as we take responsibility for *our* feelings, *our* thoughts, *our* process—then, and only then, can healing take place.

IS PSYCHOTHERAPY BASED UPON CONTROL AND MANIPULATION? Much of psychotherapy is built upon the need to control and manipulate. I have come to believe that these are often used in the service of the therapist (out of his or her unresolved issues). For example, Drake and Sederer offer the following about schizophrenic patients: "Schizophrenic patients can be harmed by individual, group or milieu therapies that invite self-disclosure and encourage emotional confrontation or open expression of anger. Instead, a therapist should promote the ability of patients to test reality, fortify their self-esteem, and provide practical advice."[130]

This simple statement can be looked at on several levels. It reveals a view that the "experts" know what a massively diverse group of "patients" need. My experience with schizophrenics since I have been doing Living Process work (and I had extensive previous experience) is that a schizophrenic break is usually a speeded-up, time-and-space-intensified deep process. When the process is "sat with" and not controlled by drugs, the person usually gets the same kind of learning from it that others get from going through their deep processes. Most treatment of psychosis involves trying to control and "manage" it. My experience hints that psychosis may be just a form of intense deep process.

DO NEW AGE HEALING TECHNIQUES EMULATE THE MODEL OF PSYCHOTHERAPY AND THEREFORE RENDER THEMSELVES HARMFUL? In essence, most New Age approaches have borrowed the techniques, interpretations, and tools of psychotherapy or have co-created new tools and have tried, by changing the content, to bring about change.

Many writers in the field who have put forth good information and ideas do not feel secure enough to trust it and let people digest it as they will. They therefore succumb to the codependent trap of adding exercises and techniques, falling into the same problem that therapists have of offering the "how to" or the "fix."

It is important to remember that spirituality is not just a "high." It certainly is not just substituting some therapy or New Age philosophy-induced high for a drug-induced high.

These are only some of the issues that arise when we ask the question, Is psychotherapy harmful? I know that many people have been temporarily helped by psychotherapy, some for long periods of time, but if in the long run it helps us adjust to a system that is destructive and destroying, is this really help?

Most psychotherapy is based upon the belief that at some level, insight and understanding are what we need for healing. I have never seen anyone heal from understanding and insight. More important, understanding and insight may well interfere with people doing their deep process work, where, I believe, healing really happens.

Does Therapy Keep People from Doing Their Deep Process Work?

Whether therapy keeps people from doing their deep process work seems almost a rhetorical question. Any approach that is so controlled, and that keeps people in their heads, looking for meaning and understanding, cannot risk letting people have their deep process. I only need to share two recent letters to illustrate this point.

> It's difficult, too, when I have people calling me that come from the same incest background who don't have anywhere to do their work. There really is so little provided by the regular services—therapists, groups, sponsors, Twelve-Step groups, other incest groups to serve that special emotional need. What to do? I refer people to you frequently when they ask me how I am recovering and what helped. That and suggesting they honor their feelings—a foreign concept to many, even those in therapy. Are you laughing? Probably heard this before, eh? Can I be of more help? I don't feel comfortable starting a process group here by myself, although I have offered to sit with two individuals who are struggling with finding a place to do their work. I empathize with them. How could I have had the courage to

stay with my process unless I had seen others do so, get up and walk away later, and see the incredible healing afterwards? I thought I would die down there and needed some basis for a faith that would allow me to proceed. I feel frustrated. I want them to have the opportunity I have had. Do you have any suggestions?

Judy

I have been living in process for almost two years now. . . . This past summer, I attended a seminar on career planning. For years I had been feeling a lot of shame about my lack of direction in a professional sense, and I thought this little weekend course would answer all my questions. Well, it did, but not at all in the way it was designed to. In these two days, we were told repeatedly that there was no such thing as "being ready," that one needs to simply "go for it" no matter how one is feeling. We were asked to sign an agreement saying that we wouldn't be late and that we would be "fully present" as long as we were there. Then, we were assigned to create a "treasure map" about our future. I was told mine wasn't ambitious enough. I left the workshop feeling very angry. I found the counselors extremely controlling and judgmental. They told *me* that my problem was that I was "afraid of commitment."

During the workshop, we were told that if feelings came up, it was "okay to cry" but we had to "keep talking." That feelings were essentially blockades that had to be broken through. In spite of this, and because of my experience in living in process, I kept encouraging my fellow students to respect and stay with their feelings. These offerings came right from my heart. For me, staying with feelings is *the most* important aspect of any work, and many people, including myself, were feeling a lot of sadness and anger about long-held beliefs that we were unworthy of abundance and unskilled. I wanted so badly to ask for and offer facilitation, but, again, we were told to "keep talking," and when we were done, to "listen to the others."

After two weeks, we came back together again. We were each asked to give a presentation on our progress, and again, the counselor delivered her opinions on our work throughout the presentations. As I sat there, I felt sicker and sicker to my stomach. Finally, I got up and said that I felt ill and had to go.

As I walked down the street, I knew more deeply than ever before how important process work was to me. How highly I valued the support and fellowship of people coming together to give sober witness to each other's disease and recovery. And how in any process, to cut off our feelings is to cut off our power, and without our power, any technique is simply a pretty band-aid (perhaps with Muppet designs on it).

H.B.

We have not only been badly abused in therapy, we have been denied the possibility of doing our deep process work and our recovery—which is deadly.

The Role of Professional Ethics

The role of ethics in the issues raised here is a confusing one but necessary to explore. I had studied the professional ethics of psychologists in my graduate training and thought that I had a pretty good grasp of them as they were then written. Basically, I thought of them as exhibiting basic common sense, human dignity, maturity, and good judgment. As I lived through the turmoil and the "freedom" of the professional world in the 1960s, I questioned the behavior of some of my mentors and colleagues (almost all my mentors, except one, slept with "clients"). I did not participate in the sexual freedom wave of the sixties, and during that time tried to develop a gyroscope inside myself for what felt ethical.

I was then hit by the cry of the feminists against male therapists who used the male-female power differential in the society and regularly slept with their clients. I was also disturbed with the violent, bloodthirsty reaction of some feminist therapists who wanted only to punish, control, and ruin these therapists. I did not believe that punishment and control were solutions. It seemed to me that the profession was being inconsistent with its own belief system, which said that people could be helped.

PSYCHOLOGISTS DO NOT AGREE ON ETHICS. There was a very interesting article in the *American Psychologist* entitled "Ethics of Practice: The Beliefs and Behaviors of Psychologists as Therapists." First of all, in reporting the results of their survey, the authors concluded, "There is an absence of comprehensive, systematically gathered data concerning psychologist's beliefs about and compliance with ethical principles."[131] In essence, we do not know whether psychologists think the ethics of the organization are ethical and whether they comply with them.

Of course, the survey only focuses upon the "behavior" of the therapists and does not even look at the scientific worldview out of which therapy has emerged. Also, because there is no real information about how much psychologists believe in or comply with the ethics as they now stand, there is no real information on how relevant they are.

For example, at least 90 percent of the respondents indicated that they engaged in behaviors involving self-disclosure with clients. This clearly is not in accordance with the objectivity and noninvolvement of the "objective scientist." It was interesting that among the items that the surveyors considered a "difficult judgment" (where at least 20 percent of respondents indicated "don't know/not sure"), one third were financial issues and one fourth sexual issues. Basically, their conclusions are that psychologists do not have "adequate guidelines to inform their choices."[132]

THE IMPOSSIBILITY OF THE CURRENT ETHICS.   The ethics of the APA are set up on a belief system that makes the client a dependent/victim and the therapist an all-powerful person. I believe that on the previous pages we have seen how this model is not healing. Unfortunately, however, the ethics are based on the myth of objectivity and the belief that the therapist can be in a caring, empathic, and perhaps even loving relationship of intimacy and at the same time both completely control that relationship and be objective.

In the study just quoted, a majority of the respondents believed that even having sexual *feelings* toward a client was unethical. The ethics of the APA are built upon the illusion of objectivity, the illusion of control, and the threat of ostracism and punishment. Therapists are not really helped to sort out the impossible predicament that the profession sets up in an intimate one-to-one setting. It is not surprising in a situation of intimacy that these "controlled" feelings erupt in acting out. Fear of punishment is not adequate to "control" someone acting out of the addictive process, and therapy itself is an addictive process the way it is designed. Our ethics ask us to be mechanical (objective) while at the same time being empathic, caring, understanding, and loving. This is at best confusing and at worst disastrous. Many of the "rules" of ethics have been set up to "control" the problems that the theory itself has generated.

The situation is similar to what we see in the church. The more repressive a church system is about sex, the more obsessed it is with sex and the more sexual acting out we find.

The ethics of the APA set up a system that does not really help the client or the therapist deal with the intimacy of therapy.

THE ONE-PARTY SYSTEM.   One of my gravest concerns about state regulatory boards in psychology, social work, medicine, and so on is the unspoken political issues that are put forth as ethical issues.

I have already mentioned the psychic healer who was accused of "practicing medicine without a license" and the battered women's shelter that was closed because it was not under the control of professionals. I have been terrified to see what seems like fascist development of a gestapo-like force that tries to wipe out any methods of working with people that do not fit into the narrow framework of a mechanistic science.

We say that we live in a pluralistic society, but licensing and regulatory boards are exerting tighter and tighter control over approaches that differ in any way from the mechanistic/scientific model. I know of at least one state where the regulatory board itself has become so Hitler-like that the alternative approaches to healing that exist in the state have successfully called for and been granted a hearing by the state legislature. One has to question whether there has developed a greater focus on protecting the professionals than protecting the public and whether the public should have the right of choice. Also, who protects the public from the aftermath of a mechanistic science?

At some metalevel, I am aware that this kind of activity on the part of regulatory boards can be historically understood as a part of the death throes of a system that is facing its demise. Yet, having lived through the Second World War, I have a fear and a concern about fascism wherever I see it, and right now I see it operating in a profession that I once cared about and have had to leave for my own survival, health, and sanity.

DUAL RELATIONSHIPS.   As I said earlier, one of the most confusing and hottest arenas in "professional ethics" right now is dual relationships.

Dual relationships are when the therapist has any kind of contact with the client other than in the therapy hour.

One state defines dual relationships as including when the client's and the therapist's children attend the same school or when the two attend the same church. The absurdity is that this is a rural state, and when local therapists follow these "rules," there is no one they can associate with in their town.

In one situation, a therapist was reprimanded because he took a guitar class in which a client was also enrolled. In another, a therapist and a client attended the same workshop, and this was seen as "unethical" on the part of the therapist. In the attempt to control harmful interactions that come out of an assumed and believed imperative power differential, the field has opted for greater and greater illusions of control.

In Europe, dual relationships are quite common. In the United States, they are quite common also. In fact, among the many thousands of therapists I meet and have interviewed, most of them report some kind of dual relationship with clients.

The whole focus upon the dual relationship issue is taking the image of the "pure," uninvolved, detached, objective experimenter to its ultimate and absurd conclusion. Most models of healing in the world involve dual relationships—the medicine man, the healer, the curandera, the kahuna—but in this country, because they are prohibited and there is a massive denial that they occur, there is no systematic recognition that they exist and no help in dealing with them. Because of the fear of censure and punishment, when therapists get into trouble with dual relationships, there is no place for them to turn for help.

Even though dual relationships are so common in therapeutic circles, my experience is that most of the persons reported to the regulatory boards are reported for political, not ethical, reasons. Dual relationships become the vehicle for trying to control someone with whom one disagrees. I have seen several people reported for dual relationships where the reporting was used as a form of professional harassment. All of them were later exonerated.

I have also seen therapists form their own Twelve-Step groups because of their fear of being accused of dual relationships if clients went to the same recovery meetings they attended. Again, in rural areas, this is impossible. Moreover, the homogeneous nature of this exclusive group often robs its members of the kind of wisdom that comes from long sobriety and the richness that comes from the participatory experience of equality in this addictive disease regardless of background or differences in the path that led us to recovery.

If George Albee was right (that we have to develop new models for prevention, healing, and health),[133] then we are going to have to work on larger and larger community levels. The model of the scientific experiment will not wash, and we are going to have to develop skills for dealing with many types of relationships occurring simultaneously.

Psychotherapy Has Ignored Organizational, Societal, and Global Issues

It is time to look at therapy from a broader perspective. As Philip Norman says, "Mental Illness, in its most common manifestations, grows out of our own experience, our own systems of belief, and especially our own choices."[134] Later in the same article he notes, "Some social scientists have even suggested that the problem of self-esteem may undergird most of our social pathology, all the way from delinquency to divorce. Such a widespread and pervasive dysfunction must have deep roots in the culture."[135]

Paul Taylor calls us back to looking at the concept of science out of which therapy has arisen:

> During the germination period of psychiatry and psychotherapy, the Cartesian-Newtonian model of the universe was enjoying great success. In this model, the universe is seen as an assemblage of immutable parts, interacting according to timeless laws. Life is then assumed to evolve from certain accidental (though lawful) assemblages of matter, and consciousness to mysteriously appear only when sufficient complexity has arisen in higher brains. All the developing scientific branches were keen to build on this foundation, not realizing that it was engineered to support a very narrow range of reality, and was soon to totally crumble under the wider scope of modern physics.
>
> Intrinsic in the Cartesian-Newtonian paradigm is the mistaken notion that it provides a definitive picture of what reality is and is not, rather than just being a useful conceptual model. Freud quite deliberately emulated Newtonian thought in laying down the principles of psychoanalysis. Psychiatry defined mental health as perceptual, cognitive

and emotional congruence with the description of the universe given by mechanistic science, and with proper social behavior of the era. Experiences outside that range indicated that there was a mental disorder or disease.

The insistence upon agreement with a paradigm-bound reality forced psychiatry to ignore the clear fact that there is a cultural and historical relativity to what is considered normal and what is pathological.[136]

We have systematically refused to see that what we thought was truth is culture-bound and very limited. Michael Lerner calls for us to take cultural factors into consideration, and we certainly need to do that and see how sexism, racism, homophobia, and many of the "isms" are tied to mechanistic science.[137] It is time to look beyond the individual and the family. It is time to look beyond Western culture, which is built on a mechanistic scientific worldview.

For me, the combination of recovery from addictions and learning to Live in Process has opened the doors for me to see the old paradigm clearly and to move into living out of a new paradigm.

Confronting and Healing the Addictive Process

I maintain that Truth is a pathless land, and you cannot approach it by any path whatsoever, by any religion, by any sect. . . . If an organization be created for this purpose, it becomes a crutch, a weakness, a bondage, and must cripple the individual, and prevent him from growing, from establishing his uniqueness, which lies in the discovery for himself of that absolute, unconditioned Truth. . . . I do not want followers. . . . The moment you follow someone you cease to follow Truth. . . . I am concerning myself with only one essential thing: to set man free.

J. Krishnamurti

In this section, I want to focus on confronting and healing the addictive process. As I lecture on this disease process, am present with people who are actively working on their recovery over time, and am actively working my own recovery, I have realized three important things: (1) that we need a unified theory about the process of recovery; (2) that my colleagues and I know much about the healing of the addictive process and we have been successfully working with this process for many years; and (3) that no one, as yet, has done any major writing

264

about the healing of the overall addictive process and where it fits into what we know about the helping professions.

As I stated in the introduction, when I initially thought about writing this book, it was going to be a book about confronting and healing the addictive process. Later I realized that though this is still an important topic, it is only a small part of what I wanted to address here.

Over time, we have developed a model that has proved exceptionally successful as an alternative to treatment for working with the addictive process. I want to share some of the salient aspects of the model we use in the Living Process Network and some theories and concepts that have emerged out of this model.

The Role of the Evolution of the Concept of Codependence

As I have said earlier, the training in the helping professions is systematized training into the disease of codependence. Therefore, it is helpful to look at the historic development of the concept of codependence as a way to understand addiction better and a way to understanding working with addiction.

♦ The Alcoholic

Early in our understanding of addictions we looked at alcoholism as the best known and most documented addiction. At that phase in our understanding, the alcoholic stood alone in the disease. Alcoholics were seen as weak-willed, bad people who basically could not and would not control their drinking. There was no recognition of a family involvement in the disease, nor was there any recognition that alcoholism was a disease.

Alcoholics were enormously isolated in their disease, and anyone who had any relationship with them tried to ignore the disease as much as possible.

The next stage was an emerging recognition that the disease of the alcoholic did not exist in isolation. There was a belief that the alcoholic was affected by family members, and some (usually counselors who were themselves alcoholics) believed that the alcoholic drank because of troubled relationships, especially with the spouse. At that point in our history of treating alcoholism, family members were seen as the enemy, and, if they were involved in treatment at all, it was usually because they were seen as potential saboteurs of the recovery process.

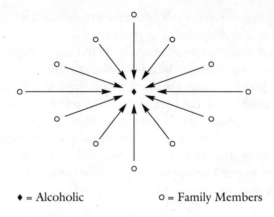

♦ = Alcoholic o = Family Members

Their help was enlisted to support the recovery of the alcoholic or, at least, to not sabotage it. During these times, treatment blatantly mirrored the disease by continuing to make the alcoholic the center of attention and encouraging family members to focus upon the alcoholic's recovery. This, of course, was exactly the setup occurring at home, so it seemed reasonable at the time. I think it is also important to note here that most of the drug and alcohol counselors at that time were recovering alcoholics who were nonrecovering codependents and relationship addicts (which, unfortunately, often continues to be true). There was frequently a great deal of unresolved hostility toward their own family members, which was then dumped on family members of the alcoholic in treatment.

Shortly after this phase, there began to be an acknowledgment and belief that family members had been injured by the disease of the alcoholic or addict and the diagram begin to look more like this:

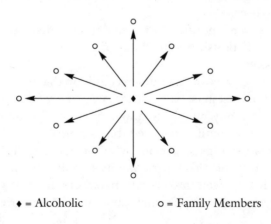

♦ = Alcoholic o = Family Members

This was the "victim" stage of understanding the effects of the disease in family members. At this stage, the disease was almost seen as contagious, and the family members were described as having contracted the disease and having been contaminated by the alcoholic. At this point, family members were seen as the heroic, if pathetic, victims of the alcoholic. This, by the way, is a typical stance of mental health professionals toward their patients, and many in the field still unconsciously hold this belief. In this belief system, family members are acted upon and are victims of their circumstances. At least there was an embryonic awareness of the interaction between the addict and the family members.

Co   Alcoholic

The next stage in our understanding was the "co" stage. We started out with the term *co-alcoholic*, and that stage still subtly reinforced the victim stance, although there was a budding recognition that "co" persons had their own issues and were not purely victims of their addicts.

There was a growing recognition that both the codependent and the alcoholic were in pain and shared many of the same characteristics. We began to see the "co" and the addict both as having a disease and co-related in that disease as counterparts to one another. There was slowly an acknowledgment that codependents generally needed their own help and support, not just in relation to the addict, and that the characteristics present in the codependent were not just alcohol and drug related. It also became apparent that many people shared the characteristics of the codependent, even when they did not seem to be related to a particular alcoholic or drug addict. At this point, we also began to look at anyone who lived or worked with an addict as a codependent, and that, of course, included therapists.

Codependent

Alcoholic

In the next stage in our thinking we began to see the same characteristics in people who were in recovery from substance addiction that we saw in codependents. Some treatment centers began to request that six months to a year after people completed treatment for chemical addiction, they return for a month-long codependency treatment program as a follow-up to their earlier treatment. There was a budding awareness that perhaps what had been defined as codependence was a more basic disease than the specific addictions and lurked behind those addictions.

At this point, my thinking was beginning to develop along somewhat different lines. I was beginning to think in terms of an underlying addictive process that was learned in the addictive society as being basic to all addictions, and I began to question whether codependence existed at all. I openly wondered whether, if we took out of codependence what should be pushed up into the addictive process and pushed down what belonged in the specific addictions, there would be anything left that could be rightfully called codependence.

Writing the book *Escape from Intimacy* helped me with this dilemma. As I was working on that book, I began to question all the "co" terms and could see that labeling myself a codependent exacerbated my disease in two ways: (1) it allowed me to feel a little superior to addicts, and (2) it was a form of external referenting. In addition, it kept me from claiming my true addictions, which were relationship and romance addictions; when we do not face our specific addictions, we do not have recovery. I checked these ideas out with other "codependents" and found their experience to be the same. Most were stuck in their recovery when they focused on being "cos." This list of "bogged-downs" included codependents, co-alcoholics or co–sex addicts, Al-Anons, and Adult Children. The promises of recovery are not ours unless we truly admit our addictions. My recovery progressed by leaps and bounds when I admitted that I was an addict just like any other addict. I began to see that codependence, like all the "co" terms, was a useful door into seeking help. The "cos," including adult children of alcoholics, were umbrella concepts, but real help was possible only when the underlying addictive process was claimed. And in that process we are all equal as addicts.

Hence, I moved to my next diagram, which more accurately fits my experience and that of other recovering addicts.

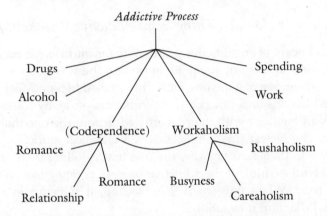

There is an underlying addictive process that is learned and based in society. We learn to be addicts. The "choice" of which addiction may be determined by genes and/or body chemistry. Addiction itself is a *process* that is *taught* by the society and *learned*. It is because addiction is a process and not something that can be understood mechanistically in terms of cause and effect that the mechanistic scientific model of mental health and medicine do not work well in the treatment of addictions. Addictions may, and usually do, have physical side effects, *and* medicine and the medical and/or psychological approach are not effective with addictions per se.

I believe there are several other major reasons that traditional mental health approaches have not proved effective with addictions: (1) the addictive process does not fit into a mechanistic science or the worldview of that science; (2) if one admits to an underlying addictive process, one has to move beyond the individual and the family and look at institutions and society and ultimately the worldview behind both; (3) as addiction treatment is progressively taken over by medicine and mental health, the very techniques used and the philosophy behind them exacerbate the underlying addictive process; (4) most if not all of the places that treat addictions are themselves very addictive organizations not even attempting organizational recovery (I believe that this is one of the reasons people are often so "at home" in treatment centers. My experience is that usually, as organizations, they just replicate the addictive family system); and (5) none really treats the underlying addictive process. They only work with specific addictions and ignore the underlying addictive process.

There Is No Such Thing as an Addictive Personality

The concept of an addictive personality fits into a static, mechanistic worldview and is not adequate to explain the way addiction functions. I have never met anyone with only one addiction. Most people switch addictions and practice their addictions in many forms. Most people start recovery with their favorite addiction, the one that is killing them the fastest (frequently, this is a chemical addiction). Then they move to their next favorite, the one that is killing them the next fastest. I tend to think of the addictive process as being like an underground river. When one channel is blocked, it switches to another channel. I diagram it as follows:

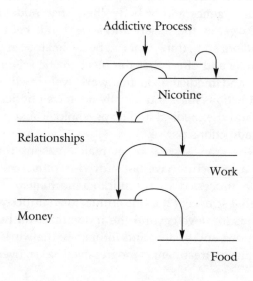

Of course, one can substitute any addiction in the diagram for others, and all are just manifestations of the underlying addictive process that is learned. Everyone who works with addicts knows that giving up the chemical is just the tip of the iceberg and being "dry" is not sober. Being sober is a completely different life process from the addictive process, and one has to learn or relearn that process to be in full recovery. The addictive process is a killer of body, mind, and spirit, and any form of the addictive process is lethal.

Because the addictive process is a process and it is learned, it takes time to unlearn it, and it is not amenable to "fixes" and techniques. Information is necessary and helpful in recovery, *and* no one ever recovered from information and understanding or insight alone. Recovery is a process that people must do for themselves. No amount of well-meaning codependence, or enabling on the part of "helpers," can really do it. This, of course, means that drugs cannot cure the addictive process and in most instances are contraindicated. I have been very concerned with the almost unlimited use of Prozac in treatment centers because it often masks the deep processes necessary for the recovery process. When the model reflects and operates in a way that supports what it is trying to change, it subtly exacerbates the disease process.

Over the years, we have developed a recovery model that has proved very effective and has resulted in creative, long-lasting recovery for many people throughout the world. It is not a therapy model. It is a recovery, Living in Process model. People who are interested in confronting their addictive process and learning to Live in Process (make a paradigm shift) sign up to come to an Intensive workshop. There is no screening process; these workshops are open to the public. We clearly state that this is not treatment or therapy.

At the Intensives all the facilitators (including myself) and participants take part. That is to say, we all check in, share our struggle with our addictive process, and do whatever work comes up for us.

After having been to an Intensive, those who are interested are eligible to sign up for a Training Year. I believe that it is important to note here that after an Intensive, those who are interested in the Training Year have an experiential knowledge of who we are and how we work and of their responsibility to do their own work and recovery. Feedback from the Intensives has been "It's the most honesty I have ever seen"; "I never felt so safe"; "Honesty and participation by everyone results in safety"; "I know that I have to do my own work here, and no one will try to pull it out of me or do it for me"; "There is hard, to-the-bone confrontation, but there is no judgment." (I believe analysis and interpretation always result in judgmentalism.)

Basically, the Intensives are fun. We do a lot of work, and those attending face into some, at times, unbelievably difficult processes (involving torture and/or sexual abuse, for example). And, we have a lot of fun. We laugh and joke a lot and have the opportunity to see just how funny our disease is.

If people feel comfortable with the recovery process and Living Process, they have the option of requesting to sign up for a year of Training. I see this as a year of commitment to oneself with the most support possible. The learning for the year is to confront one's own addictive process and to experiment with Living in Process, with support.

A big part of this program is encouraging those in the Training group to try the Twelve-Step program of Alcoholics Anonymous. Trainees are encouraged to try out various programs, to "shop" for what meets their needs. Then, when they find a program that fits well with their needs, they are encouraged to commit to that one basic program. Those in the group can fool around as much as they want with working a Twelve-Step program, and the group is never shy about giving tough feedback along the way. Those in the group often hear that going to meetings is not working a program. Going to meetings, working closely with a sponsor, reading the Big Book (and other literature), and *working* the steps is working a program. Sometimes someone in the group will suggest or volunteer to be a temporary sponsor, if they think it is needed. Again, getting a temporary sponsor is a *suggestion* and can be and is made by anybody, and it is up to the person to whom the suggestion is made to act on it, or not. There are always those in the group (including facilitators) who are talking about their struggles and growth in the Twelve-Step program. At the same time, people in the group (again including facilitators) are doing their deep process work when it comes up and sharing their struggles in relearning to Live in Process.

The Training group, as a group, meets three times during the year. Trainees are asked to attend at least one Intensive during their Training Year (and they may attend more than one). They may also attend other Training groups that I am doing in other parts of the world such as Europe, and New Zealand. In fact, I encourage Trainees to travel and experience this work and the work of recovery in different languages and cultures, because it seems to facilitate recovery and relearning our Living Process. For some, it means a very intense year of attending Training group sessions all over the world. For others, the three Training sessions and some Intensives in the U.S. are quite enough. There is so much flexibility that most can and do select what they need.

In addition to the three Training sessions, the Trainees have the option of setting up and attending Regionals. The group determines who is in what Regional, and when it will meet. These are peer groups. Most elect to meet for a weekend once a month. These groups provide a very important continuity, a place to do deep process work, check in, and build a smaller community within the larger community of the full Training group. My perception is that these groups are very important for those who elect to participate. Some opt not to. That is their choice and, I believe, their loss.

Over time, we have found that one year to confront the addictive process and begin to learn to Live in Process is not enough for most people, and we have begun to suggest that people consider two years a basic program. Many also have come to see this work as an alternative to treatment and psychotherapy. A person could do as many as five years of Training for what one month of treatment would cost in many places.

I did not "design" or "think up" this model. It has emerged (continues to emerge) as I have done my recovery, tried to stay clear with my convictions, and made a paradigm shift in my life and my work. I am sure whatever I do will continue to change as I participate in my own process and work my recovery program.

As I reflect on what we have been doing, several important elements emerge:

1. Everyone involved is in recovery, or wants to be, and all are doing their own work. We are committed to being a recovering organization and also to being in personal recovery. Everyone is encouraged to say when the group or the organization feels unclear, and we hit these issues head on.

2. Nothing breaks down the "power differential" illusion more than the "leaders" "hitting the mats" in deep process, or sharing "slips" or "relapses" into their addictive processes. This kind of sharing is done regularly by the "leaders" (the group facilitators).

3. There are no secrets. If we are concerned about someone or something in the group, it is not brought up in a "staff meeting." It is

brought up in the group. There is an assumption that whatever happens is an opportunity for learning, and we try to learn whatever we can from whatever happens. Nothing is too big or too small or too crazy to discuss in group.

4. Unlike in many treatment centers, there is a lack of emphasis upon me, the place, or the group. The emphasis, by our behavior, is on recovery as a person's responsibility in conjunction with his or her Higher Power, and that is accessible to the person all the time. Because the majority of time and the majority of focus is on persons in their home settings, working in their local Twelve-Step groups and their Regionals, the larger Training group sessions are deemphasized. They become more opportunities for reconnecting and checking in.

5. Sometimes, I will do some "teaching" or pointing out of a salient factor in the Training group, but it is always done spontaneously and it is integrated into the process of the group, which, by default, deemphasizes my role. Others will do the same thing when appropriate.

6. When my control issues or anyone else's arise, there is always someone to pick up on it and give feedback;

7. This model offers more time at less cost to confront the addictive process and puts the emphasis and the responsibility on the person, which is what recovery is all about.

8. This model is a holographic/holomovement model in that it provides an experience that is personal and global and is a process model.

9. Everyone's process is respected, and there are no goals to accomplish by a certain time.

10. It is a participatory model, with everyone present and participating and committed to do so.

11. There are no "experts," only people further along in the same process.

12. It models the new scientific paradigm without having set out to do so, which, in itself, models a process approach.

13. It does not maintain people as victims. It recognizes that people are victimized in many ways in their lives and that they may have anger, hurt, terror, and any number of other feelings about and responses to these experiences and need to work through whatever processes are there, but that if they get stuck in "victim," they will never claim their own lives and live fully. At some metalevel, in a Liv-

ing Process System, the issue is to deal with our lives whatever they have been, get the learnings, integrate them, and live.

14. The model is one of the process of self-reliance, of taking ownership for one's life and living it, whatever that means for that particular person. This means that the person does not have to live *my* agenda, their *parents'* agenda, or even *their own* agenda. They are supported to live their own life and to find out what that means. Because most of their life is spent outside the Training group during that year, they have many opportunities to explore options for themselves.

15. Because the staff and I are not responsible for everyone and their progress, we do not have therapist's "burnout," and I usually return from the Training groups relaxed and rested.

I have to say here that I love this work. I am much healthier than when I was a therapist and trying to operate out of a mechanistic, scientific model. Yet, the greatest joy is to see people really heal, even from experiences of which I was taught healing was not possible and adjustment was the best one could hope for. I feel that I am surrounded by miracles all over the world. I just finished the third session of this year's Training group in Europe, and the changes in the Trainees are phenomenal. It is so much more satisfying to see healing in myself and others and not just adjustment.

I now would like to share some of the things I have learned over the years working with the addictive process.

Early Recovery

Early recovery is a long, slow process. Early recovery is two to five years. It may be two to five years before a person who is actively working on recovery has the first experience of sobriety. To me, it is a miracle that so many people are beginning this journey when they really do not have any experiential knowledge of what it means.

In early recovery, most of the time is spent in the addictive process. Amazingly, the Living Process is always there, but often it has become so submerged and ignored that it is not much in evidence.

In early recovery, we see flights into the crazy, paranoid-like thinking of the addict and bouts with the illusion of control, dishonesty, dualistic thinking, and perfectionism, among other "character defects" as they are called in the Twelve-Step program. It is very helpful to hear from others in the group who struggle with the same issues in a participatory way and not to depend upon an "expert" who has the answers.

It is difficult to see the rewards of recovery (except, sometimes, in others) when still in early recovery, and there is often a lot of talk and complaining about how *hard* recovery is. One of the characteristics of early recovery is a lack of perspective, which frequently leads to a kind of amnesia about how hard the addictive process has been.

We often talk about the addictive process as "cunning, baffling, powerful, and patient" and forget that the Living Process is also cunning, baffling, powerful, and patient. If it weren't, it wouldn't still be around.

In early recovery, it is important to be aware that addicts have little or no memory. Often it is said that we addicts cannot learn from our mistakes because we have no memories. Also, addicts bring a large tolerance for insanity into their early recovery. This is one of the important characteristics of the disease—an increased tolerance for insanity.

One of the most important aspects of the Intensives and the Training Year, I believe, is that we have people in different stages of recovery and Living in Process. There are always enough people present with sufficient recovery so that clarity and input are not left to the staff alone. The staff just facilitates the group and sits with people. Reliance on experts, I believe, is one of the major handicaps of the treatment model as it now exists. It is designed for a homogenous group, and staff are supposed to be the models and the experts. This means that other recovering resources in the group are not used. Then, too, the staff is often handicapped in what can be accomplished by being so enmeshed in an addictive organization and in using techniques that come out of the addictive system.

In the training groups, those in early recovery also help the old-timers graphically remember what their early recovery was like, and so are important to those farther along in recovery as well. This richness is very important in a group.

Before I move on to another topic, I want to mention that one of the dangerous pitfalls of early recovery is cockiness. This disease is tricky. I marvel at how creative it is and how we can talk ourselves into or out of almost anything in order to "protect our supply." One of the ways this is often manifested in early recovery is to use recovery and the tools of recovery in order to continue to practice the disease. For example, I have heard many people use the admission, "I'm in my disease," as a way of staying in it. Or, I have seen people use recovery to hold on to the possibility of using again.

I find in early recovery that few have any notion of what sobriety really is and absolutely no idea of what it means to be willing to go to any lengths for sobriety. And, still, it is very important to hear old-timers saying that phrase and continuing to put their sobriety first.

There is only one real question that one has to ask—about everything: Does this threaten my sobriety? If it does, we addicts cannot do it. It is as simple as that.

Dualism Lincoln Logs

Recognizing and dealing with dualism is absolutely essential for recovery. Dualistic thinking is addictive thinking and comes out of a mechanistic science. Native people the world over marvel at the ability of the Western mind to set up its world in a dualism. As I said earlier, dualisms are the building blocks of an addictive society. I think of them as Lincoln Logs.

Dualism serves two major purposes in the addictive process: (1) It takes a very complex world and reduces it to two options, therefore feeding our illusion of control. (2) It keeps us stuck by keeping us going back and forth between two options that we may not even want and that we might know are not sober for us.

Anyone who works with recovery must be able to spot, name, and work with dualism. We addicts tend to set up our lives in terms of dualism:

Good-Bad

Right-Wrong

In-Out

Can do-Can't do

We also set up a complex web of dualism that supports the disease, where the two ends are intimately intertwined and cannot exist without the other:

Staying in the marriage-Getting divorced

Niceness-Dishonesty

Powerless-In control

Victim-Perpetrator

It is important to be able to see and name our own and each other's dualistic thinking. All of us need help and support in doing this, and it is a very important way to look at the addictive process.

"Sick" versus "well" itself operates out of dualistic thinking and often sees a "good" solution as somewhere in the middle. *Not so.* Whenever we are still on the Lincoln Log (the dualism), we are operating in the disease. We have to jump off the Lincoln Log and find the third option. That third option is almost always moving to our Living Process and seeing what we need to do for our own sobriety and not referencing our lives to either end of the Lincoln Log.

Dualism is a very tricky part of the disease, and it is important to learn to recognize dualistic thinking as we move into recovery.

Victimization

A dualism that I have been witnessing lately in people who are in early recovery, or not in recovery at all, is the dualism of victim-perpetrator. We tend to think of these two ends as very different, but more and more I am observing that as people seriously do their recovery, they see that they are stuck on this Lincoln Log.

Addicts tend not to want to take responsibility (ownership—not blame) for their lives and have a string of reasons why someone else is responsible for who and what they are and how they are living or not living their lives. Addicts often see themselves as victims, while others experience them as perpetrators. I have seen many people in recovery over a period of time starting out as victims and dealing with their hurt and anger and, as they gradually accept their participation in their disease, move to a place where they see that they are, indeed, perpetrators who in some way victimize others. It is only when people claim and work through both roles and jump off that dualism that they know sobriety and can begin to live their own process.

This does not mean that when people feel like victims, we push them to see themselves as perpetrators. It does mean that we need to let their recovery process take them where it will.

I have great concern about the mental health establishment and the women's movement when they buy into the mechanistic system, perpetuating the victim status, and then unknowingly move into perpetrator status. The violence that we have seen in the women's movement often reflects the very processes of the perpetrators that the woman's movement stands over against (and this is, of course, the problem: being against something). It is when we move to the third option of our Living Process and what we need that we fully become ourselves.

Any system that helps people stay victims is, itself, a victimizer. As I said earlier, victims don't get better—they get bitter.

Noticing and Naming

Because addicts are rarely present and rarely in their bodies, noticing and naming are very important processes to learn. Addicts have to relearn simple things like noticing when they are tired, hungry, lonely, angry, and so forth. Noticing and naming are vital for recovery.

Some nonrecovering people, usually from the helping professions, have been very negative about addicts calling themselves addicts and naming their addictions. This is a very interesting systems clash. When this naming behavior is viewed from the judgmental position of the addictive system (in which disease, illness, psychological problems, and so forth *are* seen as bad), then of course this noticing and naming is seen as negative and judged as "bad."

However, from a recovery and a Living Process perspective, "the truth shall set you free," and noticing and naming specific addictions becomes the door to the promises of recovery. I have often heard recovering people talk about the deep relief and hope they felt in naming their own addictions (it doesn't often help much, though, for others to name them).

Judgment

Addicts are long on "judgment against" and short on good judgment. It is important to remember this in recovery groups. To be judgmental perpetuates the disease. Often in early recovery it is important to follow the advice of an old-timer or sponsor, even when our addictive process has a million reasons to resist. It is important to remember that this: If our judgment is so good, why are we in the mess we are in? Asking that question usually helps us be more open to support. Sometimes in the Training groups we do have what has been fondly called "two-by-four encouragement" (hard confrontation by the group) to help to break through denial. It is often miraculous to see this done without judgment.

Isolation

Addictions are diseases of isolation. We isolate from ourselves, from one another, and from our spiritual base. One of the good things about the model I have presented is that there are many forms of ongoing contact for support, and the responsibility for making that contact is not just in the "aftercare" format that so many groups use. Twelve-Step programs abound worldwide. There is an international network of people who have begun to Live in Process, and good people are everywhere if we look.

Wholeness

Any recovery process must involve the wholeness of the person and offer avenues to move into wholeness. For myself, I like healthy food, good air, rest, and especially nature and hot springs. We try to have our Intensives in affordable places that offer these "necessities." We do not tell people how they should eat. We have good food. People learn from their experience, and unlearning the addictive process and the effects of the addictive process takes time. It is best done experientially. A big part of sobriety, I believe, is to experience the "commonness of sobriety." We knew it before we knew addiction.

Chemicals

If a person has a chemical addiction, my experience is that, ideally, this needs to be addressed before the process addictions. One cannot really work on relationship addiction, for example, with alcohol or even a food addiction raging in the body. Unless people are willing to start a period of abstinence or sobriety, it is often a waste of the group's time and energy to try to deal with them.

We do not, however, *require* abstinence before joining the Training, and the group does tend to zero in on its absence when people are in the group. Frequently, however, people do not *know* their ingestive or process addictions when they enter the Training and the Training group. The Trainees often laughingly remark that they must be getting sicker in the Training group because they have many more addictions than they did when they came.

Spirituality

I do not believe that recovery is possible without in some form coming to terms with our spirituality. Addiction itself is a form of alienating ourselves from the whole of the process of the universe, and recovery must in some way establish again our relationship to all things. The process of that relationship cannot be forced. It has to come. So often, critics of the Twelve-Step program criticize the "spirituality" of the program. I know that in my own case, when I got stuck on that aspect of the Twelve-Step program, I was using my "objective criticism" to avoid my recovery. When I really let myself see that my Higher Power could really take any form I wanted, I had to look at myself and my resistance. A quote I heard at a Twelve-Step meeting helped me a lot. "Even if you don't believe in a Higher Power, can you believe you ain't him?" How often I had used theological arguments to avoid my own understanding of my own spirituality!

Finding where we belong in the process of the universe is spirituality. That knowledge comes differently to each of us, and the awareness of our place is essential for recovery.

Facilitators

Who qualifies to facilitate others' recovery processes and deep process work? I believe that our best teachers in recovery are recovering addicts themselves and hopefully those who have moved beyond their specific addictions and are dealing with their underlying addictive process. Also, those who are best qualified to facilitate are those who participate—participate in their own recovery and their deep process work.

Rigid external boundary setting is not necessary for recovering people, because recovery demands more carefully defined boundaries than any external person or organization could mandate. And these boundaries are internal.

The good facilitator is a person who participates fully in his or her own process of recovery and Living Process while, at the same time, not jumping on the hooks others put out or engaging in the games of the disease. This, of course, demands a certain level of recovery and the continuation of one's own growth and healing, including deep process work as it emerges.

I have found that frequently those persons who have the most difficulty facilitating and not trying to control other's process are those trained in the helping professions. Those trained in the helping professions firmly believe they need to *help*.

Humor

Recovery is fun, and the addictive process is often funny. There is nothing funnier than watching us try to fool ourselves and others with our "con"—or believing that we can hide what we are feeling from others when we are in our addictive process. The only one fooled is ourselves.

Laughing at our disease is an important part of recovery. Some people have trouble with the humor they hear from addicts, but addicts who are in recovery know that we are often very funny in our disease.

As I have said, the mental health establishment treats our shit with such respect that it tends to make it secretive and put it on an altar to worship. There is some relief in knowing that our shit is just our shit and we can laugh about it and not have to worship it.

Summary

I think the model presented here has many advantages over what we have done with addictions and mental health in the past. The most obvious advantage is that it works and it is by design not that expensive. Working with the addictive process has, by default, opened the door to a paradigm shift and is, I believe, presenting us a key with which to achieve a paradigm shift.

The Twelve-Step program of Alcoholics Anonymous is, to my thinking, the most effective tool to deal with the addictive process, and it is most effective when combined with the Living Process and deep process work. "When you struggle with an addiction, you deal directly with the healing of your soul. You deal directly with the matter of your life."[138]

The Interface of the Living Process System and Recovery

In this section, I want to return to a diagram presented earlier that is key to understanding the ideas and the work being offered in this book. This diagram clearly shows the interface of the recovery process and the Living Process work.

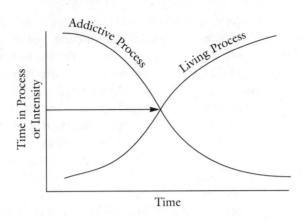

As I have stressed, transformation is not possible without recovery. Mental health, psychology, medicine, religion, and all of the helping professions have tried to bring about transformation (of some sort) without the messiness of facing the addictive process and, especially, without the inconvenience of having to look at the roots of their scientific worldview and to see that those roots grow out of the soil of the addictive process. So many of our attempts at transformation in this society, including New Age work, have tried to make transformations without doing recovery and have used addictive processes to do that. Even Marion Woodman, a person whom I admire and respect very much, said in a recent interview, "You have to try to figure out what the addictive substance means symbolically."[139] This kind of thinking, with its interpretation and control, is a good example of trying to use an addictive process to heal addiction. We cannot transform without recovery.

And, conversely, we cannot recover without transformation. People who try to recover without transformation are "dry but not sober," or abstinent but not in recovery. In order to become sober, we have to risk making a paradigm shift. As we peel away our addictions and get closer to the bottom of our addictive process, we begin to become aware of the deep processes that the addictions have been holding in check.

Again, Woodman offers a good example of the difference between traditional work and Living Process work. In the above-quoted article, she says "Reality is too painful if the bottom line is that I am not loveable."[140] This has not been my experience in deep process work. Our inner being will not feed us deep processes we are not ready to cope with, and we can cope with much more than we think we can. I find that it is more often the therapists who cannot cope, not the clients. I have found that people quite easily can tolerate the truth, even if it is that we are not lovable. Not knowing our own reality is much more painful than a painful reality. Again, Jesus said, "You shall know the truth, and the truth shall make you free." I have found this to be true. Most people can handle the truth. It is the illusions that are difficult. Deep process work heals wounds that in the past have been seen as impossible to heal. Deep process work is the bridge that connects us with the divine, within and without. Deep process work leads with the being and process and then conceptualizes. Conceptualizations that do not arise out of our being are disembodied and ultimately of little use.

In the Living Process System, theory and practice cannot be separated. They are, by definition, integrated. Living Process work also does not assume it can fix what was missed or is missing. The issue is not really what a person missed. The issue is what they need to do about what they missed.

Living in Process work accompanies the person doing the deep processing; it does not try to lead. This is one of the reasons that this work has been so easy to do in different cultures and different languages. Because the facilitator does not need to know what is going on with the participant, it is possible to be present to the person's deep work even if the person in process and the facilitator do not share the same language or culture. Living Process work is respectful and trusting of the participant's work and does not need to manipulate or control it.

In a paper written by Bill W., the co-founder of Alcoholics Anonymous, called "The Next Frontier, Emotional Sobriety," he opens the door to understanding that not drinking or not using the chemical is not enough. It is an excellent paper, and I wish I could reproduce it in its entirety. Let me, at least, share a few quotes that illustrate that recovery and a paradigm shift must go hand in hand. He starts by saying, "I think that many oldsters who have put our A.A. 'booze cure' to severe but successful tests still find they often lack emotional sobriety"[141]—no recovery without transformation.

One can still hear the illusion of control raise its ugly head when he says, "How shall our unconscious—from which so many of our fears, compulsions and phony aspirations still stream—be brought into line with what we actually believe, know and want?!"[142] This ideal usually happens when we do our deep process work and seek to live our process *and* we do not control that process.

Unfortunately, the rest of the paper is a search for a technique and yet, at the end, he says eloquently, "If we examine every disturbance we have, great or small, we will find at the root of it some unhealthy dependency and its consequently unhealthy demand."[143] In essence, we need to do recovery, and recovery and our process work are not just "gimmicks." As Bill W. writes, they involve "active transformation."[144]

Living in Process is much more active than surrendering. It is actively choosing to trust our life process and participate in it. It is not as easy as just letting someone else or something else take over. It requires our full participation. Much of the spiritual literature sets up an active-passive dualism on how to live. Living in Process is the third option—of fully participating in our life and trusting where it will take us.

Active participation in our life results in change that is organic. For example, as people do their recovery, it is important to notice the things that they feel uncomfortable with and to honor that discomfort. The result is that we gradually stop doing things that make us uncomfortable. This is how I have developed the work I do now. It has been an ongoing interaction between my recovery and my Living Process, with much deep process work along the way.

I have discovered that, as I am clearer in my sobriety, my deep process and my full participation in my Living Process have given me all the information I need. This does not mean that I do not remain open to sources of knowledge from outside myself or that I do not use my brain and intellect. Quite the contrary. I do, however, find I use outside material and my intellect in new ways—I follow with my thinking and my external sources. Often the idea has already evolved from my personal work, and then I find resources that put it into language, as happened with the works I have quoted on the "thinking" about the new paradigm. I was already *living* a new paradigm, and it helped to read what others were saying. I did not read and then try to "fix" myself and fit myself into someone else's thinking.

Living in Process does not ignore the intellect. It just does not lead with the intellect. In a Living Process System, thinking is embodied. It is tempered by feelings and participation, and it helps integrate knowledge that comes from many sources.

I have found that living and working in this way is conciliatory. Reconciliation cannot happen on any level when one or more of the parties are in their disease, being dishonest, and trying to manipulate each other. Talking to a "drunk" who is drunk is a waste of time, yet many of our attempts at reconciliation on an interpersonal or an international level are just that. One form of denial that we see in these situations is the refusal to see that one or the other of us is operating out of the addictive process.

Long ago, I quit doing couple or family work in a systems way, even though the conceptualization had been helpful. I discovered that when individuals did their recovery process and their deep process work, couple and family relationships cleared up with little effort.

Perhaps this would even happen on an international level if we did our work. I can see, for example, the possibility that we will reach a critical mass of people actively in recovery. As they do their recovery work, out of necessity they will begin to make a paradigm shift in their lives and the way they live them. Then, as they learn to live their lives in a participatory way, they might begin to develop a new worldview that would be sober and life-giving.

I have to say that with the recovery and transformation that I have seen happening as individuals face their addictions and learn to Live in Process, I believe that anything is possible and that the combination of these two processes is the greatest hope for the world that I have seen anywhere.

The New Paradigm

You cannot fight for the environment without
eventually getting into conflict with politicians.

Wangari Maathai (in Time)

Writing about the new paradigm could be a life's work and probably will be for me. I have planned to write a comprehensive book on *Living in Process* for many years and will do so in the near future. However, I do want to present here some ideas about a new paradigm that are being expressed and give some information about my own experience of a new paradigm.

I see two main groups actively struggling with the extensive implications of a new paradigm. Those two groups are theoretical scientists (mostly physicists) and people in recovery. (Willis Harman has suggested to me that he believes the number of these scientists looking at a new paradigm to be *very few.*) My experience has been that the scientists are changing theories and thinking and the recovering people are changing attitudes, feelings, and behavior *in themselves*. There are also scattered others who are writing and/or talking about a new paradigm, such as some therapists, workshop leaders, spiritual leaders, and New Age people.

In my experience, the new paradigm cannot be approached theoretically. The very nature of the paradigm is that it is a participatory paradigm. One can have ideas and assumptions about the theory and the way it *should* operate. This is very different from living it, and living it is the only way to really *know* it.

I believe that there is an inherent difficulty in trying to arrive at this new paradigm through our brains. We need to lead with our bodies and our beings and not with our brains. This issue is clearly demonstrated in recovery from addictions. No one ever recovered through *understanding* the Twelve-Step program or through understanding addiction. In recovery groups, we often hear the difference between "Talking the Talk" and "Walking the Walk." Talking the Talk is trying to recover in our heads and through understanding. Not only does this not facilitate recovery, it impedes it. Walking the Walk is living recovery until it is a process out of which comes our being.

In my experience many scientists, futurists, New Age people, and especially therapists are interested in "Talking the Talk" and not "Walking the Walk." The message and the method are often not congruent. In the Living Process Network, we have to be able to bring the message and the practice together in order to know the new paradigm.

One of the processes that I find is typical of the old paradigm or the addictive process is what I call the "girdle syndrome." In the girdle syndrome, we predetermine what and how something or somebody should be and we try to fit into it. Unfortunately, the predetermined mold is almost always several sizes smaller than reality and never really fits.

Often the *ideas* about a new paradigm are not tempered by experience or even science. It is important not to make the same political and emotional mistakes of the old mechanistic paradigm and force ourselves to accept a new paradigm because of an emotional, political, or theoretical attachment when it does not seem congruent with our experience. This very process of disembodied or nonexperiential figuring things out is, itself, the old paradigm. Often, those operating in old paradigms have changed the *content* of what is said and have clung to processes and procedures that are incongruent with that belief system.

Doing this is one of the subtle tactics we use to convince ourselves that changes are being made while in no way threatening the old paradigm and its political belief system. As is said in Twelve-Step circles, "Half measures availed us nothing," or in the words of Jesus, "Forsake all you have and follow me."

Paradigm changes are radical. Recovery is radical. I have often watched people in the helping professions who are forced into recovery because of their disease then, sadly, be willing to compromise their recovery to maintain acceptance in their professional community, trying desperately to keep a foot in each camp. I have also seen some achieve a modicum of personal recovery and then when that recovery requires them to move beyond personal and family recovery to organizational and professional recovery, choose to stay in the disease process at that level.

When we Live in Process, we are open to wherever that process takes us. Often, that is different from where we thought we were going or what we planned. It is interesting that every major religious leader has spoken in these terms, but a mechanistic scientific worldview introduced the illusion of control, and the subtlety of this illusion permeates even our thinking about the new paradigm. If the new paradigm comes out of recovery and experience, the illusion of control must be dealt with early on (and again and again).

Having said all this about leading with theory, I do want to present some salient ideas from key writers in this area and then go on to share some ideas that have emerged from my own recovery and work with Living in Process.

Theories and Thinking on the New Paradigm

I have found several books challenging and helpful in thinking about a new paradigm: *The Reenchantment of the World*, by Morris Berman; *The Reenchantment of Science: Postmodern Proposals*, edited by David Ray Griffin; and *The Holographic Paradigm and Other Paradoxes: Exploring the Leading Edge of Science*, edited by Ken Wilber. I am happy that these books came into my life after I had worked for over twenty years on my own in trusting the changes that I felt necessary in psychology and psychotherapy and had done almost ten years of work in my own recovery.

Because of that previous search and many major shifts within myself, I was open to ideas that could articulate or help articulate my experience. I had taken time out from reading scholarly books for many years in order to start from my own experience as I tried to conceptualize and bring understanding to that experience. When I finally did happen upon and tackle some of these books, it was from a position of being well grounded in Living in Process and recovery. I use the word *tackle* because, in general, I have not found writers operating on the theoretical plane very easy to read. My motivation was such that I happily hacked through what seemed like millions of footnotes and language and concepts that tired my brain *and* my patience. As I said earlier, the issue of the struggle to understand became most obvious when I asked those who were training with me to read some of the books and articles and they responded with open rebellion. Even though our Trainees are very bright people and most of them are highly educated, I finally ended up "translating" an article by one of the writers because I thought the information was important and I wanted them to have it. They simply would not read it in its original form.

I feel especially sad that this information is so hard to read because I believe in my heart of hearts that this "new" paradigm is something that is present in the DNA of the human race. We all know about it. In some deep recess in our beings, we "remember" what we have tried to forget in order to try to fit into a world governed by this mechanistic scientific worldview.

I have often said that this addictive system is an illusionary system. It is built on the illusion of control, the illusion of perfectionism, the illusion of objectivity, dishonesty, confusion, crazy thinking, and abstractions and concepts that have become completely disembodied and are not tempered by our experience or our beings. We have built that world on theoretical constructs that are unrelated to the world as it actually exists, and we have called it "reality."

Whenever we put forth *our* reality, we are told that we do not understand "reality" and that we are crazy. We have been told that the illusion is reality and reality is illusion. Is it any wonder that we are willing to accept a label of "crazy"? Is it any wonder that we feel we must give up reality in order to fit in? Is it any wonder that we need to anesthetize the pain of our loss of self, our connection with and our place in all of the created universe?

The information about the "new" (old?) paradigm is not just for scholars. People who have experienced the new paradigm in their lives must inform the scholars, and the scholars need to share their information in such a way that ordinary people can know that they already knew it.

I will share some ideas about the new paradigm that have been important for me, and maybe that will encourage a more careful reading of these writers. Please know that I do not pretend to do any of them justice.

Morris Berman: Participation and Embodiment

As I have said, Morris Berman's book *The Reenchantment of the World* was a great find for me. The two most important concepts that I gleaned from his writings were those of a participatory science and/or worldview and the disembodiment of knowledge.

For some time, I had been struggling with what I called the "myth of objectivity" in psychology and psychotherapy. I could see how objectivity was a myth and how this myth was the very basis of psychology (all science) and psychotherapy. I saw that the ethics of psychotherapy were built on the belief that objectivity was possible and good. I put that together with my growing belief that the helping professions were the systematized practice of codependence and relationship addiction and with my awareness that the function of addiction is to keep us out of touch with ourselves, and suddenly I could see why a nonparticipatory scientific worldview would result in an addictive society. We have set up a society in which we need to be out of touch with ourselves in order to tolerate the society we have created.

At the same time, I was working on my recovery, and I could see that recovery *demanded* participation. One could not send others to meetings, "observe" Step work, or "understand" addictions and change or even understand recovery. I tried. In fact, the only way fully to know recovery was to *do* it. I found myself in an intense struggle with my training, which dictated that I stay outside and "observe," and my way of living, which was to jump in and do.

I also noticed that as the Twelve-Step work demanded participation, it also became a great leveler. There were no experts, no leaders, and no authorities. The ones who were the best teachers were often those who had behaved the worst before recovery. In this disease, we were all participants. The Twelve-Step groups were the best example I found of an actual participatory worldview.

Berman was saying that we had to have a participatory scientific worldview. Was science the key? Did science have to be the central thread for the changes that needed to take place? Certainly Berman would have that perspective, because that was his background. Or, was science even capable of evolving a worldview?

I had observed that cultures that are based upon economics were not very viable, and I had been intrigued with cultures in which spirituality and the nurturing of that spirituality were core to the culture.[145] Part of the problem in Eurocentric cultures stems from building a culture based on the belief that a very limited mechanistic science is the only valid approach to truth. Is science central to where we go from here? As I write this, I believe science and the development of a new science will be important, and I do not think that science, itself, will be the core out of which the new paradigm evolves. Scientists have been the guides, the priests, the politicians, and the warriors who have led us into this modernist worldview. I am not sure they will be the ones to lead us out of it *and* I *am* sure that their cooperation *and* participation will be essential.

What does a participatory scientific worldview entail? It releases us from the myth of objectivity, for one thing. Berman says that the last really participatory science was alchemy, and he does not recommend that we return to alchemy. We have to move on. To do this, we must let go of being *disembodied*.[146]

This idea caught my attention because I had, over the years, developed a complete admiration of the material stored in our bodies. I remember remarking once a few years after graduate school that no one had ever told me about the *body* (except for Perfield's work on stimulating specific memories in the brain). I learned physiology and anatomy, but no one ever really told me that depression, memories, awareness, images, and specific sensations are stored *in the body*. I realized that in my doctoral training I had learned very little about the body, except to see it as a machine. When I thought about it, I realized that somewhere along the line in the process of my education, I had unknowingly developed the image that depression, memories, awareness, and so forth were all lurking somewhere within a foot of my head. I laugh when I think of this now, but no one ever even suggested that the body held memories that our brains did not even *remember*.

It is now obvious to me that although it was never said, my education clearly *suggested* that the brain was the most important aspect of my physical being, that it controlled the body, and that it should be *in control*. There was no real recognition that the body, too, can remember, that feelings are necessary to the brain, that the brain needs the body for full information, and that the memories and feelings stored in the body are in most instances *more* accurate than those stored in the brain. What a revelation it was in this work to see that the body often is the seat of the most clearly stored information and that the only way to participate fully in our lives is to use our bodies, brains, feelings, intuitions, awareness, and thoughts.

I also saw that the emphasis on thinking and leading with our brains had, indeed, resulted in a disembodiment of our knowing and therefore a distortion of our knowledge and an inability to receive and understand a large portion of the information that was actually available to us. It was more than a matter of not operating on all cylinders. We did not have cylinders at all. As a species and as a race, we were not using even one-tenth of the information and knowledge of which we are capable. In deep process work, I could see that not only were we able to know much more than we thought we could, we could handle it. In order to participate in our lives and in our world, we had to be in our bodies and open to the information that is stored there.

These two concepts of embodiment and participation are antithetical to a mechanistic scientific worldview. In order to participate in our lives, we have to relinquish our illusions of objectivity (staying outside and observing) and control. I could not recover from my addictions when I wanted to *observe* recovery. Only when I threw myself into full participation could I start recovery. In order to participate fully, I had to be in touch with my body and the messages it was giving me. I could not afford the illusion of safety in just thinking about my disease and recovery. Of course, as I participated, I changed.

Often, when I think of and try to imagine a fully participatory science, my mind boggles (which is probably a good sign, now that I think of it). I would like to share a recent example of a process that moved me to a new level of awareness about the immense shift that will be required in order to develop a participatory science.

I recently spent some time in Ireland for the first time. This was a very important visit for me because when I was growing up, my mother used to say to me, as an explanation for many behaviors, "We're Irish!" My mother has been dead for many, many years, but I have not forgotten her very hot temper and how she often blew up. The beauty of my mother's temper was that after she had "exploded," there was no lingering anger. She was finished with it. I realized, when I was a therapist, that credit for much of my ability to be comfortable with the rage work of my clients belonged to my mother. Anger simply wasn't dangerous. It was only dangerous when it wasn't expressed or when it was expressed *at* someone.

This type of temper was always explained as being because "we're Irish." We had a gift of gab because "we're Irish." So much of our reality was attributed to being Irish. She often accused me of having kissed the Blarney Stone. We had a quick sense of humor because "we're Irish." We grew up with a sense of never having met a stranger—only friends we hadn't made yet—because "we're Irish."

For the past few years, I have been reading the work of Irish writers and novelists, and I have been amazed at the many familiar chords struck in me. This sense of familiarity was only intensified by being in Ireland.

This current trip was precipitated, I believe, by a talk I had recently with an aboriginal elder in Australia. I was reflecting on my awareness of the amazing similarity between my belief system and theirs. She asked me what my family background was, and I said English and Irish. She said, "That explains it. The Irish are closer to the knowledge and awareness of tribal people than any other Western group." Of course, I then had to spend time in Ireland to check out what this means.

When I got to Ireland, I was astonished at how Irish I really am. Many feelings, thoughts, and realizations flooded through me. I was unconsciously drawn to areas still steeped in pre-Christian tradition and to the Irish-speaking areas, and I felt at home. Where did this come from? Certainly, from my mother. Yet, as I was driving along, I thought of her, and my "awareness" mind, *not* my thinking mind, played with my perceptions.

Clearly my mother was very Irish in her soul. Her father was Irish, and her mother was English. *But* her mother died in childbirth, and she was raised by her grandmother (her mother's mother), who was *very* English and *very* proper. This was the great-grandmother who made me put on white gloves to go to the country store when I was a little girl. My mother saw almost nothing of her father when she was growing up. Yet, she was very Irish. She and my great-grandmother were in constant conflict, my grandmother being a rigid, strict, proper Englishwoman, and my mother being a fiery, hot-tempered, intense Black Irish woman. Years after both their deaths, I had a deep process precipitated by a rolfing session in which I realized that I was the bridge between these two powerful women who never could really understand one another. I loved and understood them both and had both of them integrated in me, for which I am very grateful.

But where did my strong connection with Ireland come from? My mother had very little contact with her father or that side of the family. How did she know to be Irish? Before I went to Ireland, I talked with my aunt, who is the family historian, and I discovered that my Irish ancestors came to America in 1640. A long time ago. There are few of us left in Ireland. And, as it turns out, we came from a family of scribes and writers. My mother was a writer and a poet; my children are writers; I fought being a writer and have finally succumbed. What does all this mean? How nice it was to have the time and space to let my mind play with these thoughts and memories as I sped through the Irish countryside.

Then I began to think about the age-old issue in psychology of nature versus nurture. Are we basically determined by our genes or by our environment? It was over forty years ago that I entered the field of psychology, enough time to see the pendulum swing back and forth between these two through several cycles.

Clearly my experience with my mother would argue for nature (genes). Yet, was being a writer in the genes? That seemed a little farfetched to me. Then I realized that nature-nurture was a dualism. I have come to believe that dualistic thinking is addictive thinking, and even when you say it is a little bit of both, that is still a dualistic thinking process.

I thought again about nature-nurture. Both are part of the mechanistic worldview, and that worldview basically sets up human beings to be victims. It is a blaming, judgmental worldview that sees people as acted upon from outside and victims of that "acting upon." Suddenly, I could see how the nature-nurture argument promoted victimization. We are either victims of our genes, or we are victims of our environment. I could see how psychotherapy had played into this judgmental dualistic victimization, and frankly, I was shaken and appalled. My mother was clearly not a victim of either her genes or her rearing. Although she had many reasons to become a victim in her life, she steadfastly refused to see herself that way.

If neither of these really was relevant or if they weren't "the answer," then what was? With addictive system dualism the only way to escape dualistic thinking is to jump off and embrace the third option, which means starting with our own process and our own participation.

At that moment, I felt as though I had moved into an altered state and was in a void—not a void that was nothing, but a void that was something. I could see my mother *participating* in the holomovement that is all creation and in that *participation* pulling out what was required for her living of her life. I had a sudden deep awareness of how it was possible to see the entire universe from a completely different perspective. I know that perspective already exists, but we cannot know what it is unless we participate in it. I felt my fear and my wonderment and saw the security of the old mechanistic psychological paradigm slipping away from me before I had concepts or words to describe the new one. I could see why Willis Harman has said, "Psychology will of course be totally different."[147] It was clear to me at that moment that psychology as we know it cannot exist. I wondered if perhaps it cannot exist *at all.*

I remembered the recent work on stretchable genes[148] and wondered what full participation in our lives, working through all our deep processes and dysfunctional patterns, and full participation in the holomovement of the universe would mean for one individual and the planet and the universe. What if our full participation in our process were the answer to our genes and our environment? What if both were infinitely changeable or stretchable as we participate with ourselves? (I had seen hints of this in deep process work.) What unimagined possibilities would there be for the human race and the planet if each one of us fully participated in all the aspects of our own lives, adding worked-through personal experiences to the real evolution of the planet? What if this mechanistic scientific worldview and all the systems that have been developed to support it, including education, politics, religion, psychology, and medicine, have resulted in a blocking of the normal process of participation and growth that *is* the universe? And, what if the only real way to know this process is fully to participate in it?

I was aware of the anxiety, fear, and excitement I felt in facing the unknown and the false security that a dualistic, static, mechanistic, nonparticipatory, scientific worldview had lulled me into when, indeed, I still had to face the unknown in spite of this false security. This system did not take care of the unknown or remove the need for my participation in it. It had only not given me the tools for this participation or the faith to try it.

As I careened down narrow Irish roads, I had a true glimpse and awareness of what a fully participatory scientific worldview could mean and felt a sobering frustration with how difficult it is to articulate that knowing.

My mother was a participator. Much of her "Irishness" was, I believe, due to her willingness to participate in her life and be open to processes, forces, energies, connections, and entities that have as yet gone unnamed in a nonparticipatory worldview. She embraced the opportunity to be open to and pull out of the holomovement what she needed to be fully herself, and she put back into it that which she had to contribute—not fully, because she was plagued with a struggle to find meaning in and fit into an illusionary system.

I struggled to find neat, concise terms to articulate an understanding of this new awareness that would be as clear as nature-nurture. They did not and have not come.

I was so filled with these new ideas and new awareness that I thought I had to stop the car and write them down immediately, and yet, at night when I had time alone to write, I avoided it. I have long been aware that writing and true creativity are similar to having an orgasm. I understand that it is not possible really to write or be creative unless one is willing to let go and turn oneself over completely to the process. I know that sometimes my avoidance of my writing may look like writers' block when it is really just a fear of that letting go and plunging in and giving myself over to it. This writing felt even bigger. I sensed that if I really plunged into this awareness process it would be very powerful. I felt right on the cusp of articulating some ideas that could be the seed for a new way of thinking about psychology, about ourselves, and our universe. I did not feel ready to plunge in completely.

Right now, I feel that an understanding of these issues I have raised (stretchable genes, deep process work, participatory science, ways of knowing, the holomovement of the universe and our place in it) are right on the tip of my brain, and I am not ready to know what a fully participatory science or living worldview would be like. Yet I have an intriguing and curious glimpse, thanks to my mother and her Irishness, and I know that part of being Irish is being open to when and where this participation will take me.

Clearly, even the process that I just have described is one of a participatory way of living and thinking. I trusted my intuition to go to Ireland and explore things Irish. When my mind began to explore this awareness, I did not try to "think" about these ideas, I let *them* think *me*. When I experienced my fear and avoidance, I honored them, trusting that they are there for a reason and that if I am meant to explore these issues further and have more ability to describe what this participatory worldview has to do with my mother, I will know when the time comes. All I have to do is keep open and participate in my life.

Instead of reducing our lives and the influences of them to the nature-nurture dualism, I began to think in terms of the possibilities and options for participation. Can participation change the future? Can it change the past? What if we truly take our place in the puzzle of the universe? Does that change the entire universe? What does all this mean about the power of taking responsibility (not blame) for our lives? What if individual people took responsibility for their lives and did not turn that responsibility over to people who did not and could not have their genes (stretchable though they may be) and experiences (changeable though they may be) and therefore could not know from their perspective what kind of participation was needed in the world?

What if a new scientific paradigm encouraged and enhanced a science, a politics, an education, a religion, and even a psychology (for want of better words at this time) that supported, encouraged, allowed, and facilitated full participation in the life of the universe for all out of their own life experiences and truths? The possibilities are electrifying. What would science look like if it were not mechanistic, reductionist, and controlling? It is not the seeking to understand nature that is so destructive. It is the way that we try to use that understanding to control and exploit nature that destroys. Suppose that we sought to understand nature and the forces in the universe not by analyzing them, picking them apart, making them static, and trying to reduce them to their simplest parts? Suppose we tried to understand them with all aspects of our being by participating with them and developed a science that could do that? The possibilities are limitless.

I remember an example that I used in one of my books (I believe it was *Women's Reality*) about a realization I had at one point many years ago, listening to a news announcement. The reporter said that scientists in Washington D.C. had announced that if they had only a few million (or billion—I don't remember now) dollars for further research, they could completely control the weather. I was astounded. Who would want to do that? I used it as an example of the difference between what I then called the White Male System and the Emerging Female System. I remember thinking that in an Emerging Female System, we could spend a part of that money learning how to live more effectively with the weather (we probably could not control it anyway), which would be a participatory system, and have money left over to deal with world hunger, pollution, and other more important issues. What I described in *Women's Reality* was a participatory system. I certainly did not realize then the implications of what that meant to the extent that I do now.

Earlier, I quoted a paper by Carl Rogers called "Toward a More Human Science of the Person." In it he stressed that a mechanistic science was not "particularly suitable for, or congenial to the study of the human condition."[149] Yet he, like most of us, tended to cling to the more conventional concepts of science. He quotes Patton, Polkinghorn, and Miles and Huberman in looking at phenomenological research, hermeneutics, and qualitative research.[150] Some of these approaches suggest the possibility for a more participatory science without, I believe, really seeing the revolutionary implications of a fully participatory science. Most of these writers wanted to broaden the scope of humanistic research without moving to a new scientific paradigm. Still, they have paved the way to do just that. In this world of stretchable genes and fuzzy thinking, anything is possible. However, I believe it will be some time before we have adequate language to describe a fully participatory science. We do have some clues that move us beyond concepts like participant-observer, experimenter bias, and phenomenological concepts that still do not really explore what a fully participatory science would be. If we participate fully, we also change what we are observing. If we participate fully, we change. Mechanistic science does not give us much help in thinking in these terms.

Holographic or Holomovement Science

The first book that I read in detail about the holographic paradigm was a series of articles and interviews edited by Ken Wilber called *The Holographic Paradigm and Other Paradoxes: Exploring the Leading Edge of Science.*[151] I was totally fascinated with the concept of the hologram and utterly intrigued with David Bohm's idea of the holomovement. This was the closest I had come to anything that approximated what I had been experiencing in my work and in the writing I had been doing about the Living Process System. Richard Leviton clearly describes several key features of the hologram: (1) it has "the enormous capacity for information storage in a small space, something like 10 billion bits of information encoded in contour lines in one cubic centimeter of film"; (2) "the information is distributed in the system, such that if the hologram plate is shattered, a single fragment will regenerate the original image with only a little loss in depth-of-field and resolution"; and (3) "by changing the angle at which the laser strikes the photographic plate, multiple images can be layered on the same surface like interpenetrating or overlapping realities."[152]

I was aware that what I was reading about a holographic paradigm not only made sense in terms of the Living Process and deep process work I was doing, the holographic paradigm also was exactly what I was discovering in my study of ancient Egypt, the Mayan culture, the Native American culture, and many others in which the temples, for example, reflect the universe and the universe *is* the temple. It was what I heard when I listened to myself and my knowing as I visited these places, spoke to the native people, and did not rely upon anthropologists and others "trained" in the mechanistic paradigm.

Could the concept of the hologram make sense out of my experience of my mother's Irishness? Are we all part of a hologram in which all the parts *are* the whole and the whole *is* the parts?

I especially liked Richard Leviton's description of David Bohm's concept of the holomovement because it fit my experience of a universe in process with everything in it being a process: "Bohm rejected the randomness of quantum mechanics and proposed a holographic universe, which he called 'the implicate order.' The implicate order was the frequency domain, or blur of wave patterns, that enfolded everything—time, space, past, present, future, all opposites."[153] I had trouble with the language, yet I knew that my experience in the work I was doing with people moved much beyond Newtonian physics, relativity, and quantum physics, whereas the psychology I had learned was stuck several scientific worldviews back from where my experience was taking me. It is not unusual for social sciences to lag far behind the physical sciences; this lag was no longer acceptable as I evolved in my new learning.

Leviton goes on to say, "Our apparent world, Bohm said, is a holographic regeneration, or enfolded explicate order, of this primary frequency realm. The dynamic relations between the two Bohm calls holomovement."[154]

Although I had trouble with the language of enfolding, exfolding, explicate, and implicate, I knew what these concepts meant from my own experience and the work I was doing with others. I knew that each of us reflects the all, and the all is each of us; individuals reflect the society, and society reflects the individuals. We are the same, and all of us reflect and participate in what we have called God; that God is a process. When people are recovering from the addictions that serve to remove them from the holomovement, and they begin to operate out of their Living Process, they return to their normal state, which is to again be part of the holomovement and one with what we call God.

I was seeing this process in person after person, but my science gave me no concept or language to talk with myself or others about it. When I read about Karl H. Pribram's concept of the brain as a hologram[155] and Bohm's holomovement, I knew that I was learning a science that fit my experience. Or as John Battista, M.D., says in *The Holographic Paradigm,* "Thus a new holographic model is being developed which emphasizes the interdependent, parallel, and simultaneous processing of events."[156]

What we are seeing is, I believe, not just a model but a worldview that requires a new science. These ideas basically mean that each particular aspect of the hologram can be intimately knowledgeable about every other aspect of the hologram. This could make sense with respect to my mother and her Irishness and also the phenomena that I have observed and experienced in deep process work. Could it be that the healing work that we have been evolving is the door to what the theorists are writing about? Or, indeed, the *practice* of it. What if the two major ways of actively entering the holomovement are through dreams and deep process work? Perhaps this is what the Australian aboriginal means by Dreamtime. What if we have access to information and realms that were totally inaccessible to a mechanistic science?

In a holomovement universe, there is an acceptance of oneness and spirituality is a given. If we are one with all creation and we participate in that oneness, then we have to establish a cooperative relationship with nature, animals, and all other people because we are the same and are one. Once we remove our estrangement from our awareness of our reality as part of the one, or the holomovement, and we begin to *participate* in that oneness, our lives and the perception of our lives will change drastically. For example, we will no longer treat nature or even other people as we have under a mechanistic scientific worldview. Like so many indigenous people have known, we will have to live with nature and with each other.

The key to what Bohm is saying can be stated in his words, "An essential part of this proposal is that the whole universe is actively enfolded to some degree in each of the parts. Because the whole is enfolded in each part, so are all the other parts, in some way and to some degree."[157] Hence, what mechanistic science has called reality is what Bohm calls only the secondary order of things or what I have called the illusionary world.

Postmodern physics begins with the whole, not the reductionist parts. Perhaps an important key to this wholeness about which Bohm speaks is to bypass the reductionism of our thinking processes. Maybe our deep processes that bypass our rational, logical mind are truly vehicles into the information of the whole and the enfolded universe. I have seen that as people do their deep process work and become respectful of their own process, they begin to respect, almost by default, others' processes and the processes of the universe. Bohm says it well, "It follows that if we approach the world through enfolding its wholeness in our consciousness and thus act with love, the work, which enfolds our own being within itself, will respond in a corresponding way."[158] Can it be that what we call God is in interaction with us to generate what we all love or the love of God and that, just as in the Old Testament, God longs for and needs her or his or its people? If we seal ourselves off in our addictions, is what we call God also becoming more addicted? These are important questions, and our thought can play with them, but, ultimately, we can only answer them through participation.

Ecology and Environment

It is clear that the new scientific world paradigm will include a larger concern for ecology and the environment. When we see television specials that demonstrate that seventy-five to one hundred years of mining in Colorado, for example, have altered and polluted the ground water and that corrections for this pollution will have to be made as long as there is human life on this earth, or when we look at the crack babies and AIDS babies and also realize that our use of addictive agents such as nicotine, alcohol, prescription drugs, coffee, and probably other substances is altering the gene pool and slowly decreasing the mental and physical potential of generations to come in what are considered "normal" people, we have cause for concern. Or, as Brian Swimme has stated, "Those cathedrals are *nothing* compared to the elegance of the DNA. In terms of architectural power and beauty, the cathedrals are tin shacks in comparison. And yet we'll allow the DNA to be smashed, beat up, ruined."[159] Our denial about the role of addiction in destroying our gene pool and the support of that destruction by addiction of that DNA needs to be of concern to us all. We need to see that the internal and the external environment are all one and that both are polluted and are affecting all of creation and the creation process itself.

When we remove ourselves from full participation in the environment and we fail to see that what we do affects all of creation, we destroy creation.

Native people are acutely aware of their relationship with the environment. It is more than just a group of humans trying to save the environment. Native people know that we have to recognize that Grandmother Earth and Grandfather Sky, as well as Wakan Tonka (God, Creator, or Ultimate Process), are not separate from us and that a working relationship with all three is both necessary for survival on this planet and one of the gifts of being human. Concern for the environment must be embedded in a larger change of consciousness. Swimme says, "Anything less than a fundamental transformation of our situation is hardly worth talking about."[160]

David Griffin states clearly how we have arrived at a nonecological view of the universe:

> The bias toward the laboratory experiment in the philosophy of science has philosophically reflected the materialistic, non-ecological assumption that things are essentially independent of their environments, so that the scientist abstracts from nothing essential in (say) removing cells from the human body or animals from a jungle to study them in a laboratory, it reflects the reductionist assumption that all complex things are really no more self-determining than the elementary parts in isolation, so that they should be subject to the same kind of strong laboratory repeatability.[161]

We have developed a world order that systematically fails and refuses to see the whole and that the survival of the whole will be absolutely essential to the survival of the individual. Imagine, for example, decisions about building, mining, or number of plane flights being considered not on the basis of economics but on the basis of the needs of the environment and that each company saw the needs of the environment overriding the needs of the company.

Imagine if every conference of every group held anywhere in the world started each session the way the conference of the American Indian Science and Engineering Society does, with someone asking that, in all our deliberations, we considered and were in keeping with the needs of Grandmother Earth and Grandfather Sky.

Imagine what each of our lives would be like if we were aware of the sacredness of our internal and external environments and we were not willing to put anything in either that we would not offer to who or whatever our concept is of God.

One clear voice that sounds the need for a postmodernist ecology is that of John B. Cobb, Jr. He says, "Once we are forced to attend to the destructive consequences of our exploitation of our environment, the facts are indisputable. Because the destruction has been vastly accelerated by the individual revolution, we ask ourselves why in recent times we have been so oblivious. The answer is that we see what our worldview encourages us to see."[162]

Cobb discusses the need for an ecological worldview as absolutely essential in our world today. I could not agree more. It is not just that we need to be concerned with ecology and the environment. We need to start with a worldview that is based upon a very complex participation with the environment. Ironically, again, when we fully participate in our own lives and are aware of our participation with our environment and all life, we interchange with our worlds, and both we and our worlds are changed.

In my time with the Australian aboriginals, I was told that they had lived so completely with their environment for forty thousand years that they left almost no trace of their being there. Of all native peoples, they have had least impact on their environment and forced themselves on it least, respecting all of nature more than any other group of people on this planet.[163] We have much to learn from them, as we do from most native people, when it comes to living with our environment.

It can be seen, therefore, that a new paradigm is by necessity based upon cooperation. This is not a cooperation that comes out of a mental decision to cooperate. It is a cooperation that comes out of the process of respecting ourselves and our process, which then leads to our respect of other people, the environment, and all of creation. It is difficult for mechanistically trained minds to understand that respecting ourselves, taking care of ourselves, and listening to ourselves and our own process does not lead to self-centeredness. Ironically, the work I am doing has shown that just the opposite is true. When people are self-centered (in their addictions), they are, indeed, out of touch with themselves *and* others. It is only as recovering people begin to respect themselves that they really begin to be aware of their *connection* with all things and, interestingly enough, with their God. John Cobb puts it well, "The ecological worldview tells us that our initial mistake was the supposition that we could isolate some elements from the whole and learn the truth about them in this abstraction."[164]

We are only a part of a whole. The choice to participate in that whole is ours. One of the basic characteristics of addiction is isolation; isolation from ourselves, from others, from the environment, and from our spirituality. Recovery and the new paradigm offer the possibility of the breakdown of this isolation. It is when we participate, with respect for ourselves and our environment, that we truly begin to know the meaning of the new paradigm.

Spirituality

Years ago, theologians talked about sin as an alienation from God. Alienation from our spirituality allows us to commit all manner of destruction on ourselves, other people, and the environment. Alienation from God is an alienation from ourselves. Addictions are necessary for us to deal with the pain and to achieve a level of pseudo-functioning when we are alienated from our spirituality.

A new paradigm must, by necessity, be one that facilitates our reconnection with our spirituality. In the new paradigm, there is a recognition and an assumption that we are spiritual beings. This assumption accepts the reality that we are, by nature, connected with what we have called God and all of creation. It is through our addictions that we shut off this awareness and alienate ourselves from this natural oneness. We do not need to have this connection controlled by anyone or anything else. It exists. It is just that simple. We, and our acceptance of alienating forces and belief systems external to ourselves, are what alienate us from our spiritual connection. It is not that the connection does not already exist.

I am often shocked and appalled at the reaction to this new scientific thinking by some Christian groups. I have a good friend who is a very good person—and who belongs to a fundamentalist, charismatic Christian group. We often dined together, shared stories about our kids who grew up together, and talked about life and times. One night he was having dinner at my house and our family was discussing our excitement that my latest book had made the cover of *New Age* magazine. He was shocked, and, essentially, I have not seen him since. His church teaches that all New Age ideas are of the devil and to be avoided at all costs.

The role of the Catholic church is even more interesting. Not only did they temporarily silence a remarkable theologian like Matthew Fox for his suggestion of a positive creation theology, but they continue to see any growth in personal spirituality as a threat to Christianity (which has somehow been equated with the church). In fact, as I write this, a group of former therapists who have trained with me and are working with people to help them move toward recovery and Living in Process are under an inquisition by their Catholic bishop. Certainly, as we see the historic involvement of the church in the initiation and propagation of the modernist mechanistic scientific paradigm, this kind of reaction is not surprising. The issue that is being raised is not one of theology, spirituality, God, or even one's relationship with God. The issue being raised is one of manipulation and control. The issue being raised is one addressed by Martin Luther long ago. It is an issue of spiritual dependency. The church needs the human race to be spiritually dependent upon it to ensure its survival.

I have studied with many of the great theologians of our time, (Niebuhr, Buber, Tillich, Brown, and Casteel). I have studied the Old and New Testaments, and I find nothing in the new scientific paradigm that contradicts the teachings of the Old or New Testament. What I *do* find, however, are ideas and knowledge that threaten the *political* control of the church.

As I study the history of the mechanistic scientific worldview, I can see what an investment the church has made, politically, in this worldview. A Living Process paradigm offers the possibility of realizing the promises that Jesus and all the other great spiritual teachers have offered. Can the church, like any other addict, afford to put its personal illusion of control, self-centeredness, dualism, dishonesty, and distorted thinking above spirituality? I hope not.

When I think about it, I should not be so surprised (and hurt) by the reaction of the church. I have seen the same thing in the field of psychology. I am dismayed at the way some therapists cling to a mechanistic belief system and the illusion of control, but I have come to realize that this mechanistic scientific worldview is not just a science or a technology for some people. It is a religious belief system, and there has been more violence on this planet in support of religious belief systems than in any other one cause. There is a progression that takes place in a belief system in an addictive system: one moves from experience to belief, from belief to theory (explanation), from theory to dogma, and from dogma to fanaticism. I am seeing this movement in many sectors of society. Of course, this progression leads to a closed system and an inability to utilize those aspects of the human brain that Franck suggests are fully human.

The system that is built on the illusion of control is being seriously challenged, and it does not die easily. I find it sad that a positive, life-giving spirituality, very much attuned to all the great spiritual teachings, with the potential to move us beyond the religions that our addictive minds have constructed, is presenting itself to us and we are not greeting it with open arms. Unfortunately, such is the legacy of a static, mechanistic, reductionist, controlled worldview. If we fully participate in our lives, our spirituality comes alive.

Consciousness

This new paradigm also demands a change in consciousness. It is necessary that we move beyond a consciousness that sees human beings as the center of the universe toward one that allows us to be fully human. How ironic that our human-centered interpretation of the universe has robbed us human beings of validity and meaning!

Our human-centered focus is exactly the same as what those of us in the addictions field call self-centeredness, which is a key characteristic of addiction. When people are self-centered they not only are selfish, they define the world in terms of themselves. Everyone and everything is either for or against them (a characteristic of most major religions of the world). Anyone who is unlike them must be destroyed, because they feel so insecure in themselves that any differences are a threat (also a characteristic of most religions). When people are self-centered, they have no boundaries and do not know where they end and others begin. In fact, they do not know *that* they end and others begin; therefore, it is necessary for them to try to control everything. Addicts set up a world that is based upon the illusion of control. This is the type of world we have constructed out of the mechanistic paradigm.

In recovery, we see that as people become more in touch with themselves, they relinquish their self-centeredness; and as they relinquish their self-centeredness, they have more of a self; and when they have a self, they do not need to be so self-centered, set up such rigid impenetrable boundaries, or penetrate others' boundaries. When we change from a self-centered, human-centered form of consciousness, we have more awareness of the self and the other, and we are comfortable with oneness. Frederick Franck has suggested that reducing humans to stimulus-response and control issues reduces them to a subhuman state.[165] Can it be that as we stop defining the universe in terms of ourselves, we become more fully ourselves and what we can be? I think so.

Psychotherapy and Healing

It is not possible to use the techniques and philosophies of the mechanistic paradigm to heal the effects and devastations of that paradigm. First of all, therapists must do the work in themselves that is necessary for them to move beyond the paradigm that has led to personal burnout, systematized codependent behaviors, and perpetuation of a system that keeps clients victims and also victimizes them. As therapists do their own process work, they may move to a paradigm in which healing (not just adjustment) is really possible.

Psychotherapists cannot just learn a new technique or method or philosophy. They must initiate their own recovery from the addictive process and make a paradigm shift, themselves, in order to be able to work in any creative, healing way with others, and that will probably not *be* psychotherapy as we know it. I truly believe that we are at a place in the history and development of the field of psychotherapy in which most of the people in the field can fully embrace the kind of shift in consciousness, belief, and functioning that will be necessary if any form of the helping professions is to survive.

I have seen that as I put my sobriety first, there are more and more things I cannot do—such as interpretation, exercises, techniques, and control—yet my work life has become richer, easier, and much less stressful. The very approaches that were supposed to make my life easier actually made it more difficult.

The following chart gives an interesting look at different healing traditions. I am convinced that the paradigm of the Living Process moves beyond all three. At present, I am working on a program for recovering psychotherapists. Due to space constraints, it will be presented in its entirety at a later date in another context. Suffice it to say that I do believe that psychotherapists can recover from their enmeshment in a paradigm that does not work for us, and as we do, our work will be completely different.

307

Three Traditions of Healing

		SCIENTIFIC TRADITION
	Symbol	line/monolith
	Time span	A.D. 1500 to now
	Overall vision	homeostatic
	Disease/death	the enemy
	Cure	fix/fight
	Body view	machine
	Healer as	mechanic
	Troubled one says	"It's beyond me. I want the expert to do it."
	Healer says	"Trust the test results."
	Preferred treatments	drugs, surgery
	Health/life	young, fully functioning white male
	Health care	elite
	Characteristic	visible
	Assumes	measurable repetition
	Worldview	atomic
	Lineage	Newton, Descartes
	Overview	The whole is the same as its parts
	Place of power	machine/tests/drugs
Visions of:	Women/womb	unstable
	Snakes	caduceus
	Moon/blood	inconsequential
	The void	avoid it
	Birth	impossible
Herbal Medicine	Favorite plants	tobacco, coffee, drugs
	Sought-after plant parts	alkaloids, active ingredients
	Ideal remedy	precise, odorless, tasteless

HEROIC TRADITION	WISE WOMAN TRADITION
circle	spiral
1000 B.C. to now	50,000 B.C. to now
dualistic	holographic
result of toxins	natural allies for transformation
clean/punish	nourish
(dirty) temple of the spirit	perfect manifestation of complete being
savior/ruler	compassionate, self-loving one
"I've been bad and need someone to punish me."	"I seek support so I can let go to my depths."
"I'll save you."	"I'll play with you in the sacred garden."
stimulants, purges, enemas	unconditional love and nourishment
fully functioning white people	unimagined transformations
popular	common
alternative	invisible
endless cycles	unique variations
good/bad	interconnected web
St. Paul, Hippocrates, Galen	crone, midwife
The whole is the sum of its parts	The whole is more than the sum of its parts
healer	self
unclean	central
Ouroboros	snake and egg (void)
dangerous	fertile
will get you	source of all being
trauma	empowerment
lobelia, cayenne, goldenseal	common local weeds
medicinal ones, strong ones	vitamins, minerals, chlorophyll
complex, difficult, scarce	familiar, simple, messy, fun

Copyright ©1988 Susun Weed

Psychotherapy is harmful in that the science on which it is based sees people as objects, and those objects are only acted upon externally, denying the role of volition and self-action. This sets up a victim mentality, and victims never get better. They only get bitter. This belief system robs people of the possibility of taking ownership of their lives, and it prevents their full participation. Once we recognize victimization we need to move on to what we need to do in ourselves to heal. We can never claim our own power as long as we are stuck in blaming others and seeing ourselves as primarily "acted upon." Psychotherapy, the way we have set it up, tends to perpetuate dependency and a victim status.

As stated earlier, psychotherapy is also harmful in that it focuses upon "understanding" and "figuring out." This sets up a system in which feelings and deep processes are avoided by trying to figure out and understand. However, psychotherapy is probably most harmful in that it provides a "fix" and keeps people away from their deep process work. It is analogous to giving a drug that suppresses the immune system; when the immune system is needed, it is not there. It is like taking an aspirin for pain, only to discover that the pain was a warning to the body. When pain is suppressed, but the cause of the pain is ignored, the possibility for healing a potentially fatal disease is reduced. The aspirin helps with the symptomatic problem and gives a "fix"; it ultimately exacerbates the problem and prevents healing.

In our codependency, we have settled for the fix and the need to be needed, and we have not moved to real healing because, in some deep way, that makes us less indispensable than we are as the "fixer."

What will the new paradigm look like in healing? I do not know. I have only gone far enough in this work to know that it will be totally different from what we learn in a mechanistic scientific paradigm.

According to a recent Associated Press article entitled "Panic Disorder Often Misdiagnosed," for example, "A panel of experts says those attacks of sudden, unexplained terrors that cause rapid heartbeat, churning stomach, flushing and rapid breathing can be *controlled* if doctors and patients recognize the disorders" (emphasis mine). The "experts" further state that this is *inappropriate* fear and affects one in seventy-five Americans. People fear these attacks and feel that they are "having a heart attack, about to die, going crazy or about to commit an uncontrollable act."

A member of the panel, a New York psychologist, stated that panic attacks are often "associated with stressful life events, such as surgery, pregnancy and even such things as high intake of caffeine." Of course, women are most affected by this "disorder," and the onset is usually in the mid-teens or young adulthood.

I found the next bits of information especially interesting in demonstrating how the (addictive) mechanistic paradigm functions:

> Drugs can hold the panic attacks in check for about half of all patients, though there is a danger the disorder will rebound powerfully if the drugs are stopped.
>
> More successful treatment has come from therapy in which the patient is taught to confront and control unrealistic fears and panicky thoughts.
>
> Research is under way to determine the best combination of drugs and psychotherapy that can control the disorder.[166]

This is how a panic attack is viewed from a mechanistic scientific paradigm. First of all, the "experts" decide what the issue is, diagnose it, and prescribe from their paradigm. The experts also decide the feelings are inappropriate, even though they are linked to life experiences. This is a good example of what I have called the disrespect, violence, and arrogance of that paradigm. In a Living Process paradigm, the assumption is that feelings are valid and are not present without a reason. If the feelings are more intense than those one would expect from the current situation, that is often the clue that a deep process is coming up, one that probably has little or nothing to do with the present "door." What would happen if the public understood this about their internal healing process and viewed attacks like these as an opportunity for healing?

Also, there was a mention that these attacks could be related to a "high intake of caffeine" (a drug), but no indication of whether the investigators really asked about the relationship of these "attacks" to addiction or growing up in addictive families. My guess would be that they would find a high correlation with both.

Early in the article, they mentioned that because the syndrome had not been adequately diagnosed doctors tended to treat the symptoms and not the cause. Then they suggest the same thing: a very simplistic, mechanistic, cause-and-effect approach (to the symptoms) of drugs and a therapy modality based on the illusion of control.

Viewed from a Living Process paradigm, the attack is a symbol, a door that is probably ushering in some old issues that are ready to heal. The person needs support to stay with the feelings and see what comes up. The fact that they state that drugs are helpful for some but when the drugs are stopped the attacks come back with more force clearly supports what I have said about our deep processes. If we miss them the first time around, they will recycle, and each time they come up it will be with more force.

Then the therapy suggested is clearly one based upon the illusion of control and one that asks people to judge their feelings negatively and to try to control them. The entire focus is on *controlling the disorder,* which probably means that the issue the attack is raising will erupt in some other form.

How different it is if we respect these feelings, let the deep process run its course, and in learning to trust our deep process, learn to trust and heal ourselves.

I have been actively involved in evolving a new paradigm for emotional, psychological, and spiritual healing for almost thirty years, and only now am I realizing the true meaning of a paradigm shift. The civil rights movement and the women's movement let me know different systems, and still both are enmeshed in the old mechanistic science. I did, however, learn that I cannot understand everyone with my mind, and, most important, I cannot interpret them from a system that does not understand them.

I have also seen the importance of grass roots and self-defined groups of codependents and addicts. To heal, groups need to get away from being under the definition or "control" of the "professionals." My observation is that recovery groups that are a major impetus for paradigm shifts have come from the Midwest, not from the East or the West coasts, which are usually the centers for idea generation in the United States. Centers for the generation of ideas tend to be more embedded in the modernistic scientific paradigm than grass roots places. (This may be too simplistic, and I think there is some value to looking at regionalism and the U.S. culture.) We need to start listening to those who are participating in life and not so much to those who are thinking about it. This may well mean listening to the people of the planet who have been disenfranchised by the mechanistic, scientific worldview.

All of this work is, indeed, a process. In doing it, I have had to be willing always to be ready to let go of what was true for me yesterday (or ten minutes ago). When I Live in Process, I learn to trust that the process will take me where I need to go. This paradigm does, indeed, require a life of faith.

The new paradigm is one that comes out of being more fully human than we have ever before realized and recognizing and being fully in our bodies while being a part of and participating in all creation. It is a participatory system that requires *full* participation. In that participation, we have information and experience available to us about all of creation. In Living in Process we are part of a universe that is a hologram, and the holomovement is our reality.

In the Living Process System, at some level, nothing is ultimately bad or good. It just *is,* and our issue is to learn from the experience and integrate it into our being and within the cosmos, which results in an evolving process of all creation.

We cannot Live our Process without a concern for and participation in ecology and the environment. We are the environment, and what we do with our internal and external environment affects all of the creation.

The new paradigm recognizes and supports spirituality as a "given." There will need to be a shift of consciousness from our human-centered perception of the world. This, in turn, will change our religions and our consciousness. Reconciliation with all creation will become possible.

Finally, psychotherapy as we know it will no longer exist. The kind of healing that deep process work reaches is not amenable to modern psychological techniques and understanding. Whatever replaces psychotherapy will have to be integrated into the complete life of the individual, the planet, and the cosmos; it cannot be isolated from life and will probably be communal in form. Deep process work will be only a small part of living the paradigm. The simple skills of noticing and naming will take on new meaning as these will be very important skills in living a new paradigm.

People have often said to me that it is not surprising that Living in Process and deep process work was developed by a woman, because it is time for the feminine principle to reemerge. I do not fully agree with this. I have noticed that deep process work is like the birth process, but men can do it as well as women. Perhaps it is easier for a woman to notice these things. However, I do think that dividing the world up into a masculine-feminine dualism is part of the problem. Strength is not masculine, and softness is not feminine. Many native men are attuned to the process, often more so than Western women. If we are really talking about a holomovement here, we all participate in the all. What we have called masculine and feminine are just labels for processes that exist. We all have access to all processes, at some level beyond our understanding choosing what we need, learning what we must learn, to participate in the ongoing creation of the universe.

Concerns and Questions, Implications, and Visions

There is *mystery*—something I have sorely missed in most of my narrow life; *Living* in Process *is* mystery!

Gail G.

As I write the final words of this book, I feel excited and relieved (and, perhaps, anxious). How wonderful to be ready to present a life's work (that is still evolving) and feel good about that work. Now there's an understatement! I have literally been filled with awe and wonder as I have put these pieces together and seen the fullness of ideas emerge. This experience of awe has been a joy and a pleasure to me and has undergirded what could have, at times, become a frightening and overwhelming task.

In summing up, I do want to reiterate some gripes and concerns as well as present some questions, implications, and visions that have arisen from this work. Any work that is "worth its salt" probably should generate more questions than it has answers, and this certainly has been true for me.

Gripes and Concerns

It seems almost redundant at this point to state that I am concerned with what is happening in the helping professions, psychology and psychotherapy especially, and I do feel that a clarion call needs to be sounded. This book is that. And it is more than that.

It is not enough to say that these professions *are* not and *cannot do* the kind of healing that is necessary for individuals, a nation, and a planet, as George Albee has so ably pointed out.[167]

It is not enough to demonstrate that this very psychotherapeutic approach itself is based upon a scientific paradigm that is antithetical to that which it sets out to accomplish and that because of this, the actual *healing* that is possible is stifled, aborted, and controlled out of existence.

It is not enough to point out that the helping professions in many instances have become more political (as in supporting a particular worldview) than therapeutic and have been willing to sacrifice healing for the illusion of power and control.

It is not enough to see that the practice of the field of psychotherapy has become a vehicle for persons who are nonrecovering addicts to practice their disease, get paid for it, and through their clients and their professional organizations, wield tremendous destructive political power.

We must be open to look at a movement in our nation, and spreading throughout the Western world, that is designed to give psychotherapists even more power and control. This is the issue of dual relationships. I have alluded to this issue several times and now, in closing, want to explore it in its entirety because I think it is symbolic of the state of the field of psychotherapy. I was one of the early feminists who helped raise the concern about therapists who slept with their clients and took unfair advantage of the vulnerability of some women who put themselves in a one-down position in relation to a therapist (and probably many other persons in their lives). Coming out of the 1960s and the sexual revolution, this was a concern that needed to be addressed. Now, however, what was a legitimate concern has become so distorted and insane that the tail does, indeed, seem to be wagging the dog. I don't believe that the public realizes the extent of this insanity and the implications for so many of us and for the culture, so I want to say more about what is actually going on in this country with respect to this issue.

There is an attempt to define a dual relationship as any relationship between a "psychotherapist" and a "client" outside of the therapeutic hour. I have already demonstrated how these assumptions are based upon the belief that the therapy session is modeled after a scientific experiment and the therapist functions as a *detached* experimenter/scientist with complete power. These attempts to define therapeutic relationships this way have resulted in legislation or attempts at legislation that define dual relationships as, for example: the children of a therapist and client going to the same school; a therapist and client going to the same church; or a therapist and client being in the same class or workshop. I have already raised the issue of what happens in rural communities and the implications there, where dual relationships are a necessary reality. But what about therapists for therapists? They are, I assume, in the same professional communities. Where do they go for "help"?

Then there is the issue of not having any contact with a *former* client. When I was trained, we were told to talk with a supervisor when we felt uncomfortable with a client and if we did not feel clear, to terminate or refer them. There were no rules about further contact. Now some states are trying to pass laws that restrict any contact after termination. Laws have been passed stating that there should be no contact for one month after termination; then it was changed to six months; then changed one year. Now some are trying to change it to no contact for life. What is all this about? This trend is also present in the field of higher education, as is evidenced by a recent article in the Harvard alumni magazine.[168]

Concurrently, there have been attempts to define almost every human contact as psychotherapy and put it under the licensing controls of psychology. For example, in one state there was an attempt to have tarot card readers, psychic healers, Twelve-Step sponsors, even management consultants, put under the rubric of psychotherapy to then be controlled by the psychology/psychotherapist licensing boards that forbid "dual" relationships. Fortunately this attempt failed.

I have been appalled by the forceful energy existing around this issue and concerned about the intensity and almost violence it has generated. I addressed the implications of setting up and maintaining a victim-perpetuator dualism in relation to this issue where both therapists and lawyers are certainly the only ones who profit from maintaining this dualism, and still, I felt, there was some understanding that evaded me.

I could see how the entire setup of psychotherapy was an escape from intimacy, as is mechanistic science itself, and how the rules, controls, and threats of punishment are not very facilitative of handling what at its best (not in a mechanistic science mode) is a very intimate relationship. I could see that psychotherapy as it is designed had clearly set itself up as an escape from intimacy for the psychotherapist *and* the client. I saw how therapists avoided intimacy with themselves (objectivity), how they taught the client to avoid intimacy with themselves (analyzing, understanding, interpreting, talking *about* feelings), and how the two avoided intimacy with each other. I also have long seen that intimacy with oneself, others, nature, and the planet is the worst threat to an addictive mechanistic system that exists. I do not want to give the impression that I condone therapists' taking advantage of the intimacy that develops between therapist and client, and I think that confusion about this intimacy is not only inherent in the setup of psychotherapy, it is also inherent in codependence and relationship addiction, the model for psychotherapy. The model breeds the issue and does not have in itself a way to solve it.

We have done nothing to work with the therapist in this confusion. We need no longer to escape from intimacy. We need to learn healthy ways to deal with intimacy. I believe community and peer relationships are the answer. Still, I felt a piece was missing. Recently, it came to me.

I suddenly asked myself why, instead of instituting more and more *controls* in finer and finer details, was I not hearing any questions about the assumption that a power imbalance *had* to exist in professional relationships? I know when I *feel* a power imbalance with someone (i.e., one-down or one-up) it is *in* me and has nothing to do with the other person. I can never deal with it by trying to control the other person. That approach is only falling back into my codependency, which is evidenced by trying to deal with what is going on in me by trying to control others.

Of course, as a woman, I have had to deal with an assumed power imbalance in society against women, *and* I am the only one who can make me *feel* inferior. As Eleanor Roosevelt says, "No one can make you feel inferior without your consent." The *feeling* is in me. This does not mean that particular feeling should not be honored and worked with, and it does mean that I can never reclaim my unexperienced personal power by blaming and trying to control others.

Why were psychologists, especially women psychologists, not calling into question the assumption that a power imbalance must exist in professional relationships? Wasn't this questioning of unbalanced relationships the very basis of feminism? It was for me. I have devoted my life to calling into question the assumption of a power imbalance and trying to find ways to listen to, respect, and honor all people, nature, the earth, and the planet and to recognize that domination and oppression destroy us all. Healing and domination and oppression are mutually exclusive. An artificial power imbalance between any two parts of the creation destroys all of the creation.

I began to see that the very people who are not calling into question this assumption that a power imbalance is necessary in any professional (probably *any*) relationship actually *wanted to maintain a power imbalance*. They did not question it, *because they wanted it*. They wanted to have the illusion that they were in control of others. The structured power imbalance and the concomitant oppression are essential for the illusions of the codependent.

I remembered that in *Women's Reality* I had talked about relationships and how in the White Male System relationships were *conceived* of as one-up and one-down. In the White Male System, there was an assumption that relationships *had* to be that way. Also, I had noted that White Male System people were so wedded to this conceptualization that when they had an opportunity to be equal with someone, they would automatically go one-down rather than take the risk of being equal (and then *resent* being one-down).

In what I then (*Women's Reality* was published in 1981) called the Emerging Female System (what I now call a Living Process System), relationships are conceived of as equal. I may have more information than you (or you than I) about something, *and* as persons we are equal. Power differentials and inequality do not exist in a Living Process System. If the feeling of inequality exists in me, I need to deal with it. No one else can do that for me. Trying to maintain a belief in a power differential is to try to "protect the supply" (the illusion of control) of the addict and/or codependent. In trying to do this so desperately, the field of psychotherapy is showing the typical behavior of an addict about to hit bottom.

Finally, all this insanity made sense to me. In a holographic model, maybe the real issue is to find a form of healing that is embedded in real life, one that does not attempt the false security and illusion of control of isolating healing as we do in a mechanistic reductionist model. The Living Process work integrates healing with living and being a part of all life, where we are equals as part of the creation. In fact, it is this integration that is the spiritual basis of recovery and Living in Process. We have tried to remove healing *from* life, and what we need to do is integrate healing *into* life and make all life an opportunity for healing. Healing cannot and should not be in the hands of a few. It is the task of all creation and creating.

I grieve for the field of psychology. I grieve for those who are trying so desperately to hold onto a model that is so diseased and that can only maintain and support disease. I grieve for those of us who have entered recovery from practicing our disease of addiction and codependency in our work and have sought new models and then have been so battered by the field that we leave. I grieve that a field that has as its mandate healing and concern has, like all addicts, so often turned its violence and wrath on those closest to it and those who love it the most.

I am sad that psychology and psychotherapy have not met the challenge of true science to be open-minded, chart new courses, move into the unknown, and truly serve *all* human beings, nature, and the planet. In trying to become mechanics instead of stewards, we have lost our individual souls and our collective souls as a profession. I grieve this loss and know that we can reclaim our souls, our spirituality, if we are only willing to drop our defenses and to ask the question I posed earlier: Is the very worldview out of which we are coming antithetical to what we are trying to accomplish?

I also am concerned about what is happening in the field of addictions and what is happening between the field of mental health and the field of addiction. When I look at what the helping professions are doing in trying to maintain the status quo, to fight and control recovery from addictions, and to keep services offered under a one-party mechanistic science worldview, I feel angry and saddened.

The helping professions are putting themselves in a death struggle with the change that is necessary to save the planet and all life on this planet. We could instead be on the cutting edge of this change, facilitating and supporting it at every turn.

For example, I recently was sent an article with a Boston, Massachusetts, Associated Press byline. The title was, "Care-Giving Workers Suffer from Fatigue." This was a workshop given by Dr. Edward Poliandro at a National Association of Social Workers Conference. The workshop was on stress management, and the syndrome discussed was called "compassion fatigue." I am impressed with several things about this information. First of all, what is being described is codependence and relationship addiction, but any codependent or relationship addict would much rather be told that they have compassion fatigue than that they are addicts and are operating out of an addictive process. The term itself, *compassion fatigue*, feeds the disease.

Second, by naming this addictive process something else, the one who names gets great support for doing this while simultaneously robbing of the potential for recovery those who are suffering from an expression of the addictive process.

Third, the suggested solution actually exacerbates the problem and, as we would say in addictive circles, "protects their supply." Stress management is a technique often used to reduce stress so that individuals can continue to practice their disease and eventually kill themselves. It is like giving up hard liquor and using beer to reduce the craving. This offers a "fix," not a solution. Fixes will not deal with the underlying addictive process. "I'll take a vacation," he says (so he can recover the energy to continue to overwork). It is like workaholics using exercise and a good diet to help them continue to kill themselves.

I grieve for the trap into which the helping professions have fallen. It is as if all of us have been treating diabetes with a drug that is supposed to be the state of the art. Everyone is using it, and it has wide acceptance. Many of us even have stock in the company. Then, through research, we find that not only is the drug not helpful to diabetes (though, initially, there is a lessening of symptoms) but through very subtle chemical reactions it is actually exacerbating the disease, slowly killing the patient and having a negative effect beyond the individual. If I do not sound the alarm, how can I be responsible to my knowledge and information? I am speaking the truth as I know it and owning that I have used the drug. I am also owning that to continue to use it would be a crime for me. Not to state my research observations and my experience would be criminal. If we are a process, we have to be evolving. Nothing of *our* creation is sacred.

We cannot accept the mentality that states that if everyone has it (addiction), the concept of addiction loses its meaning. This is based on a concept that if something is statistically "normal," it is all right. In the culture we have built, to be an addict and live out of the addictive disease process is "normal." It is not healthy. The fact that this addictive process is so widespread should be a clarion call for change. It is not just a worldview that is at stake here. It is a *world*.

Alcoholics Anonymous is not political. Yet therapists, when in recovery, *are* faced with a political issue with respect to their training in the mechanistic, scientific, modernist worldview. Maybe the emotional and political violence I experience surrounding this issue is the death knell of a worldview. No worldview dies without a struggle. Certainly the present worldview did not enter upon the scene without conflict, *and* the power systems of the premodernist world were less organized than those power systems are now.

Perhaps my sadness and grieving that the helping professions are not in the forefront of these necessary changes is only an indicator that I, too, am still holding on to a profession that I loved and that I have outgrown and must leave behind.

I identify with Carl Rogers's sadness when he said that in spite of the great impact that humanistic psychology has had at the grass roots level, few, if any, colleges and universities have been affected very much by its concepts and implications. This has changed to some extent, yet if we see how difficult and laborious its acceptance has been, even when humanistic psychology was attempting to stay within the modernistic mechanistic scientific paradigm, we can grasp the problem we now face. Just imagine what a real paradigm shift will entail!

Those of us who are sounding the alarm, whether it be for psychotherapy as we now know it or for the safety of the planet, are doing so because we care so deeply and from our perception that we are in grave trouble. I have a passion for living with and loving others, animals, nature, the planet. The holomovement science–Living Process paradigm offers so many more options, not just for survival but for actually fully living, that I desperately hope we as a human race and as a planet will consider it.

Questions, Implications, and Visions

As I said earlier, I have generated many more questions than answers in doing this work. A man once asked me in a lecture if I thought "God" was becoming addictive. I was startled with the question and stopped to take a look at what he was asking. I had just drawn a diagram of the Living Process System, and in drawing that conceptualization had said that "we are affected by the process of the universe (God) and we affect the process of the universe." (I later learned that I was expressing what David Bohm calls "enfolding.") His question was, "If we are progressively becoming more addictive, is then God also becoming progressively more addictive?" A good question. A frightening possibility.

We live in a world, on a planet, that is groaning and begging for a respite, a healing. Have we pushed ourselves so far that we can no longer resist the necessity for healing? That's what the addict does. As R. D. Laing says, "We live in a culture that would absolutely fall apart if the truth were told."[169] In order to recover, addicts have to get honest. More and more people are entering recovery from various addictions. Just as we have built-in mechanisms and processes within us that we need for healing ourselves, so will perhaps the massive movement of recovery from addictions become the process for healing the culture we have created. Yet, we also need to look at other questions as they emerge.

For example, we need to ask, "Is time not really linear?" Can we truly be in two (or more) places at the same time? Is space not linear or defined as we think we know it? Is it possible to occupy two or more spaces (and times) simultaneously? I believe so. I have witnessed both these phenomena in deep process work. Australian aboriginal medicine men and American Indian healers have transcended time and space. Do we have something to learn from tribal, indigenous science? I think so.

Can we change the past? As we do our work, do we not only change the present but also the past? I believe so. I have seen it happen.

By doing our deep process work and fully living our process, can we participate in healing on a universal level? Does each person represent a stretchable gene that can transposition for a changing universe, similar to what the gene on the individual chromosome represents? I think it's a possibility. I am eager to do further exploration.

Are the possibilities really limitless and beyond our wildest imagination? I believe so. In deep process work, when people have deep processes that seem to come from a past life and are experiences that are very real to them about, for instance, the horror of war or the terror of a death camp, are these possibly the tapping into the collective unconscious or the holomovement to give us a real gut-level knowing of the horror we have created as a human race? When we get beyond our addictions and our controls so we can see and feel these experiences, is this an attempt of the hologram or the universe to send up these memories for healing on a planetary level? Can we also reach into the holomovement not only to experience the horror of all time but also the loving, spirituality, and beauty of all time? I believe so. I have experienced this.

Can we build a true global community and operate as equals with all creation as a holomovement? I believe so. Can we let go of reductionism and build, expand, encompass the whole and respond out of concern for all things? I believe we can and must.

How remarkable that we have within us a process for healing all the psychological, emotional, and spiritual trauma that we experience as a result of our participation in a society based upon a worldview that causes the very trauma from which we need to heal.

What a wonder that as we have developed a progressively detached, isolated, addictive, rationality-dominated life-style, our inner beings have been busily concocting a way to deal with the very issues we have been inventing. Not only do our stretchable genes allow us to develop and adapt to a system that is progressively lethal (which may not be as positive as it initially seems), these very same genes give us the inherent ability to cope with and heal from what we have unwittingly developed. Perhaps there is a reason that native people all over the world so readily are succumbing to the side effects of this addictive system. They encounter it before they have built up a process inside themselves to deal with it, because the normal state of the human organism is not to have to contend with the problems we have created in Western culture. Of course, ironically, the mechanistic culture that we have built is attacking the physical, psychological, emotional, and spiritual "immune system" with greater ferocity and frequency.

Yet, just perhaps, it is this very defense against this system—our addictions—that will lead us to a path of recovery and a paradigm shift. *And* we would not need this shift if we had not created the system we have created. Native peoples seem not to need to make this shift unless they become infested with Western culture. I know the theory of homeopathy holds that physically we have inside us the solutions that we need to heal ourselves. The Living Process work has shown that the same is true on the emotional, psychological, and spiritual levels (of course, affecting the physical) as well. What if we have developed an internal process to cope with the problems we have created and as we heal ourselves from the effects of a world ruled by mechanistic science we heal the system?

I want to repeat that I have nothing but awe for the process of healing that we have available to us. I have participated in building a grass roots movement for healing traumas that I never thought in my wildest imagination were even amenable to healing. I have not participated perfectly. I have glimpsed how important it is to participate in the evolution of a system in which people claim their own lives, connect with their spirituality, and live *with* the universe.

I have noticed that we often speak of "objectivity" when we mean being free of the contamination of unprocessed personal material. Frequently the most "emotional" outbursts are presented as being objective. As it is practiced, there is a great difference between being "objective" or "rational" and being clear. Clarity comes from confronting our addictive process and doing our deep process work. When we do those two, a paradigm shift is inevitable.

Living in Process does not require a predictable God or a solvable, orderly, linear reality. Nor does it require chaos. The order-chaos dualism is irrelevant. When we just trust the process and participate fully in our lives, we live the universe. We do not need a system built on the illusion of control. God is the void. God is chaos. God is organization. God is Process.

Questions abound. What I am talking about here is not nearly as simple as "creating" your own reality. *Living* our process requires faith and leaps of faith at every moment. It does not require us to be naive. As R. D. Laing says, "If you love someone who lies or is deceptive, then one is not loving them by trusting them."[170] We need to become realistic in an illusional world and we need to claim our place in it.

I have concerns about whether an open system can survive, when it supports the existence of other open and closed systems, especially when the very nature of a closed system is to destroy everything unlike itself. We see native people all over the world struggling with this issue. Yet, when we or they seek to destroy closed systems, we become one. Throughout the world peace groups, environmentalists, healers, and people embracing aliveness are struggling with this issue. I do not know the answer. I know full participation out of my living process is the only true possibility.

To me, deep process work is miraculous. I have seen healing of a kind and at a depth that I never thought possible. Deep process work can and does transcend time and space. It has pushed me to challenge my previous concepts about both as I experienced a transcendence that I never before felt possible. If the hologram (holomovement) is enfolded at all levels, does that mean that all time and all space is available to us right now? I have had experiences during my deep process that suggest this possibility.

If we have a psychological, spiritual, "immune system" process that is not just feelings and in which feelings can be a door, do we have available to us levels of growth, healing, and awareness we have not reached and yet are fully available to us? I believe so, and I have experienced these possibilities.

What does it mean that masses of people are coming up with incest and early sexual abuse memories? What if the emergence of the incest memories worldwide is coming out of enfolded reality and is the way the cosmos moves to eliminate these occurrences?

I know that I see people come alive doing this work in a way that I have never seen before. I know that I participate with people of different races, cultures, and backgrounds who globally are dealing with the same issues and are healing. Is the cosmos pushing us to a critical mass of people in recovery and people who are learning to live their process because we no longer have the luxury of nonliving? I believe so.

We have a possibility. We have an opportunity.

I only know that as I participate more fully in my life, life participates more fully in me. We have a possibility. A sacred possibility.

Notes

INTRODUCTION

1. Brian Swimme has compared the form of my work to that of Barbara McClintock, a scientist who won the Nobel Prize in genetics. She does not theorize about a new paradigm. She does her work as it unfolds and by so doing demonstrates a new scientific paradigm. See Evelyn Fox Keller, *A Feeling for the Organism* (New York: W. H. Freeman and Co., 1983).

2. This is the subject of my first book, *Women's Reality* (Minneapolis: Winston Press, 1981).

3. David Ray Griffin, ed., *The Reenchantment of Science: Postmodern Proposals* (Albany, NY: State Univ. of New York Press, 1988). I am using Griffin's definition of postmodernist science (p. x):

> The postmodernism of this series . . . seeks to overcome the modern worldview not by eliminating the possibility of worldviews as such, but by constructing a postmodern worldview through a revision of modern premises and traditional concepts. This constructive or revisionary postmodernism involves a new unity of scientific, ethical, aesthetic, and religious intuitions. It rejects not science as such but only that scientism in which the data of the modern natural sciences are alone allowed to contribute to the construction of our worldview.

4. See the "Big Book" of Alcoholics Anonymous: *Alcoholics Anonymous: The Story of How Many Thousands of Men and Women Have Recovered from Alcoholism*, 3d ed. (New York: Alcoholics Anonymous World Services Inc., 1976).

5. Martin Buber, *I and Thou*, 2d ed. (New York: Scribners, 1958).

6. Michael Lerner, "Public-Interest Psychotherapy: A Cure for the Pain of Powerlessness," *Utne Reader*, Mar./Apr. 1987, p. 41.

7. As Michael Vincent Miller says in his review of *Acts of Will*, when he writes about the reaction of Otto Rank's esteemed colleagues to his work,

What was it that stirred these distinguished students of human nature to such hostile behavior? For one thing, destroying each other's reputations seems to be a popular pastime among psychoanalysts. In tracking Rank from Vienna and Freud's early circle to his later years of wandering between Paris and New York, in exile from the psychoanalytic mainstream, Dr. Lieberman turns up backbiting, rumor-mongering, lying, possible plagiarisms, downright meanness and Machiavellian political stratagems—all practiced by the founders of psychoanalysis.

(Review of *Acts of Will: The Life and Work of Otto Rank,* by E. James Lieberman, *New York Times Book Review,* Mar. 24, 1985).

8. To be "in integrity with myself" is a phrase often used in recovery circles.

9. The work of Barbara McClintock is an excellent example.

10. Griffin, ed., *Reenchantment of Science.*

11. David Bohm, "Postmodern Science and a Postmodern World," in Griffin, ed., *Reenchantment of Science,* pp. 57–68. Also see Ken Wilber, ed., *The Holographic Paradigm and Other Paradoxes: Exploring the Leading Edge of Science* (Boulder, CO: Shambhala, 1982).

PART I. THE RISE AND DEMISE OF A PSYCHOTHERAPIST

1. See Morris Berman, *The Reenchantment of the World* (New York: Bantam, 1984).

2. Schaef, *Women's Reality,* p. 1

3. See Joreen, "Trashing: The Dark Side of Sisterhood," *Ms.,* April 1976, p. 49.

4. I have come to wonder how ethical or even legal it is to spread false rumors about a colleague and trash her. I have been celibate for many years and have not seen clients for many years, and just a few months ago a social worker reported to me that a local psychologist had told her "confidentially" that I sleep with my clients!

5. In another incident a few years ago, I was asked to speak at a large western university. Again, the caller, a licensed Ph.D. "feminist" psychologist, told the social work department (the sponsoring department) that I should not be allowed to speak, and she read off the same list of reasons! Even if I had been guilty of all the accusations, one would think that ten years later I had paid my obligation to society or psychologists or feminists or whomever I had offended. The program planners paid no attention and didn't even tell me until we were having dinner just before I was to speak.

"What did you think when she told you all this?" I asked.

"Not much," she said. "Most of us think she's a little nutty anyway."

I asked if she would be at the speech, and they all said, "Of course. She'll be right there taking notes."

"Good," I said. " Please point her out. I have never met most of these people who are after me, and almost all of them have no idea who I am or what I do."

When I walked into the lecture room, there she was, front row center. After almost ten years of these attacks, I had developed a little more chutzpah, and I walked up to her, put out my hand, and said, " Hi, I'm Anne Wilson Schaef. I understand you have some concerns about me." " I sure do," she said, and began to rattle off the timeworn list. I asked, "Would it make any difference to you if you knew I had been investigated on all these counts and fully exonerated?" There followed one of the most extraordinary experiences of my life. "No," she hissed, "I trust the women who told me this, and if they said you did these things, you did these things." She was practically foaming at the mouth as she said these words.

6. See Carol Pearson and Katherine Pope, *The Female Hero in American and British Literature* (New York: R. R. Bowker, 1981).

7. *Grok:* to know with all of one's being. From Robert Heinlein, *Stranger in a Strange Land* (New York: Putnam, 1961).

8. Anne Wilson Schaef, *When Society Becomes an Addict* (San Francisco: Harper & Row, 1987).

9. See Berman, *Reenchantment of the World.*

10. American Psychiatric Association, *Diagnostic Manual III-R: Diagnostic and Statistical Manual of Mental Disorders,* 3d ed., rev. (Washington, D.C.: American Psychiatric Association, 1987).

PART II. INTRODUCTION TO LIVING PROCESS
AND DEEP PROCESS WORK

1. Sigmund Freud, *The Interpretation of Dreams.*

2. Jeffrey Moussaieff Masson, *Final Analysis: The Making and Unmaking of a Psychoanalyst* (Reading, MA: Addison-Wesley, 1990).

3. *Postmodern* is a worldview beyond current scientific beliefs and methods.

PART III. THE SCIENTIFIC PARADIGM, PSYCHOTHERAPY,
AND THE LIVING PROCESS PARADIGM

1. Griffin, ed., *Reenchantment of Science.*

2. Jeffrey Moussaieff Masson, *Against Therapy: Emotional Tyranny and the Myth of Psychological Healing* (New York: Macmillan, 1988).

3. Anne Wilson Schaef and Diane Fassel, *The Addictive Organization* (San Francisco: Harper & Row, 1988).

4. Berman, *Reenchantment of the World.*

5. Bohm, "Postmodern Science," p. 59.

6. Bohm, "Postmodern Science," p. 57.

7. I am very grateful to David Griffin for reading through this manuscript and making the comments that are added here in the form of notes for further clarity. In a letter to me, he wrote, "In short, I would not use *empirical, linear, objective,* and *rational* as negative terms. Only certain distortions of these are objectionable, and are characteristic of modern thought."

8. Griffin and I do not see eye to eye here, and certainly he is more techni-
cally informed in philosophy and metaphysics than I am. I add his comments
for clarity:

> I'm all for empiricism, insofar as that means basing one's theories on, or
> at least seeking to be adequate to, all the relevant facts of experience. The
> problem with modern science and philosophy is that it has been based
> upon a *superficial* empiricism, limited (largely) to the facts of *sensory* per-
> ception. What is needed is a radical empiricism (William James), in which
> nonsensory perception is also included. Only through nonsensory per-
> ception (Whitehead's "prehension") do we get knowledge of values,
> causality, time, and even our knowledge that we're in a world of other
> actualities (vs. solipsism).
>
> Now for your definitions: Your first sentence is fine. . . . But none of the
> rest of your characterization *necessarily* is involved in "empiricism." You
> need to make clear whether you're speaking of a method (which is what
> empiricism really is), or a metaphysic (in which one turns a method into
> a metaphysic—which does happen, but this is not inherent in empiri-
> cism). Also, empiricism need not be limited to things that can be mea-
> sured; for example, parapsychologists and physical researchers seek to be
> empirical, in the sense of taking evidence seriously; but they deal with
> types of experience that cannot be measured and quantified. Probably
> what you need to do is add an adjective, speaking of a certain type of
> empiricism—such as "modern empiricism," in which you point out that
> empiricism, which is wholly admirable in itself, became limited by certain
> a priori notions about what kinds of "empirical facts" there could be.

9. Berman, *Reenchantment of the World,* p. 33.

10. I believe Griffin and I are making the same point. I enclose his statement to ponder. From David Griffin:

> Whatever Berman may say, Newton himself certainly did not limit him-
> self to "empiricism" as here discussed. He only went positivistic when he
> was charged with speaking of "occult" forces with regard to gravitation.
>
> Huston Smith and others may say that "empirical knowledge is essen-
> tially dependent upon controlled laboratory procedures," but that is an
> extremely reductionist view of empiricism. Historians are empirical; so
> are geologists, and astrophysicists, and all sorts of other scientists for
> whom the laboratory plays little if any role.

11. Griffin, *Reenchantment of Science,* p. 26. And Griffin's comments on this
paragraph:

> My quote at the bottom does not support your point. I'm arguing
> against those who refuse to see any difference between "science" and
> "ideology" or "propaganda." I argue that, although there are ideological
> and sometimes propandistic elements in what is generally accepted as
> "scientific" writing and research, we should not call it science unless the
> concern to discover truth is paramount. The issue of whether this concern

to discover truth is expressed through "empirical work" (in the narrow, laboratory, measurement-based sense) does not enter in.

12. Griffin, *Reenchantment of Science*, p. 26.

13. Berman, *Reenchantment of the World*, p. 30.

14. Berman, *Reenchantment of the World*, p. 30. David Griffin comments: "Newton had a very different type of 'mechanism' than did Descartes. For Descartes, mechanism entailed that all causation was by contact. In Newton's 'dynamic mechanism,' action at a distance is allowed. (See Richard Westfall, *Never at Rest* [New York: Cambridge Univ. Press, 1981])."

15. Masson, *Against Therapy*.

16. Frederick Ferré, "Religious World Modeling and Postmodern Science," in Griffin, *Reenchantment of Science*, p. 89.

17. Griffin says, "William Uttal . . . a contemporary psycho-biologist . . . says that reductionism, according to which all the activities of the mind are reducible to the most elementary levels of organization of matter, is 'the foundation upon which the entire science of psychobiology is built'" (*Reenchantment of Science*, p. 4).

18. From David Griffin:

> *Linear*: this is a most confusing, ambiguous term. In a recent paper (on Whitehead and parapsychology), I pointed out several respects in which (my type of) postmodern thought is not linear, and then one central way in which it is. It *is* linear in saying that all efficient causation goes from the past to the present, from the present to the future. There is no backward causation from the future to the present, from the present to the past. (We do not influence Descartes—although we can, of course, change the *significance* of Descartes.) This means there is no "true precognition." (I have thirteen alternative explanations, most of which are parapsychological, but do not accept the idea that future events cause present perceptions.) It is *not* linear insofar as linear means: (1) The present is totally determined by the past (which would mean that there is no self-determination in the present). (2) A present "effect" is produced by a single line of causation from the past. (The truth is that each present event is influenced by everything in the past, as Buddhists, Einstein, and Whitehead agree.) (3) Causation among enduring objects does not run only one way, such as from lower to higher types of things, which would make reductionism true. (Rather, there is also downward as well as sideways causation, so that every type of thing is causally interacting with every other type of thing. DNA molecules are surely included within this universal interaction—vs. "the central dogma" of neo-Darwinism.)

This is Griffin's input on these ideas. In deep process work, however, I have seen the present change the past, and we have more and more evidence that time is not necessarily linear, so this is an interesting concept to chew on.

19. David Griffin comments:

> Objective: Modern science has been "objectivist" in an *ontological* sense, claiming that all things, or at least all "really real" things, are mere objects,

being devoid of subjectivity, such as feeling and purposive activity. In an *epistemological* sense, however, any good science should be "objective," in the sense of letting one's conclusions be formed, as much as possible, by the "objective facts," rather than one's subjective biases or preferences or prejudices. One reason this issue has been so confused and confusing is that Jacques Monod, in claiming that science is and must be objective, oscillated between the two meanings *(Chance and Necessity)*. That is, he began with the latter, unobjectionable sense; then glided without comment into the first (objectionable) meaning, claiming that science had to describe the world without any reference to purposes within nature.

See Jacques Monod, *Chance and Necessity: An Essay on the Natural Philosophy of Modern Biology,* trans. by Austryn Wainhouse (New York: Vintage, 1971).
20. David Griffin comments:

Rational: Science must be "rational" in the sense of seeking to be self-consistent. What is objectionable is a type of "rationalistic" thought that stands in tension with being empirical; that is, when one rules out certain types of evidence (e.g., for ESP) on the a priori grounds that such types of things could not possibly occur. Another type of rationalism (in the bad sense) assumes that the human mind (especially the mind of the scientist or philosopher) is primarily and essentially rational, rather than seeing that rationality is a very rare type of experience, that we are first of all emotional, purposive beings, for whom not only self-interested but also mythic, archetypal forms of imagery are much more basic than rational thought.

21. Griffin, ed., *Reenchantment of Science,* p. 4.
22. Griffin, ed., *Reenchantment of Science,* p. 5.
23. Brian Swimme, "The Cosmic Creation Story," in Griffin, ed., *Reenchantment of Science,* p. 50.
24. Ursula Le Guin, *Dancing at the Edge of the World* (New York: Grove Press, 1989), p. 151.
25. Le Guin, *Dancing at the Edge of the World,* p. 148.
26. Jon Clark, "Macho Science, or The Science of the Patriarchal System," unpublished paper submitted to the author in personal correspondence, Sept. 1984, p. 3.
27. Clark, "Macho Science."
28. Swimme, "Cosmic Creation Story," p. 47.
29. Caroline Whitbeck, "A Different Reality: Feminist Ontology," *Beyond Domination,* ed. Carol Gould (MD: Rowman & Allenheld, 1983), p. 64.
30. Schaef, *When Society Becomes an Addict.*
31. David Griffin and Willis Harman, in Griffin, ed., *Reenchantment of Science;* Whitbeck, "A Different Reality"; Berman, *Reenchantment of the World.*
32. Griffin comments:

Dualism is probably the most ambiguous term in the English language, having at least nine or ten different meanings. I have used dualism in only one of these meanings here, this being the Cartesian idea that the mind is ontologically different in kind from the body (or its components). Some people (materialists) call dualistic any view that even distinguishes between the mind and the brain, saying that they are numerically distinct. I affirm this distinction, but argue that it should not be called dualism, unless one adds the further point that not only are they numerically distinct (two different things) but also ontologically different (two different *kinds* of things). (Being a panexperientialist, I think that the mind is only different in degree, although vastly so, from a brain cell.)

33. Whitbeck, "A Different Reality."

34. Griffin, ed., *Reenchantment of Science*, p. xiii.

35. Griffin, ed., *Reenchantment of Science*, p. 11.

36. Griffin, ed., *Reenchantment of Science*, pp. 1–2.

37. Griffin, ed., *Reenchantment of Science*, p. 12.

38. Griffin, ed., *Reenchantment of Science*, p. 11.

39. Griffin, ed., *Reenchantment of Science*, p. 11.

40. Bohm, "Postmodern Science," p. 57.

41. Whitbeck, "A Different Reality" p. 68.

42. Morris Berman, "Nature Is Not a Paradigm," *Whole Earth Review* (Summer 1987), p. 31.

43. Berman, *Reenchantment of the World*, p. 3.

44. Berman, *Reenchantment of the World*, p. 8.

45. Berman, *Reenchantment of the World*, p. 10.

46. Griffin, ed., *Reenchantment of Science*, p. 9.

47. Swimme, "Cosmic Creation Story," p. 53.

48. Bohm, "Postmodern Science," p. 58.

49. Bohm, "Postmodern Science," p. 59.

50. Bohm, "Postmodern Science," pp. 60–61.

51. Willis Harman, "The Postmodern Heresy: Consciousness as Causal," in Griffin, ed., *Reenchantment of Science*, p. 122.

52. Harman, "The Postmodern Heresy," p. 116.

53. Dane Rudhyar, "The Need for a Multi-Level, Process-Oriented Psychology," in *The American Theosophist* 68, no. 5 (May 1980), pp. 156–61.

54. Rudhyar, "Need for a Multi-Level, Process Psychology," p. 156.

55. Rudhyar, "Need for a Multi-Level, Process Psychology," p. 156.

56. I. K. Broverman, D. M. Broverman, F. E. Clarkson, P. S. Rosencrantz, and S. R. Vogel, "Sex-Role Stereotyping and Clinical Judgments of Mental Health," *Journal of Consulting and Clinical Psychology* 34 (1970), pp. 1–7; F. E. Clarkson, S. R. Vogel, I. K. Broverman, D. M. Broverman, and P. S. Rosencrantz, "Family Size and Sex-Role Stereotypes," *Science* 167 (1970), pp. 390–92; P. S. Rosencrantz, S. R. Vogel, H. Bee, I. K. Broverman, D. M. Broverman, "Sex-Role Stereotypes and Self-Concepts in College Students," *Journal of Consulting and Clinical Psychology* 32 (1968), pp. 287–95; Irene P. Stiver, "The Meaning of Care: Reframing Treatment Models," *Women's Growth in Connection: Writings from the Stone Center* (New York: Guilford, 1991), pp. 250–67.

57. Griffin, ed., *Reenchantment of Science*, pp. 9, 27. Griffin, however, sees it as only partly a projection, even if it is a *large* part.

58. Griffin, ed., *Reenchantment of Science*, p. 9. Griffin comments: "I do not endorse this view that 'many' hold. Again, I hold a both/and position, not a 'not this, but this' position."

59. Griffin, ed., *Reenchantment of Science*, p. 24.

60. Griffin, ed., *Reenchantment of Science*, p. 25.

61. Masson, *Final Analysis*, p. 177.

62. Irene P. Stiver, "The Meaning of Care"; Wendy Holloway, *Gender, Meaning and Science* (London: Sage Publications, Ltd., 1989); Daniel N. Robinson, *Systems of Modern Psychology: A Critical Sketch* (New York: Columbia Univ. Press, 1979); Murray Sidman, *Scientific Research: Evaluating Experimental Data in Psychology* (New York: Basic Books, 1960).

63. Whitbeck, "A Different Reality."

64. Griffin, ed., *Reenchantment of Science*, p. 17.

65. Griffin, ed., *Reenchantment of Science*, p. 18.

66. Berman, *Reenchantment of the World*, p. 85.

67. Harman, "The Postmodern Heresy," p. 119.

68. Harman, "The Postmodern Heresy," p. 123.

69. Carl R. Rogers, Ph.D., "Toward a More Human Science of the Person" (La Jolla, CA: Center for Studies of the Person, n.d.), pp. 1–2.

70. Rogers, "Toward a More Human Science of the Person," p. 2. I wonder if this issue is similar to something I have observed in the church? The leadership of the church is historically male. Yet the role of the minister or the priest is one that is traditionally seen as female. They wear "dresses," they serve the meal (sacraments), they minister to the sick and dying, and they are professional listeners and caregivers. Much of the function of the church is what would be considered "the feminine" in this culture. However, the church is also heavily political, and whenever politics and spirituality collide, politics usually dominate. I wonder if the resistance to ordaining women and giving women leadership in the church is not only a statement that the main concern of the church is really not a commitment to spirituality and healing. It may also be a statement about the continued hatred and disgust for what is perceived as "the feminine" or as nonmechanistic science in the culture and the belief that if real leadership were given to women, the church would not only have to change, it would also lose power and prestige in the society at large.

71. Rogers, "Toward a More Human Science of the Person," p. 4.

72. Rogers, "Toward a More Human Science of the Person," p. 5.

73. From a review of Stiver, "The Meaning of Care."

74. Michael Lerner, "Public-Interest Psychotherapy," p. 41.

75. Jon Clark, "Macho Science," p. 3.

76. Very early on, Otto Rank broke with Sigmund Freud on this issue. He "came to regard all this [sublimated instinctual conflicts] as a species of reductive determinism." This quote is from Michael Vincent Miller's review of *Acts of Will: The Life and Work of Otto Rank*, by E. James Lieberman, in the *New York Times Book Review*, Mar. 24, 1985. Miller continues: Rank "often asserted . . . that the impulse to create was even more elemental and far-reaching than the sexual urge."

77. Elaine F. Cherry and Steven N. Gold, "The Therapeutic Frame Revisited: A Contemporary Perspective," *Journal of Psychotherapy* 26:2 (Summer 1989), p. 163.

78. Frederick Franck, "On the Criteria of Being Human," *The Eastern Buddhist* 23:1 (Winter 1990), p. 127.

79. Franck, "On the Criteria of Being Human," p. 127.

80. Franck, "On the Criteria of Being Human," p. 128.

81. Franck, "On the Criteria of Being Human," p. 128.

82. Franck, "On the Criteria of Being Human," p. 129.

83. Franck, "On the Criteria of Being Human," p. 129.

84. Franck, "On the Criteria of Being Human," p. 129.

85. Franck, "On the Criteria of Being Human," p. 131.

86. Arthur L. Kovacs, "Here Comes the Iceberg," *Psychotherapy Bulletin* 24:1 (Spring 1989), p. 11.

87. Kovacs, "Here Comes the Iceberg," p. 11.

88. Thomas Maeder, "Wounded Healers," *Atlantic Monthly,* Jan. 1989.

89. Maeder, "Wounded Healers," p. 37.

90. A holomovement universe is a universe in which all things are connected, the part is reflected in the whole and the whole is the part, and all are in process.

91. Maeder, "Wounded Healers," p. 37.

92. Cherry and Gold, "Therapeutic Frame Revisited," p. 164.

93. Cherry and Gold, "Therapeutic Frame Revisited," p. 167.

94. Maeder, "Wounded Healers," p. 40.

95. The issue goes much beyond the "God Complex," as Maeder describes it. Even though Maeder clearly describes the wounded healer in terms that fit exactly with the codependent, he does not really see the connection between this and the way the role has been set up and defined. This, gratefully, is not true for all who are writing in the field.

96. Joe Reid, "Wounded Healer: Helping the Helping Professional," *CARE Network* 2:5 (Sept./Oct. 1989), p. 7.

97. Reid, "Wounded Healer," p. 9.

98. A flyer from "Nancy's Farm," RFD 1, Box 1010, Thorndike, ME 04986.

99. This is admirable in a mechanistic cause-and-effect science mode. I question how much healing it offers.

As I mentioned earlier, almost twenty years ago a group of professional and nonprofessional women here in Colorado tried to develop a graduate training school that would offer an alternative to the therapy that was available to women and men at that time. We called it the Women's Institute of Alternative Psychotherapy (WIAP). Our basic premise was that the existing training to become a psychotherapist actually trained *out* those elements in a person that were the most healing. We also believed that there was an inverse relationship between the amount of training and the "healing" ability that was left. At that time, we did not know that we were dealing with issues of the scientific worldview and codependency, and we *did* have our finger on the pulse of something important.

Fortunately, we were violently shot down by conservative women psychologists who believed that any institution such as WIAP must be under the control of licensed women psychologists. I say "fortunately" as I can see now that we would only have been trying to develop an alternative within the mechanistic scientific worldview and looking to traditional approaches for approval and would have ourselves probably fallen into training people into codependency. We did not have the awareness then about addiction and the recovery process that now, for many of us, has led to a shifting of perceptions and worldview.

100. Timmen L. Cermak, "Diagnostic Criteria for Codependency," *Journal of Psychoactive Drugs* 18 (1983), reprinted in *Patient Care* (Aug. 15, 1989), p. 133.

101. Dr. Neal Sutherland, quoted in the *Kauai Times*, Feb. 8, 1991.

102. Cermak, "Diagnostic Criteria," p. 133.

103. Masson, *Against Therapy*, p. 243.

104. Masson, *Against Therapy*, pp. 214–19.

105. Masson, *Against Therapy*, p. 219.

106. Mary Daly, *Gyn/Ecology: The Metaethics of Radical Feminism* (Boston: Beacon Press, 1978), p. 281.

107. Daly, *Gyn/Ecology*, p. 282.

108. George Albee, "Preventing Psychopathology and Promoting Human Potential," in *American Psychotherapy* 37:9 (Sept. 1982), pp. 1043–50.

109. Albee, "Preventing Psychopathology," p. 1044.

110. This was on Alkali Lake Reservation in Canada. For information, including a video series and related materials, contact the Four Worlds Project, University of Lethbridge, Alberta, CANADA T1K 3M4.

111. Albee, "Preventing Psychopathology," p. 1043.

112. Albee, "Preventing Psychopathology," p. 1044.

113. Albee, "Preventing Psychopathology," pp. 1044–45.

114. Marion K. Jacobs and Gerald Goodman, "Psychology and Self-Help Groups: Predictions on a Partnership," *American Psychologist* 44:3 (Mar. 1989), p. 536.

115. Albee, "Preventing Psychopathology," p. 1045.

116. Albee, "Preventing Psychopathology," p. 1045.

117. Lancelot Law Whyte, *The Next Development in Man* (New York: New American Library, 1948), p. 254. Quote taken from Rev. Edwin M. McMahon, Ph.D., and Rev. Peter A. Campbell, Ph.D., *"Process-Skipping:" A Mechanism that Locks In Addictive Patterns and Blocks the Experience of Grace* (Institute for Bio-Spiritual Research, 6305 Greeley Hill Road, Coulterville, CA 95311-9501), p. 7.

118. Masson, *Final Analysis*, p. 177.

119. Eugene T. Gendlin, "A Theory of Personality Change," in Philip Worchel and Don Byrne, eds., *Personality Change* (New York: John Wiley & Sons, 1964), p. 134.

120. Gerald G. May, *Addiction and Grace* (San Francisco: Harper & Row, 1988).

121. Masson, *Against Therapy*, p. xx.

122. Ari Kiev, M.D., J.D., "The Tarasoff Decision: The Psychiatrist's Duty to Warn," *Medical Tribune*, Dec. 29, 1988, p. 24.

123. Jacquelyn Small, *Transformers Notebook* 1:6 (Mar./Apr. 1984), p. 2.

124. Michael Kerr, "Chronic Anxiety and Defining a Self," *Atlantic Monthly*, Sept. 1988, p. 46.

125. Kerr, "Chronic Anxiety," p. 51.

126. Kerr, "Chronic Anxiety," p. 52.

127. Jay Efran and Michael D. Lukens, "The World According to Humberto Maturana," *Networker*, May/June 1985, p. 72.

128. Kerr, "Chronic Anxiety," p. 52.

129. Jacquelyn Small, *Transformers Notebook* 1:6 (Mar./Apr. 1984), p. 1.

130. Robert E. Drake and Lloyd I. Sederer, "Inpatient Psychosocial Treatment of Chronic Schizophrenia: Negative Effects and Current Guidelines," *Hospital & Community Psychiatry* 37 (Sept./Oct. 1986), pp. 897–901.

131. Kenneth S. Pope, Barbara G. Tabachnick, and Patricia Keith-Spiegel, "Ethics of Practice: The Beliefs and Behaviors of Psychologists as Therapists," *American Psychologist*, Nov. 1987, p. 993.

132. Pope, Tabachnick, and Keith-Spiegel, "Ethics of Practice," p. 999.

133. Albee, "Preventing Psychopathology," p. 1045.

134. Philip Norman, "Why People Are Screwed Up," *Earthmate*, Summer 1987, p. 21.

135. Norman, "Why People Are Screwed Up," p. 22.

136. Paul Taylor, Ph.D., "Science and Transformation," *Transformers Notebook* 1:6 (Mar./Apr. 1984), p. 5.

137. Lerner, "Public-Interest Psychotherapy," pp. 39–47.

138. Gary Zukav, *Seat of the Soul* (New York: Simon & Schuster, 1989), p. 160.

139. Marion Woodman, "Worshipping Illusions," *Parabola: The Magazine of Myth and Tradition* XII, no. 2 (May 1987), p. 59.

140. Woodman, "Worshipping Illusions," p. 60.

141. Bill Wilson, "The Next Frontier, Emotional Sobriety," *The AA Grapevine* (January 1958), p. 3.

142. Bill Wilson, *The Next Frontier*, p. 3–4.

143. Bill Wilson, *The Next Frontier*, p. 5.

144. Bill Wilson, *The Next Frontier*, p. 5.

145. As I have explored through my contacts with indigenous peoples and through reading, including the following references: *Serpent in the Sky: The High Wisdom of Ancient Egypt* by John Anthony West (New York: Harper & Row, 1929); *Aboriginal Australia: A Traveller's Guide*, by Burnham Burnham (North Ryde, NSW, Australia: Angus and Robertson, 1988); *The Word for World Is Forest*, by Ursula Le Guin (New York: Putnam, 1972).

146. Morris Berman, *Coming to Our Senses: Body and Spirit in the Hidden History of the West* (New York: Bantam Books, 1990).

147. Harman, "The Postmodern Heresy," p. 125.

148. The work of Barbara McClintock as described in Evelyn Fox Keller, *A Feeling for the Organism: The Life and Work of Barbara McClintock* (New York: W. H. Freeman, 1983), and Evelyn Fox Keller, *Reflections on Gender and Science* (New Haven, CT: Yale Univ. Press, 1985).

149. Rogers, "Toward a More Human Science of the Person," p. 3.

150. Rogers, "Toward a More Human Science of the Person," pp. 6, 7.
151. Wilber, ed., *Holographic Paradigm*.
152. Richard Leviton, "The Holographic Body," *East/West Journal*, Aug. 1988, p. 38.
153. Leviton, "The Holographic Body," p. 38.
154. Leviton, "The Holographic Body," p. 39.
155. Karl H. Pribram, "What the Fuss Is All About," in Wilber, ed., *Holographic Paradigm*, pp. 27–34.
156. John Battista, "The Holographic Model, Holistic Paradigm, Information Theory and Consciousness," in Wilber, ed., *Holographic Paradigm*, p. 143.
157. David Bohm, "Postmodern Science," p. 66.
158. David Bohm, "Postmodern Science," p. 67.
159. Brian Swimme, "Cosmocentric Consciousness in an Addicted Society," a speech given in 1986 at The First National Conference on Addictions and Consciousness, Brookridge Institute / 1209 Palm Ave. / San Mateo, CA 94402 / (415) 349-9675. Directors: Shirley Burton and Leo Kiley.
160. Swimme, "Cosmic Creation Story," p. 47.
161. Griffin, ed., *Reenchantment of Science*, p. 27.
162. John B. Cobb, Jr., "Ecology, Science, and Religion: Toward a Postmodern Worldview," in Griffin, ed., *Reenchantment of Science*, p. 105.
163. Burnham, *Aboriginal Australia: A Traveller's Guide*.
164. Cobb, "Ecology, Science, and Religion," p. 111.
165. Franck, "On the Criteria of Being Human," pp. 132–33.
166. All quotes are from "Panic Disorder Often Misdiagnosed," *Garden Island News*, Feb. 6, 1992.
167. Albee, "Preventing Psychopathology."
168. Edward L. Pattullo, "Sex and Secrecy at Harvard College," *Harvard Magazine* 94:3 (January/February, 1992), 68.
169. R. D. Laing, "The Lies of Love," *East/West Journal*, Sept. 1987, pp. 37–42.
170. Laing, "Lies of Love," p. 42.

Index

Addiction, 91, 192, 269, 321–23; vs. addictive process, 128; Bellevue and, 29; care-aholism, 51; course work on, 22; deep process kept at bay by, 130; and dual diagnosis, 247–48; enabling of, 128–29; facing, 78–82; family, 29–31, 80–81; and gene pool, 301–2; helping professions and, 78, 82, 94, 122–23, 227, 269–70, 319–20; intervention with, 78–79, 143–45; and isolation, 280, 304; and job vs. vocation, 236; learning about, 81–82, 84–85; medicine and, 128–29, 226, 235–36, 269–70; naming, 6, 279; objectivity and, 114–15, 202–3; and panic attacks, 311; professionals', 246; psychotherapy based on, 94, 114, 117, 233, 236–40 (*see also* Addictive process); schizophrenia and, 99–103, 161; scientific worldview and, 197, 269–70; self-centeredness in, 306; sex, 56; and spirituality, 210, 281, 304; training group and, 87; treatment centers for, 76–82, 87, 118, 269–76 passim; to Twelve-Step programs, 80; workaholics, 320. *See also* Addictive process; Alco-holism; Codependence; Recovery; Relationship addiction

Addictive Organization (Fassel & Schaef), 192

Addictive personality, 270–75

Addictive process, 4–5, 9, 69, 91, 131, 269, 320; vs. addiction, 128; and "compassion fatigue," 319–20; confronting and healing, 128–30, 131–32, 143, 189, 264–82; and defense mechanisms, 247; dualism and, 207–8; facilitators and, 169–70; "fixes" and, 133; in groups, 36, 186; psychotherapy as, 6–7, 50, 84–85, 120, 129, 131, 193–96, 233, 236–40, 241, 251, 252, 254, 260–61, 310, 315, 318; thinking, 113, 142, 283; transference/countertransference in, 250–51; willingness to confront, 169–70; in women's movement, 68. *See also* Addiction; Control; Scientific worldview

Addictive System, 84–85, 93, 127; as illusory, 289; psychotherapeutic healing and, 240; scientific worldview as, 197, 207; therapist behaviors in, 117; WIAP and, 73. *See also* Addictive process

For information about Living in Process, contact
Wilson-Schaef Associates, Inc.
PO Box 990
Boulder, MT 59632–0990